Heiner Bielefeldt

Freedom of Religion or Belief:

Thematic Reports of the UN Special Rapporteur
2010 – 2016

Religious Freedom Series (IIRF)

Volume 3

Heiner Bielefeldt

Freedom of Religion or Belief:

Thematic Reports
of the UN Special Rapporteur
2010 – 2016

Edited by Thomas Schirrmacher

WIPF & STOCK · Eugene, Oregon

Wipf and Stock Publishers
199 W 8th Ave, Suite 3
Eugene, OR 97401

Freedom of Religion or Belief
Thematic Reports of the UN Special Rapporteur 2010-2016
By Bielefeldt, Heiner and Schirrmacher, Thomas
Copyright©2017 Verlag für Kultur und Wissenschaft
ISBN 13: 978-1-5326-5451-0
Publication date 3/29/2018
Previously published by Verlag für Kultur and Wissenchaft, 2017

Contents

The content in detail

The United Nations Special Rapporteur on Freedom of Religion or Belief

An introduction to the role and the person

THOMAS SCHIRRMACHER

I. The United Nations Special Rapporteurs

The United Nations Special Rapporteurs (in some cases also termed Independent Experts) are individuals working on behalf of the United Nations (UN) according to the Special Procedures mechanisms. They receive a specific mandate by the United Nations Human Rights Council (UNHRC). The mandate either concerns the human rights situation in a specific country or within a specific area or theme, meaning a particular human right or problem. In some cases the UNHRC also appoints a working group, usually made up out of 5 members from the 5 regions of the earth.

The mandate holders are appointed by the UNHRC and act independently of any UN-superior, any government, or any other institution. The mandate by the United Nations is to "examine, monitor, advise and publicly report" on human rights problems through "activities undertaken by special procedures, including responding to individual complaints, conducting studies, providing advice on technical cooperation at the country level, and engaging in general promotional activities."

The earliest thematic appointment was the "Working Group on Enforced or Involuntary Disappearances" appointed in 1980. The first thematic Special Rapporteur was appointed in 1982 to examine "extrajudicial, summary or arbitrary executions."

Mandate holders do not receive any financial compensation for their work to assure total independence, but they receive some personnel and logistical support from the Office of the UNHRC. Thematic Special Rapporteurs are, with rare exceptions, appointed for three years, after which their mandate can be extended for another three years. Country Special Rapporteurs are appointed for one year, and their terms can be renewed every year without a given limit.

Victims of human rights violations can write to the Special Rapporteurs who then try to assess and verify their complaints. Mandate holders have the option to engage governments by sending allegations, letters or urgent appeals with a view to clarify cases brought to their attention. A very important type of instrument used by Special Rapporteurs is the fact-finding mission to particular countries. But Rapporteurs can only visit countries if they first ask the government and it accepts the request and invites the person.

Presently there are 41 Special Rapporteurs (and Independent Experts) of the UN. Ten of them report on a country, 31 have a thematic task. Some selected themes are: Adequate Housing, Contemporary Forms of Slavery, Education, Effects of Economic Reform Policies and Foreign Debt on Human Rights, Extreme Poverty and Human Rights, Right to Food, Freedoms of Peaceful Assembly and of Association, Freedom of Opinion and Expression, Human Rights Defenders, Minority Issues, Protecting Human Rights while Countering Terrorism, Racism, Racial Discrimination, Xenophobia and Related Intolerance, Sale of Children, Child Prostitution and Child Pornography, Torture, Trafficking in Persons, Violence against Women, Human Rights and Access to Safe Drinking Water and Sanitation, Human Rights and Transnational Corporations and other Business Enterprises, and Human Rights of Indigenous People.

II. The United Nations Special Rapporteur on Freedom of Religion or Belief

The position of United Nations Special Rapporteur on Freedom of Religion or Belief was established in 1986. It was a direct result of the Declaration on the Elimination of All Forms of Intolerance and of Discrimination Based on Religion or Belief, passed by the General Assembly of the UN in 1981. It was the first international legal instrument devoted exclusively to the freedom of religion. To further the goals of this declaration, the UNHRC established the "Special Rapporteur on Religious Intolerance." In 2000 the title of the position was changed to "Special Rapporteur on Freedom of Religion or Belief (FORB)" to better emphasize that the right of freedom of religion or belief protects non-religious beliefs as much as religious beliefs.

Like the other UN Rapporteurs, the UN Rapporteur on FORB is appointed by the UN Human Rights Council for three years, is independent, and is not paid. His/her mandate is to identify obstacles to the free exercise of the right to freedom of religion or belief, and to present recommendations how to overcome those obstacles.

The mandate holders so far were or are:

- Angelo d'Almeida Ribeiro (Portugal), 1986 – 1993
- Abdelfattah Amor (Tunisia), 1993 – 2004
- Asma Jahangir (Pakistan), 2004 – 2010
- Heiner Bielefeldt (Germany), since 2010.

The best way to get to know their work is to download the "Rapporteur's Digest on Freedom of Religion or Belief," which includes excerpts of the reports from 1986 to 2011 arranged by topics of the Special Rapporteur's framework for communications.[1]

III. Text of the official website of the United Nations Special Rapporteur on Freedom of Religion or Belief[2]

The Special Rapporteur on freedom of religion or belief is an independent expert appointed by the UN Human Rights Council. The mandate holder has been invited to identify existing and emerging obstacles to the enjoyment of the right to freedom of religion or belief and present recommendations on ways and means to overcome such obstacles.

1. Historical background

The United Nations Commission on Human Rights appointed, further to resolution 1986/20, a "Special Rapporteur on religious intolerance." In 2000, the Commission on Human Rights decided to change the mandate title to "Special Rapporteur on freedom of religion or belief," which was subsequently endorsed by ECOSOC decision 2000/261 and welcomed by General Assembly resolution 55/97. On 12 April 2013, the Human Rights Council adopted resolution 22/20, which, inter alia, extended the mandate of the Special Rapporteur for a further period of three years.

2. Mandate

The Special Rapporteur has been mandated through Human Rights Council resolution 6/37 (see full text in English, French, Spanish, Chinese, Arabic and Russian):

---

[1] www.ohchr.org/Documents/Issues/Religion/RapporteursDigestFreedomReligion Belief.pdf (only available in English).

[2] www.ohchr.org/EN/Issues/FreedomReligion/Pages/FreedomReligionIndex.aspx

- to promote the adoption of measures at the national, regional and international levels to ensure the promotion and protection of the right to freedom of religion or belief;

- to identify existing and emerging obstacles to the enjoyment of the right to freedom of religion or belief and present recommendations on ways and means to overcome such obstacles;

- to continue her/his efforts to examine incidents and governmental actions that are incompatible with the provisions of the Declaration on the Elimination of All Forms of Intolerance and of Discrimination Based on Religion or Belief and to recommend remedial measures as appropriate;

- to continue to apply a gender perspective, inter alia, through the identification of gender-specific abuses, in the reporting process, including in information collection and in recommendations.

3.   Working methods

In the discharge of the mandate, the Special Rapporteur:

1. transmits urgent appeals and letters of allegation to States with regard to cases that represent infringements of or impediments to the exercise of the right to freedom of religion and belief;

2. undertakes fact-finding country visits;

3. submits annual reports to the Human Rights Council, and General Assembly, on the activities, trends and methods of work.

IV. Themes of Heiner Bielefeldt's reports on FORB to the UN

Since assuming his position as United Nations Special Rapporteur on Freedom of Religion or Belief, Heiner Bielefeldt chose a major topic for each of his reports.[3] He liked to get into the middle of important topics which are often bypassed due to their complexity or emotionality, addressing themes such as conversion[4] or religious minorities. He also liked to discuss supposed clashes between different human rights, such as

---

[3]   See http://ap.ohchr.org/documents/dpage_e.aspx?m=86. Most of the reports are available there in French, Spanish, Arabic, Chinese and Russian.

[4]   See Marianne Heimbach-Steins and Heiner Bielefeldt, *Religionen und Religionsfreiheit: Menschenrechtliche Perspektiven im Spannungsfeld von Mission und Konversion* (Würzburg: ergon, 2010).

FORB and equal rights, being convinced that human rights should never be understood as opposed to each other since ultimately the many rights go hand in hand with each other.[5] The topics he has addressed also apply to the whole range of institutions of society in their relation to FORB, including the state, school, employers, and organized religion.

Thus these reports became a major forum for philosophical and legal discussions of major areas of obstacles to religious freedom reaching far beyond current reporting on specific situations. The wide spectrum of topics also assured that criticism, because of violations of FORB, does not point towards one fixed group of states or certain religions, but finds quite varied types of violations of FORB in most states and among all religions.

So far the topics he has addressed are:

1. Freedom of religion or belief in school education

2. The role of the state in promoting interreligious communication

3. Freedom of religion or belief and recognition issues

4. The right to conversion as part of FORB

5. FORB of persons belonging to religious minorities

6. FORB and the equality of men and women

7. Tackling collective manifestations of religious hatred

V. A short biography of the present United Nations Special Rapporteur on Freedom of Religion or Belief

Heiner Bielefeldt is first of all a human rights scholar. But he does not see human rights as a topic for a specific subject in academia, e.g. the law department, but as an interdisciplinary task for many university departments or faculties. He has lived this out in his own academic career and in the special university chair he presently holds.

Bielefeldt (born 1958) studied philosophy and theology at Bonn University and Tübingen University, receiving his diplomas in 1981 and 1982. He received a third undergraduate degree in history from Tübingen University in 1988. In 1989 he received his Dr. Phil. (PhD) in Philosophy from the University of Tübingen with a thesis on social contract theories. Until

---

5   See his "Misperceptions of Freedom of Religion or Belief," *Human Rights Quarterly* 35 (2013): 33-68.

1990 he worked on an interdisciplinary research project on human rights at the University of Tübingen.

Starting in 1990 Bielefeldt taught in university law faculties in the fields of legal philosophy and ethics. During 1990-1992 he worked in the Department of Philosophy of Law at the law school of the University of Mannheim, before going to the law school of the University of Heidelberg. He spent 1993 as a research fellow of the Alexander-von-Humboldt-Stiftung at the Faculty of Law of the University of Toronto. In 1995 he became a researcher at the Interdisciplinary Institute for Conflict and Violence Research at the University of Bielefeld (not to be confused with his name).

In 2000 Bielefeldt received a post-doctoral degree *(Habilitation* in German) from the University of Bremen. He then began teaching at the University of Bielefeld in the departments of law and education, developing his interdisciplinary experience. In 2007 the University of Bielefeld gave him the honorary title of professor.

From 2003 to 2009, Bielefeldt served as Director of Germany's National Human Rights Institute (NHRI) in Berlin, which monitors the human rights situation inside Germany. In this capacity Bielefeldt traveled the world, spoke with governments and at major conferences, and built up the network of knowledge and relationships he brought to his UN office. During 2008-2009 Bielefeldt chaired a sub-committee on accreditation within the International Coordinating Committee of National Human Rights Institutions.

In 2009, Bielefeldt was appointed professor at the newly created Chair of Human Rights and Human Rights Policy at the University of Erlangen/Nuremberg. Bielefeldt teaches in the areas of political science, philosophy, law, and history and can receive students for doctoral research from a wide range of disciplines. His main areas of research and publishing are the philosophy of human rights, history of political ideas, philosophical ethics, philosophy of law, intercultural philosophy, and freedom of conscience/freedom of religion and belief.

One of the areas of concern of Bielefeldt remains interreligious dialogue which led him into Muslim, Christian, and Muslim-Christian institutions in Germany, and which also led him to publish several major articles. On June 18, 2010, he was elected as United Nations Special Rapporteur on Freedom of Religion or Belief as successor of the Pakistani lawyer Asma Jahangir, assuming his office August 1, 2010. In March 2013 he was reelected.

Interview for the second edition (2017) – looking back on six years in office

Thomas Schirrmacher: If you could name three short reasons, why the UN should retain the position of a special rapporteur for FORB, what would they be?

Heiner Bielefeldt: Okay, here you have three reasons: It is important to have someone in the UN system (1) continuously raising awareness about FORB violations across the globe, (2) clarifying the meaning and significance of that specific right within the entire system of human rights, and (3) getting in-depth insights into country-specific patterns of problems as well as coping-strategies. Of course, none of this is unique in itself. And indeed, I would insist that a special rapporteur in order to make any difference has to look out for allies among civil society activists, academics, and not least from other UN agencies. This is not an exercise in splendid isolation. The work of a rapporteur only makes sense, if you see yourself as a little piece within a broader mosaic and act accordingly. Otherwise, forget it. What is unique is that you operate within the UN, but in personal independence, not belonging to the UN staff and not being subjected to any chain of command. Borrowing from Biblical language, I am sometimes tempted to say that as a special rapporteur you are "in the UN, but not of the UN". Being entitled to use the global stage of the UN in full independence is a particular possibility. It also means an enormous challenge or, if you like, a vocation to try to make the most of it.

TS: The task of the office of the special rapporteur includes that individuals whose FORB is restricted can write to you. Did people often use this chance? And where there cases in which you were able to help them?

HB: This aspect of the mandate has not attracted much attention, not even in the broader human rights community. Nonetheless, I personally consider it the backbone of the mandate, because it is only with regard to individual communications that the work of a rapporteur is actually global. Over the years I have approached governments in all parts of the world on quite a number of individual cases, requesting information and clarification or calling for certain initiatives. In a few cases, we could actually achieve direct results, for example, the stop of threatened deportation of Ahmadi refugees back to Pakistan where they might have suffered persecution. One of the advantages of that procedure is that it can be very quick. You don't even have to complete your fact-finding first, because the idea is that governments have a responsibility to clarify the facts in cases where human rights violations have been suspected. During that phase, communication is confidential. In retrospect it is made accessible on the Website of the Office of the High Commissioner on Human Rights.

TS: Is there a situation or a success that you will remember the most, when looking back in some years?

HB: Oh my goodness, I could give you lots of examples. But the important thing is: whenever we have a "success" story this is mainly due to the efforts taken by local actors. Let me give you the example of Cyprus. After my "official" mission in 2012 I re-visited the country four or five times and became part of a process called "the Religious Track of the Cyprus Peace Process" that had been initiated by local actors under the auspices of the Swedish Embassy. While the religious leaders of the big Cypriot communities, the Greek Orthodox Archbishop residing in the south of Nicosia and the Mufti residing a few kilometers further up north across the checking points, had never met over decades, the "Religious Track of Cyprus Peace Process" organized a series of meetings that later on also included other religious leaders and activists. As a result, much happened: churches in the north that had been abused as stables could be cleaned and restored to their liturgical functions; graveyards located in military compounds became more accessible; mosques in the South were repaired and reopened in the presence of Greek Orthodox clergy; some people of mainland-Turkey origin living in the north could for the first time perform a pilgrimage to a famous mosque located near Larnaca. I was lucky to be able to support the process thereby giving it additional legitimacy, stability and attention from the UN. But the work has been done by local actions, mainly. I would say this is the general pattern.

TS: You are a professor teaching human rights interdisciplinary. In how far did your academic achievements help you in the fulfillment of the task as Special Rapporteur on FORB?

HB: When working on FORB issues you are confronted with numerous misunderstandings. For example, many people seem to assume that FORB promotes religious values or even reinforces existing religious hegemonies. Of course, FORB has to do with religion – this is a trivial remark. However, the decisive point, it deals with religion from a human rights perspective, which means that right holders are human beings – like it is the case in all other human rights. With a grain of salt, you may say that FORB deals with human beings who themselves deal with religion, either affirmatively or critically. FORB does not protect belief systems in themselves (i.e. religious truth claims, identities, reputations), but rather protects the believers – and the non-believers as well. You cannot imagine how often things are terribly mixed up in this regard. Thus, conceptual clarity is really necessary, and here my academic training certainly comes in handy. I would also like to confirm the need for an interdisciplinary approach, to which you have alluded in your question. My favorite example is the term "choice" that occurs prominently in human rights, including article 18 of the International Covenant on Civil and Political Rights, which guarantees everyone's freedom to have and adopt a religion or belief of their "choice". As a legal term "choice" makes a lot of sense; it is actually indispensible. "Choice" defines a sphere that should be free from coercion. This is the function the term "choice" has in human rights language. From the inner viewpoint of many believers, however, this may be different. For many people their faith is not a matter of "choice". Instead, they would more likely use concepts, such as "destiny", "calling", "vocation". This can be a source of much confusion, especially if a legal term is mistaken for a theological proposition or the other way around. In order to see the various dimensions of human life in their distinctness, but also in their interconnectedness, a multidisciplinary approach is necessary. While international law plays an important role in defining the precise contours of FORB, other disciplines like philosophy, theology or cultural studies, should also contribute to a better understanding of FORB.

TS: Often religious and worldview communities love FORB for themselves, but either deny it for others or even though they do not deny it officially, they just do not become active on behalf of others. How did you try to convince them that FORB is indivisible?

HB: This is a matter of credibility. As long as you limit your focus on your own rights or the rights of your own community, you cannot credibly claim to do human rights advocacy. One of the most encouraging experiences in the last years has been that people can actually get out of their various boxes. This also includes cooperation across religious and denominational boundaries. For example, the Lutheran World Federation and

Islamic Relief started some cooperation on issues of refugee relief. During the last session of the UN Human Rights Council in Geneva, Christian Solidarity Worldwide (CSW) and the British Humanists jointly held a number of side event on issues of FORB. A few years ago, these two organizations would have been considered pretty unlikely partners. Their cooperation started when CSW took initiatives on behalf of an imprisoned atheist in Indonesia who had come into conflict with the Indonesian blasphemy law. To give you yet another example: Some time ago, the representative of the Baha'i community to the UN raised awareness of increasing persecution of Shia Muslims in various parts of the world. You have to let that sink in: the spokesperson of the Baha'is, i.e. a community that suffers more than any other religious minority from religious repression in the Shia-dominated Iran, actually shows the strength to support Shias who suffer persecution elsewhere. This is an amazing and wonderful example demonstrating that FORB can bring together people across religious and denominational differences.

TS: In your reports you often combined FORB with other human rights like women rights, educational rights, minority rights, freedom of expression. What is your opinion concerning conflicts between FORB and other human rights?

HB: In retrospect I can see that the interrelatedness of FORB with other human rights runs like a golden threat through many of my thematic reports, even though I had not planned this. Why? I see a danger of increasing fragmentation within the international human rights framework. Not only are the various rights sometimes treated in isolation, which would be bad enough. It can actually get worse: they are perceived – or rather misperceived – as mutually corrosive. Let's take the example of freedom of expression. After the Charlie Hebdo massacre, I was repeatedly asked in interviews whether and how freedom of expression and freedom of religion could ever be "reconciled", or how they could ever coexist? My answer was: they cannot exist without each other. Those posing the question obviously assumed that the two rights go in totally different, perhaps even opposite directions: while freedom of expression seems to signal "green light" for all sorts of artistic experimentation and provocation, FORB appears to function more like a "stop sign" – or so is the perception. Consequently, if you really want to have maximum freedom of expression, you better forget FORB, or so is the assumption, which I find highly problematic. You wouldn't believe how often I have come across such a dichotomized view of the two rights. This is really dangerous. The

same may happen when FORB is discussed in the context of gender issues. Here, too, FORB is often suspected to be a mere obstacle on the way
to gender-emancipation. However, if we see FORB and gender-
emancipation as two totally different or even contradictory rights, we
betray all those many millions of people whose life situation is characterized by complex needs, yearnings and vulnerabilities. For instance, wom-
en from religious minorities often feel confronted with the expectation
that they have to choose: either they opt for emancipation as a modern
women, which means move out of their religious tradition, or they stay
within their religious community thereby implicitly forfeiting any claims
of liberation and equality. However, what if they wish both: respect for
their religious identity as well as full equality as an emancipated woman?
This is the question we have to answer. There are so many artificial ei-
ther-or-dichotomies around these issues. If human rights are to do justice
to the complexities of human life, these artificial barriers must be re-
moved. In other words, we need a holistic understanding of human
rights, in which the various rights ultimately belong together. Within the
system of human rights, FORB plays an indispensible role. Today, it is
possibly more important than ever before.

I. Chapter: Report December 2010

I. Introduction

1. The mandate of the Special Rapporteur on freedom of religion or belief was created by the Commission on Human Rights in its resolution 1986/20 and renewed by the Human Rights Council in its resolution 6/37. On 18 June 2010, the Special Rapporteur's mandate was extended for a further period of three years by the Human Rights Council through its resolution 14/11.

2. During the fourteenth session of the Council, Heiner Bielefeldt was appointed as Special Rapporteur on freedom of religion or belief; he took office on 1 August 2010. He very much values the wealth of experience collected during the last 24 years by the three previous mandate holders: Asma Jahangir, Abdelfattah Amor and Angelo Vidal d'Almeida Ribeiro. It is his aspiration to continue this work in the spirit of cooperation with States and all relevant stakeholders. The Special Rapporteur also wishes to highlight the excellent support provided by the Office of the United Nations High Commissioner for Human Rights, in particular its Special Procedures Branch.

3. In the present report, the Special Rapporteur first gives an overview of the mandate activities since the submission of the previous report to the Human Rights Council (A/HRC/13/40) (chap. II). He then focuses on the theme of freedom of religion or belief and school education, referring to relevant international human rights documents, the elimination of stereotypes and prejudices, the issue of religious symbols in the school context and religious instruction in schools (chap. III). In his conclusions, the Special Rapporteur notes that freedom of religion or belief and school education is a multifaceted issue that entails significant opportunities as well as far-reaching challenges. He recommends that States should favourably consider a number of principles in this regard (chap. IV).

II. Activities of the Special Rapporteur

4. The Special Rapporteur's activities include sending communications to States concerning individual cases, conducting official country visits, participating in meetings with representatives of States, religious or belief communities and civil society organizations and delivering speeches and issuing public statements. In this chapter, the Special Rapporteur has

clustered the overview of recent mandate activities under five headings pursuant to Human Rights Council resolutions 6/37 and 14/11.

A. Promotion of the adoption of measures at the national, regional and international levels to ensure the promotion and protection of the right to freedom of religion or belief

5.   At the national level, the Special Rapporteur was invited to participate in an expert hearing on 27 October 2010 held by the Committee on Human Rights and Humanitarian Aid of the German *Bundestag*, the Parliament of Germany. During the public hearing in Berlin, a number of questions relating to "freedom of religion and European identity" were discussed by the experts and members of Parliament.

6.   At the regional level, the Special Rapporteur attended the Supplementary Human Dimension Meeting on Freedom of Religion or Belief held by the Organization for Security and Cooperation in Europe (OSCE) in Vienna on 9 and 10 December 2010. The meeting focused on freedom of religion or belief and the Special Rapporteur was a speaker in the panel discussion on education and religion or belief. Ahead of Human Rights Day 2010, he issued a joint statement together with the director of the OSCE Office for Democratic Institutions and Human Rights.[6] In Vienna, he also met with members of the OSCE Advisory Council of Experts on Freedom of Religion or Belief.

7.   At the international level, the Special Rapporteur issued a joint press statement on 17 September 2010 in anticipation of the High-level Plenary Meeting of the sixty-fifth session of the General Assembly on the Millennium Development Goals.[7] The 26 special procedures mandate holders argued that the implementation of the agreed outcome document (General Assembly resolution 65/1) must have a stronger focus on human rights not only to ensure the achievement of the Goals, but to also make them meaningful for the billions of people who need them most. The experts emphasized that some groups, including those who face religious discrimination, too often find themselves forgotten. They added that poverty gaps will increase unless programmes such as those to achieve the Millennium Development Goals address the unique circumstances of

---

[6]   See www.osce.org/item/48158.html.

[7]   See   www.ohchr.org/en/NewsEvents/Pages/DisplayNews.aspx?NewsID=10344& LangID=E.

these groups and the causes and effects of the discrimination that limits access to education or jobs.

B. Identification of existing and emerging obstacles to the enjoyment of the right to freedom of religion or belief and presentation of recommendations on ways and means to overcome such obstacles

8.   The Special Rapporteur has held public or bilateral meetings with representatives of States and civil society organizations to discuss existing and emerging obstacles to the enjoyment of the right to freedom of religion or belief. He met with numerous members of religious or belief communities and held public briefings with them, for example in Geneva on 23 September 2010 and in New York on 22 October 2010.

9.   Country visits offer an important opportunity for Special Rapporteurs to interact with various State officials and to meet representatives of religious or belief communities and other members of civil society. The Special Rapporteur is very grateful for the invitation by the Government of Paraguay to visit the country and he envisages conducting this mission in early 2011. Further country visits are currently being scheduled, and updated information about the Special Rapporteur's visit requests and forthcoming missions is available on the website of the Office of the United Nations High Commissioner for Human Rights.[8]

10.   Since follow-up is of central importance to the mandate, the Special Rapporteur has continued his predecessors' follow-up procedure concerning country visit reports. On 5 November 2010, he sent follow-up letters concerning those missions undertaken by the previous mandate holder in 2008, i.e. to Israel and the Occupied Palestinian Territory, India and Turkmenistan. The Special Rapporteur requested to be provided with updated information on the consideration given to his predecessor's recommendations, the steps taken to implement them, and any constraints which may prevent their implementation. The follow-up tables with the conclusions and recommendations in the related mission report, and information from the Government and relevant United Nations documents, including from the universal periodic review, special procedures and treaty bodies, are available online.[9]

---

[8]   See http://www2.ohchr.org/english/bodies/chr/special/visits.htm.
[9]   See http://www2.ohchr.org/english/issues/religion/visits.htm.

C. Examination of incidents and governmental actions incompatible with the provisions of the Declaration on the Elimination of All Forms of Intolerance and of Discrimination Based on Religion or Belief and recommendation of remedial measures as appropriate

11. The Special Rapporteur has continued to engage in constructive dialogue with States by sending them communications to seek clarification on credible allegations of incidents and governmental actions incompatible with the provisions of the 1981 Declaration on the Elimination of All Forms of Intolerance and of Discrimination Based on Religion or Belief. Since 1986, the Special Rapporteur has sent more than 1,200 allegation letters and urgent appeals to a total of 130 States. The communications sent by the Special Rapporteur between 1 December 2009 and 30 November 2010, and the replies received from Governments, are summarized in his latest communications report (A/HRC/16/53/Add.1). The Special Rapporteur continues to include in the report practical recommendations of remedial measures as appropriate in the observations to each of these cases.

12. The Special Rapporteur's communications cover a wide range of thematic issues, including allegations of disappearances, torture, arrest and detention of individuals belonging to religious minorities or belief communities. Another major issue of concern is intercommunal violence which has unfortunately resulted in the killing of hundreds of persons, including many women and children. The communications also relate to death threats against and discrimination of converts as well as statements inciting violence directed against members of religious minorities. The Special Rapporteur has also taken up allegations of public manifestations of religious intolerance, stigmatization of persons based on their religion or belief and public announcements of disrespectful acts. Further cases involve attacks on places of worship and religious tensions related to religious sites, including cemeteries. In addition, allegation letters were sent with regard to the situation of asylum-seekers who were due to be forcibly returned to their home countries where their life or freedom would be threatened on account of their religion. The Special Rapporteur has also analysed constitutional and legislative systems as well as draft legislation that fail to provide adequate and effective guarantees of freedom of thought, conscience, religion and belief to all without distinction. Some communications deal with cases of conscientious objectors who

have been sentenced, or risk imprisonment, for refusing to serve in the country's military because of their beliefs.

13. Country visits offer further opportunities to examine and analyse such incidents and governmental actions in greater detail. Conclusions and recommendations in mission reports can be tailored to the domestic legislation, bills, policies and their implementation. Since the establishment of the mandate, the Special Rapporteur has conducted 31 country visits, including one follow-up mission. A list of the country visits is contained in the Special Rapporteur's previous report to the Human Rights Council (A/HRC/13/40, para. 13). The Special Rapporteur would also like to highlight that the Universal Human Rights Index of United Nations Documents, an online research tool,[10] provides easy access to country-specific human rights information by compiling conclusions and recommendations addressed by United Nations independent experts to specific countries in view of improving the human rights situation.

D. Application of a gender perspective

14. The Special Rapporteur has continued to apply a gender perspective, inter alia, through the identification of gender-specific abuses, in the reporting process, including in information collection and in recommendations. The latest interim report submitted to the General Assembly (A/65/207) also contains a chapter on women and freedom of thought, conscience and religion or belief and related conclusions and recommendations.

15. In a joint statement of 8 March 2010, on International Women's Day, 28 special procedures mandate holders called for a new vision of women's rights, informed by the lessons learned from the 15-year review of the implementation of the Beijing Platform for Action.[11] The mandate holders emphasized that old challenges in the protection of women's rights remained, such as multiple forms of discrimination, and that new challenges had emerged. They concluded that the participation of women in all contexts, be it in peacetime or in conflict or post-conflict situations, or in other types of crisis, such as natural disasters or financial crises, was a requisite element not only for the protection of their rights, but also to achieve peace, security and sustainable human development.

---

[10] See www.universalhumanrightsindex.org.
[11] See   www.ohchr.org/en/NewsEvents/Pages/DisplayNews.aspx?NewsID=9877& LangID=E.

16. In his statement to the Third Committee of the General Assembly on 21 October 2010, the Special Rapporteur highlighted that gender-based discrimination has at least two distinct dimensions in the context of religion.[12] On the one hand, women belonging to discriminated communities often suffer at the same time from gender-based discrimination, for example if a woman is discriminated against in the labour market because she has decided, from a religious conviction, to wear a religious symbol. On the other hand, religious traditions or interpretations of religious doctrine sometimes appear to justify, or even call for, discrimination against women. In this context, the Special Rapporteur would like to reiterate that it can no longer be taboo to demand that women's rights take priority over intolerant beliefs that are used to justify gender discrimination.

E. Working with mass-media organizations to promote an atmosphere of respect and tolerance for religious and cultural diversity, as well as multiculturalism

17. To mark the World Day for Cultural Diversity for Dialogue and Development, the Special Rapporteur issued a joint statement on 21 May 2010 in which seven mandate holders stressed that defending diversity went hand in hand with respect for the dignity of the individual.[13] Cultural diversity could be protected and promoted only if human rights and fundamental freedoms, such as the freedom of expression, information and communication, freedom from discrimination of any kind, as well as the ability of individuals to choose their form of cultural expression, and their right to participate or not to participate in the cultural life of given communities, were guaranteed. The mandate holders emphasized that cultural diversity should not be used to support segregation and harmful traditional practices which, in the name of culture, sought to sanctify differences that ran counter to the universality, indivisibility and interdependence of human rights.

18. On 30 November 2010, the Special Rapporteur held an expert consultation in Geneva on the theme "Equality, non-discrimination and diversity: challenge or opportunity for the mass media?". This discussion brought together 12 experts with work experience in mass media organizations with a global outreach as well as the Special Rapporteur on the

---

[12] See www2.ohchr.org/english/issues/religion/docs/GA65statement_2010.pdf.
[13] See   www.ohchr.org/en/NewsEvents/Pages/DisplayNews.aspx?NewsID=10051& LangID=E.

promotion and protection of the right to freedom of opinion and expression and the Special Rapporteur on contemporary forms of racism, racial discrimination, xenophobia and related intolerance. In terms of their professional backgrounds, the 12 experts included a newspaper editor, television anchor, foreign correspondent, wire reporter, online blogger, head of newsgathering and representatives of an umbrella organization of journalists, an international human rights organization, the United Nations Educational, Scientific and Cultural Organization and the Alliance of Civilizations.

19. As part of the discussion, two specific cases studies were analysed, i.e. the media coverage of recent plans to burn copies of the Qur'an[14] and the challenges of reporting on post-electoral conflicts in an ethnically divided country.[15] The Special Rapporteur learned more about the decision-making processes within the different mass media organizations and the conditions for making their day-to-day judgement calls, adhering to the key principles of professionalism and independence. The experts highlighted several challenges faced by mass media, for example the increasing competitive nature of the industry and the need to provide news around the clock, coupled with a global and evolving media landscape. Drawing upon their work, the experts also reflected upon existing initiatives and guidelines used by mass media organizations to promote equality, freedom of expression and diversity.[16] They acknowledged that self-regulation for mass media is the best system, albeit imperfect, yet also emphasized that self-regulation should not lead to detrimental self-censorship or a conspiracy of silence. They also stressed the importance of skills training, including with respect to investigative reporting.

---

[14] See also the Special Rapporteurs' allegation letter dated 8 September 2010 (A/HRC/16/53/Add.1).

[15] See   www.ohchr.org/EN/NewsEvents/Pages/DisplayNews.aspx?NewsID=2122& LangID=E.

[16] See for example Aljazeera's *Code of Ethics* (http://english.aljazeera.net/aboutus/ 2006/11/2008525185733692771.html); the British Broadcasting Corporation's *Editorial Guidelines* (www.bbc.co.uk/guidelines/editorialguidelines); Article 19's *Camden Principles on freedom of expression and equality* (www.article19.org/advocacy/ campaigns/camden-principles); and the International Federation of Journalist's *The Ethical Journalism Initiative* (http://ethicaljournalisminitiative.org).

III. Freedom of religion or belief and school education

A. Introductory remarks

20. The school constitutes by far the most important formal institution for the implementation of the right to education as it has been enshrined in international human rights documents, such as the Universal Declaration of Human Rights (art. 26), the International Covenant on Economic, Social and Cultural Rights (art. 13), the Convention on the Rights of the Child (art. 28) and the Convention on the Rights of Persons with Disabilities (art. 24). The right to education is also anchored in basic documents of regional human rights protection systems.[17] There seems to be worldwide consensus that the right to education is of strategic importance for the effective enjoyment of human rights in general. Not least for this reason, article 28 of the Convention on the Rights of the Child demands that primary education be made compulsory and available free to all, whereas secondary education should be made available and accessible to every child.

21. Besides providing students with the necessary knowledge and information in different disciplines, school education can facilitate a daily exchange between people from different ethnic, economic, social, cultural and religious backgrounds. The possibility of having face-to-face interaction of students on a regular basis is not less important than the development of intellectual skills, because such regular interaction can promote a sense of communality that goes hand in hand with the appreciation of diversity, including diversity in questions of religion or belief. Experiencing the combination of communality and diversity is also a main purpose of interreligious and intercultural dialogue projects. Thus the school provides unique possibilities for such a dialogue to take place on a daily basis, at a grass-roots level and during the formative years of a young person's development.

22. The Durban Declaration and Programme of Action (2001) promotes the purpose of an "inclusive society"[18] in which people from different ethnic or social backgrounds can participate on the basis of equality.

---

[17]   See for example the first Protocol to the Convention for the Protection of Human Rights and Fundamental Freedoms (art. 2); the African Charter on Human and Peoples' Rights (art. 17, para. 1); the African Charter on the Rights and Welfare of the Child (art. 11); and the Additional Protocol to the American Convention on Human Rights in the Area of Economic, Social and Cultural Rights (art. 13).

[18]   See A/CONF.189/12 and Corr. 1, chap. I, paras. 6 and 96.

From a different angle, this goal has recently been taken up in the Convention on the Rights of Persons with Disabilities, in which the principle of inclusion features as a key concept closely related to other principles, such as respect for personal autonomy and appreciation of diverse life situations. It is in such a complex understanding that the Convention on the Rights of Persons with Disabilities lays down the right to inclusive education.[19] Although this right explicitly relates to students with disabilities, it is at least worth discussing whether and how the principle of inclusive education could also be applied to other contexts, including diversity in religion or belief in the school life. Inclusive education pertaining to the issue of religious diversity would make use of the school as a place in which students of different religious or non-religious orientations get to know each other in a natural way.

23.   Freedom of religion or belief and school education, however, require very careful handling. The main reason is that the school, besides providing a place of learning and social development, is also a place in which authority is exercised. It is during their school education that young people receive, or fail to receive, crucial diplomas on which their future life and work opportunities may depend to a large extent. Moreover, especially for young children, the teacher may represent an authority with an enormous influence, coming close to, and sometimes even superseding, the authority of parents and other adult family members. Hence school life can put persons in situations of unilateral dependency or particular vulnerability. Students may feel exposed to pressure exercised by fellow students, teachers or the school administration. Parents may fear that the school could alienate their children from the family tradition. At any rate, more so than other societal institutions the school can trigger a host of contradictory emotions ranging from hopes and high expectations to scepticism and various fears.

24.   For members of minorities, including religious or belief minorities, such ambivalent feelings are typically more pronounced. On the one

---

[19]   See art. 24, para. 1: "States Parties recognize the right of persons with disabilities to education. With a view to realizing this right without discrimination and on the basis of equal opportunity, States Parties shall ensure an inclusive education system at all levels and life long learning directed to: (a) The full development of human potential and sense of dignity and self-worth, and the strengthening of respect for human rights, fundamental freedoms and human diversity; (b) The development by persons with disabilities of their personality, talents and creativity, as well as their mental and physical abilities, to their fullest potential; (c) Enabling persons with disabilities to participate effectively in a free society."

hand, they may hope that school education can contribute to dispelling negative stereotypes and prejudices from which they may personally suffer. On the other hand, members of religious minorities – students as well as parents – may fear discrimination, mobbing or pressure in the school, perhaps even with the intention of urging them to assimilate into mainstream society by abandoning their faith. Such fears, be they justified or not, must always be taken seriously.

25.   According to article 18, paragraph 4, of the International Covenant on Civil and Political Rights, States "undertake to have respect for the liberty of parents and, when applicable, legal guardians to ensure the religious and moral education of their children in conformity with their own convictions". This has been reaffirmed by article 5, paragraph 1, of the Declaration on the Elimination of All Forms of Intolerance and of Discrimination Based on Religion or Belief which states: "The parents or, as the case may be, the legal guardians of the child have the right to organize the life within the family in accordance with their religion or belief and bearing in mind the moral education in which they believe the child should be brought up". The Convention on the Rights of the Child connects respect for parents' rights with the principle of respecting also the evolving capacities of the child. Its article 14, paragraph 2, requires States to "respect the rights and duties of the parents and, when applicable, legal guardians, to provide direction to the child in the exercise of his or her right in a manner consistent with the evolving capacities of the child".

26.   In view of this legal background, fundamental questions of school education related to issues of religion or belief – including the definition of educational principles, the compilation of the topics of the school curriculum, basic institutional and organizational arrangements, etc. – require a high degree of sensitivity. Whenever possible, these questions should not be decided without due consultation of all parties involved, including members of religious or belief communities, while taking care that international human rights standards are respected. In this context, the Special Rapporteur would like to refer to a study prepared under the guidance of his predecessor, which states:

> "Again, the main focus being human rights, what is relevant is that education on religious trends, traditions and movements as well as convictions, be provided in a fair and objective way, stimulating the curiosity of the audience, encouraging it to question their bias and stereotypes about cultures, religions and views other than the one which they see as being part of their own identity. Succeeding in portraying the others so that

they can recognize themselves provides not only a valuable and inspiring educational experience; it also help create understanding and mutual respect between different communities or world-views."[20]

B. Elimination of stereotypes and prejudices

27. Under international human rights law, States are obliged not merely to respect freedom of religion or belief but also to protect such freedom against undue interference from third parties. In addition, States should promote an atmosphere of tolerance and appreciation of religious diversity. The child should "be brought up in a spirit of understanding, tolerance, friendship among peoples, peace and universal brotherhood, respect for freedom of religion or belief of others, and in full consciousness that his energy and talents should be devoted to the service of his fellow men."[21] Moreover, article 29, paragraph 1 (d), of the Convention on the Rights of the Child indicates that States parties agree that the education of the child shall be directed to "the preparation of the child for responsible life in a free society, in the spirit of understanding, peace, tolerance, equality of sexes, and friendship among all peoples, ethnic, national and religious groups and persons of indigenous origin".

28. Given the enormous significance and potential of school education, such efforts necessarily also involve the school in all its curricular, social and organizational aspects. In this context, the Special Rapporteur would like to recommend the study of the final document adopted at the International Consultative Conference on School Education in relation to Freedom of Religion or Belief, Tolerance and Non-discrimination. This Consultative Conference took place in Madrid from 23 to 25 November 2001. It was initiated, among others, by the second mandate holder on freedom of religion or belief, Mr. Amor, who in his 2002 report to the Commission on Human Rights reproduced the full text of the Madrid final document and presented important findings (E/CN.4/2002/73, annex, appendix). In 2007, the third mandate holder, Ms. Jahangir, contributed comments during the development of the Toledo Guiding Principles on

---

[20] "The role of religious education in the pursuit of tolerance and non-discrimination", study prepared under the guidance of Abdelfattah Amor, published in *La libertad religiosa en la educación escolar*, Alberto de la Hera and Rosa María Martínez de Codes, eds. (Madrid, Ministry of Justice, 2002), pp. 55-56.

[21] Declaration on the Elimination of All Forms of Intolerance and of Discrimination Based on Religion or Belief, art. 5, para. 3.

Teaching about Religions and Beliefs in Public Schools.[22] The following observations and recommendations should be read together with the Madrid final document and the Toledo Guiding Principles, which need to be recalled and further implemented.

29. School education can and should contribute to the elimination of negative stereotypes which frequently poison the relationship between different communities and have particularly detrimental effects on minorities. This is also true with regard to religious or belief communities of different – theistic, non-theistic or atheistic – orientations. Indeed, in many countries members of religious or belief minorities experience a shocking degree of public resentment or even hatred which is often nourished by a paradoxical combination of fear and contempt. Even tiny groups are sometimes portrayed as "dangerous" because they are alleged to undermine the social cohesion of the nation, due to some mysteriously "infectious" effects attributed to them. Such allegations can escalate into fully fledged conspiracy theories fabricated by competing groups, the media or even State authorities. At the same time, members of religious or belief minorities are often exposed to public contempt based for instance on rumours that they allegedly lack any moral values. It is exactly this combination of demonizing conspiracy projections and public contempt that typically triggers violence either directed against members of minorities or occurring between different communities. Hence the eradication of stereotypes and prejudices that constitute the root causes of fear, resentment and hatred is the most important contribution to preventing violence and concomitant human rights abuses.

30. School education has a complex role to play in this endeavour. On the one hand, school education should provide fair information about different religions and beliefs. On the other hand, the school offers unique possibilities for face-to-face communication between members of different communities. Both avenues are equally important in the attempt to overcome prejudices and should, wherever possible, be pursued in conjunction.

31. Information about religions and beliefs provided in school education must be distinguished conceptually from religious instruction based on a particular faith (see also paras. 47-56 below). Whereas religious instruction aims at familiarizing students with their own religious tradition, i.e.

---

[22] Prepared by the Advisory Council of Experts on Freedom of Religion or Belief of the OSCE Office for Democratic Institutions and Human Rights. Available from www.osce.org/publications/odihr/2007/11/28314_993_en.pdf.

with theological doctrines and norms of their particular faith, information about religions, by contrast, serves the purpose of broadening the students' general knowledge about different religions and beliefs, in particular those religions and beliefs they may encounter in the society in which they live. In this sense, providing information about religions is not part of theological teaching, but instead comes closer to other disciplines, such as history or social sciences.

32. If information about religions and beliefs is to have a positive effect on the elimination of stereotypes and prejudices, however, it must be given in a non-biased and neutral way. Moreover, such forms of information about religion, given in the context of the public school, which either intentionally or in effect would amount to State propaganda in questions of religion or belief, could run counter to the right of parents and legal guardians "to ensure the religious and moral education of their children in conformity with their own convictions".[23] According to information received from various sources, however, in many countries textbooks used for providing information about religions in school education actually fall far behind the requirement of neutrality, sometimes even reinforcing existing stereotypes against minorities.[24] It is incumbent upon States to take appropriate measures to rectify this unfortunate situation.

33. Providing information about religions and beliefs in a neutral fashion is not an easy task. It may even be argued that, strictly speaking, no one can have a completely "neutral" standpoint that would be above the different horizons of meaning which competing religions or belief systems provide. Yet, without at least the aspiration to overcome biases – and to be neutral in this sense – information about religions could not unfold its beneficial effects on students' minds. One way of overcoming existing biases is to consult with members of the various communities to actively include their understanding of their own tradition and practice into school education. Such consultations are particularly useful in the process of designing textbooks and other teaching materials. They may also be part of regular trainings for teachers and other target groups on

---

[23]   International Covenant on Civil and Political Rights, art. 18, para. 4; International Convention on the Protection of the Rights of All Migrant Workers and Members of Their Families, art. 12, para. 4.

[24]   See, for example, the Special Rapporteur's reports A/54/386, para. 49; A/55/280/Add.1, para. 112; A/55/280/Add.2, para. 105; A/58/296, paras. 51-52; A/CONF.189/PC.2/22, para. 86; A/HRC/4/21, para. 50; E/CN.4/1996/95/Add.1, para. 59; E/CN.4/2002/73/Add.1, para. 80.

their task to provide fair and accurate information about religions and beliefs in the context of school education.

34. Information about religions and beliefs should always include the crucial insight that religions – as a social reality – are not monolithic; the same applies to non-religious belief systems. This message is particularly important, because it helps to deconstruct existing notions of a collective mentality that is stereotypically, and often negatively, ascribed to all followers of various religions or beliefs. In extreme cases, such ascription of a collective mentality may amount to "de-personalized" perceptions of human beings, possibly with devastating dehumanizing repercussions. Rather than being respected as irreplaceable individuals with their own personal faces as well as their own personal characters, opinions, life plans, etc., the followers of a particular religion or belief then are simply portrayed as a "faceless mass" whose members appear to be all more or less exchangeable. Needless to say, from such a point of view any serious communicative interaction is doomed to fail from the outset.

35. From the crucial insight that religions or beliefs – in social reality – are never monolithic it follows that they may also change over time. Interpretations of basic doctrines can adapt, and have in fact adapted, to different societal circumstances. Moreover, traditional practices can and have been challenged time and again by some of their adherents. When it comes to such practices that may have a negative bearing on the situation of women or girls, for example, some women have called for reforms by advocating and pursuing innovative interpretations of the respective sources, doctrines and norms.

36. Even though public schools, when informing about religions and beliefs, have no authority to decide on controversial theological issues, it is important that textbooks and other materials draw a sufficiently complex picture of the various religions or beliefs and their internal pluralism. Furthermore, existing alternative voices within religious traditions, including voices of women, should always have their appropriate and fair share of attention.[25] In general, respect for difference should not be confined to differences between various religions but should always include an awareness of internal differences as they may exist within various religious or belief communities. Only by overcoming monolithic perceptions can we become aware of the real diversity among human beings who are the rights holders in the context of human rights.

---

[25]   See also E/CN.4/2002/73, annex, appendix, para. 5.

37. Not less significant than the dissemination of fair and accurate information on religions is the day-to-day interaction of students of different religious or belief backgrounds. This is the second avenue available for dispelling adverse stereotypes and prejudices. Teachers and the school administration bear a particular responsibility to ensure that students' interaction can take place in a spirit of open-mindedness, respect and fairness. Through voluntary meetings and school exchanges, teachers and students may have the opportunity to meet with counterparts of different religions or beliefs, either at a domestic level or abroad. The goal should be to promote behaviour patterns which recognize difference, including differences in questions of religion or belief, as something "normal" in modern pluralistic societies.

38. Diversity in questions of religion and belief should be taken up in the school context in a spirit of respect and fairness. Against a typical misunderstanding, the Special Rapporteur would also like to emphasize that a respectful attitude does not require avoiding sensitive issues – for instance the situation of women – or even putting a taboo around such issues. It can be more respectful, as long as this is done in a spirit of fairness, to frankly speak about sensitive religious or belief issues, to raise questions, to open up a debate and possibly to agree to disagree. In this regard, the concepts of respect and fairness are closely intertwined.

39. With regard to the treatment of religious or belief diversity in school it is worth reiterating that from the perspective of freedom of religion or belief, the starting point must always be the self-understanding of human beings, who are the only rights holders in the context of human rights. Furthermore, freedom of religion or belief has a "positive" as well as a "negative" component, both of which equally derive from due respect for the dignity of all human beings as it is enshrined as an axiomatic principle in all basic human rights documents. The first component of freedom of religion or belief is freedom to positively express and manifest one's own religion or belief, while its (negative) flip side is freedom not to be exposed to any pressure, especially from the State or in State institutions, to perform religious or belief activities against one's own will. Given the ambivalence of the school as both a place of communication and social encounter as well as a place in which situations of particular vulnerability can occur, the positive and the negative components within freedom of religion or belief should always be considered in conjunction. Neglecting one of the two interrelated components would ultimately undermine the human right of freedom of religion or belief in its entirety.

40. Thus from a human rights perspective, it should be left primarily to pupils (or their parents or guardians, respectively) to express their religious or non-religious conviction in the school context in such a way which they themselves see fit, provided this does not conflict with the rights of others, etc. Teachers should neither play down existing religious diversity nor place undue emphasis on religious differences. Just as it would be wrong to ignore religious differences that may come up in the context of school education, it would be equally problematic to organize communication among students primarily under the auspices of inter-religious exchange between predefined groupings. Instead, respect for difference based on freedom of religion or belief requires an attitude of giving students (or their parents or guardians) the possibility to decide for themselves whether, to which degree and on which occasions they wish to manifest, or not manifest, their religion or belief. Such an atmosphere of relaxed openness provides a fertile ground for developing a sense of diversity as being a normal feature of modern pluralistic societies. It is the obligation of the State to provide an appropriate framework conducive to this goal, always bearing in mind the best interests of the child as an overarching principle laid down in article 3, paragraph 1, of the Convention on the Rights of the Child.

C. Religious symbols in the school context

41. The role of religious symbols, including wearing religious garments in school and displaying religious symbols in classrooms, has been, and continues to be, a matter of controversy in a number of countries. Students or teachers observing religious dress codes, including Islamic headscarves and Sikh turbans, have in some countries been expelled from schools, denied access to higher education or suspended from their jobs.[26] In addition, the compulsory display of religious symbols, such as the crucifix, in the exercise of public authority in relation to specific situations subject to governmental supervision, particularly in classrooms, has yielded numerous court decisions at national and regional levels.[27] Fur-

---

[26] See, for example, the Special Rapporteur's reports A/HRC/10/8, para. 51; A/HRC/10/8/Add.1, paras. 196-198; E/CN.4/2006/5, paras. 43-50; and E/CN.4/2006/5/Add.4, paras. 47-72 and 98-104.

[27] See references in E/CN.4/2006/5, para. 36 (endnote 1). See also the judgment of 3 November 2009 of the Second Section of the European Court of Human Rights in the case of Lautsi v. Italy, application No. 30814/06, which has been referred to the Grand Chamber (the final judgment was not yet published at the time of writing).

thermore, cases of imposition of religious dress codes are also of concern.[28]

42. To do justice to the complexity of the topic, one has to bear in mind a number of important distinctions. For example, given the specific role and status of the teacher, it obviously makes a difference whether religious symbols are worn by teachers or by students, and there may be good reasons for such a difference to be reflected in respective legislation or court decisions. The age of pupils could possibly be a factor for having different regulations in primary schools and in institutions of higher education. It would again be different if the presence of a particular religious symbol in classrooms of public schools was prescribed by the authorities without any exceptions and if the State itself was perceived to express a religious belief. Moreover, an important factor to be taken into consideration is the general dynamics of majority and minority religious groupings in society at large or within a particular school situation. Thus, different constellations may require different solutions which should be precisely assessed on a case-by-case basis.

43. Without prejudice to contextual specificities, however, there are nevertheless good reasons to start with a general presumption of the students' right to wear religious symbols in the school. According to article 18, paragraph 1, of the International Covenant on Civil and Political Rights, the right to freedom of thought, conscience and religion includes freedom to manifest one's religion or belief in worship, observance, practice and teaching. There can be little doubt that observing and practicing one's religion or belief may also include the wearing of distinctive clothing or head coverings in conformity with the individual's faith.[29] Moreover, freedom of religion or belief can be exercised either individually or in community with others and in public or private. The possibility to wear religious symbols in the public sphere, including in the school context, thus appears to be a natural result of the freedom to manifest one's religion or belief. In addition, religious symbols in the school may also reflect the religious diversity as it exists in society at large.

---

[28]   See, for example, the Special Rapporteur's reports A/51/542/Add.2, para. 51; E/CN.4/1998/6, para. 60; E/CN.4/2006/5, para. 38; A/HRC/7/10/Add.1, paras. 125-126.

[29]   See Human Rights Committee, general comment No. 22 (1993) on the right to freedom of thought, conscience and religion, para. 4; Human Rights Committee, communication No. 931/2000, *Hudoyberganova v. Uzbekistan*, Views adopted on 5 November 2004, para. 6.2; E/CN.4/2006/5, paras. 40-41.

44. On the other hand, the freedom to manifest one's religion or belief is not without limitations. According to the criteria set out in article 18, paragraph 3, of the International Covenant on Civil and Political Rights, limitations must be "prescribed by law and [be] necessary to protect public safety, order, health, or morals or the fundamental rights and freedoms of others". The application of the criteria for possible limitations of the freedom to manifest one's religion or belief, at any rate, requires diligence, precision and precaution. Given the ambivalence of the school situation in which students, in particular members of minorities, might at times experience situations of personal or structural vulnerability, the general presumption in favour of the possibility to wear religious symbols must thus be connected with a number of caveats. For instance, in some constellations restrictions on the freedom to manifest religion or belief by wearing religious symbols may be justifiable in order to protect minority students from pressure exercised by schoolmates or their community. Moreover, a teacher wearing religious symbols in the class may have an undue impact on students, depending on the general behaviour of the teacher, the age of students and other factors. In addition, it may be difficult to reconcile the compulsory display of a religious symbol in all classrooms with the State's duty to uphold confessional neutrality in public education in order to include students of different religions or beliefs on the basis of equality and non-discrimination.

45. Obviously, finding appropriate solutions for conflicts over religious symbols in the school is not an easy task, and there exists no general blueprint simply applicable to all constellations or situations. At the same time, it is clear that the goal must always be to equally protect the positive and the negative aspects of freedom of religion or belief, i.e. the freedom positively to manifest one's belief, for instance by wearing religious clothing, and the freedom not to be exposed to any pressure, especially from the State or within State institutions, to perform religious activities. Furthermore, any restrictions on the freedom to observe religious dress codes deemed necessary in that context must be formulated in a non-discriminatory manner. It would not be legitimate, for instance, if restrictions were linked to exception clauses in favour only of the dominant religion of the country concerned.

46. In this context, the Special Rapporteur would like to draw attention to the observations made by the previous mandate holder in her last report to the Commission on Human Rights (E/CN.4/2006/5, paras. 51-60). In that report, Ms. Jahangir developed a number of general criteria on the assessment of conflicts over religious symbols, especially in a school situ-

ation. Inter alia, she draws a distinction between regulations addressed to all religious symbols in a neutral manner and regulations which – de jure or de facto – privilege the symbolic presence of some religions, at the expense of other religions or beliefs, a practice which may be in breach of the principle of non-discrimination. She also indicated that accommodating different situations according to the perceived vulnerability of the persons involved might in certain situations be considered legitimate, e.g. in order to protect underage schoolchildren and the parents' liberty to ensure the religious and moral education of their children in conformity with their own convictions. Furthermore, women's rights, and in particular the principle of equality between men and women and the individual's freedom to wear or not to wear religious symbols, should be duly taken into account.[30]

D. Religious instruction in schools

47. As elaborated above (see paras. 27-40), it is crucial to distinguish conceptually between information about religions or beliefs on the one hand and religious instruction on the other. On a practical level there are a number of overlaps which pose problems in the actual application of that distinction.[31] In addition, different pedagogical approaches may add nuances, for example if teaching methods encourage pupils to "learn about religions"[32] or to "learn from religion"[33]. At any rate, on a normative level conceptual clarity remains of strategic importance to pursue a human rights approach and to do justice to the ambivalence of the school

[30]   See A/HRC/15/53, para. 60; A/65/207, para. 34.

[31]   One example would be a school subject that "combines education on religious knowledge with practising a particular religious belief, e.g. learning by heart of prayers, singing religious hymns or attendance at religious services". See Human Rights Committee, communication No. 1155/2003, *Leirvåg v. Norway*, Views adopted on 3 November 2004, para. 14.6.

[32]   "'Learning about religion' includes enquiry into, and investigation of, the nature of religions, their beliefs, teachings and ways of life, sources, practices and forms of expression. It covers students' knowledge and understanding of individual religions and how they relate to each other as well as the study of the nature and characteristics of religion. It includes the skills of interpretation, analysis and explanation. Pupils learn to communicate their knowledge and understanding using specialist vocabulary." (*Toledo Guiding Principles on Teaching about Religions and Beliefs in Public Schools*, pp. 45-46, footnote 52).

[33]   "'Learning from religion' is concerned with developing students' reflection on and response to their own and others' experiences in the light of their learning about religion. It develops pupils' skills of application, interpretation and evaluation of what they learn about religion." (Ibid.).

being a place of learning, social development and communicative interaction but also a place in which situations of particular vulnerability can
occur.

48. Religious instruction, i.e. instruction in a particular religion or belief
based on its tenets, can take place in different constellations. The following paragraphs will primarily focus on religious instruction given in the
public school system, i.e. the system of public education provided by the
State. While the role of private schools, including denominational
schools, will also be mentioned, the Special Rapporteur will leave aside in
this chapter those forms of religious instruction that are organized in religious institutions – such as churches, mosques, pagodas, synagogues or
temples – and attended by students outside of school.

49. In many countries religious instruction in the above defined sense
constitutes an integral part of public school teaching and maybe even of
the mandatory school curriculum. Such practice may reflect the interests
and demands of large parts of the population. Many parents may wish
that their children be familiarized with the basic doctrines and rules of
their own religion or belief and that the school take an active role in that
endeavour. In the understanding of many parents, the development of
knowledge and social skills of their children through school education
would be incomplete unless it includes a sense of religious awareness and
familiarity with their own religion or belief. Hence the provision of religious instruction in the public school system may be based on the explicit
or implicit wishes of considerable currents within the country's population.

50. However, given the ambivalence of the school situation – including
possible situations of particular vulnerability for some persons or groups
– religious instruction in the public school system must always go hand
in hand with specific safeguards on behalf of members of religious or belief minorities. The Human Rights Committee has also emphasized that
instruction in a religious context should "respect the convictions of parents and guardians who do not believe in any religion".[34] A minimum requirement would be that members of minorities have the possibility of
"opting out" of a religious instruction that goes against their own convictions. Such exemptions should also be available for persons adhering to
the very same faith on which instruction is given, whenever they feel
that their personal convictions – including maybe dissenting convictions

---

[34]   See Human Rights Committee, communications No. 40/1978, *Hartikainen v. Fin-
land*, Views adopted on 9 April 1981, para. 10.4, and *Leirvåg v. Norway*, para. 14.2.

– are not respected. Moreover, the possibility of opting out should not be linked to onerous bureaucratic procedures and must never carry with it de jure or de facto penalties. Finally, wherever possible, students not participating in religious instruction due to their different faith should have access to alternative courses provided by the school.

51. The decision whether or not to opt out of religious instruction must be left to students or their parents or guardians who are the decisive rights holders in that respect. With regard to article 18, paragraph 4, of the International Covenant on Civil and Political Rights, the Human Rights Committee has noted that "public education that includes instruction in a particular religion or belief is inconsistent with article 18.4 unless provision is made for non-discriminatory exemptions or alternatives that would accommodate the wishes of parents and guardians".[35] Moreover, attention must be given to the rights and duties of the parents and, when applicable, legal guardians, to provide direction to the child in the exercise of his or her right to freedom of thought, conscience and religion in a manner consistent with the evolving capacities of the child.[36] The concept of "evolving capacities" is crucial since it acknowledges that the child at some point "comes of age" and should be able to make personal choices in matters of religion or belief. Due weight should be given to the views of the child in accordance with his or her age and maturity, which need to be assessed on a case-by-case basis.[37]

52. Unfortunately, however, reports from various countries indicate that the above mentioned principles – which constitute an integral part of freedom of religion or belief – are not always respected. In some countries students belonging to minorities allegedly experience formal or informal pressure to attend religious instruction given on the sole basis of the country's dominant religious tradition. The same can happen to adherents of alternative interpretation of, or dissenting views on, the dominant religion on which school instruction is based. Even worse, incidents have been reported that in some schools members of minorities or persons with dissenting views have to express criticism of their own convic-

---

[35] Human Rights Committee, general comment No. 22, para. 6. See also Committee on Economic, Social and Cultural Rights, general comment No. 13 (1999) on the right to education, para. 28.

[36] Art. 14, para. 2, of the Convention on the Rights of the Child.

[37] See Committee on the Rights of the Child, general comment No. 12 (2009) on the right of the child to be heard, para. 29. With regard to the concept of "evolving capacities" in the context of the child's right to freedom of religion or belief see A/64/159, paras. 26-28.

tion as a precondition to take their school examinations. Exemptions for students adhering to religions or beliefs other than those instructed in school, if available at all, are sometimes linked to onerous application procedures or stigmatizing practices, with the result that students and parents often refrain from making use of them.

53.   In this context, it is worth emphasizing that practices which forcibly expose students to religious instruction against their own will violate article 18, paragraph 2, of the International Covenant on Civil and Political Rights which states that "no one shall be subject to coercion which would impair his freedom to have or adopt a religion or belief of his choice". This *forum internum* component of freedom of religion or belief enjoys particularly strong protection under international human rights law as no derogation from article 18 of the Covenant may be made, not even in a time of public emergency which threatens the life of the nation.[38] In addition, coercive practices may also violate the rights of parents "to ensure the religious and moral education of their children in conformity with their own convictions" (art. 18, para. 4, of the Covenant).

54.   The situation of religious instruction in private schools warrants a distinct assessment. The reason is that private schools, depending on their particular rationale and curriculum, might accommodate the more specific educational interests or needs of parents and children, including in questions of religion or belief. Indeed, many private schools have a specific denominational profile which can make them particularly attractive to adherents of the respective denomination, but frequently also for parents and children of other religious or belief orientation. In this sense, private schools constitute a part of the institutionalized diversity within a modern pluralistic society. States are not obliged under international human rights law to fund schools which are established on a religious basis, however, if the State chooses to provide public funding to religious schools, it should make this funding available without any discrimination.[39]

55.   Furthermore, the existence of private denominational schools – or the possibility of their establishment – cannot serve as an excuse for the State not to pay sufficient attention to religious and belief diversity in public school education. Even though private denominational schools

---

[38]   International Covenant on Civil and Political Rights, art. 4; see also Human Rights Committee, general comment No. 22, para. 1.

[39]   Human Rights Committee, communication No. 694/1996, *Waldman v. Canada*, Views adopted on 3 November 1999, para. 10.6.

may be one way for parents to ensure a religious and moral education of their children in conformity with their own convictions, the public school system must also respect religious and belief diversity. In this context, the inaugural session of the Forum on Minority Issues, held in December 2008, recommended that "where separate educational institutions are established for minorities for linguistic, religious or cultural reasons, no barriers should be erected to prevent members of minority groups from studying at general educational institutions, should they or their families so wish".[40]

56. Another caveat concerns situations in which private denominational schools have a de facto monopoly in a particular locality or region, with the result that students and parents have no option to avoid school education based on a denomination different from their own religious or belief conviction. In such situations it falls upon the State, as the guarantor of human rights, to ensure that freedom of religion or belief is effectively respected, including the right of students not to be exposed to religious instruction against their will as well the right of parents to ensure a religious and moral education of their children in conformity with their own convictions.

IV. Conclusions and recommendations

57. Freedom of religion or belief and school education is a multifaceted issue that entails significant opportunities and far-reaching challenges. The school is the most important formal institution for the realization of the right to education. It provides a place of learning, social development and social encounter. At the same time, the school is also a place in which authority is exercised and some persons, including members of religious or belief minorities, may find themselves in situations of vulnerability. Given this ambivalence of the school situation, safeguards to protect the individual's right to freedom of religion or belief are necessary. Special attention must be given to the forum internum component of freedom of religion or belief which enjoys the status of an absolute guarantee under international human rights law. With regard to the freedom to manifest one's religion or belief, both the positive and the negative aspects of that freedom must be equally ensured, i.e. the freedom to express one's conviction as well the freedom not to be exposed to any pressure, especially

---

[40] See the report of the independent expert on minority issues (A/HRC/10/11/Add.1), para. 27.

from State authorities or in the State institution, to practice religious or belief activities against one's will.

58. Schools may offer unique possibilities for constructive dialogue among all parts of society and human rights education in particular can contribute to the elimination of negative stereotypes that often adversely affect members of religious minorities. However, freedom of religion or belief and school education has also sparked controversy in many societies, particularly with regard to contentious issues such as religious symbols in the school context and religious instruction (see paras. 20-56 above).

59. With regard to religious symbols, especially in public schools, the Special Rapporteur would like to reiterate that each case has to be decided according to its own circumstances. If restrictions on the wearing of religious symbols are deemed necessary, these restrictions should not be applied in a discriminatory manner and they must be directly related and proportionate to the specific need on which the restrictions are predicated. At the same time, for example, the rights of the child and their parents or legal guardians may justify limiting the freedom of teachers who wish to manifest their religion or belief by wearing a religious symbol. In all actions concerning children, the "best interests" of the child shall be a primary consideration. With regard to the State-prescribed mandatory display of religious symbols in classrooms, States should uphold confessional neutrality in public education in order to include students of different religions or beliefs on the basis of equality and non- discrimination.

60. In general, educational policies should aim to strengthen the promotion and protection of human rights, eradicating prejudices and conceptions incompatible with freedom of religion or belief, and ensuring respect for and acceptance of pluralism and diversity in the field of religion or belief as well as the right not to receive religious instruction inconsistent with one's conviction. Efforts should be made to establish advisory bodies at different levels that take an inclusive approach to involving different stakeholders in the preparation and implementation of school curricula related to issues of religion or belief and in the training of teachers.

61. The Special Rapporteur would like to refer to his predecessors' reports on these issues and to their involvement in the elaboration of the final document of the International Consultative Conference on School Education in relation to Freedom of Religion or Belief, Tolerance and

Non-discrimination and the Toledo Guiding Principles on Teaching about Religions and Beliefs in Public Schools. In this context, the Special Rapporteur reiterates that States, at the appropriate level of Government and in accordance with their educational systems, should favourably consider:

a) Providing teachers and students with voluntary opportunities for meetings and exchanges with their counterparts of different religions or beliefs;

b) Encouraging exchanges of teachers and students and facilitating educational study abroad;

c) Strengthening a non-discriminatory perspective in education and of knowledge in relation to freedom of religion or belief at the appropriate levels;

d) Ensuring equal rights to women and men in the field of education and freedom of religion or belief, and in particular reinforcing the protection of the right of girls to education, especially for those coming from vulnerable groups;

e) Taking appropriate measures against all forms of intolerance and discrimination based on religion or belief which manifest themselves in school curricula, textbooks and teaching methods;

f) Evaluating existing curricula being used in public schools that touch upon teaching about religions and beliefs with a view to determining whether they promote respect for freedom of religion or belief and whether they are impartial, balanced, inclusive, age appropriate, free of bias and meet professional standards;

g) Assessing the process that leads to the development of curricula on teaching about religions and beliefs to make sure that this process is sensitive to the needs of various religious and belief communities and that all relevant stakeholders have an opportunity to have their voices heard;

h) Examining to what extent existing teacher-training institutions are capable of providing the necessary professional training for teaching about religions and beliefs in a way that promotes respect for human rights and, in particular, for freedom of religion or belief;

   i) Determining the extent to which teacher-training institutions provide sufficient knowledge of human rights issues, an understanding of the diversity of religious and non-religious views in society, a firm grasp of various teaching methodologies (with particular attention to those founded on an intercultural approach) and significant insight into ways that one can teach about religions and beliefs in a respectful, impartial and professional way.

62. Finally, the Special Rapporteur would like to reiterate that the role of parents, families and legal guardians is an essential factor in the education of children in the field of religion or belief. Consequently, special attention should be paid to encouraging positive attitudes and, in view of the best interest of the child, to supporting parents to exercise their rights and fully play their role in education in the field of tolerance and non-discrimination, taking into account the relevant provisions of the Universal Declaration of Human Rights, the International Covenant on Civil and Political Rights, the International Covenant on Economic, Social and Cultural Rights, the Declaration on the Elimination of All Forms of Intolerance and Discrimination Based on Religion or Belief and the Convention on the Rights of the Child.

2.   Chapter: Report July 2011

I. Introduction

1.   Twenty-five years ago, the mandate of the Special Rapporteur on freedom of religion or belief was created by the Commission on Human Rights pursuant to its resolution 1986/20. The Human Rights Council renewed the Special Rapporteur's mandate in its resolution 6/37 and extended it for a further period of three years through resolution 14/11. During the fourteenth session of the Council, Heiner Bielefeldt was appointed as Special Rapporteur on freedom of religion or belief; he took office on 1 August 2010.

2.   In section II of the present report, the Special Rapporteur provides an overview of his activities since the submission of the previous report to the General Assembly (A/65/207). In section III, the Special Rapporteur puts a thematic focus on the role of the State in promoting interreligious communication. His conclusions and recommendations with regard to interreligious communication are reflected in section IV.

II. Activities of the Special Rapporteur

3.   Activities include sending allegation letters and urgent appeals to States concerning individual cases; conducting official country visits; participating in meetings with representatives of States, religious or belief communities, national human rights institutions and civil society organizations; and issuing public statements. The present overview of activities since 1 August 2010 is organized under five headings pursuant to Human Rights Council resolutions 6/37 and 14/11.

A. Promotion of the adoption of measures at the national, regional and international levels to ensure the promotion and protection of the right to freedom of religion or belief

4.   The Special Rapporteur continues to promote the right to freedom of religion or belief at the national, regional and international levels. At the national level, the Special Rapporteur participated in an expert hearing on 27 October 2010, held by the Committee on Human Rights and Humanitarian Aid of the German Parliament. During the public hearing in Berlin, a number of questions relating to the topic "freedom of religion and Eu-

ropean identity" were discussed by the experts and members of Parliament.[41]

5.   At the regional level, the Special Rapporteur attended the Supplementary Human Dimension Meeting on Freedom of Religion or Belief held by the Organization for Security and Cooperation in Europe (OSCE) in Vienna on 9 and 10 December 2010. Ahead of Human Rights Day 2010, he also issued a joint statement together with the director of the OSCE Office for Democratic Institutions and Human Rights, calling upon States to remove undue restrictions on freedom of religion or belief.[42] In addition, on 15 March 2011, the Special Rapporteur met with members of the European Commission and the Human Rights Working Group of the Council of the European Union in Brussels. On 26 May 2011, the Special Rapporteur was invited by the European Parliament's Subcommittee on Human Rights for a hearing on freedom of religion or belief.

6.   At the international level, the Special Rapporteur joined a press statement on 17 September 2010 in anticipation of the High-level Plenary Meeting of the sixty- fifth session of the General Assembly on the Millennium Development Goals.[43] In their joint press statement, the 26 special procedures mandate holders argued that the implementation of the agreed outcome document (General Assembly resolution 65/1) must have a stronger focus on human rights, not only to ensure the achievement of the Millennium Development Goals, but to also make them meaningful for the billions of people who need them most. The mandate holders emphasized that some groups, including those who face religious discrimination, too often find themselves forgotten. The mandate holders added that poverty gaps would increase unless programmes such as those to achieve the Millennium Development Goals addressed the unique circumstances of those groups and the causes and effects of the discrimination that limits access to education and jobs.

---

[41]   See www.bundestag.de/bundestag/ausschuessel7/a17/anhoerungen/Religionsfreiheit/.
[42]   See www.osce.org/odihr/74525.
[43]   See www.ohchr.org/en/NewsEvents/Pages/DisplayNews.aspx?NewsID=10344&LangID=E.

B. Identification of existing and emerging obstacles to the enjoyment of the right to freedom of religion or belief and presentation of recommendations on ways and means to overcome such obstacles

7.   The Special Rapporteur has held public or bilateral meetings with representatives of States and civil society organizations to discuss existing and emerging obstacles to the enjoyment of the right to freedom of religion or belief. He met with numerous members of religious or belief communities and held public briefings with them, for example in Asunción; Barcelona, Spain; Brussels; Geneva; New York; Oslo; and Toronto, Canada.

8.   In Vienna (9 and 10 February 2011) and Nairobi (6 and 7 April 2011) the Special Rapporteur participated in two expert workshops on the prohibition of incitement to national, racial or religious hatred. In 2011, the Office of the United Nations High Commissioner for Human Rights (OHCHR) is holding a series of such workshops to gain a better understanding of legislative patterns, judicial practices and policies with regard to the concept of incitement to national, racial or religious hatred, while also ensuring full respect for freedom of expression as outlined in articles 19 and 20 of the International Covenant on Civil and Political Rights. For the various regional workshops the Special Rapporteur presented joint submissions together with the Special Rapporteur on the promotion and protection of the right to freedom of opinion and expression and the Special Rapporteur on contemporary forms of racism, racial discrimination, xenophobia and related intolerance.[44]

9.   The Special Rapporteur conducted a country visit to Paraguay from 23 to 30 March 2011, and he is very grateful for the cooperation of the Government. At the conclusion of his visit, he commended the open and tolerant atmosphere in Paraguay at both the governmental and societal levels.[45] At the same time, he stressed that there was still much room for improvement with regard to more effective implementation of human rights, particularly in terms of non-discrimination. The Special Rapporteur drew special attention to the indigenous peoples' long history of suffering from discrimination, neglect, harassment and economic exploitation. While noting that the indigenous representatives he met mostly agreed that the general attitude towards their traditional beliefs and

---

[44]   See www2.ohchr.org/english/issues/opinion/articles1920_iccpr/index.htm.
[45]   www.ohchr.org/EN/NewsEvents/Pages/DisplayNews.aspx?NewsID=10903&LangID=E.

practices had become more respectful in recent years, he stressed that the imposition of religious doctrines and practices, possibly against the indigenous peoples' will, was not a matter of the past only but persisted to a certain degree today. The Special Rapporteur encouraged the Government of Paraguay to continue supporting the interreligious forum initiated two years ago, while at the same time ensuring open and transparent participation by all interested groups and sectors of society.

10. Continuing his predecessors' follow-up procedure concerning country visit reports, the Special Rapporteur on 5 November 2010 sent follow-up letters with regard to those missions undertaken by the previous mandate holder in 2008; to Israel and the Occupied Palestinian Territory, India and Turkmenistan. The Special Rapporteur requested updated information on the consideration given to his predecessor's recommendations, the steps taken to implement them and any constraints that may prevent their implementation. The follow-up tables containing the conclusions and recommendations of the related mission report, and information from the Government and relevant United Nations documents, including from the universal periodic review, special procedures and treaty bodies, are available online.[46]

C. Examination of incidents and governmental actions incompatible with the Declaration on the Elimination of All Forms of Intolerance and of Discrimination Based on Religion or Belief and recommendation of remedial measures

11. The Special Rapporteur has continued to engage in constructive dialogue with States by sending them allegation letters and urgent appeals for clarification of credible allegations of incidents and governmental actions incompatible with the provisions of the 1981 Declaration on the Elimination of All Forms of Intolerance and of Discrimination Based on Religion or Belief. Since the creation of the mandate, the Special Rapporteur has sent some 1,250 allegation letters and urgent appeals to a total of 130 States. The communications sent by the Special Rapporteur between 1 December 2009 and 30 November 2010 and the replies received from Governments are summarized in his latest communications report (A/HRC/16/53/Add.1), which also includes recommendations of remedial measures.

---

[46] See www.ohchr.org/EN/Issues/FreedomReligion/Pages/Visits.aspx.

12. The Special Rapporteur's communications report provides evidence of worrying allegations of the disappearance, torture, arrest and detention of individuals belonging to religious minorities or belief communities. He is very much concerned about intercommunal violence, which has resulted in the killing of hundreds of persons, including many women and children. His communications also relate to death threats and discrimination against converts, as well as statements inciting violence directed against members of religious minorities. The Special Rapporteur has also taken up allegations of public manifestations of religious intolerance, stigmatization of persons based on their religion or belief and public announcements of disrespectful acts. Further cases involve attacks on places of worship and religious tensions related to religious sites. The Special Rapporteur has also analysed problematic legislation, including on blasphemy. In his statement to the Human Rights Council on 10 March 2011, he referred to horrific consequences of related controversies, including loss of life, and extended his deepest condolences to the families affected.[47]

13. Country visits offer further opportunities to examine and analyse incidents and governmental actions in greater detail. Since the establishment of the mandate, the Special Rapporteur has conducted 32 country visits, including one follow-up mission. The Special Rapporteur is grateful for the invitation by the Government of the Republic of Moldova to undertake a fact-finding mission in September 2011. Updated information about the Special Rapporteur's visit requests and forthcoming missions is available on the OHCHR website.[48]

14. On 10 March 2011, the twenty-fifth anniversary of the establishment of the mandate, the Special Rapporteur launched a reference e-book with observations and recommendations by the four mandate holders who have served as Special Rapporteur on freedom of religion or belief since 1986. The "Rapporteur's digest on freedom of religion or belief"[49] is a 108-page downloadable compilation of relevant excerpts from thematic and country-specific reports produced by Angelo d'Almeida Ribeiro (serving from March 1986 to March 1993), Abdelfattah Amor (serving from April

---

[47] See www.ohchr.org/Documents/Issues/Religion/HRC16statement_March2011.pdf and the press statement condemning the killing of the Pakistani Minister for Minority Affairs on 2 March 2011 (www.ohchr.org/en/NewsEvents/Pages/DisplayNews.aspx?NewsID=10786&LangID=E).

[48] See www.ohchr.org/EN/Issues/FreedomReligion/Pages/Visits.aspx.

[49] See www2.ohchr.org/english/issues/religion/docs/RapporteursDigestFreedomReligionBelief.pdf.

1993 to July 2004), Asma Jahangir (serving from August 2004 to July 2010) and Heiner Bielefeldt (serving since August 2010). For ease of reference, the digest is arranged according to the five topics of the mandate's framework for communications, as outlined in the last thematic report submitted to the Commission on Human Rights: (a) freedom of religion or belief, (b) discrimination, (c) vulnerable groups, (d) intersection of freedom of religion or belief with other human rights, and (e) cross-cutting issues (see E/CN.4/2006/5, paras. 28-35 and annex).

D. Application of a gender perspective

15. As requested by the Human Rights Council, the Special Rapporteur has continued to apply a gender perspective — inter alia, through the identification of gender-specific abuses — in the reporting process, including in information collection and in recommendations made. A number of allegation letters and urgent appeals summarized in the Special Rapporteur's communications reports specifically address practices and legislation that discriminate against women and girls, including with regard to the exercise of their right to freedom of thought, conscience and religion or belief.

16. In his statement to the Third Committee of the General Assembly on 21 October 2010 (see A/C.3/65/SR.25), the Special Rapporteur emphasized that gender-based discrimination had at least two distinct dimensions in the context of religion. On the one hand, women belonging to communities that are discriminated against also often suffer from gender-based discrimination — for example, if a woman is discriminated against in the labour market because she has decided to wear a religious symbol. On the other hand, religious traditions or interpretations of religious doctrine sometimes appear to justify, or even call for, discrimination against women. In this context, the Special Rapporteur would like to reiterate that it can no longer be taboo to demand that women's rights take priority over intolerant beliefs that are used to justify gender discrimination.

17. In his statement to the Human Rights Council on 10 March 2011, the Special Rapporteur stressed that religions or beliefs change over time.[50] In the case of practices that may have a negative bearing on the situation of women or girls, for example, some women have called for reform by advocating and pursuing innovative interpretations of the respective sources, doctrines and norms. The Special Rapporteur stressed the im-

---

[50]   www.ohchr.org/Documents/Issues/Religion/HRC16statement_March2011.pdf.

portance of ensuring that textbooks and other information materials in public schools draw a sufficiently comprehensive picture of the various religions or beliefs and their internal pluralism. Existing alternative voices within religious traditions, including voices of women, should have their fair share of attention. With regard to wearing religious symbols, the Special Rapporteur emphasized that any restrictions on the freedom to observe religious dress codes deemed necessary in a certain context must be formulated in a non-discriminatory manner. Women's rights, and in particular the principle of equality between men and women and the individual's freedom to wear or not wear religious symbols, should be duly taken into account.

E. Working with mass media organizations to promote an atmosphere of respect and tolerance for religious and cultural diversity, as well as multiculturalism

18. The Human Rights Council, in its resolution 14/11, called upon the Special Rapporteur to work with mass media organizations to promote an atmosphere of respect and tolerance for religious and cultural diversity, as well as multiculturalism. In this context, supported by the OHCHR, the Special Rapporteur held an expert consultation in Geneva on the theme "Equality, non-discrimination and diversity: challenge or opportunity for the mass media?". This consultation, on 30 November 2010, brought together the Special Rapporteurs on freedom of religion or belief, on freedom of opinion and expression and on racism and 12 experts with experience in mass media organizations having a global outreach, including a newspaper editor, a television anchor, a foreign correspondent, a wire service reporter, a blogger and a head of news-gathering, and representatives of an umbrella organization of journalists, an international human rights organization, the United Nations Educational, Scientific and Cultural Organization and the Alliance of Civilizations.

19. As part of the discussion, two case studies were analysed: the media coverage of plans to burn copies of the Koran (see also A/HRC/16/53/Add.1, paras. 414-421) and the challenges of reporting on post-electoral conflicts in an ethnically divided country.[51] The Special Rapporteur learned more about the decision-making processes within the different mass media organizations and the conditions for making their day-to-day judgement calls, adhering to the key principles of pro-

---

[51] See   www.ohchr.org/EN/NewsEvents/Pages/DisplayNews.aspx?NewsID=2122& LangID=E.

fessionalism and independence. The experts highlighted several challenges faced by mass media, for example the increasingly competitive nature of the industry and the need to provide news around the clock, coupled with a global and evolving media landscape.

20. Drawing upon their work, the experts also reflected on existing initiatives and guidelines used by mass media organizations to promote equality, freedom of expression and diversity.[52] They acknowledged that self-regulation for mass media is the best system, albeit imperfect, yet also emphasized that self-regulation should not lead to detrimental self-censorship or a conspiracy of silence. The mass media experts also emphasized the importance of skills training, including with respect to investigative reporting.

III. The role of the State in promoting interreligious communication

21. The General Assembly and Human Rights Council have stressed "the importance of a continued and strengthened dialogue in all its forms, including among and within religions or beliefs, and with broader participation, including of women, to promote greater tolerance, respect and mutual understanding" (General Assembly resolution 65/211 and Human Rights Council resolution 16/13). In this context, the Special Rapporteur has decided to put a thematic focus in the present report on the role of the State in promoting interreligious communication. He understands "interreligious communication" to include various forms of exchange of information, experiences and ideas of all kinds between individuals belonging to different theistic, atheistic or non-theistic beliefs or not professing any religion or belief.

22. The Special Rapporteur has held discussions with people from different religious or belief backgrounds who have long-term experience in interreligious communication. He is generally very impressed by the high degree of commitment that countless individuals have shown in this field. Moreover, members of minority groups — even those who so far

---

[52] See for example Al-Jazeera's Code of Ethics (http://english.aljazeera.net/aboutus/2006/11/2008525185733692771.html); the British Broadcasting Corporation's Editorial Guidelines (www.bbc.co.uk/guidelines/ editorialguidelines); the Camden Principles on Freedom of Expression and Equality (www.article19.org/resources.php/resource/1214/en/the-camden-principles-on-freedom-of-expression-and-equality); and the Ethical Journalism Initiative (http://ethical journalisminitiative.org).

have been largely excluded from existing dialogue projects — have repeatedly expressed their hopes that interreligious communication may help to improve their situations. Therefore, the Special Rapporteur wishes to encourage States to continue and further increase promotional activities in the field of interreligious communication. They should be conducted in a spirit of inclusiveness, non-discrimination and respect for every human being's freedom of religion or belief. Moreover, the Special Rapporteur extends his utmost appreciation to all those who, sometimes under complicated circumstances, have engaged in interreligious communicative projects designed to eliminate prejudices, stereotypes and hostility.

A. Communication and human rights in general

23. The relationship between communication and human rights is complex. A vigorous culture of communication and public debate constitutes a crucial element for human rights to become a reality. This includes the possibility of organizing protests against human rights abuses and exercising public criticism of existing or emerging obstacles to the full enjoyment of human rights. Human rights include free communication, with freedom of expression being the most prominent example. Other examples include freedom of assembly, the right to participate in cultural life, minority rights (e.g., rights of linguistic minorities), the right of accused persons to be heard in criminal trials and, last but not least, freedom of religion or belief. Open and critical communication is also needed to eradicate negative stereotypes, which themselves constitute root causes of mutual suspicion, discrimination, hostility or violence and concomitant human rights abuses.

24. This multifaceted relationship between communication and human rights also manifests itself in the area of freedom of religion or belief, which like other human rights, can flourish only in a climate of open public discourse. At the same time, the right to freedom of religion or belief itself encompasses various forms of freely chosen communication, including the freedom to communicate within one's own religious or belief group, to share one's conviction with others, to broaden one's horizons by communicating with people of different convictions, to cherish and develop contacts across State boundaries, to receive and spread information about religious or belief issues and to try to persuade others by means of peaceful communication. There can be no doubt that activities of intrareligious and interreligious communication in the broadest sense

fall within the scope of freedom of religion or belief.[53] In addition, the necessity of dispelling existing stereotypes by promoting communication between members of different religious or belief groups has rightly received particular attention in recent years, given the many incidents of religiously motivated violence (see for example A/HRC/13/40; A/HRC/16/53/Add.1; A/HRC/13/40/Add.1; and A/HRC/10/8/Add.1).

25.   Violence between religious or belief groups is often triggered by a dangerous combination of paranoia and public contempt against minorities. Sometimes even tiny minorities are confronted with allegations of undermining peace or national cohesion due to some mysteriously "infectious" effects attributed to them. Such allegations can escalate into fully fledged conspiracy theories fabricated by competing groups, the media or even State authorities. At the same time, members of religious or belief minorities often see themselves exposed to public manifestations of contempt — for instance, based on rumours that they supposedly lack moral values. It is exactly this combination of demonizing conspiracy projections and public contempt that typically triggers violence either directed against members of minorities or occurring between different communities. Hence the eradication of stereotypes and prejudices that constitute the root causes of fear, resentment and hatred must be part and parcel of any policy of preventing violence and concomitant human rights abuses. Intrareligious and interreligious communication must play a crucial role in this continuous endeavour.

26.   Unfortunately, we sometimes witness the outbreak of violence despite existing inter-group communication, including interreligious communication. The most notorious examples are civil wars in which former neighbours, who used to live peacefully side by side over many years, attack one another violently. Not infrequently, such violence occurs under the auspices of ascribed or actual religious differences. Ample evidence indicates that communication per se does not provide a guarantee for peaceful coexistence between different groups of people. Yet it would be dangerous to use this disturbing observation as an argument for downplaying the significance of communication. Rather, what is needed are effective policies for improving the conditions for a sustainable culture of communication.

---

[53]   Article 6 (i) of the Declaration on the Elimination of All Forms of Intolerance and of Discrimination Based on Religion or Belief provides that the right to freedom of thought, conscience, religion or belief includes the freedom "to establish and maintain communications with individuals and communities in matters of religion and belief at the national and international levels".

27. Research in social psychology has confirmed that communication is generally conducive to peaceful, non-violent relations, provided the following conditions are met: (a) people, or groups of individuals, encounter each other on an equal footing; (b) communication has a long-term perspective (i.e., it goes beyond mere superficial brief encounters); (c) elements of common interest are identified and clarified; (d) there is encouragement from society at large, including from political authorities, in the sense of a general appreciation of inter-group communication.

28. Human rights, in particular the rights to freedom of thought, conscience, religion, opinion and expression and the principle of non-discrimination, can help to bring about circumstances of improved communication, which, in turn, enhance the general prospects for the practical enjoyment of human rights by all. The Special Rapporteur would like to reiterate a quote from Boutros Boutros-Ghali, the former Secretary-General: "Human rights, when viewed from a universal perspective, force us to face the most demanding of all dialectics: the dialectics of identity and otherness, of 'self' and 'other'. They teach us, in the most direct way, that we are, at one and the same time, the same and different" (see E/CN.4/2003/66, para. 119).

29. Many interlocutors with expertise in the field of interreligious dialogue have expressed to the Special Rapporteur their experience-based conviction that regular encounters between individuals and groups, if conducted on an equal footing and with a long-term perspective, foster a better mutual understanding across religious divides. At the same time, it is important to be aware of possible frustrations which participants in dialogue projects might experience. It can happen that, as a result of serious attempts at getting to know one another, people may feel they are further apart than they had previously thought. And yet it would be wrong to contend that communication in such cases has been useless or even an outright failure. On the contrary, however frustrating the experience of limits of mutual understanding may be, a concrete lack of understanding is still generally better than an abstract lack of understanding, as an abstract lack of understanding, in the sense of ascribing complete "otherness" to a person or group typically renders groups of people vulnerable to uninhibited and dangerous negative projections, including conspiracy theories and scapegoating communications in which participants experience the limits of mutual understanding are clearly preferable to an attitude of refusing communication in general. This clarification is intended to encourage people to continue dialogue

projects even in the face of frustrating experiences that may at times occur.

B. Formal and informal interreligious communication

30. The underlying understanding of interreligious communication is broad so as to conceptually include individuals holding different religious as well as non-religious convictions. From a human rights perspective, it is crucial to work on the basis of such a broad, inclusive approach. Indeed, this requirement mirrors the universalistic nature of freedom of religion or belief as a human right that is based on the recognition of the inherent dignity of all members of the human family.[54] As the Human Rights Committee rightly pointed out, freedom of religion or belief "protects theistic, non-theistic and atheistic beliefs, as well as the right not to profess any religion or belief" (see CCPR/C/21/Rev.1/Add.4, para. 2). It furthermore includes members of newly established communities, small communities and minority groups as well as minorities within minorities.

31. Interreligious communication can take place in formal or informal settings. The Special Rapporteur understands formal interreligious communication to mean dialogue projects in which the participants meet explicitly in their capacity as followers of their respective religions or beliefs. In informal communication, people may well be aware of, and may, if they wish, talk about, their different religious or non-religious affiliations without organizing their dialogue explicitly along those differences. Informal settings such as multicultural neighbourhoods, schools, clubs, Internet exchange forums and other public services may be conducive to constant interaction as a part of daily life. In a society where there are no boundaries on the basis of religion or belief, constant interaction is much more likely, thus enhancing the prospects of mutual understanding (see A/HRC/10/8, para. 21).

32. There have been interesting examples of countries that have decided to organize inclusive debates about diversity and non-discrimination, bringing together all stakeholders to discuss how to better live together. Indeed, interreligious communication does not exclusively take place in a framework specifically dedicated to religious issues. It can also be part of more general discussions and exchanges, for example about diversity and non-discrimination. Integrating religious issues into the broader dimension of diversity also has the advantage of illustrating that religions and

---

54   See preamble to the Universal Declaration of Human Rights (resolution 217 A (III)).

beliefs represent one element of diversity among several others. This could contribute to attenuating differences built or perceived exclusively on religious lines. By expanding the scope of issues discussed, this sort of dialogue can also open up new horizons for seeking possible solutions and compromises.

33.   There seems to be a tendency in international forums to narrow the concept of interreligious communication to formal dialogue projects while paying comparatively little attention to the reality, potential and significance of informal communication. However, there are good reasons to understand the two forms as equally relevant because they can complement each other. Formal interreligious dialogue makes it possible, for instance, to tackle stereotypes or prejudices based on an explanation of the self-understanding of the various religious or belief groups involved in such dialogue. Informal interreligious communication can more easily accommodate individuals who do not want to be identified publicly with their religious or belief convictions or people who are less knowledgeable about, or less interested in, theological and philosophical issues. Thus, there are good reasons to further explore the potential of informal interreligious communication, thereby roadening the options of promoting encounters between individuals and groups of different religions and beliefs. In general it seems advisable always to take both approaches into account when designing political strategies. Moreover, promoting a combination of formal and informal interreligious communication is one way to do justice to the requirement of conceptual inclusiveness, which itself mirrors the universalistic nature of freedom of religion or belief as a human right.

C.   Appreciating diversity of interreligious communication

34.   Interreligious communication harbours an inexhaustible diversity of possible settings, forums, agendas, themes, goals and procedures, with the result that any attempts at a comprehensive mapping exercise would necessarily fail. To start with, interreligious settings range from rather exclusive groupings to projects that aspire to be as inclusive as possible. Conducting or promoting exclusive dialogue settings does not, per se, violate the requirement of conceptual inclusiveness, provided some important safeguards are respected (see sect. E below). Bilateral forums may be preferable, for instance, if two religious groups sharing a difficult and painful history of misunderstanding want to communicate intensively for the purpose of overcoming traditional obstacles and improving their coexistence. Religious communities that feel specific theological affinities

towards one another may also prefer somewhat exclusive communicative settings that allow them to further develop existing ties. By contrast, politically oriented dialogue projects, for instance those aiming to foster national, regional or international peace, typically require a maximum of inclusiveness in the sense that people from the most widely differing religious or belief backgrounds should have a chance to participate. Moreover, traditionally marginalized persons, such as women, may wish to come together across religious divides in order to identify patterns of discrimination in different religious or philosophical traditions and to envisage strategies that may help rectify that state of affairs. Examples of such settings are interreligious conferences or research projects by feminist theologians.

35. Thematically, interreligious communication can address a multitude of different issues. Dialogue projects may pursue a theological agenda by dealing with methods of analysing sacred texts or the understanding of rites and ceremonies in different traditions. As a result, discussants may discover similarities, overcome traditional misunderstandings and develop respect for remaining theological differences. Other forums of interreligious communication, in particular those supported by international organizations, are devoted chiefly to promoting a broad consensus on political issues, such as protection of the environment, international peace or respect for human rights. On the municipal level, interreligious round tables have been established, for instance, for the purpose of solving neighbourhood conflicts over the construction of religious buildings. Of special importance are educational and training projects designed to familiarize young people or specific groups, such as journalists or other media practitioners, with religious or belief diversity. Finally, there are examples of people across religious divides coming together to work in common on artistic projects. These projects can include creative collaboration, using theatre, festivals and other live events as ways of experiencing a common passion for the arts. Renowned orchestras have been created to demonstrate that music can break down barriers that were once considered impossible to overcome.

36. Interreligious dialogue may manifest itself in concrete events, such as public conferences or ceremonies, as well as in long-term forums or projects. It can take place at a grass-roots level or on the level of religious leadership, or in a combination thereof. Communication can be formally institutionalized or evolve spontaneously. Another important difference concerns the role of the State. While many participants of dialogue projects will probably appreciate active State involvement, others might be

more sceptical or generally favour interreligious communication without the presence of State representatives.

37. It is important to appreciate a legitimate diversity of interreligious communication with regard to settings, themes, goals and modes of operation. The conceptually inclusive approach to interreligious communication does not, per se, preclude the possibility of more exclusive communicative personal or group settings, provided some safeguards are respected. As no specific dialogue setting or project may ever claim a monopoly, there must always be room for other forms, themes, settings, goals and projects of interreligious communication. Last but not least, it is advisable to take into account the differences between formal and informal interreligious communication, which can complement each other. It may well be that informal dialogue leads to a more formal process or vice versa depending on the specific context.

D. State responsibility in promoting dialogue

38. Under international human rights law, States are obliged not merely to respect freedom of religion or belief but also to actively protect such freedom against undue interference from third parties. In addition, they should promote an atmosphere of tolerance and appreciation of religious diversity.[55] The General Assembly has repeatedly encouraged activities aimed at promoting interreligious and intercultural dialogue in order to enhance social stability, respect for diversity and mutual respect in diverse communities and to create, at the global, regional, national and local levels, an environment conducive to peace and mutual understanding (see resolutions 64/81 and 65/138).

39. The significance of promotional activities of States has recently attracted increasing attention within the entire United Nations system, including from the United Nations Educational, Scientific and Cultural Organization (UNESCO), the Alliance of Civilizations, the United Nations Population Fund, the United Nations Children's Fund, the Joint United Nations Programme on HIV/AIDS, OHCHR, the Department of Public Information and the Department of Economic and Social Affairs (see A/64/325 and A/65/269). The General Assembly, in its resolution 62/90, proclaimed 2010 the International Year for the Rapprochement of Cul-

---

[55] The general obligation of the State as guarantor of human rights has been divided into the three duties to respect, protect and fulfil human rights. The promotion of societal tolerance can be understood as falling within the field of the duty to "fulfil".

tures; more than 700 activities were undertaken in this context by States, United Nations agencies, intergovernmental and non-governmental organizations, the private sector and UNESCO institutes and chairs.[56] During its sixty-fifth session, the Assembly proclaimed the first week of February every year the World Interfaith Harmony Week between all religions, faiths and beliefs (see resolution 65/5), and requested the Secretary-General to further solicit views of Member States on the possibility of proclaiming a United Nations decade for interreligious and intercultural dialogue and cooperation for peace (see resolution 65/138). The Human Rights Council called upon States to foster a domestic environment of religious tolerance, peace and respect, inter alia by encouraging the creation of collaborative networks to build mutual understanding, promoting dialogue and inspiring constructive action towards shared policy goals and the pursuit of tangible outcomes (see Human Rights Council resolution 16/18).

40.   One recent activity, for example, is the launch of a global campaign to create a grass-roots movement of people who advocate for diversity, with an emphasis on creating a stronger link between those working at the local and global levels. The "Do One Thing" campaign was launched by the Alliance of Civilizations and UNESCO on United Nations World Day for Cultural Diversity. It involves a campaign calling on individuals to take an action that is relevant to their lives and that promotes diversity and inclusion, for example in the form of culture, an exhibition, a film or even a particular food. The sharing of experience is to be promoted through the use of social media, website postings and videos. The campaign also has the support of the private sector and large corporations, which allows the project to receive greater visibility.

41.   The options for State activities in the field of interreligious communication are manifold and include symbolic or financial support and facilitating or infrastructural activities. The possible impact of symbolic public acknowledgement and encouragement of interreligious communication by representatives of the State should not be underestimated. Social psychological research has underscored the significance of an encouraging societal and political environment for human encounters in yielding productive and sustainable results. In addition to the Government, members of legislative bodies and representatives of other State organizations can play an important role in this regard. States can also

[56]   See www.unesco.org/en/2010-international-year-for-the-rapprochement-of-cul tures.

designate a particular period of the year for interreligious communication activities (e.g., holding an interfaith week and giving symbolic, financial and infrastructural support to such a project. This approach can also be used as an opportunity to highlight the smaller initiatives, practical projects, art exhibitions and seminars that would otherwise go largely unnoticed.

42. The State can also provide financial support for existing or new interreligious dialogue projects. Not only high-level projects, such as public meetings of religious leaders, but also grass-roots movements warrant attention and appreciation in this regard and should be able to benefit from financial subsidies and infrastructure support. States should favourably consider providing teachers and students with voluntary opportunities for meetings and exchanges with their counterparts of different religions or beliefs, encouraging exchanges of teachers and students and facilitating educational study abroad (see A/HRC/16/53, para. 61 and E/CN.4/2002/73, appendix, para. 10). This can be in the form of annual summer camps or workshop projects that bring together students from different regions for an intensive training course on human rights education, interreligious dialogue and conflict resolution. Providing space and opportunity for participants to meet, interact and engage with their peers can also be a good basis for not only getting rid of negative stereotypes, but also for taking back to their respective countries the skills and techniques acquired in such camps and for perhaps replicating the initiatives in different countries or communities.

43. In addition, the State has the ability to directly invite representatives of religious or belief groups to meetings, thus taking the role of host and facilitator. This can be done at all levels of government, including at the municipal level. Indeed, reports indicate that many successful dialogue projects have actually been initiated by mayors or other municipal actors. Such invitations can have various advantages. The "neutral" framework of the State may facilitate dialogue even between groups which, owing to a history of conflicts or other negative factors, would not be likely to meet at their own initiative (see also para. 50 below). The establishment of interreligious forums facilitated by the State can provide new space for dialogue among groups of different religions, philosophical orientations and other sections of society, including indigenous and small belief communities. Another advantage of State invitations concerns the proposal of constructive agendas for interreligious dialogue projects. The presence by the State in the role of host of interreligious dialogue may

also be particularly useful whenever themes of general public interest are to be discussed.

44.   Finally, State institutions, such as public schools, provide a very important venue for both informal and formal interreligious communication. States have an obligation to make use of the manifold options inherent in the school system by providing appropriate teaching material, offering interreligious training for teachers and facilitating encounters among pupils. As the Special Rapporteur emphasized in his annual report to the Human Rights Council at its sixteenth session, school education has an enormous communicative potential in this regard (see A/HRC/16/53, para. 21).[57] This can include the distribution of interfaith toolkits at school or on campus, for example through students unions, with a view to increasing dialogue and mutual understanding between different religious groups. Such projects can aim to share resources, offer good practice and training to alleviate possible tensions between certain groups in schools or on university campuses and ultimately strengthen good relations in educational institutions. Moreover, schools and university campuses are seen as pivotal places where interreligious communication occurs.

45.   Public museums, at national or municipal levels, can also serve as platforms for facilitating interreligious dialogue projects. For instance, projects that encourage students from both denominational and non-denominational schools to explore interreligious issues can be documented, with the materials being made accessible to the wider community. Museums can also showcase stories told and discussions held, which can further facilitate and initiate discussions with students and the local communities. Furthermore, the mandate of public service broadcasters should require them to promote intercultural understanding and to foster a better understanding of different communities and the issues they face (see principle 9.2 of the Camden Principles12).

E.   Important caveats

46.   State-sponsored interreligious communication, if conducted in an inappropriate manner, can unfortunately have serious negative side ef-

---

[57]   See also Human Rights Council resolution 16/13, which underlines that educational institutions may offer unique possibilities for constructive dialogue among all parts of society, and that human rights education in particular can contribute to the elimination of negative stereotypes that often adversely affect members of religious minorities.

fects. If the State is perceived to take sides in favour of one particular religion or one specific strand within the predominant religion, then other
religious communities may — for perfectly understandable reasons —
prefer not to participate in a State-sponsored dialogue initiative. For instance, in one particular country, a minority community has been pressured by the State in recent years to join the mainstream branch of its
particular religion. The frustration felt by the community members ultimately led them to boycott the dialogue project initiated by the State. In
another country, the manner in which political leaders conducted debates on the prohibition of wearing religious garments caused a boycott
of an interreligious dialogue project by a particular community. These
examples illustrate that interreligious dialogue projects may also lead to
alienation of the very communities those projects should seek to engage.
Moreover, some reports indicate that interreligious forums have been
manipulated politically, including for electoral purposes or other political gains.

47. Therefore, the Special Rapporteur would like to reiterate that the
general starting point for designing dialogue projects must be the insight
that freedom of religion or belief has the status of an inalienable human
right based on the recognition of the inherent dignity of all human beings. Hence, when supporting interreligious communication, the State
remains under the obligation to always respect the freedom of religion or
belief. This general caveat leads to a number of more specific requirements, such as refraining from monopoly claims for State- supported dialogue projects, respecting the voluntary nature of participation, observing the principle of State neutrality and doing justice to the idea of
conceptual inclusiveness.

48. State-initiated or State-supported interreligious dialogue projects,
for all the symbolic and practical significance they may have, must never
claim a monopoly in this area. As mentioned earlier, the possibility of in-
tra- and interreligious communication itself has the status of a universal
human rights claim within the scope of freedom of religion or belief. It is
therefore clear that religious or belief communities always remain free to
establish dialogue projects on their own initiative, without depending on
State approval. State-promoted dialogue projects must also be open to
public criticism.

49. State-initiated or State-supported interreligious dialogue projects
must always proceed on a voluntary basis. They should be presented and
perceived as an offer addressed to religious or belief communities, rather
than as an obligation imposed on them by the State. If some religious or

belief groups prefer not to participate in a given project or generally wish to preserve distance from the State or from other religious groups, such an attitude of reserve must be respected as a part of their freedom of religion or belief. However, reports from different countries indicate that this is not always the case and that some communities have been negatively branded as a result of their decisions not to get involved in specific dialogue projects.

50. When initiating or promoting interreligious communication, the State should refrain from identifying itself with one particular religion or belief — or with one specific type of religion, such as a monotheistic religion. States should aspire to remain neutral in this respect. If, by contrast, the State were to participate in interreligious projects while identifying itself with one particular religion or belief, this would almost inevitably lead to discrimination against followers of other religions or beliefs. In such a situation, encounters between communities on the basis of equality would be nearly impossible. The principle of State neutrality in questions of religion or belief has been and continues to be a matter of controversy. Neutrality has sometimes been portrayed as indicating a lack of State commitment in this field. Against such a misinterpretation of the concept of neutrality, however, the Special Rapporteur would point to the positive significance of that concept, which lies in the State's obligation to be fair to the members of different religions or beliefs, on the basis of equality, and to refrain from any discriminatory treatment. State neutrality in this sense can be understood as a normative principle deriving from the obligation of a non-discriminatory implementation of freedom of religion or belief. Consequently, it should have an impact also on any promotional activities of the State in the area of interreligious communication. Again, there is evidence that some States fail to comply with this principle, with the effect that interreligious dialogue projects may in some cases amount to undue pressure placed by the State on members of religious or belief minorities. For instance, some State initiatives in interreligious dialogue were reportedly connected to pressure exercised on particular religious groups to limit their religious activities, pending recommendations from the respective Government ministries.

51. The sum total of State-promoted interreligious dialogue projects must, as far as possible, meet the criterion of conceptual inclusiveness. There is a legitimate diversity of dialogue settings, all of which may warrant State support. There may be good reasons for the State also to promote some concrete forms of "exclusive" bilateral communication, for example between certain religious or belief communities that have a his-

tory of mutual distrust. This does not in itself present a problem. However, the general balance of State support for interreligious communication should reflect the requirement of conceptual inclusiveness in the sense that all religious or belief groups that would like to participate and benefit from State support should get their fair share of attention and options. An important test question in this regard is the fair inclusion of groups that in a given society have traditionally been neglected, marginalized or completely ignored. Unfortunately, reports indicate that in many countries religious or belief minorities who would like to benefit from State-promoted dialogue continue to suffer from more or less systematic exclusion.

52.   From a practical point of view, it may be virtually impossible to fully accomplish the requirement of the concept of inclusiveness. Paying more attention to the often underestimated potential of informal interreligious communication can, however, at least indirectly, help the State come closer to that benchmark. Since informal interreligious communication does not require individuals to identify themselves explicitly as members of a particular religious group, it has the advantage of being open to the participation of people adhering to typically neglected groups, including individuals generally less interested in, or less knowledgeable about, questions of religion or belief. This example reinforces the advisability of combining formal and informal communicative settings between individuals or groups of different religions or beliefs.

F.   Addressing adverse side effects

53.   Calls for interreligious dialogue have recently attracted increasing attention in international forums, including in the United Nations. For good reasons, such calls typically receive broad or even unanimous applause. It is important, however, to be aware of possible adverse side effects that may occur and to develop appropriate coping strategies. The following remarks do not relate only to State-initiated or State-supported dialogue projects, but may also have a bearing on other forms of interreligious communication.

54.   It has been observed that focusing on interreligious diversity may lead to an underestimation of intrareligious diversity, with a possible negative impact on internal pluralism as well as "dissident voices" within the participating communities.[58] A telling metaphor frequently used to describe the general purpose of interreligious dialogue projects is the

---

[58]   The same is true for intercultural or inter-civilizations dialogue projects.

"building of bridges". This metaphor seems to imply the possibility of clearly locating the discussant groups on two opposite sides of a river or a valley. Moreover, it is often said in this context that sustainable bridge-building presupposes "solid pillars" in the sense that a clear awareness of the respective religious identities is required on both sides of the bridge. This metaphor is revealing in that it obviously presupposes a bipolar jux-taposition of "us and them". Indeed, even dialogue projects that are de-signed to prevent a "clash of civilizations" sometimes operate implicitly on the basis of a global map of predefined religious and cultural group-ings that are thought to be rigid and inflexible. Against such mispercep-tions, the Special Rapporteur would argue that we should not construe an antagonistic scenario of "us and them" living on different islands. On the contrary, we very much live on one common mainland with multifaceted layers of interconnections, identities and complexities not based solely on religion or belief.

55. The relevance and degree of intrareligious diversity should never be undervalued. To avoid the danger of underestimating or even downplay-ing pluralism within religious or belief communities, a good combination of intra- and interreligious communication is advisable. Only on the basis of such a combination is it possible to do justice to the real diversity of human beings in questions of religion or belief. This must also include a substantive and substantial participation of women, who unfortunately continue to be marginalized, especially in high-level interreligious dia-logue events. The Special Rapporteur would like to reiterate that dia-logue projects would greatly benefit from the views of women. Moreover, women from different religions or beliefs have been very effective hu-man rights advocates in situations of communal tensions (see A/HRC/10/8, para. 19; A/HRC/13/40, para. 61; and A/HRC/16/53, paras. 35-36).

56. Another problem connected with the underestimation of internal diversity is a possibly too-stereotypical picture of other religious com-munities. The apparently assumed bipolar pattern in metaphors such as "bridge-building" seems indeed to imply that the addressees of interreli-gious dialogue are generally located "on the other side" of the bridge. Thus, in the intention of reaching out widely across imagined divides, it may happen that somewhat "unusual" manifestations of minority beliefs receive undue attention because they may appear to be more attractive for outreach purposes than less salient religious manifestations. It is a great irony that, in spite of the explicit intention of finding common ground, some dialogue projects may thus inadvertently solidify existing

stereotypes. This danger is particularly pronounced in short-term dialogue projects. In order to counter such dangers, due account needs to be taken of the existing or emerging internal pluralism within the various religious or belief communities. Long-term dialogue projects will more likely reveal the relevance of internal diversity, which in some settings may be more significant than the differences between religious or belief groups.

57.   Yet another problem that may occur in interreligious dialogue projects concerns the false pretence of inclusiveness. As elaborated above, conceptual inclusiveness functions as an indispensable reminder that State-promoted interreligious dialogue projects — at least in their sum total — should do justice to all interested parties. However, no concrete dialogue project will ever be able to fully represent that idea of inclusiveness. Bearing this in mind, it is important to refrain from making a problematic pretence of full inclusiveness. For instance, if a Government claims to have invited "all relevant actors" to a given project, this will most likely imply the marginalization of some groups. To symbolically demonstrate the awareness that human diversity in questions of religion or belief will never fully be reflected in any concrete communicative setting, it might be a good idea to reserve and publicly display some empty seats as a reminder of those not represented.

58.   It is not easy to develop appropriate coping strategies for the purpose of overcoming or at least alleviating the unintended side effects mentioned above, and no one can present a blueprint suitable for all contexts and communicative settings. Again, one way to at least alleviate the problem is by paying more systematic attention to informal interreligious communication. As mentioned earlier, it would be wrong to see formal and informal interreligious communication as contradictory; rather, they mutually complement each other. Creating better conditions for informal interreligious communication can be one way of coping with risks and unintended side effects of formal interreligious dialogue projects, such as downplaying internal pluralism, bipolarization or false pretence of inclusiveness.

59.   Whereas formal interreligious projects have been increasingly recognized in their significance for the promotion of a culture of religious tolerance, the potential of informal interreligious communication still needs to be further explored. In his latest thematic report to the Human Rights Council, the Special Rapporteur, addressing freedom of religion or belief in the context of public schools, makes the point that, just as it would be wrong to ignore religious differences that may come up, it

would be equally problematic to organize communication primarily under the auspices of interreligious exchange between predefined groupings. Instead, respect for difference based on freedom of religion or belief requires an attitude of giving individuals the possibility to decide for themselves whether, to which degree and on which occasions they wish to manifest, or not manifest, their religion or belief. Such an atmosphere of relaxed openness provides a fertile ground for developing a sense of diversity as being a normal feature of modern pluralistic societies (see A/HRC/16/53, para. 40).

IV. Conclusions and recommendations

60. Interreligious communication has an important role to play in the continuous endeavour to eliminate prejudices and stereotypes which constitute the root causes of resentment, fear, paranoia, hatred, hostility, violence and concomitant human rights abuses. In order to contribute to this purpose, communication between individuals or groups should be conducted on an equal footing and with a long-term perspective. Pursuing common practical projects can help to accomplish sustainability in interreligious communication.

61. Besides its instrumental role in the eradication of stereotypes and prejudices, intra- and interreligious communication falls within the scope of freedom of religion or belief. Therefore, States have to respect, protect and promote the freedom to communicate within one's own religious or belief group, to share one's conviction with others, to broaden one's horizons by communicating with people of different convictions, to cherish and develop contacts across State boundaries, to receive and spread information about religious or belief issues and to try to persuade others by means of peaceful communication.

62. States should take a constructive role in promoting interreligious communication (i.e., the various forms of exchange of information, experiences and ideas between individuals or groups holding different religions or beliefs). As a consequence of the universalistic nature of freedom of religion or belief, interreligious communication must be broadly construed and include theistic, atheistic or non-theistic beliefs as well as the possibility not to profess any religion and belief.

63. Interreligious communication harbours an inexhaustible diversity of themes, settings, goals and procedures. Thus, there can be no one-size-fits-all approach with regard to interreligious dialogue. Keeping that cru-

cial insight in mind, States have a number of general options at their disposal to promote interreligious communication, including by:

a) Encouraging interreligious communication by publicly expressing their appreciation for well-defined dialogue projects;

b) Providing financial subsidies to existing or newly created projects;

c) Facilitating dialogue between members of various religious or belief groups in the framework of the State itself;

d) Using and developing forums of regular encounters among people of different religious or belief affiliations.

64. Promotion of interreligious dialogue by the State must always be based on respect for every human being's freedom of religion or belief as an inalienable human right. Therefore, when promoting formal or informal dialogue projects States should take into account a number of important caveats:

a) States should refrain from monopolizing interreligious communication;

b) States should not identify themselves with one particular religion or belief;

c) States should endeavour to be inclusive, in the sense that the overall balance of State-promoted interreligious dialogue projects must be fair and non-discriminatory;

d) States should meticulously respect the principle of voluntary participation and should refrain from negatively branding those communities that decide not to participate in an interreligious dialogue project.

65. Interreligious dialogue projects should be undertaken with a critical view to avoid adverse side effects, which are more likely to occur in short-term projects. Examples of problematic side effects are neglect or even marginalization of internal diversity within a particular religious community, a false emphasis on "unusual" manifestations of minority beliefs and the exclusion of marginalized religious or belief communities from dialogue projects. Working on a long-term perspective of communication seems the best way of preventing or overcoming such negative side effects.

66. Substantive and substantial participation by women in formal interreligious dialogue projects should be a priority in order to address the

current imbalance in the composition of high-level interreligious dialogue events where women tend to be marginalized.

67.   Besides promoting formal interreligious dialogue, States should also become more aware of the potential of informal interreligious communication (i.e., communication across different groups that is not organized explicitly along denominational lines and may include informal settings in multicultural and multireligious neighbourhoods, schools, clubs and other public services). In other words, interreligious communication does not necessarily need to take place in a framework specifically dedicated to religious issues. Both approaches — formal as well as informal interreligious communication — have their specific advantages and thus should be promoted in conjunction.

68.   In general, interreligious communication should not undervalue the dissident voices or existing intrareligious diversity within the participating communities. Rather than focusing only on "building bridges" between "us and them" seemingly living on different islands, the Special Rapporteur would encourage that "we" should aim for a mutual understanding and appreciation of living on one common mainland with multifaceted layers of interconnections, identities and complexities.

69.   The Special Rapporteur is impressed by the high degree of commitment that countless people show in the field of interreligious communication. He furthermore wishes to extend his high appreciation to all those who, often under complicated circumstances, have engaged in communicative projects designed to eliminate prejudices, stereotypes and hostility.

3. Chapter: Report December 2011

I. Introduction

1. The mandate of the Special Rapporteur on freedom of religion or belief was established by the Commission on Human Rights in its resolution 1986/20 and renewed by the Human Rights Council in its resolution 6/37. On 18 June 2010, the Special Rapporteur's mandate was extended for a further period of three years by the Human Rights Council through its resolution 14/11.

2. During the fourteenth session of the Council, Heiner Bielefeldt was appointed as Special Rapporteur on freedom of religion or belief. Since taking office on 1 August 2010, the Special Rapporteur has been committed to continuing the work of the previous mandate holders, in a spirit of cooperation with States and all relevant stakeholders. The Special Rapporteur wishes to highlight the excellent support provided by the Office of the United Nations High Commissioner for Human Rights, in particular its Special Procedures Branch.

3. In the present report, the Special Rapporteur first gives an overview of the mandate activities since the submission of the previous report to the Human Rights Council (A/HRC/16/53) (chap. II). He then focuses on the theme of freedom of religion or belief and recognition issues, referring to due respect for the status of right holders, fair provision of legal personality status and questions concerning privileged status positions for certain religious or belief communities (chap. III). In his conclusions, the Special Rapporteur notes the importance of clearly distinguishing different meanings within the concept of State recognition in order to avoid possible misunderstandings that could negatively affect the implementation of freedom of religion or belief, or undermine its status as a universal human right (chap. IV).

II. Activities of the Special Rapporteur

4. The Special Rapporteur's activities include sending communications to States concerning individual cases, conducting official country visits, participating in meetings with representatives of States, religious or belief communities and civil society organizations, as well as delivering speeches and issuing public statements. In this chapter, the Special Rapporteur has clustered the overview of recent mandate activities under

five headings pursuant to Human Rights Council resolutions 6/37 and 14/11.

A. Promotion of the adoption of measures at the national, regional and international levels to ensure the promotion and protection of the right to freedom of religion or belief

5.   At the national level, the Special Rapporteur held consultations with members of the executive and legislative bodies during his country visits to Paraguay and the Republic of Moldova in 2011, with a view to promoting and protecting the right to freedom of religion or belief. In Paraguay, the Special Rapporteur participated in a session of the Human Rights Network of the Executive, chaired by the Ministry of Justice, in which possibilities of adopting measures to promote and protect freedom of religion or belief in Paraguay, especially with regard to members of indigenous peoples, were discussed. In the Republic of Moldova, the Special Rapporteur was invited to participate in a round table on the revision of the 2007 Law on Religious Denomination and their Component Parts, organized by the Ministry of Justice and the United Nations in the Republic of Moldova on 6 September 2011, to which religious communities and civil society organizations had also been invited. The Special Rapporteur is grateful for the opportunity to attend this consultation, by which the Government set a positive example of transparency and dialogue with civil society.

6.   At the regional level, on 15 March 2011, the Special Rapporteur met with members of the European Commission and the Human Rights Working Group of the Council of the European Union in Brussels. Furthermore, on 26 May 2011, the Special Rapporteur was invited by the European Parliament"s Subcommittee on Human Rights for a hearing on freedom of religion or belief. On 7 December 2011, the Special Rapporteur attended a briefing with the European Commission against Racism and Intolerance in Strasbourg.

7.   At the international level, on 12 December 2011, the Special Rapporteur attended a two-day meeting in Washington entitled the "Istanbul Process for Combating Intolerance and Discrimination Based on Religion or Belief". It focused on concrete and positive measures that States can take to combat religious intolerance in the implementation of Human Rights Council resolution 16/18 on combating intolerance, negative ste-

reotyping and stigmatization of, and discrimination, incitement to violence and violence against, persons based on religion or belief.

B. Identification of existing and emerging obstacles to the enjoyment of the right to freedom of religion or belief and presentation of recommendations on ways and means to overcome such obstacles

8. The Special Rapporteur has held public or bilateral meetings with representatives of States and civil society organizations to discuss existing and emerging obstacles to the enjoyment of the right to freedom of religion or belief. He met with numerous members of religious or belief communities and held public briefings with them, including in Asunción, Barcelona, Baku, Berlin, Brussels, Cairo, Chisinau, Geneva, Nairobi, New York, Oslo, Oxford, Santiago de Chile, Toronto and Vienna.

9. Country visits offer an important opportunity for Special Rapporteurs to interact with various State officials and to meet representatives of religious or belief communities and other members of civil society. In 2011, the Special Rapporteur undertook two country missions to Paraguay and the Republic of Moldova, respectively. The country reports on his visits to Paraguay (A/HRC/19/60/Add.1) and Moldova (A/HRC/19/60/Add.2) will be submitted to the Council at its nineteenth session. The Special Rapporteur would like to thank both States for the excellent cooperation they extended during his respective missions. He hopes that the recommendations issued following the country visits will contribute to overcoming existing and emerging obstacles to the enjoyment of the right to freedom of religion or belief in the concerned countries.

10. Further country visits are currently being scheduled, and updated information about the Special Rapporteur's visit requests and forthcoming missions is available on the website of the Office of the United Nations High Commissioner for Human Rights.[59]

11. Since follow-up is of central importance to the mandate, the Special Rapporteur has continued his predecessors' follow-up procedure concerning country visit reports. On 30 November 2011, he sent follow-up letters concerning those missions undertaken by the previous mandate holder in 2009, i.e. to the Lao People's Democratic Republic, to Serbia, including visit to Kosovo, and to the former Yugoslav Republic of Macedonia. The Special Rapporteur requested to be provided with updated in-

---

[59] See http://www2.ohchr.org/english/bodies/chr/special/visits.htm.

formation on the consideration given to his predecessor's recommendations, the steps taken to implement them, and any constraints which may
prevent their implementation. The follow-up tables with the conclusions
and recommendations in the related mission report, and information
from the Government and relevant United Nations documents, including
from the universal periodic review, special procedures and treaty bodies,
are available online.[60]

C. Examination of incidents and governmental actions incompatible with the provisions of the Declaration on the Elimination of All Forms of Intolerance and of Discrimination Based on Religion or Belief and recommendation of remedial measures as appropriate

12. The Special Rapporteur has continued to engage in constructive dialogue with States by sending them communications to seek clarification
on credible allegations of incidents and governmental actions incompatible with the provisions of the 1981 Declaration on the Elimination of All
Forms of Intolerance and of Discrimination Based on Religion or Belief.
Since 1986, the Special Rapporteur has sent more than 1,250 letters of allegation and urgent appeals to a total of 130 States. The communications
sent by the Special Rapporteur between 1 December 2010 and 30 November 2011, and the replies received from Governments, are summarized in
the latest joint communications reports (A/HRC/18/51 and Corr.1 and
A/HRC/19/44). Both reports demonstrate an innovative approach as they
contain hyperlinks to scanned communications sent by the Special Rapporteur and to the full replies received from Governments during the
above stated period.

13. The Special Rapporteur's communications cover a wide range of
thematic issues, including allegations of disappearances, arrest and detention of individuals belonging to religious minorities or belief communities. Key issues of concern include death threats and discrimination
against converts, as well as violent attacks against and killings of members of religious communities and statements inciting violence directed
against members of religious minorities. The Special Rapporteur has also
taken up allegations of public manifestations of religious intolerance and
stigmatization of persons based on their religion or belief. Recent cases
involve attacks on places of worship and religious tensions related to religious sites and cases of peaceful protests and assembly in this context.

---

[60] See www.ohchr.org/EN/Issues/FreedomReligion/Pages/Visits.aspx.

In addition, the Special Rapporteur has also analysed problematic constitutional and legislative systems and draft legislation that fail to provide
adequate and effective guarantees of freedom of thought, conscience, religion and belief to all without distinction or provide additional burdensome practices of recognition and identity for members of religious or
belief communities.

14. Country visits offer further opportunities to examine and analyse
such incidents and governmental actions in greater detail. Conclusions
and recommendations in country visit reports can be tailored to the domestic legislation, bills, policies and their implementation. Since the establishment of the mandate, the Special Rapporteur has conducted 33
country visits, including one follow-up mission. A list of the country visits is contained in the Special Rapporteur's report to the thirteenth session of the Human Rights Council (A/HRC/13/40, para. 13). The Special
Rapporteur would also like to highlight that the Universal Human Rights
Index of United Nations Documents, an online research tool,[61] provides
easy access to country-specific human rights information by compiling
conclusions and recommendations addressed by United Nations independent experts to specific countries with the view of improving the
human rights situation.

15. On 10 March 2011, the twenty-fifth anniversary of the establishment
of the mandate, the Special Rapporteur launched a reference e-book with
observations and recommendations by the four mandate holders who
have served as Special Rapporteur on freedom of religion or belief since
1986. The *Rapporteur's Digest on Freedom of Religion or Belief*[62] is a 108-page
downloadable compilation of relevant excerpts from thematic and country-specific reports produced by Angelo d'Almeida Ribeiro (serving from
March 1986 to March 1993), Abdelfattah Amor (serving from April 1993 to
July 2004), Asma Jahangir (serving from August 2004 to July 2010) and
Heiner Bielefeldt (serving since August 2010). On the occasion of the thir-
tieth anniversary of the Declaration on the Elimination of All Forms of
Intolerance and of Discrimination Based on Religion or Belief, the Special
Rapporteur delivered a speech at a conference in Oxford on "New Fron-
tiers of Protection of Freedom of Religion or Belief under International
Law".

---

[61]   See www.universalhumanrightsindex.org.
[62]   Available from www.ohchr.org/Documents/Issues/Religion/RapporteursDigest
FreedomReligionBelief.pdf.

D. Application of a gender perspective

16. The Special Rapporteur has continued to apply a gender perspective, inter alia, through the identification of gender-specific abuses, in the reporting process, including in information collection and in recommendations. One of the key concerns raised includes allegations of forced conversion of women, especially if they belong to religious minorities.

17. The Special Rapporteur's latest interim report submitted to the General Assembly (A/66/156) also highlights the important role of women when the State is promoting interreligious communication. In his statement to the Third Committee of the General Assembly on 20 October 2011, the Special Rapporteur emphasized that substantive and substantial participation by women in formal interreligious dialogue projects should be a priority in order to address the current imbalance in the composition of high-level interreligious dialogue events where women tend to be marginalized.[63]

E. Working with mass-media organizations to promote an atmosphere of respect and tolerance for religious and cultural diversity, as well as multiculturalism

18. In Vienna (9 and 10 February 2011), Nairobi (6 and 7 April 2011) and Santiago de Chile (12 and 13 October 2011), the Special Rapporteur participated in three expert workshops on the prohibition of incitement to national, racial or religious hatred. The series of workshops, organized by the Office of the United Nations High Commissioner for Human Rights, was aimed at gaining a better understanding of legislative patterns, judicial practices and policies with regard to the concept of incitement to national, racial or religious hatred, while also ensuring full respect for freedom of expression as outlined in articles 19 and 20 of the International Covenant on Civil and Political Rights.

19. The Special Rapporteur presented to the regional workshops joint submissions with the Special Rapporteur on the promotion and protection of the right to freedom of opinion and expression and the Special Rapporteur on contemporary forms of racism, racial discrimination, xenophobia and related intolerance.[64] During the workshops the Special

---

[63] The statement is available from www.ohchr.org/Documents/Issues/Religion/ GA66statement_SRFreedomReligion.pdf.

[64] Information on the workshops is available from www2.ohchr.org/english/is sues/opinion/articles1920_iccpr/index.htm.

Rapporteurs looked at the strategic response to hate speech, which should include efforts to educate about cultural differences, promote diversity, empower and give a voice to minorities. An example of this is through the support of community media and its representation in mainstream media. In this context, the Special Rapporteur would like to refer to the Camden Principles on Freedom of Expression and Equality,[65] which recommend a public policy framework for pluralism and equality, for example, by making an equitable allocation of resources, including broadcasting frequencies, among public service, commercial and community media, so that together they represent the full range of cultures, communities and opinions in society.

III. Freedom of religion or belief and recognition issues

A. Introductory remarks

20. "Recognition" is one of the key terms regularly referred to in debates on freedom of religion or belief. On closer examination, however, it turns out that this concept harbours a variety of meanings which should be kept clearly distinct in order to avoid confusion. Striving for conceptual clarity on the different meanings of "recognition" in the field of freedom of religion or belief is not a purely academic enterprise. Indeed, in dealing with practical cases, the Special Rapporteur is often confronted with widespread misunderstanding about the concept of recognition and the role of the State in this regard. Such misunderstandings, however, can have a direct negative impact on the enjoyment of freedom of religion or belief, since they may seriously obscure the applicable international human rights obligations of States.

21. In this chapter, the Special Rapporteur focuses on three different meanings of recognition which relate to different levels of the conceptualization and implementation of freedom of religion or belief.

22. The first and most fundamental meaning is "recognition" in the sense of the due respect for the status of all human beings as rights holders in the area of freedom of religion or belief, a status finally deriving from the inherent dignity of all members of the human family.

---

[65] Article 19: Global Campaign for Free Expression (London, 2009). Available from www.article19.org/resources.php/resource/1214/en/camden-principles-on-freedom-of-expression-and-equality

23. The second meaning relates to the necessary provision by the State of a legal personality status, which religious or belief communities need in order to be able to take collective legal actions. Obtaining such a legal status typically requires undergoing some administrative "recognition procedures", which should be designed so as not to pose undue obstacles, either de jure or de facto, to the accessibility of the required legal personality status.

24. The third meaning concerns privileged status positions, often connected with practical advantages such as tax exemption and financial subsidies, which certain religious or belief communities enjoy in many States. In this context, the term "recognition" is also typically used.

25. All of the above three dimensions are relevant for the implementation of the right to freedom of religion or belief. However, they have different implications for the role of the State in the following regard. While the status of all human beings as rights holders cannot legitimately become a matter of administrative "recognition procedures", some procedures may indeed seem necessary to provide certain religious or belief communities with the status of a legal personality. However, given the practical significance of such a legal personality status for the full enjoyment of freedom of religion or belief, States should ensure that the respective procedures are quick, transparent, fair, inclusive and non- discriminatory. Lastly, unlike the general status of a legal personality, the granting by States of a more specific legal position connected with some practical advantages such as tax exemption or financial subsidies does not necessarily follow from the right to freedom of religion or belief. However, if States decide to offer such a position, they should do this in accordance with the principles of equality and non-discrimination.

B. Due respect for the status of rights holders

26. It is no coincidence that the term "recognition" already occurs at the very beginning of the mother document of international human rights protection, the 1948 Universal Declaration of Human Rights. The preamble of the Universal Declaration of Human Rights starts by postulating that "recognition of the inherent dignity and of the equal and inalienable rights of all members of the human family is the foundation of freedom, justice and peace in the world". This first sentence of the preamble of the Universal Declaration of Human Rights has been cited in many subsequent international human rights standards, including the International Covenant on Civil and Political Rights. It clearly has a fundamental significance for the understanding of human rights in general.

27. The term "recognition" as used in the opening sentence of the Universal Declaration of Human Rights represents the insight into the axiomatic status of human dignity on which the entire system of human rights protection is based. This dignity is further said to be "inherent" in all human beings, which means it has a normative rank prior to, and independent of, any acts of State approval. Indeed, the dignity of all members of the human family calls for unconditional respect for every human being by the State and society at large.

28. The concept of human dignity has a long history and strongly resonates within most different religious, philosophical and cultural traditions. For the concept of human dignity to function as a normative reference in international human rights law, however, it is crucial to make sure that the notion of dignity is not claimed as a monopoly by any of those traditions, but rather remains open for a wide diversity of religious or philosophical readings. This openness does not mean emptiness, though. For all the different interpretations of what human dignity may signify in the framework of philosophical or theological reasoning, this concept at the time has the precise and indispensable function of reminding us of the universalistic nature of those basic rights which all human beings have a claim to simply because they are human beings.

29. The preamble of the Universal Declaration of Human Rights furthermore links the "inherent dignity" of all human beings to their "equal and inalienable rights". Respect for human dignity thus receives an institutional backing in terms of internationally binding rights. At the same time, it is this very focus on human dignity that accounts for the specific qualification of human rights as "equal and inalienable rights". The principle of equality ultimately follows from the axiomatic status of human dignity which does not depend on any particular qualities, talents or societal status positions that an individual may happen to have or not to have. Likewise, the specific rank of human rights manifests itself in the "inalienability" of those rights that are aimed at the legal protection of everyone's dignity. The same connection between human dignity and human rights also occurs in the first sentence of article 1 of the Universal Declaration of Human Rights, which in clear terms confirms that "all human beings are born free and equal in dignity and rights." As a universal human right, the right to freedom of thought, conscience, religion or belief must be interpreted strictly in keeping with the opening sentence of the Universal Declaration of Human Rights and similar provisions. Hence it is not that the State could "grant" certain individuals or groups of individuals this right. Rather, it is the other way around: the State has

to respect everyone's freedom of religion or belief as an inalienable – and thus non-negotiable – entitlement of human beings, all of whom have the status of right holders in international law by virtue of their inherent dignity.

30.   Hence the starting point for defining the application of freedom of religion or belief must be the self-understanding of human beings – all of them – in the field of religion or belief. Such self-understandings obviously can be very diverse. As the Human Rights Committee has rightly pointed out, freedom of religion or belief should therefore be broadly construed so as to protect "theistic, non-theistic and atheistic beliefs, as well as the right not to profess any religion or belief".[66] Already in a study published in 1960, the then Special Rapporteur of the Sub-Commission on Prevention of Discrimination and Protection of Minorities, Arcot Krishnaswami, stated that "the term „religion or belief' is used in this study to include, in addition to various theistic creeds, such other beliefs as agnosticism, free thought, atheism and rationalism".[67]

31.   The Special Rapporteur subscribes to this wide understanding, which appropriately reflects respect for the status of all human beings as rights holders by virtue of their human dignity. He furthermore would like to reiterate that freedom of religion or belief equally includes followers of traditional and non-traditional religions or beliefs, members of large or small communities, minorities and minorities within minorities, converts or re-converts and dissenters or other critical voices. One must also not forget the rights of women, who continue to have only marginalized positions within many religious traditions.

32.   The Special Rapporteur has noted with concern, however, that some States seem to limit freedom of religion or belief to a given list of religious options. For instance, while in a number of States only the followers of monotheistic religions can fully enjoy their religious freedom, other States take concepts like "traditional religions", "patriotic religious associations" or "known religions" as the starting point, with the result that members of lesser known, new or alternative communities are officially excluded from the full and equal protection of their freedom of re-

---

[66]   Human Rights Committee, general comment No. 22 (1993) on the right to freedom of thought, conscience and religion, para. 2; the same formulation was also used in the Final Document of the International Consultative Conference on School Education in relation to Freedom of Religion or Belief, Tolerance and Non-Discrimination (E/CN.4/2002/73, appendix, footnote 1).

[67]   Study of Discrimination in the Matter of Religious Rights and Practices, document E/CN.4/Sub.2/200/Rev.1, p. 1, footnote 1.

ligion or belief or are discriminated against. In some countries, the enjoyment of freedom of religion or belief is limited to mainstream manifestations of religions, at the expense of members of so called "heterodox" currents within those religions. Other States have resorted to a differentiation between "religions" and "sects" to exclude members of small communities from the protection of freedom of religion or belief. The Special Rapporteur also regrets that a few States still make citizenship dependent on affiliation with a particular religion or deny members of non- recognized religions access to official documents such as identity cards, passports, birth certificates and marriage licences.[68] However, the Special Rapporteur has noted with appreciation that judgments of domestic courts in a State have ended a discriminatory

33. policy of not issuing official documents to individuals who do not belong to the three religions officially recognized by that State.[69]

34. Regardless of whether a list of recognized religions or beliefs is short or long, the human rights problem remains that, based on such an understanding, freedom of religion or belief could de facto or de jure unfold only within a set of permissible options that are more or less clearly predefined by the State. From the point of view of normative universalism, however, such limitations are problematic, as the right holders are "all members of the human family" whose most diverse self-understandings in the area of religion or belief constitute the starting point for the conceptualization and implementation of freedom of religion or belief as a universal human right.

35. A typical objection to a wide application of freedom of religion or belief points to harmful practices that may occur in the name of religions or beliefs, practices which may in fact require restrictions enacted by States to protect the rights of others or important public order interests. Such concerns are often associated with small communities sometimes negatively branded as "sects" or "cults". They also frequently target members of non- traditional communities or groups perceived as not fitting into the cultural makeup of the country.

36. The Special Rapporteur would like to clarify two related points. First, even though harmful practices undoubtedly do occur in the name of religions or beliefs, it would be unacceptable to simply identify such prob-

---

[68]   See interim report of the Special Rapporteur on freedom of religion or belief, A/63/161, paras. 27–36.

[69]   See interim report of the Special Rapporteur on freedom of religion or belief, A/65/207, para. 25.

lems with particular communities or types of communities, such as small groups or new religious movements. Allegations of harmful practices must always be based on clear empirical evidence and should not be presented as mere conjectures or negative projections, which often turn out to reflect existing stereotypes and prejudices.

37.   Second, restrictions deemed necessary by States to protect the rights of others or important public interests against harmful religious manifestations must be enacted in strict conformity with the provisions laid down in article 18, paragraph 3, of the International Covenant on Civil and Political Rights. Accordingly, restrictions can only be permissible if they are legally prescribed and if they are clearly needed to pursue a legitimate aim – the protection of public safety, order, health, or morals or the fundamental rights and freedoms of others. In addition, restrictions must meet the requirements of proportionality; they must be limited to a minimum of interference and furthermore must be enacted in a strictly non- discriminatory manner. All these criteria are important to preserving the substance of the human right to freedom of religion or belief, even in situations of a conflict with other human rights or important public order interests.

38.   As a precondition for restricting certain external manifestations of freedom of religion or belief, States have to bear a burden of justifying any limitation, as required by article 18, paragraph 3, of the International Covenant on Civil and Political Rights. However, some States try to circumvent that burden of justification when imposing limitations on some religious or belief manifestations. For this purpose, sometimes restrictive definitions are used to exclude certain religious or belief communities from the very protection of their freedom of religion or belief. Such an approach often negatively affects members of minority religions, adherents to non-traditional religions or beliefs, or members of groups that are perceived as not fitting into the religious or cultural make-up of the country. Such use of restrictive definitions would clearly go against the universalistic spirit of human rights based on respect for everyone's human dignity.

39.   Against such tendencies of resorting to restrictive definitions, the Special Rapporteur has always interpreted the scope of application of the freedom of religion or belief in a large sense, in line with the principle "*in dubio pro libertate*", bearing in mind that manifestations of this freedom may be subject to such limitations as are prescribed by law and are necessary to protect public safety, order, health, or morals or the fundamen-

tal rights and freedoms of others.[70] Only can such an open and broad understanding do justice to the real diversity existing among human beings, all of whom are rights holders in the context of universal human rights.

C. Fair provision of legal personality status

40. The second dimension of "recognition" relevant in the field of freedom of religion or belief pertains to the status of a legal personality, which religious or belief communities may require to be able to exercise important collective functions. Many States have registration procedures to award legal personality status to religious or belief communities. However, some registration practices actually limit the right to freedom of religion or belief of certain communities (see subsection 1 below), thus leading to huge difficulties for organizing their community life with a long-term perspective (see subsection 2). Consequently, it seems vital that the State implements any existing registration procedures in a fair and non-discriminatory manner and in the service of the human right to freedom of religion or belief (see subsection 3).

1.   Issues pertaining to registration procedures

41. Freedom of religion or belief is a right held by all human beings because of their inherent dignity. According to article 18, paragraph 1 of the International Covenant on Civil and Political Rights this includes the freedom, "either individually or in community with others and in public or private, to manifest [their] religion or belief in worship, observance, practice and teaching". The possibility of engaging in various forms of community activities thus clearly falls within the scope of freedom of religion or belief. Thus registration should not be compulsory, i.e. it should not be a precondition for practising one's religion, but only for the acquisition of a legal personality status. Some of the collective activities of religious or belief communities typically require the status of a legal personality in the sense of becoming recognized as a legal entity with corporative legal responsibilities and corporative legal options.

42.   While the axiomatic status position of human beings as rights holders in the area of freedom of religion or belief has a normative rank prior to, and independent of, any administrative procedures, some such proce-

---

[70]   See reports on the implementation of the Declaration on the Elimination of All Forms of Intolerance and of Discrimination Based on Religion or Belief, E/CN.4/1990/46, para. 110, and E/CN.4/1997/91, para. 99; and report of the Special Rapporteur on freedom of religion or belief, A/HRC/4/21, paras. 43–47.

dures are generally required as a prerequisite for groups obtaining the status of a legal personality. For instance, those wishing to be registered as a legal personality typically have to provide some certified information about membership, organization, the purpose of the group or the structure of internal responsibility. This sort of information may be needed for the administration to take a decision on the attribution of legal personality status.

43. Such an administrative decision should not be misconceived as an act of mercy, however. Under international law, States are obliged to take an active role in facilitating the full enjoyment of human rights, including freedom of religion or belief. By not providing appropriate legal options that, de jure and de facto, are accessible to all religious or belief groups interested in obtaining a legal personality status, States would fail to honour their obligations under the human right to freedom of religion or belief.

44. Unfortunately, the Special Rapporteur has received numerous complaints that registration procedures have been used as a means to limit the right to freedom of religion or belief of members of certain religious or belief communities. In some States, certain communities are de facto or even de jure excluded from the possibility of obtaining the status of a legal person or suffer from discriminatory treatment in this regard. Once again, such discriminatory practices disproportionately affect small or non-traditional groups. Often the threshold defined for obtaining legal personality status – for example the provision of a minimum number of followers – does not appropriately take into account the needs of smaller communities. In some States, religious or belief communities are also required to document that they have long existed in the country. Other cases of obstruction relate to the requirement that the registration application be signed by all members of the religious organization and should contain their full names, dates of birth and places of residence. However, some members may legitimately wish to keep their religious affiliation confidential and those who were not included in the registration application might subsequently face difficulties when taking part in religious activities of their fellow believers. Furthermore, some States seem to require in practice not only registration at the national level, but also a separate registration of local branches of religious or belief communities, which in turn leaves local authorities with wide discretionary powers for approving or rejecting the local registration applications.

2. Difficulties encountered by unregistered religious or belief communities

45. As a result of such obstacles, members of unregistered religious or belief communities typically encounter huge difficulties when trying to organize their community life in a stable environment and with a long-term perspective.

46. For instance, without the status of a legal personality, religious or belief communities cannot open bank accounts or engage in financial transactions. As a result, the ownership of places of worship frequently remains precarious, in that real estate assets or other important property only belong to private individuals who informally operate in the service of the community. Whether in the case of death, their successors will continue such activities on behalf of the community or claim the inherited property for different purposes may be questionable. Furthermore, the construction of larger places of worship seems hardly conceivable under such insecure circumstances. In this context, the Special Rapporteur would like to recall that the right to freedom of thought, conscience, religion or belief includes, inter alia, freedom to establish and maintain places of worship and freedom to solicit and receive voluntary financial and other contributions from individuals and institutions.[71]

47. Similarly, communities lacking legal personality status are faced with additional obstacles when trying to establish private denominational schools. This in turn may have negative repercussions for the rights of parents or legal guardians to ensure that their children receive religious and moral education in conformity with their own convictions – a right explicitly enshrined in international human rights law as an integral part of freedom of religion or belief.[72]

48. It may be even more difficult to establish institutions of higher education, including theological training institutes, which are vital to intellectually further develop and convey the tenets of a faith to the next generation. This may seriously hamper the freedom to teach a religion or belief in places suitable for these purposes and the freedom to train ap-

---

[71] Article 6 (a) and (f) of the Declaration on the Elimination of All Forms of Intolerance and of Discrimination Based on Religion or Belief.

[72] Article 18, paragraph 4, of the International Covenant on Civil and Political Rights. See also article 13, paragraph 3, of the International Covenant on Economic, Social and Cultural Rights; article 14, paragraph 2, of the Convention on the Rights of the Child; and article 5 of the Declaration on the Elimination of All Forms of Intolerance and of Discrimination Based on Religion or Belief.

propriate leaders called for by the requirements and standards of any religion or belief.[73] In some situations, the denial of legal personality status might jeopardize the long-term survival chances of a religious or belief community.

49. In addition, if communities do not enjoy legal personality status, their members may encounter administrative problems with regard to making, acquiring and using to an adequate extent the necessary articles and materials related to the rites or customs of their religion or belief.[74] This may also negatively affect their opportunities of celebrating holidays and ceremonies in accordance with the precepts of their religion or belief.[75]

50. Moreover, religious or belief communities lacking legal personality status are barred from employing staff in an official manner. People serving for the community either have to do this on a purely voluntary basis or conclude working contracts with a private employer, which again is a situation detrimental to any long-term planning. Yet, the right to freedom of thought, conscience, religion or belief includes, inter alia, freedom to establish and maintain appropriate charitable or humanitarian institutions.[76]

51. Another problem concerns the establishment of radio stations or other media. In the absence of the status of a legal personality, it would again require individual members of the community to take all the financial responsibilities and risks in their private capacities. It seems clear that media work is extremely complicated under such conditions. This, however, will most likely have negative effects on the possibilities to reach out to parts of the community living in remote areas or in other countries and to participate in public debates. However, international human rights law also protects the freedom to write, issue and disseminate relevant publications and the freedom to establish and maintain communications with individuals and communities in matters of religion and belief at the national and international levels.[77]

---

[73]   Art. 6 (e) and (g) of the Declaration on the Elimination of All Forms of Intolerance and of Discrimination Based on Religion or Belief.
[74]   Ibid., art. 6 (c).
[75]   Ibid., art. 6 (h).
[76]   Ibid., art. 6 (b).
[77]   Ibid., art. 6 (d) and (i).

3.   Provision of fair and non-discriminatory registration procedures

52.   The above-mentioned practical problems and their human rights implications show that a lack of legal personality status may adversely affect virtually the whole catalogue of manifestations protected under the non-exhaustive list in article 6 of the Declaration on the Elimination of All Forms of Intolerance and of Discrimination Based on Religion or Belief. Furthermore, the Human Rights Council and the General Assembly have repeatedly urged States to step up their efforts to protect and promote freedom of thought, conscience and religion or belief and, to this end "to review, whenever relevant, existing registration practices in order to ensure that such practices do not limit the right of all persons to manifest their religion or belief, either alone or in community with others and in public or private".[78]

53.   The Human Rights Committee has also expressed concern about the use of criminal laws to penalize the apparently peaceful exercise of religious freedom and that a large number of individuals have been charged, detained and sentenced in this context (CCPR/CO/83/UZB, para. 22). Moreover, the Human Rights Committee has dealt with registration issues in individual cases, for example by finding a violation of article 18, paragraph 1, of the International Covenant on Civil and Political Rights following a State's refusal to register a community as a religious association, which made impossible such activities as establishing educational institutions and inviting foreign religious dignitaries to visit the country.[79]

54.   Providing non-discriminatory registration procedures therefore falls within the responsibility of States under international human rights law. Even though a standard procedure for all States does not exist, it is clear that such domestic procedures should be established and implemented in the service of the human right to freedom of religion or belief. From this it follows that any procedures for the registration of religious or belief communities as legal persons should be quick, transparent, fair, inclusive and non- discriminatory.[80]

---

[78]   Human Rights Council resolution 16/13 and General Assembly resolutions 63/181, 64/164 and 65/211. See also Human Rights Council resolution 6/37 and General Assembly resolutions 60/166 and 61/161.

[79]   Human Rights Committee, communication No. 1207/2003, *Malakhovsky and Pikul v. Belarus*, Views adopted on 23 August 2005, para. 7.6.

[80]   See report submitted by Asma Jahangir, Special Rapporteur on freedom of religion or belief, E/CN.4/2005/61, paras. 56–58; and the "Guidelines for Review of Legislation Pertaining to Religion or Belief", prepared by the Organization for

55. Members of religious or belief communities interested in obtaining such a status should not be confronted with unnecessary bureaucratic burdens or with lengthy or even unpredictable waiting periods. Indeed as repeatedly highlighted by the Special Rapporteur, a number of existing registration practices need to be reviewed by States to ensure that such practices do not limit the right of all persons to manifest their religion or belief, either alone or in community with others and in public or private. Domestic registration requirements often appear to be used as a means to limit the rights of members of certain religious minorities.[81] Such procedures should not be used as control instruments but, rather, should be enacted in the interest of enabling members of religious or belief communities to fully exercise their human rights.

56. For these reasons, the registration procedures must be accessible – on the basis of fairness, inclusiveness and non-discrimination – to all those who wish to achieve legal personality status for their communities. No religious community should have the possibility to exercise a "veto" or otherwise influence the decision to register or not to register another religious or belief group. All registration decisions must be based on clearly defined formal elements of law and in conformity with international law. Registration should neither depend on extensive formal requirements in terms of the number of members and the time a particular community has existed, nor should it depend on the review of the substantive content of the belief, the structure of the community and methods of appointment of the clergy. In addition, provisions which are vague or which grant excessive governmental discretion in giving registration approvals should be avoided. Members of religious or belief communities who have been denied registration must have access to remedies, including informal conflict management and formal legal measures to challenge a negative registration decision.

57. Furthermore, the Special Rapporteur has observed with concern a recent trend of Governments enacting legislation with a view to stripping some denominations of their previous registration status as a religious community. Some domestic laws even provide for discriminatory exemptions of certain religious communities considered "traditional", while

---

Security and Cooperation in Europe/Office of Democratic Institutions and Human Rights (OSCE/ODIHR) Advisory Panel of Experts on Freedom of Religion and Belief in consultation with the Council of Europe's Venice Commission. Available from www.osce.org/odihr/13993.

[81] Interim report of the Special Rapporteur on freedom of religion or belief, Asma Jahangir, A/65/207, paras. 20–23.

small or new religious movements would need to submit new applications to be re- registered – an option often connected with lengthy and costly bureaucratic procedures. Such State policies of depriving some religious or belief groups of a previously held status may be pursued for different purposes; for example, to exercise control over some religious or belief movements or marginalizing groups deemed not to fit into the cultural, religious or political makeup of the country. From the perspective of freedom of religion or belief and in view of the principle of non-discrimination underlying human rights in general, such practices are highly problematic, as they are likely to create an atmosphere of legal insecurity and political intimidation detrimental to the free and equal enjoyment of freedom of religion or belief by everyone. Provisions that operate retroactively or that fail to protect vested interests should be avoided and if new rules are introduced there should be at least adequate transition provisions.

58. A legal personality status made available for religious or belief communities should be understood as an option, not an obligation imposed on them by the State. If some communities, for whatever reasons, prefer not to obtain such a status and generally wish not to be registered as a legal entity by the State, such a decision clearly deserves respect and should not be penalized. Unfortunately, however, the Special Rapporteur has received information that in a number of countries members of "non-registered" religious communities have experienced police harassment, surveillance or even criminal sanctions, as their activities are deemed illegal by the State or certain State agencies, such as the police or the secret service. Restrictive measures include the closing of places of worship, confiscation of property, financial sanctions possibly causing financial ruin, imprisonment and in some cases even the use of torture. Target groups may include communities that have been denied registration status against their will and communities not wishing to obtain any such legal status. Against such unacceptable practices, the Special Rapporteur would like to reiterate that the enjoyment of the freedom of religion of belief as such does not depend on any acts of State approval or administrative registration. Moreover, States have an obligation to provide information and clear instructions to those working in law enforcement and other agencies that religious manifestations of members of "non- registered" groups must be respected as part of their freedom of religion or belief.

D. The issue of privileged status positions for certain religious or belief communities

59. Many States provide for a privileged status position to be accorded to certain religious or belief communities or – in most cases – to only some of them. Such a specific status position typically goes way beyond the general possibilities attached to the status of a legal personality and may include practical privileges, such as tax exemption, financial subsidies, or membership in public broadcasting agencies. The term "recognition" is often used with reference to such a privileged status position, which some denominations may enjoy while others might be excluded.

60. While States have a clear human rights obligation to offer the possibility for religious or belief communities to obtain a general status of a legal personality, the provision of a more specific status position on behalf of religious or belief communities does not directly follow from the human right to freedom of religion or belief. States have different options in this regard. There is room for a broad range of possibilities. Whereas many States have offered such a specific status position as part of their promotional activities in the field of freedom of religion or belief, other States have decided not to do so and to take different routes to discharge their obligation to promote freedom of religion or belief.

61. Should States provide for specific status positions on behalf of religious or belief communities, they should ensure that these provisions are conceptualized and implemented in a non-discriminatory manner. Non-discrimination is one of the overarching principles of human rights. It relates to human dignity, which should be respected for all human beings in an equal and thus non-discriminatory way. To quote the Universal Declaration of Human Rights once more, all human beings are "born ... equal in dignity and rights" and must be treated accordingly. Moreover, the principle of non-discrimination undoubtedly also prohibits discrimination on the grounds of religion or belief. This has been explicitly enshrined in numerous human rights instruments, including the Universal Declaration of Human Rights, the International Covenant on Civil and Political Rights and the Declaration on the Elimination of all Forms of Intolerance and of Discrimination Based on Religion or Belief.

62. Unfortunately, the Special Rapporteur has received a lot of information on existing discriminatory practices and policies of States when it comes to providing specific status positions and concomitant privileges to some denominations, while withholding the same position from others. In many cases, the criteria applied remain vaguely defined or are

even not defined at all. In a number of other cases, general reference is made to the cultural heritage of the country in which some religious denominations are said to have played predominant roles. While this might be historically correct, one has to wonder why such a historical reference should be reflected in a legal text or even in a Constitution. Reference to the predominant historical role of one particular religion can easily become a pretext for a discriminatory treatment of the adherents to other religions or beliefs. There are numerous examples indicating that this is actually the case.

63. Moreover, quite a number of States have established an official State religion, a status position often even enshrined in State Constitutions. Although, in most cases, only one religion has been accorded such an official position, there are also examples of two or more State religions existing in one country. The practical implications of the establishment of a State religion can be very different, ranging from a more or less symbolic superior rank of one religion to rigid measures aimed at protecting the predominant role of the State religion against any denominational competition or against public criticism. In some extreme cases, only followers of the official State religion are allowed to manifest their religious or belief-based convictions. There are also examples of States rendering citizenship dependent on adherence to the State religion.[82] In quite a number of States, those who wish to take up important positions within the State apparatus – such as president, prime minister, member of parliament, king, queen, attorney-general, chief justice or member of the national human rights institution – must be affiliated with a particular religion or denomination and have to publicly declare allegiance to this religion by taking an oath.[83] Providing some denominations with a privileged status position or establishing an official State religion is sometimes part and parcel of a State policy of fostering national identity. Ample experience shows, however, that this harbours serious risks of discrimination against minorities, for instance, against members of immigrant religious communities or new religious movements.

64. The Special Rapporteur would like to reiterate in this context that, while the notion of State religions is not per se prohibited under international human rights law, States have to ensure that this does not lead to a de jure or de facto discrimination of members of other religions and beliefs. The burden of proof in this regard falls on the State. In this context,

---

[82]   See A/63/161, paras. 28–30.
[83]   See ibid., para. 38.

the Special Rapporteurs fully subscribes to the position taken by the Human Rights Committee in its general comment No. 22, paragraph 9, which emphasizes that "the fact that a religion is recognized as a State religion or that it is established as official or traditional or that its followers comprise the majority of the population, shall not result in any impairment of the enjoyment of any of the rights under the Covenant, including articles 18 and 27, nor in any discrimination against adherents to other religions or non-believers. In particular, certain measures discriminating against the latter, such as measures restricting eligibility for government service to members of the predominant religion or giving economic privileges to them or imposing special restrictions on the practice of other faiths, are not in accordance with the prohibition of discrimination based on religion or belief and the guarantee of equal protection under article 26."

65.   The Special Rapporteur would also like to reiterate warnings against aggravated discrimination following the adoption of a State religion. While the mere existence of a State religion may not in itself be incompatible with human rights, this concept must neither be exploited at the expense of the rights of minorities nor lead to discrimination on the grounds of religion or belief.[84] Formal or legal distinction between different kinds of religious or belief communities carries the seed of discrimination insofar as such a distinction in their status implies a difference in rights or treatment.

66.   Indeed, it seems difficult, if not impossible, to conceive of an application of the concept of an official "State religion" that in practice does not have adverse effects on religious minorities, thus discriminating against their members. As an earlier mandate holder, Abdelfattah Amor, has rightly pointed out in this context, "to the extent that everything ultimately depends on the goodwill of the State, the personality of those in office at any given moment, and other unpredictable or subjective factors, there is no serious guarantee in law that the State will at all times respect minority ethnic and religious rights".[85] When the State itself announces its religion in the Constitution, the law arguably ceases to reflect

---

[84]   See interim report on the elimination of all forms of religious intolerance concerning a visit to Greece, prepared by Abdelfattah Amor, Special Rapporteur of the Commission on Human Rights, A/51/542/Add.1, para. 132; his report on a visit to Sudan, A/51/542/Add.2, para. 134; his report on a visit to Pakistan, E/CN.4/1996/95/Add.1, para. 81; and his report on a visit to the Islamic Republic of Iran, E/CN.4/1996/95/Add.2, para. 88.

[85]   Reports, studies and other documentation for the Preparatory Committee and the World Conference, A/CONF.189/PC.1/7, annex, para. 119.

the ethnic and religious variety of the society, opening the floodgates to arbitrary action and religious intolerance.[86] Furthermore, if one religion is recognized as a State religion, then women belonging to religious minorities, or those who do not follow the mainstream interpretation of the State religion, may face aggravated discrimination; for example when the State or society seeks to impose its view of women.[87] Both with regard to State religions and other religious or belief communities, the State should never try to take control of religion by defining its content and concepts or by imposing limitations, apart from those which are strictly necessary pursuant to article 18, paragraph 3, of the International Covenant on Civil and Political Rights.[88]

IV. Conclusions and recommendations

67. The concept of State recognition has many repercussions in the field of freedom of religion or belief. It is important to clearly distinguish different meanings within that concept in order avoid possible misunderstandings which could negatively affect the implementation of freedom of religion or belief, or even undermine its status as a universal human right.

68. The Special Rapporteur has proposed differentiation between three relevant meanings of recognition pertinent to freedom of religion or belief: (a) "recognition" in the sense of due respect for the status of all human beings as right holders by virtue of their inherent dignity; (b) "recognition" in terms of States providing for the possibility of obtaining the status of legal personality, which religious or belief groups typically need for the exercise of important communitarian aspects of their freedom of religion or belief; and (c) "recognition" in the sense of States according a specific privileged status position to some religious or belief communities.

69. The Special Rapporteur would like to emphasize that States have obligations related to all of the above-mentioned meanings of recognition.

70. In keeping with the universalistic understanding of human rights, States must ensure that all individuals can enjoy their freedom of thought, conscience, religion or belief on the basis of respect for their

---

[86] Ibid., para. 120.
[87] See the Special Rapporteur's study on freedom of religion or belief and the status of women in the light of religion and traditions, E/CN.4/2002/73/Add.2, para. 188.
[88] E/CN.4/1996/95/Add.1, para. 81.

self-understanding in this entire area. Respect for freedom of religion or belief as a human right does not depend on administrative registration procedures, as freedom of religion or belief has the status of a human right, prior to and independent from any acts of State approval.

71. Furthermore, States should offer appropriate options for religious or belief communities to achieve the status of legal personality on a domestic level, a status needed for undertaking important community functions relevant for the full exercise of freedom of religion or belief. Registration procedures for obtaining legal personality status should be quick, transparent, fair, inclusive and non- discriminatory.

72. Moreover, if States decide to provide for specific status positions connected with particular financial and other privileges, they should make sure that such a specific status does not amount to de jure or de facto discrimination against members of other religions or beliefs. With regard to the concept of an official "State religion", the Special Rapporteur would argue that it seems difficult, if not impossible, to conceive of an application of this concept that in practice does not have adverse effects on religious minorities, thus discriminating against their members.

73. From the above considerations, the Special Rapporteur would like to make the following recommendations:

a) States should systematically ground any activities in the area of religion or belief in a clear understanding of the due respect for every person's freedom of religion or belief as a universal human right based on the inherent dignity of all members of the human family;

b) States should refrain from exercising pressure on religious or belief groups whose members prefer not to be registered as legal entities under domestic law;

c) States should instruct members of law enforcement and other State agencies that religious activities of non-registered religious or belief communities are not illegal, as the status of freedom of religion or belief prevails over any acts of State registration;

d) States should offer appropriate options and procedures for religious or belief communities to achieve a status of legal personality if they so wish. Administrative procedures for obtaining such a status should be enacted in a spirit of servicing the full enjoyment of freedom of religion or belief for everyone and should thus be quick, transparent, fair, inclusive and non-discriminatory;

e) All registration decisions must be based on clearly defined formal elements of law and in conformity with international law. Registration should neither depend on extensive formal requirements in terms of the number of members and the time a particular community has existed, nor should it depend on the review of the substantive content of the belief, the structure of the community and methods of appointment of the clergy;

f) States should ensure that no religious community has, de jure or de facto, the possibility to exercise a "veto" or otherwise influence the decision to register or not to register another religious or belief group;

g) States have to provide effective legal remedies for individuals or groups complaining about the denial or arbitrary delay of registration as a legal personality;

h) States should refrain from arbitrarily stripping certain religious or belief communities of legal status positions they had possessed before as an instrument of exercising control or marginalizing groups deemed not to fit into the cultural make-up of the country;

i) When offering a privileged legal status position for certain religious or belief communities or other groups, such a specific status should be accorded in strict conformity with the principle of non-discrimination and should fully respect the right to freedom of religion or belief of all human beings;

j) Any specific status positions given by the State to certain religious or belief communities or other groups should never be instrumentalized for purposes of national identity politics, as this may have detrimental effects on the situation of individuals from minority communities.

4. Chapter: Report October 2012

I. Introduction

1.   In 1986, the Commission on Human Rights created the mandate of the Special Rapporteur on freedom of religion or belief by its resolution 1986/20. In 2007, the Human Rights Council renewed the Special Rapporteur's mandate in its resolution 6/37 and, in 2010, extended it for a further period of three years in its resolution 14/11. Heiner Bielefeldt was appointed Special Rapporteur on freedom of religion or belief at the fourteenth session of the Council and assumed his function on 1 August 2010.

2.   In section II of the present report, the Special Rapporteur provides an overview of his activities since the submission of his previous report to the General Assembly (A/66/156). In section III, he focuses on the right of conversion as part of freedom of religion or belief. Section IV provides his conclusions and recommendations to various actors in this regard.

II. Activities of the Special Rapporteur

3.   The Special Rapporteur conducted various activities between 1 August 2011 and 31 July 2012 pursuant to Human Rights Council resolutions 6/37 and 14/11.

A. Country visits

4.   The Special Rapporteur undertook country visits to the Republic of Moldova (1 to 8 September 2011) and Cyprus (29 March to 5 April 2012). The report on his visit to the Republic of Moldova (A/HRC/19/60/Add.2) was presented at the nineteenth session of the Human Rights Council in March 2012 and the report on his visit to Cyprus is to be presented at the Council's twenty-second session.[89] The Special Rapporteur expresses his appreciation to all his interlocutors and officials for the excellent cooperation they extended to him during his visits. He hopes that the recommendations provided following the visits will be considered and implemented to overcome any existing or emerging obstacles and to reinforce

---

[89]   The Special Rapporteur's statement at the conclusion of his visit to Cyprus is available from www.ohchr.org/EN/NewsEvents/Pages/DisplayNews.aspx?NewsID=12042&LangID=E.

efforts towards promoting and protecting the right to freedom of religion or belief.

5.   Additional country visits are currently being scheduled. Updated information about the Special Rapporteur's visits and related requests is available on the website of the Office of the United Nations High Commissioner for Human Rights (OHCHR).[90]

6.   On 30 November 2011, the Special Rapporteur sent follow-up letters concerning country visits undertaken by the previous mandate holder in 2009, including her missions to the Lao People's Democratic Republic, Serbia (including a visit to Kosovo) and the former Yugoslav Republic of Macedonia. Follow-up tables with the conclusions and recommendations from the related mission report and information from the Government and relevant United Nations documents, including from the universal periodic review, special procedures and treaty bodies, are available online.[91]

B. Communications

7.   The Special Rapporteur deals with individual cases or issues of concern brought to his attention. He sends allegation letters and urgent appeals to States seeking clarification on credible allegations of incidents and governmental action possibly incompatible with the provisions of the 1981 Declaration on the Elimination of All Forms of Intolerance and of Discrimination Based on Religion or Belief (1981 Declaration) (see General Assembly resolution 36/55). Since the creation of the mandate, the Special Rapporteurs have sent more than 1,250 allegation letters and urgent appeals to a total of 130 States. The communications sent by the Special Rapporteur between 1 July 2011 and 15 March 2012 and the replies received from Governments before 15 May 2012 are included in the latest communications reports (A/HRC/19/44 and A/HRC/20/30).

8.   The Special Rapporteur's communications cover a wide range of thematic issues, including allegations of attacks, arbitrary detention and disappearances of individuals belonging to religious minorities or belief communities and converts facing "blasphemy" and "apostasy" charges that may even carry death sentences. He has also taken up allegations of public manifestations of religious intolerance and stigmatization of persons based on their religion or belief. Recent cases show an increasing tendency towards religious intolerance that involves attacks on places of worship and religious sites such as cemeteries. Moreover, manifestations

---

90   See www2.ohchr.org/english/bodies/chr/special/countryvisitsa-e.htm.
91   See www.ohchr.org/EN/Issues/FreedomReligion/Pages/Visits.aspx.

of one's religion or belief have been restricted in particular in cases of peaceful assembly and protest or in attempts to express one's opinion via the media. In addition, the Special Rapporteur has analysed problematic legislative systems or draft legislation that fail to ensure the enjoyment of freedom of thought, conscience, religion or belief by all without discrimination or that prescribe burdensome administrative procedures of registration for religious or belief communities to obtain "recognition" or legal personality status.

9.   As requested by the Human Rights Council, the Special Rapporteur has continued to apply a gender perspective through, inter alia, the identification of gender-specific abuses, in the reporting process, including in the collection of information and recommendations. A number of allegation letters and urgent appeals summarized in the communications reports specifically address practices and legislation that discriminate against women and girls, including in the exercise of their right to freedom of thought, conscience and religion or belief.

C. Other activities

10. On 12 and 13 October 2011, the Special Rapporteur participated in an expert workshop in Santiago de Chile on how best to respond to advocacy of national, racial or religious hatred that constitutes incitement of discrimination, hostility or violence. The workshop was part of a series of four regional workshops organized by OHCHR.

11. At the four regional workshops, the Special Rapporteur presented joint submissions together with the Special Rapporteur on the promotion and protection of the right to freedom of opinion and expression and the Special Rapporteur on contemporary forms of racism, racial discrimination, xenophobia and related intolerance.[92] The Special Rapporteurs analysed a strategic response to hate speech, which should include efforts to educate people about cultural differences; promote diversity; and empower and give a voice to minorities, for example, through the support of community media and their representation in mainstream media. In this context, the Special Rapporteur refers to the Camden Principles on Freedom of Expression and Equality,[93] which recommend the adoption of a public policy framework for the media that promotes pluralism and

---

[92] See   www.ohchr.org/EN/Issues/FreedomOpinion/Articles19-20/Pages/Experts Papers.aspx.

[93] See www.article19.org/resources.php/resource/1214/en/camden-principles-on-freedom-of-expression-and-equality.

equality, by, for example, making an equitable allocation of resources, including broadcasting frequencies, among public service, commercial and community media, so that together they represent the full range of cultures, communities and opinions in society.

12. On 7 December 2011, the Special Rapporteur held a discussion in Strasbourg, France, with the European Commission against Racism and Intolerance on the question of racial and religious hate speech. On 12 and 13 December, he attended a two-day meeting in Washington, D.C., entitled the "Istanbul Process for Combating Intolerance, Discrimination and Violence on the Basis of Religion or Belief". The meeting focused on concrete and positive measures that States can take to eliminate religious intolerance in the implementation of Human Rights Council resolution 16/18 on combating intolerance, negative stereotyping and stigmatization of, and discrimination, incitement to violence and violence against, persons based on religion or belief.

13. On 22 and 23 May 2012, the Special Rapporteur attended an expert seminar in Vienna on enhancing the effectiveness of international, regional and national human rights mechanisms in protecting and promoting the rights of religious minorities, together with the Independent Expert on minority issues and other relevant experts. He spoke about the protection of religious minorities under international human rights standards, including the 1981 Declaration and articles 18, 26 and 27 of the International Covenant on Civil and Political Rights.

14. The Special Rapporteur held many meetings with Government representatives, religious or belief communities, civil society organizations and academic experts working in the area of freedom of religion or belief. In this context, he participated in national and international conferences, including in Baku, Berlin, Brussels, Budapest, Geneva, Lucerne, Switzerland, and Salzburg, Austria.

III. Right to conversion as part of freedom of religion or belief

A. Introduction

15. Countless reports of grave violations of the right to freedom of religion or belief relate to converts and those who try to convert others by means of non-coercive persuasion. This has become a human rights problem of great concern which occurs in various parts of the world and seems to stem from different motives. For instance, abuses are perpetrat-

ed in the name of religious or ideological truth claims, in the interest of promoting national identity or protecting societal homogeneity, or under other pretexts such as maintaining political and national security. While some undue restrictions on the rights of converts or those trying non-coercively to convert others are undertaken by State agencies, other abuses, including acts of violence, stem from widespread societal prejudices. Violations in this sensitive area also include forced conversions or reconversions, again perpetrated either by the State or by non-State actors. In addition, the rights of converts or those trying non-coercively to convert others are sometimes questioned in principle. The Special Rapporteur has therefore decided to put a thematic focus on this issue in the present report in order to contribute to a clarification of the rights of converts and those trying non-coercively to convert others as inextricable dimensions of freedom of religion or belief.[94]

16. The right to freedom of thought, conscience, religion or belief has manifold facets. In the area of conversion, at least four subcategories warrant systematic attention: (a) the right to conversion (in the sense of changing one's own religion or belief); (b) the right not to be forced to convert; (c) the right to try to convert others by means of non-coercive persuasion; and (d) the rights of the child and of his or her parents in this regard. It is important to clearly distinguish these dimensions since they differ with respect to the precise content and degree of legal protection attached to them under international human rights law. At the same time, one should not lose sight of the close links among the various dimensions in the attempt to ensure respect for every person's freedom of religion or belief.[95]

---

[94] Issues relating to conversion have already been discussed by previous mandate holders; see, for example, A/51/542/Add.1, paras. 11-12 and 134; E/CN.4/2005/61, paras. 45-47; and A/60/399, paras. 40-68.

[95] From a strictly normative perspective, there is no meaningful difference between conversion and reconversion. As part of his empirical observations, the Special Rapporteur nonetheless occasionally refers explicitly to both converts and reconverts or to acts of conversion and reconversion.

B. International human rights framework

1. Right to conversion (in the sense of changing one's own religion or belief)[96]

17. Article 18 of the Universal Declaration of Human Rights explicitly guarantees the "freedom to change" one's religion or belief as an inextricable component of the human right to freedom of religion or belief. While subsequent United Nations instruments use slightly different wording, the right to conversion remains fully protected. Article 18 of the International Covenant on Civil and Political Rights provides that freedom of thought, conscience and religion includes "freedom to have or adopt a religion or belief of his choice". Article 18 (2) was included partly to reinforce the protection of the right to conversion, stating that "[n]o one shall be subject to coercion which would impair his freedom to have or adopt a religion or belief of his choice". Article 1 of the 1981 Declaration refers to everyone's "freedom to have a religion or whatever belief of his choice".

18. As early as 1987, the then Special Rapporteur of the Sub-Commission on Prevention of Discrimination and Protection of Minorities, Elizabeth Odio Benito, concluded that while these provisions varied slightly in wording, they "all meant precisely the same thing: that everyone has the right to leave one religion or belief and to adopt another, or to remain without any at all" (see E/CN.4/Sub.2/1987/26, para. 21). In its general comment No. 22 (1993), the Human Rights Committee also interprets the "have or adopt" formulation of the International Covenant on Civil and Political Rights to include the right to conversion — an interpretation to which the Special Rapporteur clearly subscribes: In general comment No. 22, the Committee observes that "the freedom 'to have or to adopt' a religion or belief necessarily entails the freedom to choose a religion or belief, including the right to replace one's current religion or belief with another or to adopt atheistic views, as well as to retain one's religion or belief".[97]

19. It is generally agreed that within the ambit of freedom of religion or belief, the *forum internum*, namely, the internal dimension of a person's religious or belief- related conviction, enjoys absolute protection. In this

---

[96]   In the present report, formulations like "right to conversion" or "freedom of conversion" always relate to the dimension of changing one's own religion or belief.

[97]   See CCPR/C/21/Rev.1/Add.4, para. 5.

regard, the *forum internum* differs from external manifestation of religion or belief, which can be restricted under certain conditions and in accordance with certain criteria. As pointed out by the Human Rights Committee, the *forum internum* also covers everyone's freedom to have or adopt a religion or belief of one's choice and this freedom is protected unconditionally.[98] Consequently, the right to conversion has the rank of an absolutely protected right within freedom of religion or belief and does not permit any limitations or restrictions for any reason.

20. The Special Rapporteur reiterates the Human Rights Committee's clarification that freedom of religion or belief should be broadly construed so as to protect "theistic, non-theistic and atheistic beliefs, as well as the right not to profess any religion or belief".[99] Since the application of article 18 of the International Covenant on Civil and Political Rights is not limited "to traditional religions or to religions or beliefs with institutional characteristics or practices analogous to those of traditional religions",[100] such a broad understanding must also guide the various human rights questions that occur in the field of conversion.

21. States therefore have a number of obligations vis-à-vis the right to conversion. First, States should respect everyone's right to conversion as a *forum internum* component within freedom of religion or belief, for example, by abolishing punishments against converts and removing administrative obstacles. Moreover, States are obliged to protect the right to conversion against possible third-party infringements, such as violence or harassment against converts by their previous communities or their social environment. In addition, States should promote a societal climate in which converts can generally live without fear and free from discrimination.

2.   Right not to be forced to convert

22. The right not to be forced to convert also falls within the ambit of the *forum internum*, which has the status of absolute protection. In a sense, it is already implied in the right to conversion itself which, as a right to freedom, necessarily means voluntary, namely, non-coerced

---

[98]   Ibid., para. 3.

[99]   Ibid., para. 2; the same formulation was also used in the Final Document of the International Consultative Conference on School Education in Relation to Freedom of Religion or Belief, Tolerance and Non-Discrimination (see E/CN.4/2002/73, appendix, footnote 1).

[100]   Ibid., para. 2.

conversion. However, the right not to be forced to convert entails specific obligations on the State and hence warrants a separate discussion.

23. Above all, States must meticulously ensure that the specific authority of State agents and State institutions is not used to coerce people to convert or reconvert. One area that requires particular attention in this regard is the school which, besides being a place of learning and education, is also an institution that wields a high degree of authority over children, namely, young persons who may be particularly vulnerable to pressure from teachers or peers (see A/HRC/16/53, paras. 20-62). Other institutions that typically expose individuals to situations of increased vulnerability include the police force, the military and penal institutions. In all these and other State institutions, Governments have a special responsibility to guarantee everyone's protection against possible coercion to convert or reconvert to a religion or belief against their will.[101] The Human Rights Committee has emphasized that policies or practices having the intention or effect of compelling believers or non-believers to convert, for example, by restricting access to education, medical care or employment, are inconsistent with article 18 (2) of the International Covenant on Civil and Political Rights.[9]

24. The right not to be forced to convert is also relevant to non-State actors or to third parties, namely, private individuals or organizations. If individuals or organizations try to convert people by resorting to means of coercion or by directly exploiting situations of particular vulnerability, protection by States against such practices may prove necessary. This may amount to limiting the right to try to persuade others, which itself constitutes an important part of the *forum externum* dimension of freedom of religion or belief. As will be further discussed in section III.B.3 below, such restrictions can, however, only be justified if they strictly meet all the criteria set out in article 18 (3) of the International Covenant on Civil and Political Rights.

25. States also have the responsibility to ensure that forced conversions do not occur in the context of marriage or marriage negotiations. The obligation to guarantee effective protection, especially for women and sometimes minors, in this sensitive field follows from the right to freedom of religion or belief as well as from the duty of States to combat all forms of violence and discrimination against women. According to article 16 (1) (b) of the Convention on the Elimination of All Forms of Discrimination against Women, States parties "shall take all appropriate

---

[101] See recent communications in A/HRC/16/53/Add.1, paras. 88-98 and 346-350.

measures to eliminate discrimination against women in all matters relating to marriage and family relations and in particular shall ensure, on the basis of equality of men and women [...] the same right freely to choose a spouse and to enter into marriage only with their free and full consent".

3.   Right to try to convert others by means of non-coercive persuasion

26.   Freedom of religion or belief is not confined to the dimension of a person's *forum internum* but also includes the freedom to manifest one's religion or belief in external acts, such as "worship, observance, practice and teaching".14 Such *forum externum* manifestations can be undertaken "either individually or in community with others and in public or private".[102] It cannot be denied that this covers non-coercive attempts to persuade others, sometimes also called "missionary work".[103] Communicative outreach activities aimed at persuading others, including religious discourse, can be further based on article 19 (2) of the International Covenant on Civil and Political Rights, which provides that the right to freedom of expression shall include "freedom to seek, receive and impart information and ideas of all kinds, regardless of frontiers, either orally, in writing or in print, in the form of art, or through any other media of his choice".[104]

27.   Similar to freedom of expression, freedom of religion or belief has a strong communicative dimension which includes, inter alia, the freedom to communicate within one's own religious or belief group, share one's conviction with others, broaden one's horizons by communicating with people of different convictions, cherish and develop contacts across State boundaries, receive and disseminate information about religious or belief issues and try to persuade others in a non-coercive manner. Indeed, freedom of religion or belief and freedom of expression are two mutually reinforcing human rights.[105] In this spirit, article 6 of the 1981 Declaration

---

[102]   See article 18 (1) of the International Covenant on Civil and Political Rights.

[103]   Formulations such as "missionary work" or "missionary activities", when occasionally used in the present report, are not intended to reflect specifically denominational concepts. Similar concepts include "bearing witness", "da'wa" (the call), "invitation", etc.

[104]   See Human Rights Committee, general comment No. 34 on article 19: freedoms of opinion and expression, CCPR/C/GC/34, para.

[105]   See statements made by the High Commissioner for Human Rights at the 2008 expert seminar on the links between articles 19 and 20 of the International Covenant on Civil and Political Rights (A/HRC/10/31/Add.3, para. 3) and at the 2011 series of expert workshops on the prohibition of incitement to national, racial or

confirms that the right to freedom of thought, conscience, religion or belief includes the freedoms "(d) to write, issue and disseminate relevant publications in these areas", "(e) to teach a religion or belief in places suitable for these purposes", and "(i) to establish and maintain communications with individuals and communities in matters of religion or belief at the national and international levels".

28.   Unlike the *forum internum* dimension as discussed above (namely, the right to conversion and the right not to be forced to convert), manifestations of one's religion or belief in the *forum externum* do not enjoy absolute protection. However, the decisive point in international human rights law is that the burden of proof always falls on those who argue on behalf of restrictions, not on those who defend a right to freedom. The relationship between freedom and its possible limitation is a relationship between rule and exception. In case of doubt, the rule prevails and exceptions always imply an extra burden of argumentation, including clear empirical evidence of their necessity and appropriateness. Moreover, any restrictions imposed must meet all the criteria set out in article 18 (3) of the International Covenant on Civil and Political Rights, according to which "[f]reedom to manifest one's religion or belief may be subject only to such limitations as are prescribed by law and are necessary to protect public safety, order, health, or morals or the fundamental rights and freedoms of others". Thus, limitations imposed on the right to try to convert others require a legal basis; they must pursue one of the legitimate aims exhaustively listed in article 18 (3); they should be clearly and narrowly defined; they must be proportionate; and they should not be implemented in a discriminatory manner. By contrast, general provisions against "proselytism", a term that often remains undefined or merely vaguely circumscribed while typically carrying negative connotations would not suffice to meet the criteria prescribed in article 18 (3).

29.   The Special Rapporteur notes that some religious communities, interfaith organizations and non-governmental organizations have developed voluntary ethical guidelines or voluntary codes of conduct on how to undertake and not to undertake missionary activities.[106] Those sub-

---

religious hatred (www.ohchr.org/Documents/Issues/Expression/ICCPR/HCMessageWorkshops.pdf).

[106]   See World Council of Churches, Pontifical Council for Interreligious Dialogue, World Evangelical Alliance, "Christian Witness in a Multi-Religious World: Recommendations for Conduct" (Bangkok, 2011). See also Organization for Security and Cooperation in Europe (OSCE)/Office for Democratic Institutions and Human Rights, "Guidelines for Review of Legislation Pertaining to Religion or Belief",

scribing to such guidelines commit to respecting ethical principles, such as avoiding negative stereotypes, showing sensitivity for different cultural contexts and not linking charity work or humanitarian aid to expectations of conversion. While appreciating the significance of such ethical guidelines, which can have a beneficial effect on interreligious communication and cooperation, the Special Rapporteur emphasizes that they should be respected as voluntary and cannot be enforced by States. Moreover, reference to such voluntary guidelines or codes of conduct must not become a pretext for States to circumvent the criteria set out in article 18 (3) of the International Covenant on Civil and Political Rights when imposing limitations on the right to try to convert others by means of non-coercive persuasion.

4.   Rights of the child and of his or her parents

30.   Pursuant to article 18 (4) of the International Covenant on Civil and Political Rights, States parties undertake "to have respect for the liberty of parents and, when applicable, legal guardians to ensure the religious and moral education of their children in conformity with their own convictions". This provision has been reaffirmed by article 5 (1) of the 1981 Declaration, which states: "The parents or, as the case may be, the legal guardians of the child have the right to organize the life within the family in accordance with their religion or belief and bearing in mind the moral education in which they believe the child should be brought up."

31.   At the same time, the Convention on the Rights of the Child recalls that parents' rights must always be seen in conjunction with the human rights of the child. Article 14 (1) of the Convention requires States to "respect the rights of the child to freedom of thought, conscience and religion". Article 14 (2) obliges States parties to "respect the rights and duties of the parents and, when applicable, legal guardians, to provide direction to the child in the exercise of his or her right in a manner consistent with the evolving capacities of the child". The requirement to take into account the evolving capacities of the child reflects the insight

---

2004; Oslo Coalition on Freedom of Religion or Belief, "Missionary Activities and Human Rights: Proposing a Code of Conduct regarding Missionary Activities", 2008; International Federation of Red Cross and Red Crescent Societies and the International Committee of the Red Cross (ICRC), "Code of Conduct for the International Red Cross and Red Crescent Movement and Non-Governmental Organizations (NGOs) in Disaster Relief", 1994, available from www.ifrc.org/en/ publications-and-reports/code-of-conduct/.

that children themselves are rights-holders in international human rights law and, consequently, that their own convictions deserve respect.

32. This is further specified in article 12 (1) of the Convention, which provides that the views of the child have to be given "due weight in accordance with the age and maturity of the child". Concerning the question of how to determine the maturity of the child, the Special Rapporteur is inclined to favour a case-by-case approach rather than any fixed age limits. The Committee on the Rights of the Child has also emphasized that "[t]he more the child himself or herself knows, has experienced and understands, the more the parent, legal guardian or other persons legally responsible for the child have to transform direction and guidance into reminders and advice and later to an exchange on an equal footing. This transformation will not take place at a fixed point in a child's development, but will steadily increase as the child is encouraged to contribute her or his views".[107]

33. When convictions of the parents about religious or belief matters differ, the best interests of the child shall be a primary consideration. This also includes respect for his or her right to be heard and giving due weight to the views of the child in accordance with his or her age and maturity. It is important for the State to ensure that conflicts possibly arising from parents having different convictions are settled in an unbiased and non-discriminatory manner.

34. There can be no question that these provisions also apply to the right of conversion and its correlate, namely, the right not to be forced to convert or reconvert. Converts have the right for their new religious or belief affiliation to be respected in the religious upbringing of their children, in a manner consistent with the evolving capacities of the child. Any attempts, especially by the State or in State institutions, to alienate the children of converts from their family in religious or belief-related questions — for instance, by stipulating that children of converts must receive religious instruction in schools that goes against their will or the will of their parents — would thus infringe upon freedom of religion or belief and disregard the best interests of the child.

---

[107] See Committee on the Rights of the Child, general comment No. 12, CRC/C/GC/12, para. 84; see also A/64/159, para. 27.

C. Violations of freedom of religion or belief in the area of conversion

35. In his daily work, the Special Rapporteur regularly receives complaints of serious violations of freedom of religion or belief in relation to conversion in the four subcategories mentioned in the previous section. Typical targets include converts and their families or members of minorities or new religious movements who are subjected to pressure to convert or reconvert to mainstream religions or beliefs. Another problem concerns restrictions on the right to try to convert others by means of non-coercive persuasion which, in many countries, fall short of the criteria set out in article 18 (3) of the International Covenant on Civil and Political Rights. Moreover, both converts and persons trying non-coercively to convert others are often exposed to stereotypes and prejudices that may cause violent actions against them. The following non-exhaustive overview is structured along the four categories elaborated in the previous section.

I.   Violations of the right to conversion

36. In various regions of the world, converts are confronted with difficulties when trying to live in conformity with their convictions. Some States have criminal law sanctions according to which acts of conversion can be punished as "apostasy", "heresy", "blasphemy" or "insult" in respect of a religion or of a country's national heritage. In extreme cases, this can include the death penalty. In a number of countries, converts run the risk of having their marriage nullified, being excluded from the right to inheritance or losing custody of their children (see A/63/161, para. 37). Such sanctions in family law or other areas of civil law can have dramatic consequences for a person and her or his family.

37. Various administrative obstacles against conversion are an even more widespread phenomenon. In some cases, passports and other official documents continue to reflect the previous religious adherence of converts, often against their explicit will. Reportedly, children of converts have been registered under a different religion than their own, for instance the predominant religion of the country or the religion from which their parents converted. The result can be that the children are obliged to take religious instruction in school that does not reflect their own religion or belief. Such forms of systematic administrative disrespect can also target persons who have been born into a community whose

members are collectively stigmatized as "apostates" or "heretics" (see A/HRC/19/60, paras. 40-51).

38. Converts frequently suffer from systematic discrimination in virtually all sectors of society, such as education, housing, employment or health care. Moreover, registration requirements are used for the purpose of exposing converts, possibly with systematic discriminatory intention or effect. This can be the result of deliberate State policies to exclude converts or members of new religious movements stigmatized as "apostates" or "heretics" from higher education and other important societal institutions. Sometimes they cannot even obtain the official documents they need in order to travel, apply for jobs, participate in public elections or enrol their children in school.

39. In other cases, discrimination chiefly stems from societal prejudices often also stoked by public or private media, some of which may present converts as "inimical forces" who allegedly threaten the society's identity and cohesion. Moreover, converts sometimes experience pressure and mobbing even within their own families or in their close social environment. In extreme cases, this can lead to abductions, ill treatment and killings. It is a bitter irony that they may even experience suspicion within their new religious communities, owing to fear of "fake converts" potentially being planted by a hostile administration to test their political loyalty.

40. As a result of systematic discrimination, widespread hostility, manifestations of public contempt, State repression and persecution, some converts decide to leave their country of origin and try to find a new home elsewhere. When applying for asylum, they may again be treated with suspicion in that the genuineness of their conversion is questioned or even denied.[108] Extraditions of converts to theircountries of origin, even in the face of obvious risks of persecution, have at times been justified with the cynical recommendation that they could simply "conceal" their new faith, a recommendation that shows a flagrant disrespect for freedom of thought, conscience, religion or belief. The Special Rapporteur reiterates that extraditions or deportations that are likely to result in violations of freedom of religion or belief may themselves amount to a violation of this human right. In addition, such extraditions violate the

---

[108] See A/HRC/16/53/Add.1, paras. 399-407; A/HRC/7/10/Add.3, para. 56; and A/64/159, para. 24. Also, any conversion post departure should not give rise to the presumption that the asylum claim is fabricated (see A/HRC/6/5, para. 31).

principle of *non-refoulement*, as enshrined in article 33 of the 1951 Convention relating to the Status of Refugees.[109]

2.   Violations of the right not to be forced to convert

41.   Violations of the right not to be forced to convert are perpetrated both by States and non-State actors. Reportedly, some States exercise pressure on converts in order to reconvert them to their previous religion or on members of minorities to make them join mainstream religions or the official religion of the country. Means used for such illegitimate purposes include the threat of criminal sanctions, systematic discrimination, exclusion from higher education or other important societal sectors, denial of citizenship, non-registration of marriages, involuntary exposure of religion or belief in passports and other official documents, verbal abuse and even the threat or application of physical violence. Sometimes pressure is also exercised on children, a phenomenon discussed separately (see paras. 48-50 below).

42.   The problem also involves non-State actors. Some country reports indicate that non-State actors intimidate people by launching terrorist attacks in areas where religious minorities reside with the purpose of converting them. Furthermore, private individuals or organizations may exercise pressure with the purpose of converting people against their will. This can include the exploitation of situations of particular vulnerability, for instance in the context of humanitarian disasters, when some people may be in urgent need of humanitarian support measures that themselves are linked to a clear expectation of conversion. However, whether specific missionary activities in such situations of increased vulnerability amount to coercion should be established on a case-by-case basis, examining the context and circumstances in each individual situation (see A/60/399, paras. 64-68).

43.   The right not to be forced to convert also has an obvious gender dimension, since involuntary conversions can occur in the context of marriage or marriage negotiations. In a number of countries, obstacles to interreligious marriage still exist despite the provision in article 16 (1) of the Universal Declaration of Human Rights according to which the right

---

[109]   Moreover, article 3 of the Convention against Torture and Other Cruel, Inhuman or Degrading Treatment or Punishment provides that no State shall expel, return ("refouler") or extradite a person to another State where there are substantial grounds for believing that he or she would be in danger of being subjected to torture.

to marry and found a family may not be limited on grounds of religion. Such obstacles are sometimes formally enshrined in legal statutes and enforced by State authorities, including the judiciary. While men are sometimes expected to convert against their will in order to be able to marry a woman of a different religious affiliation, women are particularly affected by formal or informal pressure to convert to the religion of their prospective husbands. Although many such conversions may be undertaken on a voluntary basis, there are also cases of threats or coercion. The Special Rapporteur has received disturbing reports about the abduction and forced conversion of women, sometimes minors, especially from religious minorities. He is concerned that such incidents seem to occur in a climate of impunity, thus leading to the impression that law enforcement agencies systematically fail to provide effective protection for women and girls. There are still countries that, on the basis of custom, religious beliefs or the ethnic origins of particular groups of people, permit forced marriages or remarriages. The Committee on the Elimination of Discrimination against Women has recommended that "States parties should resolutely discourage any notions of inequality of women and men which are affirmed by laws, or by religious or private law or by custom." (see general recommendation No. 21, para. 44).

3.   Violations of the right to try to convert others by means of non-coercive persuasion

44. A number of States restrict religious outreach activities under the heading of "proselytism", a term that typically conjures up negative sentiments but rarely receives a clear conceptual or legal definition. Prohibitions of "proselytism" or of other vaguely defined "offences" under domestic legislation are sometimes enshrined in the constitution or in criminal law statutes. As a result, non-coercive attempts to persuade others may lead to criminal prosecution because of "proselytism", "unethical conversion", "disruption of public order", "blasphemy" or related "offences".[110] Often the mere existence of such legislation has a chilling effect on communicative outreach activities. Some States have enacted explicit anti-conversion laws, some of which supposedly are intended to provide protection only from so-called "fraudulent" conversion, a term that, again, often remains ill- defined and thus opens the floodgates to restrictive practices. States that claim to protect people against exploitation in situations of particular vulnerability often fail to provide clear

---

[110]   See A/51/542/Add.1, para. 134; A/60/399, paras. 60-61 and 66.

empirical evidence that certain missionary activities amount to coercion. Moreover, law enforcement agencies often confiscate and destroy such religious materials as prayer books, information sheets, video messages or education programmes. In some States, the mere possession of such material can trigger criminal or administrative sanctions, including long-term imprisonment. Non-citizens suspected of engaging in unwelcome missionary activities frequently risk deportation or the denial of visa-extension.[111]

45. In addition to criminal and administrative sanctions imposed by States or other restrictive State measures, individuals or groups trying to persuade others are often confronted with societal prejudices that some-times escalate into fully fledged paranoia and concomitant acts of mob violence.[112] This can even affect persons or communities who merely of-fer peaceful invitations. Members of religious communities that have a reputation of being generally committed to missionary work may suffer from harassment, hostility and violence, regardless of whether or not they are personally engaged in any such activities.

46. Unlike the rights to convert and not to be forced to convert, which are protected unconditionally, the right to try to convert others by means of non-coercive persuasion can be limited in conformity with the criteria prescribed in article 18 (3) of the International Covenant on Civil and Political Rights. However, the Special Rapporteur has the strong im-pression that many of the legislative or administrative restrictions im-posed by States fall far short of satisfying those criteria. For example, vague and overly broad definitions of "proselytism", "unethical conver-sion" and related "offences" may create an atmosphere of insecurity in which law enforcement agencies can restrict acts of religious communi-cation in an arbitrary manner. Some States have started to require indi-viduals seeking to conduct missionary activities to register, sometimes on an annual basis. However, in view of the right to try to convert others by means of non-coercive persuasion, registration should not be a precondi-tion for practising one's religion or belief, including through missionary activities.[113]

47. The Special Rapporteur has also noted with concern that restrictions are often conceptualized and implemented in violation of the principle of

---

[111] See A/63/161, paras. 25-66; A/61/340, paras. 55-61.
[112] See A/HRC/10/8/Add.1, paras. 45-49; A/HRC/10/8/Add.3, paras. 11 and 47-52.
[113] See E/CN.4/2005/61, paras. 55-58; A/61/340, paras. 52-54; and A/HRC/19/60, pa-ra. 41.

non-discrimination. In particular, States that have an official religion frequently seem to encourage missionary activities on behalf of the country's official religion, while at the same time prohibiting or restricting any attempts to convert people to another religion or belief. With regard to the concept of an official "State religion", the Special Rapporteur reiterates that it seems difficult, if not impossible, to conceive of an application of this concept that in practice does not have adverse effects on religious minorities, thus discriminating against their members (see A/HRC/19/60, para. 66). There are also some discriminatory domestic legal provisions that give preferential treatment to so-called "reconversions" to the forefathers' original religion (see A/HRC/10/8/Add.3, para. 48). Such policies and practices violate the principles of equality and non-discrimination on which the entire architecture of human rights, including the right to freedom of religion or belief, is based.

4. Violations of the rights of the child and of his or her parents

48. Violations of freedom of religion or belief in the broad field of conversion sometimes include State pressure or societal pressure on children, a phenomenon that warrants special discussion, since it goes against the rights of parents or guardians to ensure the religious and moral education of their children in conformity with their own convictions and in a manner consistent with the evolving capacities of the respective child.

49. The Special Rapporteur is deeply concerned by reports of repressive measures targeting children, since they occur in a considerable number of countries. As well as directly violating the rights of the affected children, such practices often seem to pursue the illegitimate purpose of exercising pressure on their parents or guardians. The intention may be to reconvert them to their previous religion or put pressure on members of minorities or non-traditional religions to convert to socially "accepted" religions or beliefs that are thought to be more in line with the traditional makeup of the country. Measures used for such purposes include involuntary participation of children in religious instruction as part of the mandatory school curriculum. Sometimes, children of converts or children from a religious minority are even urged to actively participate in religious prayers or practice religious rituals in public schools.

50. Parents from minorities or converts may run the risk of losing the right to have custody of their own children. In conflicts between parents of different religious or belief-related orientations, for example in the context of divorce settlements, parents from minorities or converts fre-

quently suffer discriminatory treatment. In such situations, children often cannot express their views in an open, non-intimidating atmosphere, which is required to respect their right to be heard. As a result of an insensitive or discriminatory handling of such complicated situations, children are alienated from their parents or families, with traumatic consequences for all. This can amount to grave violations of the rights of the child, as well as a serious violation of freedom of religion or belief of the parents.

D. Widespread misunderstandings

51. Freedom of religion or belief in the broad field of conversion is not only violated in practice; it is sometimes also questioned in principle. In discussions with representatives of Governments, members of various religious or belief communities and other stakeholders in society and academia, the Special Rapporteur has come across perceptions and conceptualizations that may lend intellectual support to undue infringements, in particular of the rights of converts and those trying to convert others by means of non-coercive persuasion. He therefore briefly addresses some typical misunderstandings.

1.   Disruption of peace and harmony

52. The most widespread objection against the right to try non-coercively to convert others concerns the fear that this may lead to a disruption of societal peace and interreligious harmony. A number of Governments have taken up such objections and turned them into a general argument of "public order" which they use to restrict the right to try to convert others even if such attempts are undertaken by means of strictly non-coercive persuasion. In many cases, such restrictions, for example against "proselytism" or "unethical conversions" (see A/60/399, paras. 44-45) remain overly broad, vaguely defined or even discriminatory, thus failing to satisfy the criteria set out in article 18 (3) of the International Covenant on Civil and Political Rights.

53. With regard to this issue, the Special Rapporteur emphasizes that he obviously shares an interest in promoting peaceful relations among people of different religions or beliefs. He further notes that freedom of religion or belief itself should be seen as conducive to peace. This is reflected, for example, in the 1948 Universal Declaration of Human Rights, which proclaims in its preamble that respect for human rights constitutes "the foundation of [...] freedom, justice and peace in the world".

54. The peace facilitated by human rights in general and freedom of religion or belief in particular is built on due recognition of people's most diverse convictions and concomitant practices. This includes respect for the rights of individuals to communicate on questions of religion or belief, reach out across communities and State boundaries, broaden their own horizons or try to persuade others in a non-coercive manner. Thus, a society respectful of freedom of religion or belief for everyone, as guaranteed in international human rights law, will likely be a religiously pluralistic society, with open boundaries among different communities and subcommunities, and will also be open to peaceful competition and intellectual controversies on religious and belief-related questions.

55. The specific concept of peace underlying international human rights clearly differs from the authoritarian control agendas that are sometimes also put forward in the name of "peace" or "harmony". However, a peace based on respect for the dignity and freedom of all human beings goes deeper and has a better chance of sustainability than any societal order organized around such ideas as hegemony, customs or mere authority. Respect for human dignity, in turn, is not conceivable without recognition of every human being's freedom to communicate about issues of religion or belief, including the right to try to persuade others in a non-coercive manner.

2.   Threatened erosion of moral values

56. Restrictions on freedom of religion or belief are sometimes implemented in the name of protecting moral values based on a particular religious tradition that often is the tradition of the majority in a country. From that point of view, missionary activities may be perceived by some Governments as challenging the predominance of a religious tradition with allegedly adverse consequences for the moral fabric of society as a whole. Restrictive measures imposed by States to prevent such a development may target not only those who try to convert others by means of non-coercive persuasion, but also persons who themselves have converted or wish to convert away from the dominant religion of the country. This problem frequently occurs in countries where there is a State religion.

57. In this context, it is important to bear in mind that the Human Rights Committee has argued for a pluralistic understanding of the concept of "morals", a concept listed among the possible grounds for limiting manifestations of freedom of religion or belief in article 18 (3) of the International Covenant on Civil and Political Rights. In its general com-

ment No. 22, the Human Rights Committee clarifies that the concept of morals "derives from many social, philosophical and religious traditions; consequently, limitations on the freedom to manifest a religion or belief for the purpose of protecting morals must be based on principles not deriving exclusively from a single tradition". In its recent general comment No. 34 on freedoms of opinion and expression, the Committee adds that "[a]ny such limitations must be understood in the light of the universality of human rights and the principle of non-discrimination" (see CCPR/C/GC/34, para. 32). The Special Rapporteur welcomes this clarification, which must also be applied to any restrictions imposed on manifestations of freedom of religion or belief.

58. Restrictions on manifestations of freedom of religion or belief, including non-coercive attempts to convert others, thus cannot be justified by the invocation of a closed understanding of a moral order based on one particular religious or philosophical tradition. Instead, any restrictions deemed necessary by States must meet all the specific criteria prescribed in article 18 (3) of the International Covenant on Civil and Political Rights. Moreover, the interest of protecting certain moral or religious values may never be invoked to restrict the freedom of conversion itself which, as part of the absolutely protected *forum internum* dimension of freedom of religion or belief, does not permit any limitations whatsoever. For the same reason, the notion of moral values cannot be used to legitimize pressure on converts or members of minorities, for example to make them reconvert to their previous religion or to follow mainstream religions or beliefs.

3.   Freedom of "choice" — appropriateness of the term

59. The most fundamental objection against the right to freedom of religion or belief in the field of conversion is directed at the concept of "choice", which lies at the very heart of this human right. It has been argued that the language of "choice" does not appropriately reflect the existential dimension of a deep religious or philosophical conviction and the sense of belonging and loyalty that goes with any profound conviction. The Special Rapporteur shares the view that religion or belief is not just an item within a catalogue of commodities that individuals may take or leave according to their personal tastes or preferences. However, a similar statement could be made about marriage and partnership and other important human life issues. Obviously, the "choice" of a spouse should not resemble the selection of an item from a catalogue. So again, the language of "choice", as it comes up in human rights discourses on

marriage and family life, inevitably fails to reach the existential significance of such an intimate relationship and sense of profound loyalty to which it is attached. Yet, having a right to free "choice" concerning partnership and marriage, as enshrined in international human rights documents, remains important, especially in the face of such phenomena as enforced marriage or child marriage, which, to this day, continue to exist.

60. The concept of "choice" makes sense especially in the sphere of law, including human rights law. Obviously, the language of law cannot reflect the full range of human experiences. In this regard, law has insurmountable limitations that one should always bear in mind. It remains true that a person's existential experience, be it in the field of religion or belief or in relation to marriage and other important human life issues, may go far beyond the understanding of just making a "choice". The legal language of human rights is not supposed to replace such experience, and it is by no means intended to lead to a "commodified" understanding of religion or belief or other significant issues relating to human life and human communities. The opposite is true. By establishing legal safeguards against different forms of coercion, human rights norms can arguably even contribute to the achievement of higher degrees of sincerity, earnestness, authenticity, profoundness, loyalty and commitment in questions of religion or belief.

61. It would thus be utterly wrong to delegitimize the concept of "choice" in the area of religion or belief, a concept particularly important when it comes to safeguarding the human rights of converts or those trying to convert others by means of non-coercive persuasion. Protecting every human being's freedom of "choice" is a perfectly appropriate way to institutionalize, in the specific sphere of human rights law, the axiomatic respect that is due to all human beings by virtue of their inherent human dignity. Respect for human dignity, however, necessarily implies respecting the various deep convictions and commitments of all human beings by legally guaranteeing their freedom to have and adopt a religion or belief of their own "choice".

IV. Conclusions and recommendations

62. The General Assembly has repeatedly and by consensus urged States to ensure that their constitutional and legislative systems provide adequate and effective guarantees of freedom of thought, conscience and religion or belief to all without distinction, inter alia, by providing access to

justice and effective remedies in cases where the right to freedom of thought, conscience and religion or belief or the right to freely practise one's religion, including the right to change one's religion or belief, is violated (see General Assembly resolutions 60/166, 61/161, 62/157, 63/181, 64/164, 65/211 and 66/168).

63. In his daily work, however, the Special Rapporteur receives numerous reports of grave violations of the right to freedom of religion or belief in the broad area of conversion. In the present report, he has discussed this topic, distinguishing four subcategories that deserve systematic attention: (a) the right to conversion (in the sense of changing one's own religion or belief); (b) the right not to be forced to convert; (c) the right to try to convert others by means of non-coercive persuasion; and (d) the rights of the child and of his or her parents in this context.

A. Right to conversion

64. In addition to being exposed to manifestations of social pressure, public contempt and systematic discrimination, converts often face insurmountable administrative obstacles when trying to live in conformity with their convictions. Moreover, in a number of countries, they run the risk of losing jobs and educational opportunities, having their marriage nullified, being excluded from the right to inheritance or even losing custody of their children. In some States, converts may also face criminal prosecution, at times even including the death penalty, for such offences as "apostasy", "heresy", "blasphemy" or "insult" in respect of a religion or the country's dominant tradition and values. When seeking asylum, they may find that the genuineness of their conversion is questioned and may be deported back to their countries of origin where they may be confronted with aggravated risks to their life, freedom, well-being and security.

B. Right not to be forced to convert

65. Serious violations also occur in respect of the right not to be forced to convert against one's will. While some members of religious or belief minorities experience pressure to join a religion or belief deemed more "acceptable" in society, converts are often exposed to pressure to reconverting to their previous religion. Such pressure can be undertaken both by Government agencies and by non-State actors, including by directly linking humanitarian aid to expectation of conversion. The Special Rapporteur is particularly concerned about pressure or threats experienced

by women, sometimes in the context of marriage or marriage negotiations, to convert to the religion of their (prospective) husband.

C. Right to try to convert others by means of non-coercive persuasion

66. In addition, many States impose tight legislative or administrative restrictions on communicative outreach activities. This may unduly limit the right to try to convert others by means of non-coercive persuasion, which itself constitutes an inextricable part of freedom of religion or belief. Moreover, many such restrictions are conceptualized and implemented in a flagrantly discriminatory manner, for instance, in the interest of further strengthening the position of the official religion or dominant religion of the country while further marginalizing the situation of minorities. Members of religious communities that have a reputation of being generally engaged in missionary activities may also face societal prejudices that can escalate into paranoia, sometimes even leading to acts of mob violence and killings.

D. Rights of the child and of his or her parents

67. The Special Rapporteur has also received reports of repressive measures targeting children of converts or members of religious minorities, including with the purpose of exercising pressure on them and their parents to reconvert to their previous religion or to coerce members of minorities to convert to more socially "accepted" religions or beliefs. Such repressive activities may violate the child's freedom of religion or belief and/or the parents' right to ensure an education for their children in conformity with their own convictions and in a manner consistent with the evolving capacities of the child.

E. Recommendations to various actors

68. In general, the Special Rapporteur calls upon States to consistently respect, protect and promote the human right to freedom of religion or belief in the area of conversion. He reiterates that the right of conversion and its correlate, the right not to be forced to convert or reconvert, belong to the *forum internum* dimension of freedom of religion or belief, which has the status of unconditional protection under international human rights law. Furthermore, freedom of religion or belief includes the right to try to persuade others in a non-coercive manner. Any restrictions on missionary activities deemed necessary by States must

therefore meet all the criteria set out in article 18 (3) of the International Covenant on Civil and Political Rights. The rights of the child and of his or her parents must be effectively guaranteed, including in the context of conversion issues.

69. With regard to domestic legal provisions, including constitutions, legal statutes, by-laws and official interpretations of laws, the Special Rapporteur recommends that:

a) States should clarify that the human right to freedom of religion or belief includes the right to convert and the right not to be forced to convert, both of which are unconditionally protected;

b) States should repeal any criminal sanctions that directly or indirectly threaten punishment against converts;

c) States should reform any family law provisions that may amount to de jure or de facto sanctions against converts and their families. This concerns the various areas of family law, including custody of children and inheritance laws;

d) States should issue anti-discrimination legislation with a view to providing effective protection against discrimination on the grounds of religion or belief in various areas of society. Such legislation should also address the vulnerable situation of converts;

e) States should ensure that no individual is exposed to pressure to convert against her or his will in the context of marriage and marriage negotiations. In this regard, States should pay particular attention to the situation of women. Aligning family laws with article 16 (1) of the Universal Declaration of Human Rights, according to which religious difference should not be an obstacle to the right to marry a person of one's choice, could be one important way of protecting potential spouses from pressure to convert against their will;

f) States should further clarify that freedom of religion or belief includes the right to try to convert others by non-coercive means of communication and persuasion. This includes, inter alia, the dissemination of literature and other material relating to religion or belief;

g) States should repeal vague provisions against so-called "proselytism", "unethical conversion", "apostasy" and "blasphemy" and should reform respective legislation to align it with the provisions of article 18 (3) of the International Covenant on Civil and Political Rights.

70. With regard to different areas of administration, the Special Rapporteur recommends that:

a) States should ensure that converts are able to have their new religious or belief orientation registered or not registered in official documents as they wish. This should also include the religion or belief of their children, in keeping with the provisions of the Convention on the Rights of the Child. When issuing official documents, States should always ensure that no person is publicly exposed in her or his religion or belief against her or his will;

b) States should ensure that no person is exposed to situations in which she or he may experience pressure to convert or reconvert against her or his will, especially in State-controlled institutions, such as the police force, the military or penal institutions;

c) States should develop strategies on how to provide effective protection of converts from acts or threats of violence and other pressure from non-State actors;

d) States should give clear direction and training to law enforcement and similar agencies to ensure that they refrain from unduly infringing on the right to try to convert others by means of non-coercive persuasion;

e) States should not use visa rules to restrict non-coercive religious outreach activities;

f) States should ensure that when applying for asylum, converts are given a fair hearing of their claims, in conformity with international standards. Converts seeking refugee status must never be expelled or returned to the frontiers of territories where their life or freedom would be threatened on account of their religion or belief.

71. With regard to the area of school education, the Special Rapporteur recommends that:

a) States should ensure that when attending school, children are not exposed to religious instruction against their will or against the will of their parents or legal guardians, respectively. Moreover, no child should be at risk of being pressured to attend religious ceremonies or rituals in school against their will or against the will of their parents or guardians. In this regard, particular attention should be given to the situation of children of converts and members of religious or belief minorities;

b) States should ensure that school curriculums, when providing information on religious or belief-related issues, contribute to the elimination of negative stereotypes and prejudices against converts and persons or groups engaged in non-coercive missionary activities. This should also be a guiding consideration for assessing the quality of textbooks used in schools;

c) States should prescribe, organize and provide training for teachers to sensitize them about the particular needs and challenges of children of converts and children from religious minorities in the school situation.

72. With regard to non-State actors, the Special Rapporteur recommends that:

a) Civil society organizations working on human rights should pay attention to the particularly vulnerable situation of converts and members of religious or belief minorities at risk of being forced to convert or reconvert against their will. They should develop strategies to empower such people based on the understanding that conversion constitutes an inextricable part of freedom of religion or belief;

b) Public and private media should provide fair and accurate information about converts and persons or groups engaged in non-coercive missionary activities with a view to overcoming negative stereotypes and prejudices. Self-regulation mechanisms within the media can play an important role in this regard;

c) Religious leaders and opinion formers should become aware and acknowledge that not only is conversion to their own religion or belief protected, but that any decision to replace one's current religion or belief with a different one or to adopt atheistic views is equally protected;

d) Religious communities, interfaith groups and civil society and development aid organizations are encouraged to address issues of conversion and missionary activities in voluntary codes of conduct. They should use this as an opportunity to also promote more respectful attitudes towards converts and persons engaged in non-coercive missionary activities.

5.　Chapter: Report December 2012

I.　Introduction

1.　The mandate of the Special Rapporteur on freedom of religion or belief was created by Commission on Human Rights resolution 1986/20 and renewed by Human Rights Council resolution 6/37. On 18 June 2010, the Human Rights Council adopted resolution 14/11 and subsequently appointed Heiner Bielefeldt as the mandate holder as from 1 August 2010.

2.　In chapter II, the Special Rapporteur gives a brief overview of his activities since the submission of his previous report to the Human Rights Council (A/HRC/19/60). The Special Rapporteur focuses in chapter III on the protection of freedom of religion or belief of persons belonging to religious minorities. In chapter IV, he provides conclusions in this regard and addresses recommendations to various stakeholders.

II.　Activities of the Special Rapporteur

3.　The Special Rapporteur has conducted various activities pursuant to Human Rights Council resolutions 6/37, 14/11 and 19/8. In this chapter, he presents a brief overview of his mandate activities from 1 December 2011 to 30 November 2012.

A.　Country visit

4.　Since the submission of his previous report to the Human Rights Council, the Special Rapporteur has undertaken a country visit to Cyprus, from 29 March to 5 April 2012. He appreciates the cooperation and information provided by all his interlocutors and officials before, during and after his visit. He encourages all stakeholders to consider his recommendations and cooperate with each other in the implementation of the recommendations provided in the mission report (A/HRC/22/51/Add.1).

5.　During the reporting period, the Special Rapporteur has sent country visit requests to the Governments of Bangladesh, Indonesia, Jordan, Uzbekistan and Viet Nam. He is grateful for the invitation extended by the Government of Viet Nam to conduct a visit in 2013.

B. Communications

6.   The Special Rapporteur continues to receive many complaints about human rights violations perpetrated against individuals and groups from various religious or belief backgrounds. These allegations include physical attacks, arbitrary detention and involuntary disappearances of individuals belonging to religious minorities or belief communities, "apostasy" and "blasphemy" charges against converts or dissidents, public manifestations of religious intolerance and stigmatization of persons based on their religion or belief, and attacks on places of worship and religious sites, such as cemeteries or monuments of other historical and cultural value. In addition, there are reports of individuals being deported from some States to their country of origin where they may face religious persecution and serious punishment. There are also concerns about forced conversion, targeting members of some religious minorities.

7.   The Special Rapporteur seeks to clarify allegations of certain actions possibly incompatible with the provisions of the 1981 Declaration on the Elimination of All Forms of Intolerance and of Discrimination Based on Religion or Belief (1981 Declaration)[114] by sending allegation letters and urgent appeals to States. The communications sent by the Special Rapporteur between 1 December 2011 and 30 November 2012 are included in the latest communications reports (A/HRC/20/30, A/HRC/21/49 and A/HRC/22/67).

8.   As requested by the Human Rights Council, the Special Rapporteur has continued to apply a gender perspective, inter alia, through the identification of gender-specific abuses, in the reporting process, including information gathering and recommendations. A number of allegation letters and urgent appeals summarized in the communications reports specifically address practices and legislation that discriminate against women and girls, including in the exercise of their right to freedom of thought, conscience and religion or belief.

C. Other activities

9.   On 22 and 23 May 2012, the Special Rapporteur joined the Independent Expert on minority issues, Rita Izsák, at an expert seminar in Vienna that focused on "Enhancing the effectiveness of international, regional and national human rights mechanisms in protecting and promoting the rights of religious minorities". He spoke about the protection of religious

---

[114]   General Assembly resolution 36/55.

minorities under international human rights standards, including the 1981 Declaration and articles 18, 26 and 27 of the International Covenant on Civil and Political Rights.

10. On 1 October 2012, the Special Rapporteur participated in a conference organized by the Office for Democratic Institutions and Human Rights (ODIHR) of the Organization for Security and Co-operation in Europe (OSCE) on developments and challenges that OSCE member States face in the context of freedom of religion or belief.

11. The Special Rapporteur also participated in a wrap-up expert workshop in Rabat on 4 and 5 October 2012, on how best to respond to advocacy of national, racial or religious hatred that constitutes incitement to discrimination, hostility or violence. The experts jointly adopted the Rabat Plan of Action,[115] which contains conclusions and recommendations emanating from the series of four regional workshops organized by the Office of the High Commissioner for Human Rights (OHCHR) in 2011.

12. On 27 November 2012, the Special Rapporteur took part in the fifth session of the Forum on Minority Issues in Geneva. He spoke about the rights of religious minorities and presented recommendations on the positive measures that could be taken to protect and promote their rights.

13. In addition, the Special Rapporteur held many meetings with government representatives, religious or belief communities, civil society organizations and academic experts working in the area of freedom of religion or belief. In this context he participated in national and international conferences, including in Berlin, Brussels, Budapest, Geneva, Heidelberg, Lucerne, New York, Nijmegen, Salzburg, Vienna and Warsaw.

III. Protecting the freedom of religion or belief of persons belonging to religious minorities

A. Introductory remarks

14. The vulnerable situation of persons belonging to religious or belief minorities has attracted increased international attention in recent

---

[115] See www.ohchr.org/Documents/Issues/Opinion/SeminarRabat/Rabat_draft_outcome.pdf.

years.[116] States, civil society organizations, national human rights institutions, the media and other stakeholders have expressed their interest in developing strategies for more efficient protection of the rights of persons belonging to religious minorities worldwide. Such debates have also repeatedly taken place in United Nations forums, including the General Assembly, the Human Rights Council and the Forum on Minority Issues.

15.   Although people from all religious or belief backgrounds may be exposed to anti- minority victimization when living in a minority situation, certain religious communities have a particularly long-lasting history of discrimination, harassment and even persecution. Human rights violations perpetrated against members of religious or belief minorities are multifaceted in motives and settings while the perpetrators may be States or non-State actors or both (see III. C. below). These violations account for the need for concerted action.

16.   Besides the problem of ongoing human rights violations, the issue of the rights of persons belonging to religious minorities also poses a number of conceptual challenges which require systematic clarification. Misunderstandings and misperceptions, such as frequently occur in this field, may have adverse implications for the consistent conceptualization and implementation of the rights of persons belonging to religious minorities. Hence, overcoming existing conceptual misunderstandings is not merely an academic endeavour but has practical relevance.

B.   Conceptual clarifications

I.   The human rights framework in general

17.   The rights of persons belonging to religious or belief minorities should be consistently understood from a human rights perspective, and must be protected in conjunction with all other human rights. This clarification, which prima facie may seem trivial, is necessary since minority issues are often associated with concepts of minority protection that historically emerged outside of the human rights framework. It seems fair to acknowledge the historical merits of some of those protection systems in having facilitated the peaceful coexistence of different communities. However, one should be aware that they may differ conceptually from the norms and principles of universal human rights. Nonetheless, com-

---

[116]   For example, Human Rights Council resolution 19/8 includes nine references to religious minorities, whereas neither the Universal Declaration of Human Rights nor the 1981 Declaration explicitly mentions religious minorities.

ponents of different forms of minority protection continue to play an
important political role and can even permeate the rhetoric of human
rights without always being conceptually consistent with the human
rights-based approach. This is a source of much confusion with possibly
adverse implications for the practical implementation of the rights of
persons belonging to religious minorities.

18. For example, minority protection systems that were developed in
the framework of bilateral or multilateral peace agreements typically resulted in political or legal safeguards on behalf of specifically listed minority groups and their members. Although these safeguards might have
provided practical advantages for the identified minority groups, such
protection systems were not always human rights-based. Instead of
building on the principles of universality, freedom and equality, they typically protected only the members of certain predefined groups. Moreover, the political context of bilateral or multilateral agreements har-
boured the risk that the specific minorities were seen as receiving
protection by certain foreign powers. As a result, some of these minority
protection mechanisms were eventually turned against the very groups
they were supposed to protect.

19. The human rights- based approach also differs from theologically
defined concepts of minority protection in which different status positions may depend on the degree of closeness to, or distance from, the
predominant religion of the State. This would again result in reserving
protection for a predefined list of religious communities while not appropriately taking into account the right to freedom of religion or belief
of those individuals or groups who do not, or do not seem to, fit into the
setting of theologically accepted religions, such as members of other minorities, individual dissenters, minorities within minorities, atheists or
agnostics, converts or people with unclear religious orientation.

20. It is important to reiterate that the rights of persons belonging to
religious minorities as established in the context of international human
rights law, share all the characteristics of the human rights approach
based on the principles of universality, freedom and equality. This is in
the spirit of article 1 of the Universal Declaration of Human Rights, which
emphasizes that "[a]ll human beings are born free and equal in dignity
and rights". Moreover, the preamble to the Universal Declaration takes as
its starting point the "recognition of the inherent dignity and of the
equal and inalienable rights of all members of the human family". This
proclamation, which has been reiterated in several international human

rights conventions, must also guide the interpretation and implementation of the rights of persons belonging to religious minorities.

2.   Free development of individual and communitarian identities

21.   Article 27 of the International Covenant on Civil and Political Rights provides that "[i]n those States in which ethnic, religious or linguistic minorities exist, persons belonging to such minorities shall not be denied the right, in community with the other members of their group, to enjoy their own culture, to profess and practise their own religion, or to use their own language".[117] According to the wording used in this provision, rights holders are individual persons who exercise their rights within their communities. The same structure can also be found in the 1992 Declaration on the Rights of Persons Belonging to National or Ethnic, Religious and Linguistic Minorities (1992 Minorities Declaration).[118] As the title indicates, rights holders are again individual persons in relation to their communities.

22.   The Human Rights Committee, in its general comment No. 23 (1994) on article 27 (rights of minorities), further defines the overarching purpose of article 27 as facilitating the long-term development of minority communities and their identities, stressing that "[t]he protection of these rights is directed towards ensuring the survival and continued development of the cultural, religious and social identity of the minorities concerned, thus enriching the fabric of society as a whole".[119] This general purpose of minority rights is also laid down in a more comprehensive manner in the 1992 Minorities Declaration, whose article 1(1) provides that "States shall protect the existence of the national or ethnic, cultural, religious and linguistic identity of minorities within their respective territories and shall encourage conditions for the promotion of that identity."

23.   In the context of human rights, the identity of a person or a group must always be defined in respect of the self-understanding of the human beings concerned, which can be very diverse and may also change over time. While generally applying to different (ethnic, linguistic, etc.) cate-

---

[117] See also the similar wording in article 30 of the Convention on the Rights of the Child with regard to children who belong to a minority or who are of indigenous origin.

[118] General Assembly resolution 47/135.

[119] Human Rights Committee general comment No. 23 (1994) on the rights of minorities, para. 9.

gories of identity, this principle of respecting every person's self- understanding is even more pronounced when it comes to defining religious or belief identities, since the development of such identities relates to the human right to freedom of thought, conscience, religion or belief. This human right has received international recognition in a number of instruments, including article 18 of the Universal Declaration, article 18 of the International Covenant and the 1981 Declaration. Freedom of religion or belief empowers all human beings to freely find their own ways in the broad field of religion or belief, as individuals and in community with others. They have the freedom, inter alia, to retain, adopt or change their religion or belief; to broaden their horizons by communicating with members of their own communities or with people holding different convictions; to hold religious ceremonies alone or with others; to educate their children in conformity with their own faith; to import religious literature from abroad and to network with co-religionists across State boundaries. Individuals also have the right not to be exposed publicly in their religious or belief-related orientations against their will and to keep their convictions to themselves.

24. Measures used to promote the identity of a specific religious minority always presuppose respect for the freedom of religion or belief of all of its members. Thus, the question of how they wish to exercise their human rights remains the personal decision of each individual. Strictly speaking, this means that the State cannot "guarantee" the long- term development or identity of a particular religious minority. Instead, what the State can and should do is create favourable conditions for persons belonging to religious minorities to ensure that they can take their faith-related affairs in their own hands in order to preserve and further develop their religious community life and identity.

25. Positive measures are often urgently needed to facilitate the long-term development of a religious minority and its members. The added value of article 27 of the International Covenant and similar minority rights provisions is that they call upon States to undertake such measures, which thus become an obligation under international human rights law. According to article 4(2) of the 1992 Minorities Declaration, States should "take measures to create favourable conditions to enable persons belonging to minorities to express their characteristics and to develop their culture, language, religion, traditions and customs, except where specific practices are in violation of national laws and contrary to international standards". This requires a broad range of activities. For instance, support measures may include subsidies for schools and train-

ing institutions, the facilitation of community media, provisions for an appropriate legal status for religious minorities, accommodation of religious festivals and ceremonies, interreligious dialogue initiatives and awareness-raising programmes in the larger society. Without such additional support measures the prospects of the long-term survival of some religious communities may be in serious peril, which, at the same time, would also amount to grave infringements of freedom of religion or belief of their individual members.

3.   Equality and non-discrimination

26.   The preamble to the Universal Declaration links the "inherent dignity" of all members of the human family to "their equal and inalienable rights", thus highlighting the significance of equality as one of the architectural principles of human rights in general. Equality must always be interpreted in conjunction with the principle of freedom, which likewise derives from respect for human dignity. Otherwise equality could easily be mistaken for uniformity or "sameness", a misunderstanding that sometimes occurs. Such a misunderstanding, however, could have serious negative implications for the rights of persons belonging to religious minorities, possibly even exposing them to policies of forced assimilation. It is important to point out that human rights in general represent the aspiration to empower human beings – on the basis of equal respect and equal concern for everyone's freedom – to develop and pursue their own diverse life plans, to enjoy respect for their irreplaceable personal biographies, to freely manifest their different religious or belief-related convictions and to practise their religion or belief alone and in community with others. Working for the implementation of human rights for everyone on the basis of equality will make societies more diverse and more pluralistic, including with regard to religion and belief.

27.   In practical terms, equality primarily requires systematic endeavours to eliminate all forms of discrimination, including on grounds of religion or belief. Article 2(1) of the 1981 Declaration corroborates this task by stressing that "[n]o one shall be subject to discrimination by any State, institution, group of persons, or persons on the grounds of religion or other belief." Article 3 of the 1981 Declaration sends a clear message by stating that "discrimination between human beings on the grounds of religion or belief constitutes an affront to human dignity and a disavowal of the principles of the Charter of the United Nations [...]".

28.   Combating discrimination on the grounds of religion or belief is obviously a complex task which implies State obligations at different levels.

First, it requires a consistent policy of non-discrimination within State institutions, including the accessibility of public positions in administration, public services, police forces, the military and public health to everyone regardless of their religious or belief orientations. If persons belonging to religious minorities suffer from a long history of exclusion from public institutions, it may be necessary to adopt special measures to encourage members of those minorities to apply for public positions, and to promote their opportunities. Furthermore, States should combat discriminatory practices in labour and housing markets, the media, welfare systems, etc. This requires promotional activities that go beyond policies of non-discrimination, such as positive outreach and promotional measures on behalf of minorities. Finally, States should critically address the root causes of societal discrimination, including existing stereotypes and prejudices against members of religious minorities; and should foster a general climate of societal openness and tolerance, for example by providing fair information about different religious or belief traditions as part of the school curriculum, facilitating encounters between people from different denominations, and encouraging interreligious communication.

29. Besides problems of direct and open discrimination, members of religious minorities may also suffer from hidden forms of discrimination, such as structural or indirect discrimination. For instance, seemingly neutral rules relating to dress codes in schools or other public institutions, although not openly targeting a specific community, can amount to discrimination against persons belonging to a religious minority who feel religiously obliged to obey a particular dress code. Similar problems can occur with regard to dietary rules, public holidays, labour regulations, public health norms and other issues. It may be the case that large parts of the population are not even aware of the possibly adverse implications that prima facie neutral rules may have on the rights of persons belonging to religious minorities. To prevent or rectify discriminatory consequences, States should generally consult with representatives of religious minorities before enacting legislation that may infringe on their religious or belief-related convictions and practices, and they should develop and promote policies of "reasonable accommodation" for individual members of minorities to enable them to live in conformity with their convictions.

30. Moreover, systematic attention should be given to multiple and intersectional forms of discrimination, such as discriminatory patterns in the intersection of religious and gender discrimination. It may happen that measures undertaken to combat religious or belief- related discrimi-

nation implicitly follow a male understanding of the needs and require-ments of the respective communities, while programmes aimed at elimi-nating gender-related discrimination may be largely shaped by the expe-riences of women from the mainstream population. As a result, even in States that pursue proactive policies of non-discrimination there may be a serious risk that women belonging to certain religious minorities large-ly fail to benefit from anti-discriminatory measures. When designing programmes to overcome such blind spots, States should also be guided by the Convention on the Elimination of all Forms of Discrimination against Women.

4.   Broad application in the spirit of universalism

31. Based on the assumption that all human beings are rights holders in international human rights law, they all deserve respect for their self-understanding in the area of religion or belief. However, given the expe-rience that self-understandings of human beings in questions of religion or belief can be very diverse, freedom of religion or belief must have a broad scope of application and should be implemented in an open and inclusive manner accordingly. This requirement follows from the univer-salistic nature of human rights. The Human Rights Committee has clari-fied that article 18 of the International Covenant "protects theistic, non-theistic and atheistic beliefs, as well as the right not to profess any reli-gion or belief. The terms "belief" and "religion" are to be broadly con-strued. Article 18 is not limited in its application to traditional religions or to religions and beliefs with institutional characteristics or practices analogous to those of traditional religions."[120]

32. A broad and inclusive understanding must also guide the interpreta-tion of the rights of persons belonging to religious minorities in the un-derstanding of article 27 of the International Covenant and the 1992 Mi-norities Declaration. Accordingly, the term "religious minority" should be conceptualized in such a way as to cover all relevant groups of per-sons, including traditional as well as non-traditional communities, and both large and small communities. One should also take into account the situation of internal minorities, i.e. minority groups within larger minori-ties.

---

[120] CCPR/C/21/Rev.1/Add.4, para. 2. Questions related to the definition of religion or belief were also discussed in the Special Rapporteur's previous annual report (A/HRC/19/60, paras. 22-73).

33. Against a widespread misunderstanding, the Special Rapporteur would like to emphasize that the rights of persons belonging to religious minorities are not anti- universalistic privileges reserved to the members of certain predefined groups. Rather, all persons de facto living in the situation of a religious or belief minority should be able to fully enjoy their human rights on the basis of non-discrimination and benefit from measures which they may need to develop their individual and communitarian identities. The question of which individuals or groups of individuals fall under the specific guarantees of article 27 of the International Covenant and similar minority rights provisions should be established on the basis of the self-understanding of the persons concerned in conjunction with a transparent empirical assessment of their actual need for promotional measures.

34. States' obligations to respect, protect and fulfil the human rights of persons belonging to religious minorities in any case cannot be limited to the members of those communities which already happen to possess a specific status as recognized religious minorities. Rather, specifically recognized status positions can become an instrument for facilitating more effective enjoyment of freedom of religion or belief of people who de facto live in a minority situation. Moreover, the Human Rights Committee has pointed out that the enjoyment of the rights of persons belonging to minorities cannot be confined to nationals, citizens or permanent residents of a particular State, but that migrant workers also and even visitors constituting such minorities should not be denied the exercise of those rights.[121]

35. Specific status positions accorded by the State can never be the point of departure when it comes to defining the application of human rights, since this would turn the normative order of rights upside down and would violate the overarching human rights principle of normative universalism. Rather, positive measures on behalf of members of religious minorities should serve the purpose of providing efficient protection for all those people who may be in need of such measures to be able to fully enjoy their freedom of religion or belief on the basis of non-discrimination and to have long-term prospects of upholding and developing their group-related religious identities.

---

[121] CCPR/C/21/Rev.1/Add.5, para. 5.2.

C. Violations

1. Multifaceted motives and settings

36. Violations of freedom of religion or belief of persons belonging to religious minorities occur in various regions of the world and originate from many different motives. For instance, they may be perpetrated in the name of religious or ideological truth claims, in the interest of fostering national cohesion, under the pretext of defending law and order or in conjunction with counter-terrorism agendas. Existing stereotypes and prejudices against minorities are sometimes connected with historical traumas and national mythologies and may also be publicly stoked for purposes of political mobilization or to target scapegoats.

37. Violations of the rights of persons belonging to religious minorities are perpetrated by States or non-State actors or – quite frequently – a combination of both. The likeliness of human rights violations by the State usually increases when a tight law and order agenda blends with political invocations of national identity, a pattern occurring in quite a number of countries. Typical targets of such restrictive policies are members of those religious or belief groups that have, or are said to have, a tendency to evade State control and, at the same time, are perceived as not really fitting into the historical and cultural makeup of the country.

38. Furthermore, in situations of protracted conflict, de facto authorities exercising government-like functions may also target members of religious minorities, especially if they are regarded as being "on the other side". In this context, the Special Rapporteur would like to reiterate that the international community, Member States and all relevant de facto entities exercising government-like functions should direct all their efforts to ensuring that there are no human rights protection gaps and that all persons can effectively enjoy their fundamental rights, including freedom of religion or belief, wherever they live.

39. Violations perpetrated by non-State actors frequently occur in a political climate of impunity, thus indicating direct or indirect State involvement or even a human rights protection vacuum. At times incidents of discrimination or violence seem to break out spontaneously. Even then, they typically occur, however, against a background of widespread prejudices that may escalate into political paranoia, sometimes deliberately stoked by politicians. At the same time, minorities can become targets of public contempt, for instance, by being vilified as allegedly failing to honour any moral principles. In response to strangely combined sen-

timents of paranoia and contempt, two sources of aggressiveness can merge into a toxic mix, i.e. aggressiveness from a feeling of being threatened and aggressiveness from the pretence of one's own moral superiority.

40. While in some cases one can clearly distinguish between perpetrators and victims, in other situations applying such a distinction appears to be complicated or even outright impossible. It may also happen that a religious community whose members suffer terribly from persecution in one country is actively involved in human rights abuses in another country. Sometimes minorities exercise pressure against internal critics or dissidents in order to keep their ranks closed, possibly resulting in the violation of the rights of internal minorities or individual members.

2.   Specific areas of violations

41. The following violations of the rights of persons belonging to religious minorities constitute a non-exhaustive list of patterns observed by the mandate holders during their country visits and in communications sent to States.

(a)   Unnecessary bureaucratic restrictions

42. Religious minorities are often confronted with disproportionate bureaucratic requirements which, instead of facilitating freedom of religion or belief, have the effect of imposing discriminatory burdens and unjustifiable restrictions.[122] In some countries minority communities have to register on an annual basis to be recognized by the administration.[123] Members of affected groups have complained about registration procedures becoming more and more costly and time-consuming. Failure to register, or re-register periodically, could lead to legal vulnerability that also exposes the religious minorities to political, economic and social insecurity.[124] Furthermore, application procedures for being allowed to construct places of worship – churches, mosques, prayer halls, syna-

---

[122] In Angola, the Muslim community encountered difficulties in obtaining the necessary registration as the law required 100,000 signatures in order to legalize a religious community (A/HRC/4/21/Add.1, para. 18).

[123] In Paraguay, religious or belief communities have to register annually with the Vice Ministry of Worship, while the Catholic Church is exempted from this requirement (A/HRC/19/60/Add.1, para. 34).

[124] The Belarusian Evangelical Church was unsuccessful in seeking re-registration under the 2002 Religious Law and was subsequently liquidated (A/HRC/4/21/Add.1, para. 53).

gogues, temples etc. – can be extremely complicated; in some cases they have been delayed over decades.[125]

(b) Denial of an appropriate legal status

43. Most religious communities – albeit not all of them – wish to have the status of a collective legal personality. Such a status position may be needed for them to be able to undertake important community functions, such as opening bank accounts, purchasing real estate, constructing houses of worship, employing professionals (including professional clergy), establishing denominational schools and running their own community media. Without an appropriate legal status, the development of a communitarian infrastructure and the long-term survival prospects of a religious minority may be in serious peril. Nevertheless, some States fail to facilitate appropriate legal status positions. For instance, certain States do not allow associations to pursue any religious or belief-related purposes, with the implication that religious groups per se cannot obtain any legal status under the law of association. Recognition procedures may also be lengthy and overly complicated, with the intentional or non-intentional effect of discouraging certain minorities from even applying.[126] In some instances, religious organizations may be deprived of their status and de-registered, thus losing key rights and privileges afforded to registered religious organizations. (Re)-registration procedures may stipulate conditions such as a minimum number of followers or years of existence in a particular country that a priori exclude smaller or new groups.[127] An administration may also arbitrarily use negative labels, such as "sect"[128] or "cult", to generally prevent certain groups from obtaining legal personality status. Non-recognized communities typically live in situations of increased legal insecurity and structural vulnerability.

---

[125] Chin Christian Minorities in Myanmar allegedly cannot build or renovate churches or erect crosses due to the multi-tiered permissions required and the lengthy process involved (A/HRC/22/67).

[126] The law on Freedom of Conscience, on Religious Associations and Other Organizations in Tajikistan established burdensome registration procedures for religious organizations (A/HRC/7/10/Add.1, paras. 245-249).

[127] In Hungary, the Law on the Right to Freedom of Conscience and Religion and on Churches, Religions and Religious Communities requires re-registration of most religious organizations to be backed with evidence of at least 20 years of operation and regulations on its structure and operation (A/HRC/19/44, p. 35).

[128] In France, the Protestant movement of the Plymouth Brethren faced restrictions after it was listed in the MIVILUDES (Inter-ministerial Mission to monitor and combat abuse by sects) report (A/HRC/4/21/Add.1, paras. 137-145).

There are also examples of de facto authorities prohibiting and disrupting meetings of members of religious minorities on the mistaken assumption that such activities could not be undertaken by unregistered communities.[129]

(c)   Structural discrimination and exclusion

44.   Persons belonging to religious minorities often suffer from systematic discrimination in various sectors of society, such as educational institutions, the labour market, the housing market or the health-care system. Scores of examples account for structural discrimination in those and other important societal areas. Minorities are frequently underrepresented in the public sectors as well, including in the police force, the military, public media and high-level posts in public universities. Members of certain groups, once identified as such, may not have access to higher education[130] or certain public positions, or may be expelled from previously held positions. Moreover, many members of religious minorities experience multiple, intersectional and otherwise aggravated forms of discrimination, for instance a discriminatory link between scheduled caste status and affiliation to specific religions,[131] or a combination of religion and ethnicity-based violence.[132] Women or girls often have tocope with gender-based and religious discrimination, for example dress code regulations that discriminate against persons belonging to religious minorities, in particular women.[133]

---

[129]   In 2010, religious meetings of Jehovah's Witnesses living in Nagorno-Karabakh were disrupted by local "police" and several Jehovah's Witnesses were arrested (A/HRC/16/53/Add.1, paras. 6-24); however, the Special Rapporteur was subsequently informed that upon appeal the de facto "courts" overturned the initial administrative convictions, relying on the International Covenant on Civil and Political Rights and the Special Rapporteur's observations that registration cannot be a precondition for holding peaceful religious meetings.

[130]   In the Islamic Republic of Iran, members of the Bahá'í faith are being prevented from entering public and private universities and vocational training institutions (A/HRC/10/8/Add.1, paras. 91-92; A/HRC/19/44, p. 13).

[131]   See country visit report on India (A/HRC/10/8/Add.3, paras. 27-28 and 71).

[132]   See violence by Boko Haram in northern Nigeria (A/HRC/20/30, p. 67).

[133]   France has prohibited pupils from manifesting "ostentatious" religious signs, a provision which mainly affects members of certain religious minorities, notably Muslims   and   Sikhs   (E/CN.4/2005/61/Add.1,   paras.   110-122; E/CN.4/2006/5/Add.4, paras. 66 and 98).

(d) Discriminatory implications of family laws

45. An issue warranting special attention concerns discriminatory family laws, especially if personal status matters are adjudicated by religious courts. Some countries continue to restrict marriages between individuals from different denominations, thus violating article 16 of the Universal Declaration on Human Rights, which provides that men and women of full age have the right to marry and to found a family, without any limitation due to religion. Members of religious minorities, in particular women, may feel compelled to change their religion or belief as a precondition for marrying a person with a different religious affiliation. Depending on the specific cases, this may amount to a violation of article 18(2) of the International Covenant on Civil and Political Rights, which prohibits subjecting anyone to coercion in questions of religion or belief. Furthermore, individuals belonging to religious minorities may also experience discriminatory treatment in divorce settlements, a problem that often affects women. It is reported that judgements of family courts and religious courts in child custody cases have been biased against the parent who belongs to a religious minority.[134]

(e) Alienation and indoctrination of children

46. Parents from religious minorities also face difficulties in exercising the right to educate their children in conformity with their own convictions, as enshrined in article 18(4) of the International Covenant. A particularly sensitive area in this regard is school education. In some States, children from religious or belief minorities are exposed to religious instruction against their will or the will of their parents or guardians. They may have no option to obtain an exemption from religious instruction, or exemptions may remain linked to a high threshold or humiliating circumstances. There are also reports about children from minorities facing pressure in public schools to participate in rituals and ceremonies of a religion other than their own or being baptized by a priest without the parents' prior consent.[135] Reportedly, children have even been urged to

---

[134] In Serbia, Jehovah's Witnesses reported that some of their members have lost custody of their children when they were involved in divorce cases with a spouse who was not a Jehovah's Witness (A/HRC/13/40/Add.3, para. 24). The Shia religious court of the Kingdom of Bahrain denied an alleged Safara believer the right to custody of her children after divorcing (A/HRC/16/53/Add.1, paras. 25-32).

[135] In Georgia, there were reports of children being baptized by Orthodox priests without the prior permission of their parents (A/HRC/4/21/Add.1, paras. 146-151).

distance themselves from their own religion as a precondition for passing their school exams. Students who refuse to follow certain religious instruction at school are also allegedly punished or assaulted by their teachers.[136] In extreme cases, such pressure can amount to violations of the right not to be forced to convert. There are also cases where exemption from religious instruction is granted but due to the lack of resources in certain public schools, children exempted from religious instruction may have to remain in the classroom, which means that in practice they are still exposed to religious instruction that may go against their convictions.[137]

(f)   Publicly stoked prejudices

47. Rather than combating existing prejudices against religious minorities, Governments and public officials at times even stoke and exploit prejudices for political purposes, such as fostering national homogeneity or blaming political failures on scapegoats. In this context, minorities have been negatively portrayed as undermining the moral fabric of society. For instance, minorities who tend to refuse military service on conscientious grounds have been held responsible for military defeats and other national traumas. Surprisingly often, stoked political paranoia targets small groups of people who are demonized as wielding some mysteriously "infectious" power by which they allegedly pose a fatal threat to societal cohesion.[138] There are also examples of religious minorities being stigmatized by politicians or radio hosts as "a fifth column"[139] who supposedly act in the interest of hostile foreign powers, thus violating the interest of the nation. The spread of negative stereotypes and prejudices obviously poisons the relationship between different communities and puts people belonging to religious minorities in a vulnerable situation. Unfortunately, stigmatizing prejudices also continue to exist in school-

---

[136]   In Sri Lanka, a Buddhist monk teacher allegedly assaulted a 14-year-old student when he refused to learn Buddhism at school, stating that he was Catholic (A/HRC/22/67).

[137]   See country visit report on Cyprus (A/HRC/22/51/Add.1, para. 62).

[138]   In Saudi Arabia, the Imam of Riyadh mosque allegedly called Shi'as "traitors" and called for the elimination of all Shi'a believers in the world, including those residing in Saudi Arabia (A/HRC/16/53/Add.1, paras. 362-366).

[139]   In the United States of America, a radio host reportedly said during his talk show "that Muslims in this country are a fifth column. [...] The reason they are here is to take over our culture and eventually take over our country" (E/CN.4/2005/61/Add.1, para. 298).

books and teaching material for children who, given their tender age, can easily be impressed by anti-minority propaganda.

(g) Acts of vandalism and desecration

48. There are many incidents of vandalism directed against symbols, sites or institutions of religious minorities, including the demolition of places of worship[140] and the desecration of cemeteries[141] or tombs of historical and cultural heritage value.[142] Such attacks often constitute symbolic violence by which the perpetrators aim to send a message to members of religious minorities that they are not welcome in the community or country.[143] This can become a trigger for physical violence,[144] including expulsions and other extreme manifestations of hostility. There are also numerous incidents where development or construction plans end up destroying sacred sites of religious minorities or indigenous peoples.[145]

(h) Obstacles against religious rituals or ceremonies

49. Persons belonging to minorities may have difficulties when wishing to perform rituals that they consider as essentially belonging to their re-

---

[140] In the Bolivarian Republic of Venezuela, the Tiferet Israel Synagogue in Caracas was vandalized with anti-Semitic graffiti twice in January 2009 (A/HRC/13/40/Add.1, paras. 248-258).

[141] Israeli State authorities allowed the construction of a museum on a portion of the Ma'man Allah cemetery in Jerusalem that reportedly involved the excavation or exposure of hundreds of graves where there has been a Muslim burial ground for more than 1,000 years (A/HRC/16/53/Add.1, paras. 206-215).

[142] In press statements issued in 2012, the Special Rapporteur referred to the destruction and desecration of religious sites and cemeteries in Cyprus (www.ohchr.org/en/NewsEvents/Pages/DisplayNews.aspx?NewsID=12042&Lang ID=E), Mali (www.ohchr.org/en/NewsEvents/Pages/DisplayNews.aspx?NewsID= 12337&LangID=E) and Libya (www.ohchr.org/en/NewsEvents/Pages/Display News.aspx?NewsID=12485&LangID=E).

[143] In Greece, unknown persons reportedly nailed a pig's head to the entrance door of a mosque in Western Thrace (A/HRC/18/51, p. 85).

[144] In Egypt, a bomb attack targeted Coptic Christian worshippers who had emerged from a New Year's mass in the Al-Qiddissin Church in Alexandria, killing 23 Coptic Christians and injuring at least 97 others (A/HRC/18/51, p. 29).

[145] In Guatemala, concerns were raised regarding the construction of condominiums over Maya Tulam Tzu, an important cultural site used for religious ceremonies (A/HRC/4/21/Add.1, paras. 159-167). In Australia, concern was expressed at the destruction of a sacred indigenous rock art complex, housing hundreds of sacred sites for indigenous peoples in Dampier Archipelago (A/HRC/7/10/Add.1, paras. 4-10).

ligious identities. This includes rituals of religious socialization of children, for example male circumcision.[146] Members of religious minorities may also face administrative obstacles when holding processions or celebrating religious ceremonies in public. A number of governments pursue unduly restrictive policies in this regard, sometimes with reference to unspecified "public order" interests at variance with the criteria enshrined in article 18(3) of the International Covenant. It also happens that public ceremonies or gatherings are disrupted by the police or by non-State actors with the police merely standing by, thus conveying the impression that State authorities do not care or even implicitly approve of such acts.[147] Furthermore, funerals have been disrupted by crowds of people who claim that the cemeteries, albeit owned by the municipality, should be reserved for the adherents of the predominant religion and not be used by "heretics". As a result, persons from religious minorities at times cannot bury their dead family members in a quiet, dignified way.[148]

(i) Threats and acts of violence against members of religious minorities

50. Acts of violence against members of religious minorities, perpetrated by States or non-State actors, have unfortunately included cases of torture, ill-treatment, abductions, involuntary disappearances and other atrocities. They can occur spontaneously or be orchestrated by political leaders who exploit and further stoke existing stereotypes, prejudices and paranoia for political gains. The motives may be manifold and include "taking revenge" for natural disasters, national traumas or political failures mysteriously blamed on minorities or alleged self-defence against foreign powers supposedly represented by some minority groups as their "fifth columns". Violence may also be used to preserve the hegemony of the predominant religion of the country against unwelcome

---

[146] In Germany, a decision of the district court of Cologne of 7 May 2012 triggered a partially aggressive debate on the legal permissibility of religiously motivated male circumcision of children. However, the German Federal Parliament called on the Federal Government to present a draft law in the autumn of 2012, stressing that Jewish and Muslim religious life must continue to be possible in Germany (CCPR/C/DEU/Q/6/Add.1, para. 86); the Federal Parliament adopted the law in December 2012.

[147] In Eritrea, a wedding ceremony was disrupted with the arrest of 30 evangelical Christians; ultimately they were released after signing a document promising not to participate in such events in future (E/CN.4/2005/61/Add.1, para. 96).

[148] Country visit report on the Republic of Moldova (A/HRC/19/60/Add.2, para. 37).

competitors or immigrants.[149] In addition, acts of violence are perpetrated with the purpose of expelling minorities from the country,[150] or of intimidating and blackmailing them, for instance to extract "protection money". Reportedly there also have been cases of kidnapping and violence to force persons belonging to religious minorities to renounce their faith and convert to mainstream religions.[151] Beside killing and injuring people, acts of violence may also cause serious damage to historical buildings of religious communities in order to further destroy any long-term survival prospects of such groups in the country.

(j)   Disrespect of internal autonomy

51. Some States unduly interfere in the internal affairs of religious communities, with the purpose of exercising tight political control. This can include the appointment by the Government of religious community leaders in ways which contradict the self- understanding of the respective group and their traditions, thereby violating their autonomy. In some cases this has led to splits within a community and poisoned the relationship between different sub-groups, as a result endangering the long-term development of the affected religious community at large. There have also been reports from members of minorities about State agents being implanted in religious institutions, including monasteries,[152] in order to further tighten control over the religious life. Some leaders of religious groups are even arrested or detained over a long period of time.[153]

---

[149]   Concerns were raised at the assertion that members of the Rohingya minority in Myanmar were treated as illegal immigrants and stateless persons and it was stressed that the inter-communal violence in Rakhine State must not become an opportunity to permanently remove an unwelcome community (www.ohchr.org/en/NewsEvents/Pages/DisplayNews.aspx?NewsID=12716&LangID=E).

[150]   In Indonesia, Shi'as and Ahmadiyah communities face persistent challenges of harassment and attacks (A/HRC/22/67). Furthermore, the President of the National Islamic Council in Guinea-Bissau appealed to the authorities to expel the Ahmadiyah community from the country (A/HRC/4/21/Add.1, paras. 168-169).

[151]   In Bangladesh, a woman belonging to the Hindu minority was reportedly kidnapped, forcefully converted and subsequently beaten, which led to her death (A/HRC/16/53/Add.1, paras. 33-39).

[152]   In China, it is allegedly required to establish an unelected "Monastery Management Committee" in every monastery in Tibet, with up to 30 lay officials stationed in each monastery (A/HRC/22/67).

[153]   In the Islamic Republic of Iran, seven Bahá'í members who coordinated the community's religious and administrative affairs were detained and sentenced to long-term imprisonment by a Revolutionary Court in Teheran

(k)　Confiscation of property and unfair restitution policies

52. Religious minorities have suffered from confiscation of their community property,[154] in some cases to such a degree that the infrastructure needed for ensuring the community's long-term development has been destroyed. Often only insufficient or no compensation at all has been paid.[155] When trying to get back their property, religious minorities may face many obstacles, including bureaucratic stipulations.[156] States that meanwhile have embarked on programmes of restitution for previously confiscated property to religious communities sometimes fail to include minority groups in a transparent, fair and non-discriminatory manner. This can create or exacerbate resentments between different religious communities.

(l)　Criminal sanctions

53. Persons belonging to religious minorities are frequently exposed to increased risks of criminalization. Some domestic criminal law provisions specifically target members of minorities or persons otherwise deviating from the predominant religious or belief tradition of the country. When manifesting their religious or belief convictions, persons belonging to minorities may run the risk of being accused of "blasphemy,"[157] a charge which in some countries carries harsh sanctions, including even the death penalty. At times the mere possession of certain religious literature has given rise to criminal prosecution leading to long-term imprison-

---

(A/HRC/16/53/Add.1, paras. 185-196; Opinion No. 34/2008 of the Working Group on Arbitrary Detention).

[154] In Turkey, the Court of Cassation ruled to grant substantial parts of St. Gabriel Monastery (Mor Gabriel) to the Turkish Treasury; members of the Assyro-Chaldean community faced long-term difficulties in property and land registration procedures (A/HRC/18/51, p. 75).

[155] In Tajikistan, the authorities in Dushanbe demolished the city's only synagogue in 2006, offering the congregation a plot of land on the edge of Dushanbe but without providing any other compensation to build the new synagogue (A/HRC/4/21/Add.1, paras. 279-285).

[156] In southern Russia, three confessions regarded as "traditional", namely the Greek Orthodox, the Muslims and the Jews, had all failed to regain their places of worship ,which had been confiscated by the State in Communist times (E/CN.4/2006/5/Add.1, paras. 318-326).

[157] In Pakistan, the implementation of the blasphemy provisions has allegedly triggered a general atmosphere of fear (A/HRC/18/51, p. 38); for example, a member of the Christian minority was given a death sentence for blasphemy in 2010 (A/HRC/16/53/Add.1, paras. 326-335).

ment. Furthermore, members of minorities have been tried for engaging in non-coercive communicative outreach activities which some Governments negatively brand as "proselytism".[158] There are even cases in which persons who had converted away from the dominant religion of the country were accused of "apostasy"[159] and condemned to death, in disregard of, inter alia, the right to conversion, which constitutes an inextricable part of religion or belief. In general, the threat of criminal sanctions typically has far- reaching intimidating effects on members of religious minorities, many of whom may decide to hide their convictions or refrain from practising their religion or belief.

(m) Denial of asylum

54. As a result of discrimination, repression and persecution, some members of religious minorities decide to leave their country of origin and try to find a new home elsewhere. When applying for asylum, however, they may again experience being unwelcome and may not even be granted a fair hearing of their asylum claims. There are also cases in which persons belonging to religious minorities may face deportation or extradition, even in the face of obvious risks of persecution in their country of origin.[160] The Special Rapporteur would like to reiterate that extraditions or deportations which are likely to result in violations of freedom of religion or belief may themselves amount to a violation of human rights. In addition, such extraditions violate the principle of non-refoulement, as enshrined in article 33 of the 1951 Geneva Convention relating to the Status of Refugees.

---

[158] In Egypt, members of the Ahmadiyah community were charged for holding and promoting "extremist ideas" (A/HRC/16/53/Add.1, paras. 99-106).

[159] In the Islamic Republic of Iran, Pastor Youcef Nadarkhani was found guilty of apostasy and given a death sentence in 2010 (A/HRC/18/51, p. 26; A/HRC/19/44, p. 41); in September 2012, however, he was released after three years in prison (http://www.ohchr.org/en/NewsEvents/Pages/DisplayNews.aspx?NewsID=12551&LangID=E).

[160] The United Kingdom rejected the asylum applications of a member of Falun Gong and two Iranian converts despite the threat of torture or death as apostates in their countries of origin (E/CN.4/2006/5/Add.1, paras. 390-392, A/HRC/7/10/Add.1, paras. 264-274; A/HRC/16/53/Add.1, paras. 399-407).

IV. Conclusions and recommendations

A. Conclusions

55. In his daily work, the Special Rapporteur receives many reports of grave violations of freedom of religion or belief of persons belonging to religious minorities in all parts of the world. Such violations are perpetrated by States and/or non-State actors, often in a climate of impunity, and they may originate from different political, religious, ideological or personal motives.

56. Human rights violations against persons belonging to religious minorities include disproportionate bureaucratic restrictions; denial of appropriate legal status positions needed to build up or uphold a religious infrastructure; systematic discrimination and partial exclusion from important sectors of society; discriminatory rules within family laws; indoctrination of children from minorities in public schools; publicly stoked prejudices and vilification sometimes connected with historic traumas and national mythologies; acts of vandalism and desecration; prohibition or disruption of religious ceremonies; threats and acts of violence; interference in the community's internal affairs; confiscation of community property; criminal sanctions; denial of asylum, possibly resulting in extraditions and exposure to serious risks of persecution.

57. Given the number and gravity of human rights violations, the need for concerted action to better safeguard the human rights of persons belonging to religious minorities is more than obvious. Such activities must be based on the principles of universality, freedom and equality that underpin the human rights-based approach in general as well as comply with the International Covenant, the 1992 Minorities Declaration and other international human rights instruments.

58. The rights of persons belonging to religious or belief minorities should therefore be consistently interpreted from a human rights perspective, and must be implemented in conjunction with all other human rights. The term "religious minority" should be broadly construed to cover all relevant groups of persons, including traditional and non-traditional communities or large and small communities; it also covers atheistic and non-theistic believers. One should furthermore take into account the situation of internal minorities, i.e. minority groups within minorities. Special attention should be given to women from religious or belief minorities, many of whom may suffer from multiple or intersectional forms of discrimination.

59. The rights of persons belonging to religious minorities are not anti-universalistic privileges reserved to the members of certain predefined groups. Rather, all persons de facto living in the situation of a religious or belief minority should be enabled to fully enjoy their freedom of religion or belief, in full respect for their self-understanding, on the basis of effective non-discrimination and equality, and with prospects of freely developing their community-related religious or belief identities.

B. Recommendations

1. General policies on the promotion of the rights of religious minorities

60. Stakeholders engaged in political advocacy on behalf of religious or belief- related minorities should consistently base their activities on the principle of normative universalism. They should pay attention that their advocacy does not inadvertently play the game of those who demonize minorities on the basis of religion or belief. This presupposes some knowledge of historically sensitive issues, which could sometimes turn against the interests of the respective minorities. Placing solidarity activities on behalf of religious minorities systematically in the framework of normative universalism is the best way of avoiding any misunderstandings.

61. Stakeholders engaged in human rights work should always base their activities on respect for the self-understanding of the human beings concerned. They should thus take into account that the minority terminology should never be used against the interest of the respective communities and their members who, depending on their situation, may prefer not to be called minorities in the public political arena. Decisions on such sensitive terminological issues should, whenever possible, be based on broad and regular communication with representatives of the various communities.

62. Positive measures enacted with the purpose of improving the situation of religious or belief minorities, including measures of "reasonable accommodation", should be consistently based on respect for the self-understanding of the members of such communities, who are the natural interpreters of their best interests. Taking the self-understanding of human beings as the starting point for advocacy activities also requires sensitivity to possible internal diversities of convictions and interests within minorities.

63. The Special Rapporteur particularly recommends that States implement the Rabat Plan of Action on the prohibition of advocacy of national, racial or religious hatred that constitutes incitement to discrimination, hostility or violence. The Rabat Plan notes with concern that incidents which indeed reach the threshold of article 20 of the International Covenant on Civil and Political Rights are not prosecuted and punished, while at the same time members of minorities are de facto persecuted, with a chilling effect on others, through the abuse of vague domestic legislation, jurisprudence and policies. The Rabat Plan contains a list of related recommendations and also refers to Human Rights Council resolution 16/18 as a promising platform for effective, integrated and inclusive action by the international community, which requires implementation and constant follow-up by States at the national level.

2. Domestic legal provisions

64. States should enact legislation to protect members of religious or belief minorities, with a clear understanding of the universal normative status of freedom of thought, conscience, religion or belief, a human right that covers individual, communitarian and infrastructural aspects as well as private and public dimensions of religion or belief.

65. States should hold consultations with representatives of religious or belief minorities when drafting legislation that could impact on their convictions and practices such as observation of holy days, dietary provisions, dress codes in public institutions, labour laws, participation in public or cultural life, etc.

66. States should repeal any criminal law provisions that penalize apostasy, blasphemy and proselytism as they may prevent persons belonging to religious or belief minorities from fully enjoying their freedom of religion or belief.

67. States should reform family law and personal status law provisions that may amount to de jure or de facto discrimination against persons belonging to religious or belief minorities, for example in inheritance and custody matters.

68. States should issue anti-discrimination legislation with a view to protecting persons belonging to religious or belief minorities effectively from any grounds of discrimination based on religion or belief in education, employment, housing, welfare systems, media, public positions, etc. In particular where religious or belief minorities suffer from a long history of structural discrimination, positive measures are required to reach

out to members of such minorities, to encourage them to apply for positions and to promote their opportunities.

3.   Administration and procedures

69. Administrative procedures for obtaining legal personality status should be established in a spirit of facilitating the full enjoyment of freedom of religion or belief for all religious or belief communities, including minorities. States should ensure that such procedures are facilitated in a quick, transparent, fair, inclusive and non- discriminatory manner. In addition, they should favourably take into account the specific conditions of minorities, for example in defining quota and thresholds.

70. Indication of one's religious affiliation in official documents should be optional and not be used as the basis for discriminatory treatment. When issuing official documents, States should always ensure that no one is publicly exposed with regard to their religion or belief against their will.

71. States should develop outreach programmes facilitating regular encounters between State representatives in different areas (administration, police forces, health system, etc.) and representatives of religious or belief minorities in order to proactively avoid misunderstandings and concomitant conflicts. Building trust in a long-term perspective helps to de-escalate fears and resentments in crisis situations.

72. States should organize training for civil servants, police forces and other representatives of public authority to raise awareness about the rights and specific needs of persons belonging to religious or belief minorities, including unregistered religious communities.

73. States should develop policies of providing effective protection of persons belonging to religious or belief minorities against threats or acts of violence from non- State actors. This should also cover acts of vandalism or desecration of religious sites and cemeteries. To counter possible perceptions of impunity, States should send a clear and credible message that such acts cannot be tolerated.

74. States should consider listing important religious sites or places of worship of minorities as official national or international cultural heritage and promote the preservation of such sites in consultation with the representatives of the relevant communities.

75. States should ensure that the members of religious or belief minorities who seek asylum get a fair hearing of their claims, in conformity

with international standards. Moreover, States must send no one to any country or places where one's life or freedom would be threatened on account of one's religion or belief.

4.   *Education, public media, inter-religious communication and awareness-raising*

76.   States should organize training for teachers to sensitize them with regard to the particular needs and challenges of children belonging to religious minorities in schools. This should include training programmes aimed at discovering mobbing by peers and providing support measures in such situations.

77.   States may consider employing professional communicators from members of religious or belief minorities with the purpose of building confidence between the school administration and parents who belong to minorities.

78.   States should ensure that children attending school are not exposed to religious instruction against their will or against the will of their parents or legal guardians. Religious instruction as part of the general school curriculum must always include the option of exemptions. Appropriate monitoring should ensure that this option can actually be used.

79.   States have a responsibility to ensure that no child is at risk of being pressured to attend religious ceremonies or rituals in public schools against their will or against the will of their parents or legal guardians. In this regard, particular attention should be given to the situation of children from religious or belief minorities.

80.   Education in public and private schools should cater for the specific needs of members of religious minorities. Teaching materials on religious and belief diversity should present a fair picture of different religions and beliefs, in particular minorities, which can best be achieved through direct consultation with representatives of the relevant communities.

81.   States should support the development of community media which may help improve communication between members of a religious or belief minority within the country and/or across State borders. Such media can also enhance the prospects for minorities to effectively participate in general public debates within the society at large.

82.   Public media should open up for persons belonging to religious or belief minorities, who should be able to take an active role within media catering for the society at large. Depending on the situation, this may re-

quire structural reforms within public media and outreach activities towards religious or belief minorities. Furthermore, a public policy framework for pluralism and equality should ensure an equitable allocation of resources, including broadcasting frequencies, among public service, commercial and community media, so that together they represent the full range of cultures, communities and opinions in society. In this context, the Special Rapporteur recommends the implementation of the Camden Principles on Freedom of Expression and Equality.161

83.   Public and private media should provide fair and accurate information about religious or belief minorities and their members, with a view to overcoming negative stereotypes and prejudices. Self-regulation mechanisms within the media can play an important role in this regard.

84.   Whenever appropriate, States should establish truth and reconciliation commissions which can play an important role in the attempt to better come to terms with a complicated history, to overcome historical traumas and to dispel national myths that may have negative effects on the situation of religious or belief minorities.

85.   States should develop awareness-raising programmes to inform the population at large about the situation of members of religious or belief minorities as well as their human rights. Such programmes could be established in cooperation with civil society actors and representatives of various communities.

86.   International human rights organizations should raise awareness about the complicated situation of persons belonging to religious or belief minorities in different parts of the world. This should also be a part of their regular monitoring activities.

87.   In consultation with religious and belief communities, States should encourage, promote and facilitate interreligious communication. When taking place under appropriate conditions of equal footing and sustainability, interreligious communication, including at the grassroots level, is one of the most important means to enhance mutual understanding and dispel negative stereotypes which are the root causes of hatred, discrimination and violence. State initiatives in this regard should generally be open to minorities, including small groups which are often ignored in such projects.

---

161   www.article19.org/resources.php/resource/1214/en/camden-principles-on-freedom-of-expression-and-equality.

88.   States should establish a policy of public symbolic actions by which to send a clear message that religious or belief minorities are part of the larger society. An example of such symbolic presence is the participation of political representatives in ceremonies held by minorities, for instance funerals when victims of violence are publicly mourned.

89.   Civil society organizations, religious communities, national human rights institutions and other actors can and should play a crucial role in countering incitement to hatred directed against religious or belief minorities by speaking out in support of those minorities. It is important that target groups of hatred feel they have not been left alone. Public expressions of solidarity can also prevent further escalation and violence and create an atmosphere of inter-communal trust.

6. Chapter: Report August 2013

I. Introduction

1.   The mandate of the Special Rapporteur on freedom of religion or belief was created by the Commission on Human Rights by its resolution 1986/20 and renewed by the Human Rights Council in its resolution 6/37. At the fourteenth session of the Council, Heiner Bielefeldt was appointed as mandate holder and assumed his function on 1 August 2010. The Council, in its resolution 22/20, renewed the mandate for a further period of three years and requested the Special Rapporteur to report annually to the Council and to the General Assembly in accordance with their respective programmes of work.

2.   In section II of the present report, the Special Rapporteur provides an overview of his activities since the submission of his previous report to the General Assembly (A/67/303). In section III, he focuses on the freedom of religion or belief and equality between men and women. Section IV provides his conclusions and recommendations to various actors in this regard.

II. Activities of the Special Rapporteur

3.   The Special Rapporteur conducted various activities between 1 August 2012 and 31 July 2013 pursuant to Human Rights Council resolutions 6/37, 14/11 and 22/20.

A. Country visits

4.   The Special Rapporteur undertook a country visit to Sierra Leone from 30 June to 5 July 2013.[162] He expresses his appreciation to all his interlocutors and officials for the excellent cooperation they extended to him during his visit.

5.   Additional country visits are currently being scheduled. This includes an agreed visit to Jordan in September 2013. During the reporting period, the Special Rapporteur also sent requests for country visits to the

---

[162] The report of the visit to Sierra Leone will be presented to the Human Rights Council at its 25th session, in March 2014; the Special Rapporteur's statement, presented at the end of his visit, is available at www.ohchr.org/EN/News Events/Pages/DisplayNews.aspx?NewsID=13506.

Governments of Bangladesh, Indonesia, Kazakhstan, Uzbekistan and Viet Nam. Updated information about the Special Rapporteur's visits and related requests is available on the website of the Office of the United Nations High Commissioner for Human Rights (OHCHR).[163]

B. Communications

6.   The Special Rapporteur deals with individual cases or issues of concern brought to his attention. He sends allegation letters and urgent appeals to States seeking clarification on credible allegations of incidents and governmental action possibly incompatible with the provisions of the Declaration on the Elimination of All Forms of Intolerance and of Discrimination Based on Religion or Belief (General Assembly resolution 36/55).

7.   Since the creation of the mandate, the Special Rapporteurs have sent more than 1,290 allegation letters and urgent appeals to a total of 130 States. The communications sent by the Special Rapporteur between 1 June 2012 and 28 February 2013 and the replies received from Governments before 30 April 2013 are included in the latest communications reports (A/HRC/22/67 and Corr.1 and 2 and A/HRC/23/51).

C. Other activities

8.   The Special Rapporteur participated in a conference organized by the Office for Democratic Institutions and Human Rights of the Organization for Security and Cooperation in Europe (OSCE) on 1 October 2012, on developments and challenges that OSCE member States face in the context of freedom of religion or belief.

9.   On 4 and 5 October, the Special Rapporteur participated in the final expert workshop organized by OHCHR, in Rabat, on how best to respond to advocacy of national, racial or religious hatred that constitutes incitement of discrimination, hostility or violence. The experts jointly adopted the Rabat Plan of Action on the prohibition of advocacy of national, racial or religious hatred that constitutes incitement to discrimination, hostility or violence (see A/HRC/22/17/Add.4).

10.   On 27 November 2012, the Special Rapporteur took part in the fifth session of the Forum on Minority Issues in Geneva. He spoke about the rights of religious minorities and presented recommendations on the

---

[163]   See www.ohchr.org/EN/HRBodies/SP/Pages/CountryandothervisitsSP.aspx.

positive measures that could be taken to protect and promote their rights.

11. On 12 and 13 December 2012, the Special Rapporteur attended the Office of the United Nations High Commissioner for Refugees (UNHCR) Dialogue on Protection Challenges, entitled "Faith and protection".

12. On 17 and 18 January 2013, during the session of the Working Group on the issue of discrimination against women in law and in practice, the Working Group had a preliminary discussion with the Special Rapporteur on the issue of gender equality and freedom of religion and belief.

13. On 21 February 2013, the Special Rapporteur took part in the high-level launching event in Geneva of the Rabat Plan of Action. On 22 February, he also participated in the seminar on "Preventing incitement to atrocity crimes: policy options for action".

14. On 27 and 28 February, the Special Rapporteur attended the fifth Global Forum of the United Nations Alliance of Civilizations, in Vienna, which focused on the theme "Responsible leadership in diversity and dialogue".

15. From 4 to 8 March 2013, the Special Rapporteur attended the twenty-second session of the Human Rights Council. During that week, he also participated in several side events and dialogues organized by various civil society organizations.

16. The Special Rapporteur held many meetings with Government representatives, religious or belief communities, civil society organizations and academic experts working in the area of freedom of religion or belief. In this context, he participated in national and international conferences and workshops, including in Berlin, Colombo, Geneva, London, Lusaka, Luxembourg, Oslo, Oxford (United Kingdom of Great Britain and Northern Ireland), Rabat, Salzburg (Austria), Tbilisi, Uppsala (Sweden), Vienna and Yerevan. In addition, he held video conferences with stakeholders across different continents.

III. Freedom of religion or belief and equality between men and women

A. Introduction

17. Countless individuals are affected by human rights violations in the intersection of freedom of religion or belief and equality between men and women. While many such violations stem from stereotypical gender

roles which are frequently also defended in the name of religion or belief, other violations may originate from stereotyped perceptions of individuals based on their religion or belief. Gender stereotypes and stereotypical pictures of believers often exist in tandem, a problem disproportionately affecting women from religious minorities. As a result, many women suffer from multiple or intersectional discrimination or other forms of human rights violations on the grounds of both their gender and their religion or belief.

18. Anti-discrimination programmes or other programmes aimed at promoting human rights do not always adequately address the complex problems existing in the intersection of freedom of religion or belief and women's right to equality. Measures undertaken to combat religious discrimination may implicitly follow a male understanding of the needs and requirements of concerned religious communities, while programmes aimed at eliminating discrimination against women may lack sensitivity in questions of religious diversity. The same can happen with human rights policies outside of the specific context of anti-discrimination programmes. To avoid the danger of persons affected by multiple or intersectional discrimination and related violations of their human rights remaining excluded from activities relating to the promotion and protection of human rights, such complex phenomena deserve systematic attention. On the normative level, this requires a holistic approach in dealing with the various grounds of discrimination as well as a holistic understanding of human rights in general.

19. The holistic understanding of human rights has found expression in a frequently cited principle formulated at the World Conference on Human Rights, held in Vienna in 1993, that "[a]ll human rights are universal, indivisible and interdependent and interrelated".[164] The Special Rapporteur is furthermore guided by the insight formulated at the World Conference that all human rights be treated "globally in a fair and equal manner, on the same footing, and with the same emphasis".[165] In other words, on the normative level, human rights norms must be interpreted in such a way that they are not corrosive of one another but rather reinforce each other. Upholding a holistic human rights approach has direct consequences for human rights practice, in particular for those numer-

---

[164] Vienna Declaration and Programme of Action, A/CONF.157/24 (Part I), chap. III.

[165] Human Rights Council resolution 6/37, para. 18 (d). See also Commission on Human Rights resolutions 1996/23, 1997/18, 1998/18, 1999/39, 2000/33, 2001/42, 2002/40, 2003/54, 2004/36 and 2005/40, as well as General Assembly resolutions 60/166 and 61/161.

ous persons who are exposed to combined forms of vulnerability in the intersection of different human rights norms.

20.　Of course, the holistic understanding of human rights does not give an a priori guarantee of practical synergies with regard to all human rights issues that come up in this context. It has been a general experience that issues promoted under different human rights norms can collide. This is obviously also the case in the interplay of the two human rights norms discussed in the present report, namely, freedom of religion or belief and equality between men and women.

21.　The role of freedom of religion or belief within related conflicts is complex and is frequently misunderstood. Widespread misperceptions have even given rise to the idea that freedom of religion or belief and equality between men and women are norms standing in opposition to each other. However, although complicated conflicts in this area are obvious, it remains important not to draw wrong conclusions from this experience. In particular, one should not turn concrete conflicts between (seemingly or factually) competing human rights issues into abstract antagonisms on the normative level itself. This would be a systematic mistake. It would also mean to give up the holistic understanding of human rights, with the risk that the human rights approach in general might become ever more fragmented. This in turn would have detrimental effects, in particular for the human rights of many millions of persons whose problems fall in the intersection of freedom of religion or belief and equality between men and women.

22.　In order to highlight the multifaceted practical problems and contribute to a clarification of important conceptual questions, the Special Rapporteur has decided to focus the present report on the relationship between freedom of religion or belief and equality between men and women. This is in accordance with his mandate which requests him to continue to apply a gender perspective in his activities. In doing so, the Special Rapporteur builds upon the work of his predecessors in their reports to the Commission on Human Rights, the General Assembly and the Human Rights Council.[166]

---

[166]　See, for example, E/CN.4/2002/73/Add.2; A/HRC/4/21 (paras. 34-39); A/64/159 (paras. 59-63); and A/65/207 (paras. 14-16 and 69).

B. General observations on the role of freedom of religion or belief in the field of equality between men and women

1. The human person as rights holder

23. Prima facie it seems plausible to assume that freedom of religion or belief protects religious or belief-related traditions, practices and identities, since this is what the title of the right appears to suggest. This assumption, however, is misleading, because in line with the human rights approach in general, and article 1 of the Universal Declaration of Human Rights in particular, freedom of religion or belief always protects human beings in their freedom and equality in dignity and rights. To cite a frequently used short formula, freedom of religion or belief protects "believers rather than beliefs". Of course, both aspects are inextricably intertwined: no one can earnestly speak about believers without considering their beliefs and vice versa. And yet it remains true that human rights address that interrelatedness between believers and beliefs consistently from the angle of the human being. Hence it is only indirectly that religions or beliefs, encompassing their truth claims, religious scriptures, normative rules, rituals and ceremonies, organizations and hierarchies, come into the focus of human rights.

24. For a discussion of the complex relationship between freedom of religion or belief and equality between men and women it is important to bear in mind the indirectness that characterizes the relationship between human rights and religions and beliefs. In the framework of human rights, legal recognition cannot be accorded to the particular contents of religions or beliefs, namely, their doctrines, truth claims, practices and value systems, among other aspects, but is due to human beings as the responsible actors who hold, profess, cherish and develop their various religious or belief orientations, as individuals and in community with others.

25. The consistent focus on the human person as rights holder does not mean to adopt an anthropocentric worldview in which the human being figures as "the measure of all things". For many (not all) people, religious convictions, spiritual values and norms that claim a transcendent origin constitute a most important part of their daily lives and possibly the backbone of their personal and communitarian identities. The Declaration on the Elimination of All Forms of Intolerance and of Discrimination Based on Religion or Belief states that "religion or belief, for anyone who

professes either, is one of the fundamental elements in his conception of life". Thus, freedom of religion or belief serves the purpose of respecting and protecting this reality in the specific mode of universal human rights guarantees.

26. However, to take religions and beliefs in all their dimensions seriously also implies taking pluralism seriously, including sometimes irreconcilable differences in world views and practices. If the State protects the doctrinal and normative contents of one particular religion as such, this will almost inevitably lead to discrimination against adherents of other religions or beliefs, which would be unacceptable from a human rights perspective. It is not least for this reason that human rights epitomize a shift of focus from beliefs to believers, in order to appreciate existing religious or belief diversity on the basis of non-discrimination and equality. Accordingly, the human right to freedom of religion or belief does not protect religious traditions per se, but instead facilitates the free search and development of faith-related identities of human beings, as individuals and in community with others.

2. Synergies and conflicts

27. On the phenomenological level, the question of how freedom of religion or belief relates to gender issues does not find one general answer, but largely depends on how people actually make use of their human rights. Obviously, the ways in which individuals resort to their right to freedom of religion or belief differ widely. Freedom of religion or belief is a norm to which liberals and conservatives, feminists and traditionalists, and others, can refer in order to promote their various and often conflicting religious or belief-related concerns, including conflicting interests and views in the field of religious traditions and gender issues.

28. Freedom of religion or belief, in conjunction with freedom of expression, helps open up religious traditions to systematic questions and debates. In discourses on religious issues everyone should have a voice and a chance to be heard, from adherents of conservative or traditional interpretations to liberal critics or reform theologians. However, by also empowering groups who traditionally experience discrimination, including women and girls, freedom of religion or belief can serve as a normative reference point for questioning patriarchal tendencies as they exist in different religious traditions. This can lead to more gender-sensitive readings of religious texts and far-reaching discoveries in this field. In virtually all traditions one can indeed find persons or groups who make use of their freedom of religion or belief as a positive resource for the

promotion of equality between men and women, often in conjunction with innovative interpretations of religious sources and traditions. This accounts for the possibility of direct synergies between freedom of religion or belief on the one hand and policies for promoting the equal rights of women on the other. Impressive examples of initiatives undertaken by women and men of different religious persuasions clearly show that synergetic efforts in this regard actually exist and should not be underestimated.

29. At the same time, one has to face the reality of conflicting interests in this area. For instance, some religious community leaders have rejected anti-discrimination stipulations imposed by the State, in which they may see an undue infringement of their right to internal autonomy. There are also cases of parents objecting to gender-related education programmes becoming part of the school curriculum, since they fear this may go against their religious or moral convictions. Dealing with such complicated conflicts requires a high degree of empirical precision, communicative openness and normative diligence with a view to doing justice to all human rights claims involved.

30. Moreover, the Special Rapporteur notes with concern that such harmful practices as female genital mutilation, forced marriage, honour killings, enforced ritual prostitution or denying girls their rights to education are defended in the name of religious traditions. Such defence is frequently controversial within the various religious communities themselves, and many followers of the respective communities (possibly their overwhelming majority) may be heavily opposed to such practices and also voice their opposition publicly. If those still performing harmful practices try to invoke religious freedom for their actions, this must become a case for restricting the freedom to manifest one's religion or belief. The Special Rapporteur would like to reiterate what his predecessor pointed out in her final report to the General Assembly: "The Special Rapporteur strongly believes that the mandate needs to continue highlighting discriminatory practices that women have had to suffer over centuries and continue to do so, sometimes in the name of religion or within their religious community. It can no longer be taboo to demand that women's rights take priority over intolerant beliefs used to justify gender discrimination." (see A/65/207, para. 69). The current mandate holder fully shares the assessment formulated by his predecessor. Indeed, as a human right, freedom of religion or belief can never serve as a justification for violations of the human rights of women and girls.

31. When arguing for limitations of a right to freedom, it remains crucial to exercise empirical and normative diligence at all times. Sometimes supposed conflicts between freedom of religion or belief and equality between men and women may rest on mere conjectures. Moreover, restrictions on freedom of religion or belief cannot be legitimate unless they meet all the criteria prescribed for limitations in article 18, paragraph 3, of the International Covenant on Civil and Political Rights. The reasonable assumption that promoting equality between men and women always constitutes a legitimate purpose does not in itself suffice to justify restrictions; such restrictions must also have a legal basis, they must actually be conducive to pursuing the said purpose and one has to demonstrate that less restrictive means are not available. Finally, freedom of religion or belief strictly prohibits any restrictions in the *forum internum*, that is to say, the freedom to have or to adopt a religion or belief of one's choice.

3. Practical relevance of a holistic approach

32. The reality of manifold and complicated conflicts in the field of freedom of religion or belief and equality between men and women has led some to the view that the two human rights norms themselves stand in opposition to one another. As a result, the relationship between these two norms may appear close to a simple zero- sum game: any progress concerning gender equality seems to indicate a defeat of religious freedom, and any insistence on freedom of religion or belief seems to hinder gender-related anti-discrimination policies, or so it is at times misperceived.

33. Not only are such antagonistic views mostly based on a total misunderstanding of freedom of religion or belief and a disregard of its human rights nature; they can also produce protection gaps with serious practical implications. One of the resulting problems is that the potential for synergies between freedom of religion or belief and promoting women's right to equality remains systematically underexplored. Existing human rights activities in this field do not receive the attention they need and deserve. Sometimes such activities are even delegitimized by antagonistic views which wrongly assume that gender-related anti-discrimination agendas would be weakened by integrating sensitivity for freedom of religion or belief or, vice versa, that work in defence of religious freedom would be diluted by combining it with the promotion of equality between men and women and related human rights issues.

34. Above all, antagonistic views of the two human rights norms would further diminish the prospects of persons whose human rights problems fall in the intersection of freedom of religion or belief and equality between men and women. Indeed, human rights violations in the intersection of the two norms are a reality for many women. One obvious example is forced conversion in combination with forced marriage. In a number of countries, women or girls from religious minorities unfortunately run the risk of being abducted, with the purpose of forcing them to convert to the mainstream religion, often in connection with an unwanted marriage. Another example, albeit much less extreme, concerns dress code regulations in public institutions which disproportionately target women from religious minorities, thus preventing them from achieving important professional or public positions.

35. Being frequently caught between gender stereotypes and stereotypical perceptions of their religious identities, many women from religious minorities feel exposed to the expectation that they have to choose one of two seemingly contradictory options: allegedly, they can either emancipate themselves by more or less abandoning their religious tradition, or they can keep their religious heritage, thereby forfeiting their claims to freedom and equality. Such an artificial antagonism, however, fails to do justice to women's multifaceted realities, experiences, challenges and wishes. Any assessment of presumed or factual conflicts in this area should therefore take seriously the complexities of women's life-worlds and appreciate their creative potential.[167]

C. Typological analysis of challenges in the intersection of freedom of religion or belief and equality between men and women

36. In the present chapter, the Special Rapporteur analyses practical challenges in the intersection of freedom of religion or belief and equality between men and women. The described phenomena and patterns are examples; they certainly do not cover the whole range of existing challenges as they may develop in ever new facets. To avoid a possible misunderstanding, the Special Rapporteur would like to underline from the outset that each case and each situation must always be examined carefully on their own merits.

---

[167] One may assume that the same is true for individuals from the lesbian, gay, bisexual, transgender and intersex community, many of whom are religiously interested and practising, which is a reality so far largely unexplored.

*I.　Addressing religious stereotypes in conjunction with gender stereo-
types*

37.　Overcoming discrimination against women is a paramount human
rights obligation to be found in the Charter of the United Nations, the
Universal Declaration of Human Rights, the International Covenant on
Civil and Political Rights and countless other binding human rights documents. The Convention on the Elimination of All Forms of Discrimination Against Women plays the pivotal role in this regard. In its article 2,
States parties "condemn discrimination against women in all its forms,
agree to pursue by all appropriate means and without delay a policy of
eliminating discrimination against women [...]".

38.　Pursuant to article 5 (a) of the Convention, States parties are obliged
to take all appropriate measures "to modify the social and cultural patterns of conduct of men and women, with a view to achieving the elimination of prejudice and customary and all other practices which are
based on the idea of the inferiority or the superiority of either of the sexes or on stereotyped roles for men and women". To fulfil this obligation,
States parties must critically address cultural practices that accord men
and women unequal roles, positions and opportunities in family life, labour markets, public and political life and society at large. Examples include obstacles to women pursuing professional careers or attending institutions of higher education; restrictions on their right to travel;
underrepresentation of women in public positions; obstacles to women's
freedom to find a spouse of their own choice; child marriage, frequently
amounting to marital rape; humiliating treatment of widows, including
denial of their right to remarry a spouse of their own choice; female genital mutilation; rigid dress code regulations imposed on women against
their will; male-child preference, sometimes leading to sex-selective
abortion or female infanticide; non-acceptance of any way of life outside
of a traditional family context; denigration of the image of women in
public life, including in media and advertisements; violence against
women, sometimes even leading to so-called "honour killings"; denial of
property rights and of equal rights of succession; denial of the right to
seek a divorce and exposure to the threat of unilateral repudiation; and
the assumption that women generally cannot live without male protection, which may seriously hamper their freedom to lead their lives in
conformity with their own wishes, convictions and plans.[168] Needless to

---

[168]　See relevant general recommendations of the Committee on the Elimination of
　　Discrimination against Women, including No. 12 (1989) on violence against

say, this list of examples is far from exhaustive. Discrimination based on stereotypical roles of men and women is one of the most widespread human rights violations worldwide. It can assume cruel forms and deprives many women and girls of their rights to life, freedom and respect for human dignity. The need for concerted action to eliminate such violations, including by addressing their cultural root causes, is more than obvious.

39. Deeply rooted cultural patterns of expected conduct of men and women are frequently interwoven with religious norms and practices. In many cases they even claim a direct religious justification. The previous mandate holder stressed that in many countries "gender discrimination is in fact founded on cultural and/or religious practices" and that a large number of reservations to the Convention on the Elimination of All Forms of Discrimination Against Women "have been made by States on exclusively religious grounds referring to a perception of society and the law in relation to women's personal status" (see E/CN.4/2002/73/Add.2, para. 58).

40. When dealing with this problem, one should take into account that the relationship between culture and religion in general shows manifold facets both between and within religious traditions. This topic is typically also controversial within religious communities themselves. While some members of a religious community may appreciate broad overlaps between religion and culture as something quite natural, others may fear that the specific profile of religious messages and norms becomes unrecognizable if religion and culture are simply amalgamated. Moreover, using a conceptual distinction between religion and culture has become one of the most important methodological tools for reformers, including feminist theologians, operating within different religious or belief contexts with the purpose of redefining the boundaries of religion and culture. It also plays a crucial role in projects of distinguishing core elements of religious messages and norms from traditional cultural practices, with a view to promoting women's human rights within their religious communities. For any analysis of conflicts between religious traditions and the human rights principle of equality between men and women it remains utterly important to bear in mind that religion and culture, albeit interwoven in manifold ways, are not identical and that

women; No. 13 (1989) on equal remuneration for work of equal value; No. 14 (1990) on female circumcision; No. 18 (1991) on disabled women; No. 19 (1992) on violence against women; No. 21 (1994) on equality in marriage and family relations; and No. 23 (1997) on women in political and public life.

their relationship can be exposed to critical questions and reform agendas, often based on initiatives that originate from the midst of religious communities themselves.

41. Unsurprisingly, State policies for eliminating deeply rooted gender stereotypes frequently come into conflict with persons, organizations or institutions that defend existing hierarchies between men and women. In situations in which such patterns are perceived as being based on religious prescriptions, this also frequently leads to conflicts with representatives and members of religious communities. There are in fact numerous examples of religious leaders opposing gender-related anti-discrimination policies. Although such opposition may mobilize parts of religious communities against anti-discrimination programmes, there may be other currents within the same communities who hold more moderate views or are openly supportive of broad anti-discrimination programmes. Taking interreligious and intrareligious pluralism into account is of paramount importance when dealing with conflicts in this field in order to find appropriate solutions and to do justice to the human beings involved in such conflicts.

42. Given the frequent experience of religiously motivated opposition and, at times, fierce resistance, some promoters of gender-related anti-discrimination policies may feel inclined to treat certain religions, or even religions in general, as mere obstacles in the development of societies free from discrimination. However, such an attitude would be problematic for a number of reasons. It fails to do justice to the complex realities and wishes of many human beings, in particular women living in different religious communities. Although frequently suffering from discrimination within their religious communities, many women nonetheless feel attached to their religions and may wish their attachment to be recognized as part of their freedom of religion or belief. Moreover, internal differences, developments and dynamics often do not receive sufficient systematic attention. This in turn can lead to stereotypical perceptions of religions or beliefs which may further exacerbate existing prejudices against persons adhering to those religions or beliefs. Ample experience indicates that this danger disproportionately affects women from religious minorities. Indeed, it is a bitter irony that policies aimed at eliminating stereotypes in the field of gender may themselves produce or reproduce stereotypes and prejudices in a different area, namely in the area of religion or belief. There are even examples of right-wing populist or extremist movements utilizing elements of gender-related anti-

discrimination programmes with the ill-concealed intention of stoking collective resentments against unwelcome religious minorities.

43. Freedom of religion or belief does not shield religious traditions, or religions as such, against criticism, nor does it protect members of religious communities from critical questions. However, States should contribute to the elimination of negative stereotypes against individuals on the basis of their religion or belief, in particular members of religious minorities. Stereotypical perceptions can lead to a depersonalization of the human person. By being subordinated to a seemingly closed collective mentality, individuals have few opportunities to make their personal views, interests and assessments heard. They seemingly lose their faces and voices, as it were. Obviously, such de-personalization goes against the spirit and the letter of human rights which empower human beings to express their convictions, views and interests freely and without discrimination. States are therefore obliged to develop effective strategies to eliminate stereotypes, including gender-related stereotypes and stereotypical images of persons based on their religion or belief. Education programmes, awareness-raising campaigns, interreligious and intercultural dialogue initiatives and other measures can help broaden horizons towards an appreciation of the real diversity and creativity of human beings in this broad field.

44. Policies for eliminating gender-related stereotypes, in fulfilment of State obligations under the Convention, should therefore be pursued in conjunction with policies for avoiding and dispelling stereotypical perceptions of persons based on their religion or belief, in keeping with the Declaration on the Elimination of All Forms of Intolerance and of Discrimination Based on Religion or Belief.

45. There is no inherent normative contradiction between those two tasks. Taking freedom of religion or belief into account in gender-related anti-discrimination agendas may prima facie lead to additional complications. However, there is ultimately no legitimate way to ignore the complex realities, wishes and claims of human beings whose problems fall in the intersection of freedom of religion or belief and gender equality. Freedom of religion or belief should thus be systematically integrated into gender related anti-discrimination programmes as an element of their own quality management. Vice versa, policies promoting freedom of thought, conscience, religion or belief should systematically integrate a gender perspective in order to uphold the universalistic aspirations that define the human rights approach in general. Criteria for imposing limitations on freedom of religion or belief

46. Measures to eradicate violations of women's human rights necessarily include State-enforced prohibitions of harmful practices. An extreme example is female genital mutilation, which leads to lifelong and far-reaching health problems, as well as grave forms of traumatization. Whether this practice has religious root causes remains controversial and ultimately doubtful. However, religious leaders may play an important role by clarifying religious views and by publicly calling on their believers to end this cruel practice.[169] The same holds true for forced marriages, a widespread practice sometimes justified in the name of religion, and at other times, challenged in the name of religion. Other examples of harmful practices include enforced "sacred prostitution", burning or other forms of ill-treatment of widows, honour crimes often perpetrated in a climate of impunity or in which such crimes are condoned, dowry killings and many manifestations of extreme disrespect. Whether they have a religious basis typically remains controversial between and within religious communities. Be that as it may, freedom of religion or belief clearly does not protect such cruel practices. If individuals or groups were to invoke their right to freedom of religion or belief in order to get permission to perform such harmful practices, this must become a case for restricting these manifestations of religion or belief, in conformity with the criteria laid down in article 18, paragraph 3, of the International Covenant on Civil and Political Rights.

47. Before resorting to restrictions on the freedom to manifest one's religion or belief, legislators or representatives of the judiciary should always analyse the respective cases with empirical and normative precision. However, States sometimes impose restrictive measures in a rather loose way, beyond the confines of article 18, paragraph 3, of the International Covenant. This may also happen in the context of gender-related anti-discrimination policies. Based on overly simplistic perceptions, according to which religions per se constitute obstacles to the development of societies free from discrimination, some States may even be tempted to turn the principle of *in dubio pro libertate* upside down by restricting in case of doubt manifestations of religion or belief without providing the required empirical and normative evidence.

48. The Special Rapporteur would like to reiterate in this context that when States wish to impose restrictions they always bear the burden of proof, both at the level of empirical evidence and at the level of normative reasoning. Furthermore, for limitations to be legitimate, they must

---

[169] See A/HRC/4/21, para. 38 and E/CN.4/2002/73/Add.2, paras. 104-110.

meet all criteria set out in article 18, paragraph 3, of the International Covenant. Accordingly, limitations must be legally prescribed and they must be clearly needed to pursue a legitimate aim, the protection of "public safety, order, health, or morals or the fundamental rights and freedoms of others". In addition, restrictions must remain within the realm of proportionality which, inter alia, means they must be limited to a minimum of interference.[170] Finally, the *forum internum* dimension of freedom of religion or belief does not allow for any restrictions whatsoever, according to article 18, paragraph 2, of the International Covenant.

49. A much discussed issue in the context of limitations of freedom of religion or belief concerns restrictions on the wearing of religious symbols, including headscarves, turbans, kippas or religious jewellery, such as a cross attached to a necklace. In many cases those restrictions particularly affect women from religious minorities. Although there may be reasons for imposing limitations for specific situations, the Special Rapporteur has noted that some of the measures taken in this regard fail to meet all the requirements of article 18, paragraph 3, of the International Covenant. For instance, laws prohibiting the Islamic headscarf in public institutions are frequently based on conjectures that women do not wear such head garments of their own free will. The empirical evidence for these conjectures often remains questionable. Moreover, if there are some clear cases of impositions, this experience will not necessarily suffice to justify general or broad prohibitions of the headscarf in public life or by users of such public institutions as schools, universities or public administration.

50. Under the principle of proportionality, States have always to look for less far- reaching and less intrusive restrictions before issuing legislation that infringes on freedom of religion or belief. Another part of the proportionality test concerns the question of whether limitations are actually conducive to the legitimate purpose they are supposed to foster. It may happen that measures do not only fail to serve the said purpose; they may actually worsen the situation of many individuals, particularly women, for instance by further restricting their spaces of personal movement and infringing their rights to education and participation in public life.

---

[170] See General Comment No. 22 of the Human Rights Committee, CCPR/C/21/Rev.1/Add.4, para. 8.

2. Gender and sexuality in school education programmes

51. According to article 13 of the International Covenant on Economic, Social and Cultural Rights, every human being has the right to education. This has been confirmed in other important human rights documents, including in article 28 of the Convention on the Rights of the Child and article 24 of the Convention on the Rights of Persons with Disabilities. The right to education, inter alia, functions as an indispensable right for empowerment that facilitates the more effective use of many other human rights, such as freedom of expression, the right to work, participation in public life, cultural rights and freedom of religion or belief. In order to secure the right to education for everyone, States should make elementary school education mandatory, as requested by the Committee on Economic, Social and Cultural Rights and by the Committee on the Rights of the Child.[171] Given the fact that in many countries or regions the right to education continues to be denied for girls and women, this provision has a particular significance for them.

52. To realize its potential for empowerment, education must also cover human rights education, which necessarily includes the two human rights norms under discussion here. Indeed, education plays a crucial role in all policies for eliminating stereotypical gender roles and ideas of inequality of men and women, and it is important to educate individuals about sexual and reproductive health issues and their human rights in this regard. Likewise, education is of great significance in policies for combating discrimination based on religion or belief by critically addressing existing stereotypes and prejudices in this field. The voices of women, including their different and possibly conflicting assessments, should always be part of the broader picture when informing about religions and beliefs.

53. Within the broad field of education, school education warrants specific attention. Besides providing a place of learning in which students can realize their right to education, the school is also a place in which authority is exercised (see A/HRC/16/53, para. 23). In particular, children of a tender age typically experience the teacher as a person wielding a high degree of authority. In addition, students may be exposed to pressure from their peers. For some students, particularly those belonging to

---

[171] See Committee on Economic Social and Cultural Rights, General Comment No. 11 (1999), E/C.12/1999/4, paras. 1 and 6; and General Comment No. 13 (1999), E/C.12/1999/10, paras. 10 and 51; and Committee on the Rights of the Child, General Comment No. 7 (2005), CRC/C/GC/7/Rev.1, para. 28.

ethnic, linguistic, religious or other minorities, this harbours the risk of creating a vulnerable situation. Parents from minorities may furthermore fear that the school could alienate their children from the family, including from the religion of their family. All of this calls for systematic attention with a view to dispelling fears, building trust, avoiding risk situations and overcoming the vulnerable situations of students and their families.

54. From a normative perspective, school education falls in the focus of a number of human rights, including the right to education, minority rights, equality between men and women, and freedom of religion or belief. As a subcategory to freedom of religion or belief, article 18, paragraph 4 of the International Covenant on Civil and Political Rights demands respect for the "liberty of parents and, when applicable, legal guardians to ensure the religious and moral education of their children in conformity with their own convictions". This provision should not be interpreted in isolation but should be read in conjunction with article 5 and article 14, paragraph 2, of the Convention on the Rights of the Child, which require parents and legal guardians to provide appropriate direction and guidance "in a manner consistent with the evolving capacities of the child". With regard to adolescents, the Committee on the Rights of the Child emphasizes that States parties should provide them "with access to sexual and reproductive information, including on family planning and contraceptives, the dangers of early pregnancy, the prevention of HIV/AIDS and the prevention and treatment of sexually transmitted diseases".[11] The Committee furthermore insists that adolescents should "have access to appropriate information, regardless of [...] whether their parents or guardians consent".[172]

55. School curricula or other programmes addressing gender or sexuality issues have sometimes triggered resistance on the part of parents who fear that this might go against their moral convictions. Quite frequently, such opposition results from religious or other conscience-based positions, thereby possibly becoming an issue under freedom of religion or belief. There is no general recipe for handling such conflicts in practice. Each individual case requires a careful analysis of the specific context and of the human rights norms invoked by the conflicting parties. One should bear in mind that neither the right to education, including educa-

---

[172] Committee on the Rights of the Child, General Comment No. 4, CRC/GC/2003/4, para. 28.

tion "in the spirit of ... equality of sexes",[173] nor the right to freedom of religion or belief can be dispensed with, since both have the status of inalienable human rights. It is always advisable to try to prevent or de-escalate conflicts, for instance by training teachers, dispelling mistrust and misunderstandings and establishing outreach programmes towards particular communities.

56. The Special Rapporteur would like to reiterate in this context that, according to article 18, paragraph 2, of the International Covenant, the *forum internum* dimension of freedom of religion or belief receives unconditional protection and does not allow any restrictions or infringements, for any reason.[174] Even the undeniably significant aim of promoting gender equality and using school education for that purpose cannot justify forms of teaching that may amount to violation of a student's *forum internum*. States are therefore obliged to exercise due diligence in this area, for instance by sensitizing teachers, employing professional mediators and establishing suitable monitoring mechanisms.

3. Religious institutions

57. Freedom of religion or belief also covers the right of persons and groups of persons to establish religious institutions that function in conformity with their religious self-understanding. This is not just an external aspect of marginal significance. Religious communities, in particular minority communities, need an appropriate institutional infrastructure, without which their long-term survival options as a community might be in serious peril, a situation which at the same time would amount to a violation of freedom of religion or belief of individual members (see A/HRC/22/51, para. 25). Moreover, for many (not all) religious or belief communities, institutional questions, such as the appointment of religious leaders or the rules governing monastic life, directly or indirectly derive from the tenets of their faith. Hence, questions of how to institutionalize religious community life can have a significance that goes far beyond mere organizational or managerial aspects. Freedom of religion or belief therefore entails respect for the autonomy of religious institutions.

58. It is a well-known fact that in many (not all) denominations, positions of religious authority, such as bishop, imam, preacher, priest, rabbi or reverend, remain reserved to males, a state of affairs that collides with

---

[173] Article 29, para. 1 (d), of the Convention on the Rights of the Child.
[174] See also CCPR/C/21/Rev.1/Add.4, para. 3.

the principle of equality between men and women as established in international human rights law. Unsurprisingly, this has led to numerous conflicts. While the Special Rapporteur cannot provide a general recipe for handling such conflicts in practice, he would like to point to a number of relevant human rights principles and norms in this regard.

59. It cannot be the business of the State to shape or reshape religious traditions, nor can the State claim any binding authority in the interpretation of religious sources or in the definition of the tenets of faith. Freedom of religion or belief is a right of human beings, after all, not a right of the State. As mentioned above, questions of how to institutionalize community life may significantly affect the religious self-understanding of a community. From this it follows that the State must generally respect the autonomy of religious institutions, also in policies of promoting equality between men and women.

60. At the same time, one should bear in mind that freedom of religion or belief includes the right of internal dissidents, including women, to come up with alternative views, provide new readings of religious sources and try to exercise influence on a community's religious self-understanding, which may change over time. In situations in which internal dissidents or proponents of new religious understandings face coercion from within their religious communities, which sometimes happens, the State is obliged to provide protection. It should be noted in this regard that the autonomy of religious institutions falls within the *forum externum* dimension of freedom of religion or belief which, if the need arises, can be restricted in conformity with the criteria spelled out in article 18, paragraph 3, of the International Covenant, while threats or acts of coercion against a person may affect the *forum internum* dimension of freedom of religion or belief, which has an unconditional status. In other words, respect by the State for the autonomy of religious institutions can never supersede the responsibility of the State to prevent or prosecute threats or acts of coercion against persons (e.g., internal critics or dissidents), depending on the circumstances of the specific case.

61. In addition, freedom of religion or belief includes the right to establish new religious communities and institutions. The issue of equality between men and women has in fact led to splits in quite a number of religious communities, and meanwhile, in virtually all religious traditions, reform branches exist in which women may have better opportunities to achieve positions of religious authority. Again, it cannot be the business of the State directly or indirectly to initiate such internal developments, which must always be left to believers themselves, since they remain the

relevant rights holders in this regard. What the State can and should do, however, is to provide an open framework in which religious pluralism, including pluralism in institutions, can unfold freely. An open framework facilitating the free expression of pluralism may also improve the opportunities for new gender-sensitive developments within different religious traditions, initiated by believers themselves.

4.   Protection gaps in family law

62. Religions and belief systems frequently include normative rules regulating community life. Communitarian norms originating from religious or other conscientious convictions are generally covered by freedom of religion or belief which, inter alia, protects "practice" in the broad sense of the word. However, it is important to bear in mind that this happens in the indirect mode that characterizes the human rights approach in general. As explained earlier, human rights protection cannot be directly accorded to religious norms or value systems as such. Rather, human rights empower human beings as rights holders, inter alia by facilitating the free profession of their normative convictions and by enabling them to organize their community life in conformity with their religious and ethical persuasions. States should create suitable conditions for religious or belief communities in this regard, while at the same time bearing in mind the rights of individuals who should be able to develop their own life plans and to express their personal convictions, including critical and dissenting views. This is not an easy task.

63. Additional complications emerge in States that directly enforce religious norms in certain areas of society, particularly norms concerning issues of marriage, family life, child custody, divorce and inheritance. Denominational family laws and personal status laws enforced by the State are a reality in many countries. They mostly reflect traditional understandings of gender roles connected with unequal rights of men and women. Many such denominational family laws may restrict women's rights to choose a spouse according to their own wishes; they may reflect unequal rights of men and women in questions of divorce, sometimes even permitting the husband to repudiate his wife unilaterally; they may furthermore assume unequal rights concerning family property and inheritance; they may give the husband a privileged legal position in issues of child custody; and some of these laws allow men to contract polygamous marriages.

64. While from the perspective of equality between men and women the critical focus will naturally fall on discriminatory gender roles existing in

many denominational family laws, one also has to address the problem of State enforcement of religious norms. The enforcement of religious norms by State agencies necessarily gives rise to critical questions from the perspective of freedom of religion or belief, which is a right of human beings, not of States. In most (not all) such systems, State enforcement of denominational family laws accommodates a certain degree of religious pluralism. Accordingly, members of different religious communities, including recognized minorities, can regulate their family-related legal affairs in conformity with the normative precepts of their own religious traditions. In spite of pluralistic conceptualizations, however, the element of State enforcement of denominational family laws remains problematic from the perspective of freedom of religion or belief. Although each of the existing systems would require an assessment based on their specific merits, systems of State enforced denominational family laws typically fail to do justice to the human rights of persons living outside of the recognized religious communities, for example atheists or agnostics, members of small religions or new religious movements. However, as the Human Rights Committee has pointed out, article 18 of the International Covenant "protects theistic, non-theistic and atheistic beliefs, as well as the right not to profess any religion or belief. The terms belief and religion are to be broadly construed. Article 18 is not limited in its application to traditional religions or to religions and beliefs with institutional characteristics or practices analogous to those of traditional religions."[175]

65. Moreover, individuals may change their religious orientations. The freedom to do so constitutes an integral part of the *forum internum* dimension of freedom of religion or belief. However, this right can hardly be appropriately accommodated within a system of State-enforced denominational family laws. Many of the resulting problems concern women. For instance, it happens that women stemming from religious minorities who have converted in the context of a marriage wish to reconvert to their previous religion when the marriage breaks down. When trying to do so, they may encounter enormous difficulties in securing the right to have custody of their children. Losing custody of a child can be one of the worst experiences for a parent. This is only one example of serious human rights problems in this field in which violations of freedom of religion or belief and discrimination against women coincide.

66. It should be noted in this context that there have also been cases of custody denials based on prejudices against certain religious minorities

---

[175] See CCPR/C/21/Rev.1/Add.4, para. 2.

within secular family law systems. This shows the need for sensitizing judges and other professionals dealing with such matters in all systems of family law. At the same time, there is a clear need for structural reforms in order to close relevant protection gaps. What is required in order to overcome the risk of human rights violations in this important field is family law systems that unequivocally respect the equality of men and women while at the same time doing justice to the broad reality of diversity of religion or belief, including persuasions beyond the realm of traditionally recognized religions and also bearing in mind the human right to change one's religion or belief. Again, this presupposes a holistic understanding of freedom of religion or belief and equality between men and women as mutually reinforcing human rights norms.

IV. Conclusions and recommendations

67. The relationship between freedom of religion or belief and equality between men and women displays many facets and is exposed to numerous political, jurisdictional, theological and philosophical controversies. In the face of conflicting human rights concerns put forward in the name of freedom of religion or belief and/or in the name of equality between men and women, the two human rights norms themselves are sometimes perceived as standing in general opposition to one another. While acknowledging the reality of complicated conflicts in this field, the Special Rapporteur emphasizes that one must not draw the wrong conclusions from this experience. In particular, it would be problematic to turn concrete conflicts between different human rights issues into an abstract antagonism on the normative level itself.

68. Unfortunately, the idea that freedom of religion or belief and equality between men and women represent essentially contradictory human rights norms seems to be widespread and has even gained currency in parts of the larger human rights community. As a result, possible synergies between freedom of religion or belief and equality between men and women remain underexplored. Even worse, existing human rights work in this field is sometimes openly discouraged or delegitimized. Moreover, an abstractly antagonistic construction of the two human rights norms cannot do justice to the needs, wishes, experiences and specific vulnerabilities of many millions of women whose life situations falls within the intersection of discrimination on the grounds of their religion or belief and discrimination on the ground of their sex or gender. This problem disproportionately affects women from religious minorities.

69. In keeping with the formula coined at the World Conference on Human Rights that "[a]ll human rights are universal, indivisible and interdependent athe Special Rapporteur underlines the positive interrelatedness of freedom of religion or belief and equality between men and women. Upholding this holistic approach even in complicated situations is important for a number of practical reasons: it encourages the search for synergies in this area and facilitates an appreciation of sufficiently complex human rights approaches; it provides the horizon for coping appropriately with perceived or factual conflicts in a manner that does justice to all human rights norms involved in such conflicts; and it is the precondition for systematically addressing the human rights concerns of persons whose specific problems and vulnerabilities fall in the intersection of different human rights norms.

70. Abstractly antagonistic constructions of the relationship between freedom of religion or belief and equality between men and women are often based on a misunderstanding of the human rights nature of freedom of religion or belief. As a human right, freedom of religion or belief does not protect religions per se (e.g. traditions, values, identities and truth claims) but aims at the empowerment of human beings, as individuals and in community with others. This empowerment component is something which freedom of religion or belief has in common with all other human rights. Only on this basis is it possible to develop and defend a holistic understanding of the complex interplay between freedom of religion or belief and equality between men and women.

71. In discourses on contentious religious issues, everyone should have a voice and everyone should have a chance to be heard. However, by also empowering groups who traditionally experience discrimination, including women and girls, freedom of religion or belief can serve as a normative reference point for projects that challenge patriarchal tendencies as they exist in virtually all religious traditions. This can lead to more gender-sensitive readings of religious sources and far-reaching discoveries in this field.

72. When dealing with supposed or factual problems in the intersection of freedom of religion or belief and gender equality, the existing diversity of human beings must always be taken seriously. This includes an awareness of interreligious as well as intrareligious pluralism. The voices of women, including their different and possibly conflicting assessments, should always be part of the broader picture. Failure to recognize existing and emerging pluralism frequently leads to stereotypes, which in turn can become a source of human rights abuses.

73. Integrating a gender perspective into programmes designed for protecting and promoting freedom of religion or belief is a requirement that ultimately follows from the universalistic spirit of human rights. Vice versa, integrating sensitivity for issues of freedom of religion or belief broadens and solidifies the human rights basis of gender-related anti-discrimination programmes.

74. In this spirit the Special Rapporteur formulates the following recommendations addressed to different stakeholders, including States, civil society organizations, religious or belief communities, media representatives and persons in charge of education:

   a) States should ratify all core international human rights instruments, including the International Covenant on Civil and Political Rights and the Convention on the Elimination of All Forms of Discrimination Against Women. They are also encouraged to withdraw existing reservations, including any reservations with regard to religious traditions of the country. The interpretation of religious traditions is not the business of the State and should be left to the followers of the various convictions, who are the rights holders of freedom of religion or belief;

   b) States and other stakeholders should search for practical synergies between freedom of religion or belief and equality between men and women and encourage positive developments in this regard. In situations of perceived or factual conflicts, those in charge of taking legislative, policy or juridical decisions must do justice to all human rights issues involved, which implies upholding a holistic human rights understanding even in complicated situations. Taking interreligious and intrareligious pluralism into account is of paramount importance when dealing with conflicts in this field in order to find appropriate solutions and to do justice to all persons involved in such conflicts;

   c) States and other stakeholders should develop effective strategies to eliminate negative stereotypes, including gender-related stereotypes as well as stereotypical depictions of persons based on their religion or belief. This requires a holistic human rights approach in order to avoid measures employed to combat stereotypes in one area inadvertently producing or reinforcing negative stereotypes in another area;

d) Policies designed to empower individuals exposed to gender-related discrimination cannot claim credibility unless they pay careful attention to the self-understandings, interests and assessments voiced by the concerned persons themselves, including women from religious minorities. This principle should always be observed, in particular before setting legislative or jurisdictional limits to a right to freedom, for example the right to wear religious garments;

e) Legislative or jurisdictional restrictions on freedom of religion or belief deemed necessary for eradicating harmful practices and for promoting equality between men and women must be undertaken with the appropriate degree of empirical and normative diligence and must meet all criteria laid down in article 18, paragraph 3, of the International Covenant on Civil and Political Rights;

f) States and other stakeholders should reinforce educational efforts in order to promote respect for diversity, including diversity in the areas of gender and religion or belief. In the process of designing and implementing educational programmes, concerned persons should be consulted and should have a chance to take an active role;

g) Educational programmes to promote respect for diversity should become part of the regular school curriculum. In this regard, special attention should be given to the possible vulnerability of students, in particular children from religious minorities. In addition, the liberty of parents and legal guardians to educate a child in conformity with their own moral or religious convictions must be respected, while they also have to provide appropriate direction and guidance in a manner consistent with the evolving capacities of the child;

h) Outreach programmes towards certain religious communities and the employment of mediators can help to build trust between the school and religious communities, which may be important for dispelling misunderstandings and prevent conflicts around issues of gender equality and ethical norms based on religious or other convictions. Fears expressed by students or parents, even if seemingly based on misunderstandings, should be taken seriously and deserve respectful responses;

i) States should identify and close human rights protection gaps in personal status laws, including denominational family laws, which disproportionately affect women from religious or belief minorities. The purpose must be to create family law systems that fully respect equality between men and women while at the same time do justice to the broad reality of religious or belief diversity, including persuasions that go beyond the realm of traditionally recognized religions;

j) States should provide an open framework in which existing and emerging religious pluralism can unfold freely and without discrimination. Ensuring free expression of pluralism may also improve the opportunities for new gender-sensitive developments within different religious traditions, which cannot be initiated by the State but must be left to the respective believers themselves who are the rights holders in the context of freedom of religion or belief.

7.   Chapter: Report December 2013

I. Introduction

1.   The mandate of the Special Rapporteur on freedom of religion or belief was created by the Commission on Human Rights pursuant to its resolution 1986/20 and renewed by the Human Rights Council in its resolutions 6/37, 14/1 and 22/20. The Council appointed Heiner Bielefeldt as the mandate holder as from 1 August 2010; in 2013, Mr. Bielefeldt's appointment as Special Rapporteur was renewed for a further three-year term

2.   In chapter II, the Special Rapporteur provides a brief overview of his activities since the submission of his previous report to the Human Rights Council (A/HRC/22/51). The Special Rapporteur focuses in chapter III on the need to tackle manifestations of collective religious hatred. In chapter IV, he provides conclusions in this regard and addresses recommendations to various stakeholders.

II. Activities of the Special Rapporteur

3.   The Special Rapporteur has conducted various activities pursuant to Human Rights Council resolutions 6/37, 14/11 and 22/20. In this chapter, he presents a brief overview of his mandate activities from 1 December 2012 to 30 November 2013.

A. Country visits

4.   The Special Rapporteur undertook two country visits during the reporting period: to Sierra Leone, from 30 June to 5 July 2013, and to Jordan, from 2 to 12 September 2013.[176] He expresses his appreciation to all interlocutors and to the Government officials of Jordan and Sierra Leone for the excellent cooperation they extended to him during his visits.

5.   Additional country visits are currently being scheduled. This includes an agreed visit to Kazakhstan during the first quarter of 2014 and an agreed visit to Viet Nam later in 2014. Updated information about the Special Rapporteur's visits and related requests is available on the web-

---

[176] For the reports on the visits to Sierra Leone and to Jordan, see A/HRC/25/58/Add.1 and A/HRC/25/58/Add.2, respectively.

site of the Office of the United Nations High Commissioner for Human Rights (OHCHR).[177]

B. Communications

6.   The Special Rapporteur deals with individual cases or issues of concern brought to his attention. He seeks to clarify allegations of certain actions possibly incompatible with the provisions of the 1981 Declaration on the Elimination of All Forms of Intolerance and of Discrimination Based on Religion or Belief by sending allegation letters and urgent appeals to States. Since the creation of the mandate, the Special Rapporteurs have sent more than 1,290 allegation letters and urgent appeals to a total of 130 States. The communications sent by the Special Rapporteur between 1 December 2012 and 30 November 2013 are included in the latest communications reports (A/HRC/23/51, A/HRC/24/21 and A/HRC/25/74).

C. Other activities

7.   On 12 and 13 December 2012, the Special Rapporteur attended the Office of the United Nations High Commissioner for Refugees (UNHCR) Dialogue on Protection Challenges, entitled "Faith and Protection".

8.   During the session of the Working Group on the issue of discrimination against women in law and in practice, held on 17 and 18 January 2013, a preliminary discussion was held with the Special Rapporteur on the issue of gender equality and freedom of religion and belief.

9.   On 21 February 2013, the Special Rapporteur took part in the high-level event, held in Geneva, to launch the Rabat Plan of Action. On 22 February, he also participated in the seminar on "Preventing incitement to atrocity crimes: policy options for action" organized by the Office of the Special Adviser on the Prevention of Genocide.

10. On 27 and 28 February 2013, the Special Rapporteur attended the fifth Global Forum of the United Nations Alliance of Civilizations, held in Vienna, which focused on the theme "Responsible leadership in diversity and dialogue".

11. From 4 to 8 March 2013, the Special Rapporteur attended the twenty-second session of the Human Rights Council. During that week, he also participated in several events organized by various civil society organizations.

---

[177]   See www.ohchr.org/EN/HRBodies/SP/Pages/CountryandothervisitsSP.aspx.

12. The Special Rapporteur held many meetings with Government representatives, religious or belief communities, civil society organizations and academic experts working in the area of freedom of religion or belief. In this context, he participated in national and international conferences and workshops, including in Berlin, Colombo, Fès, Geneva, Helsinki, London, Lusaka, Luxembourg, Oslo, Oxford, Rabat, Richmond (Virginia), Salzburg, Stockholm, Tbilisi, Uppsala, Vienna and Yerevan. In addition, he held video conferences with stakeholders across different continents.

13. On 12 September 2013, the Special Rapporteur participated in the first interreligious round table held in Cyprus, organized by the Office of the Religious Track of the Cyprus Peace Process, under the auspices of the Embassy of Sweden, and in cooperation with OHCHR.[178]

14. On 29 October 2013, the Special Rapporteur presented his interim report to the General Assembly (A/68/290) at its sixty-eighth session; the report focused on the interplay between freedom of religion or belief and equality between women and men. During that week, he also participated in several initiatives organized by civil society organizations.

15. On 27 November 2013, the Special Rapporteur participated in the sixth session of the Forum on Minority Issues, held in Geneva, as well as in a number of related side events.

III. Tackling manifestations of collective religious hatred

A. Introductory remarks

16. Manifestations of collective hatred poison relationships between communities, threaten individuals and groups and are a source of innumerable human rights violations perpetrated by State agencies and/or non-State actors. The various forms of collective hatred also include religious hatred. While a generally agreed definition of this phenomenon does not exist, the Special Rapporteur understands by "collective religious hatred" any joint manifestations of intense and irrational emotions of opprobrium, enmity and animosity towards a specific target group or individual[179] that are proclaimed in the name of a particular religion or

---

[178] See paragraph 44 for further information regarding this round table.
[179] See the definition of "hatred" in principle 12.1 (i) of the Camden Principles on Freedom of Expression and Equality. Available from www.article19.org/data/

belief. Such manifestations may be made with the intention of defending certain religious or belief-related truth claims, practices, norms or identities against perceived or imagined threats.[180] While frequently targeting believers of a competing persuasion, or non-believers, religiously motivated hatred may also affect internal critics, dissidents, "heretics", or converts from within one's own religious community.

17.   In practice, manifestations of collective religious hatred frequently overlap with national, racial, ethnic or other forms of hatred, and in many situations it may seem impossible to clearly separate these phenomena. As a result, the label "religion" can sometimes be imprecise and problematic when used to describe complex phenomena and motives of collective hatred. Nevertheless it remains obvious that religions and beliefs can serve as powerful demarcators of "us-versus-them" groupings. Unfortunately, there are many examples testifying to this destructive potential of religion. At the same time, one should always bear in mind that anti-hatred movements exist within all religions and that most adherents of the different religious and belief traditions are committed to practising their faith as a source of peace, charity and compassion, rather than of hostility and hatred.

18.   The Special Rapporteur's rationale for focusing the present thematic report on manifestations of collective religious hatred is twofold. On the one hand, collective religious hatred is a source of many violations of the right to freedom of thought, conscience, religion or belief as enshrined in article 18 of the Universal Declaration of Human Rights, article 18 of the International Covenant on Civil and Political Rights and other international human rights instruments. A better understanding of this disturbing phenomenon is required in order to prevent human rights abuses in this area. On the other hand, securing freedom of religion or belief alongside other human rights can help eliminate the root causes of collective religious hatred by establishing trust within societies and between communities on the basis of respect for everyone's religious or belief-related convictions and practices.

---

files/pdfs/standards/the-camden-principles-on-freedom-of-expression-and-equality.pdf.

[180]   See also A/HRC/13/40.

B. Collective religious hatred and its root causes

1. Not a "natural phenomenon"

19. Manifestations of collective hatred, including religious hatred, can set in motion a seemingly unstoppable negative dynamic. However, manifestations of hatred do not "erupt" like a volcano. Rather, they are caused by human beings, that is, by human action and omission. For instance, populist politicians attract followers by offering simplistic explanations for complex societal problems; advocates of hatred poison intergroup relations by stirring up resentment for short-sighted political or economic gains; lack of trust in public institutions may exacerbate an existing atmosphere of suspicion in society; and parts of the population may be all too willing to replace political common sense with the snappy slogans of hatred.

20. What renders policies of hatred so unfortunately "attractive" in the eyes of their followers is that they provide scapegoats on whom to project multiple fears. Obviously, fear is a basic emotion and feature of human life. Unlike animals, whose fears are triggered by imminent dangers to their physical survival, human beings can imagine a broad range of potential threats — even far-fetched or statistically unlikely ones — to which they feel directly or indirectly exposed. Moreover, given the complexity of the human condition, fears can be connected to many different interests, such as social and economic status, the educational prospects of one's children or the long-term development of one's community. People may also fear for their religious identities — both as individuals and as communities. For instance, rapid changes in societies may cause feelings of a gradual dissolution of one's familiar religious lifeworld and concomitant fears of a decline in religious values.

21. Fear is a necessary and useful sentiment as long as it is balanced by common sense and realistic analysis. However, fear is often quite a "narcissistic emotion".[181] Unlike compassion, which requires openness to the perspectives of others and a readiness to move beyond one's own selfish interests, fear can breed narrow-mindedness among individuals and groups. The emotional under-complexity of fear, combined with an over-complexity of imagined reasons for being fearful, creates a demand for answers which are at the same time simplistic and all-encompassing.

---

[181] Martha C. Nussbaum, *The New Religious Intolerance: Overcoming the Politics of Fear in an Anxious Age* (Cambridge/Massachusetts, Harvard University Press, 2012), pp. 20 ff.

People wish to know — and sometimes pretend to know — on whom they can project their multiple fears.

22. Objects of fear are typically imagined as both powerful and, at the same time, deserving of contempt. For example, the Special Rapporteur once heard malicious rumours that members of a religious minority running an underwear factory allegedly contaminate female underwear with a chemical substance in order to reduce the fertility rate of the majority population. As a result of those rumours, the factory was likely to be driven into bankruptcy. However bizarre this example may sound, this type of rumour-mongering is in fact quite typical of hate propaganda, in that religious or belief minorities — including even tiny minorities — are frequently portrayed as wielding some surreptitious power by which they allegedly pose a threat to the majority society. Moreover, the way in which they are said to exercise their mysterious power is imagined as clandestine, unfair and utterly contemptible. In the above-mentioned case, the suggestion of surreptitious attacks against women may furthermore evoke atavistic male attitudes of wishing to protect female community members from external threats — this is only one example indicating that hate propaganda also needs to be studied systematically from a gender perspective (see A/68/290).

23. The combination of fear and contempt occurs regularly in hate propaganda, including in manifestations of collective religious hatred. Fear can even escalate into collective paranoia, and contempt can lead to acts of public dehumanization. Anti-Semitic conspiracy theories may be the most intensively studied and one of the most malign examples. While ascribing to the Jews some manipulative power by which they would allegedly threaten societies, the Nazis at the same time maliciously portrayed Jews as being allegedly driven by greed, malevolence and other primitive motives, an approach also employed by other promoters of anti-Semitism, both past and present.

24. The peculiar pattern of combining fear and contempt displays itself in numerous hate manifestations targeting members of religious minorities or individual dissenters who are imagined as clandestinely operating in the interest of foreign powers or otherwise exercising some pernicious influence. In response to these combined sentiments of fear and contempt, two sources of aggressiveness can merge into a toxic mix, that is, aggressiveness stemming from imagined threats and aggressiveness stemming from the pretence of one's own collective superiority.

2.   Aggravating political circumstances

(a) Endemic corruption

25. The likelihood of collective manifestations of religious hatred largely depends on the general climate, and the overall context, of a society. One widespread negatively contributing factor is that of endemic corruption, that is, corruption pervading a society to such a degree that it largely shapes social interaction and expectations in general. In a country in which people experience corruption as affecting all sectors of societal life, they can hardly develop a reasonable trust in the fair functioning of public institutions. However, public institutions play an indispensable role in facilitating the peaceful coexistence of people of diverse religious and belief-related orientations. Without reasonable trust in public institutions, a public space to which everyone has equal access and in which religious, philosophical, ethical and political pluralism may freely unfold cannot be sustained. Moreover, persons living in a society characterized by endemic corruption may not have many alternatives to organizing their lives within their own more or less narrow networks, groups or communities. This can foster an inward-looking mentality, in which people strongly cling to their own groupings while largely avoiding meaningful communication with people outside of their own circles. There are many examples of religion becoming a defining feature of such groupings, thus further contributing to the overall fragmentation of society and the hardening of "us-versus-them" demarcations. By undermining the institutional and legal foundations of society, and providing a sense of a moral and legal vacuum, uncertainty and insecurity, endemic corruption may create a breeding ground for collective religious narrow-mindedness in which religious diversity is generally perceived as threatening the position of one's own group. This may explain some of the extreme hostility that religious communities at times display towards the admission of other religions or beliefs, even minority ones, into the existing infrastructure of their society.[182]

(b) Political authoritarianism

26. Another aggravating factor is a climate of political authoritarianism which discourages people from communicating openly and participating actively in public debates. Indeed, the most important antidote to existing, or emerging, mistrust between groups of people is the reality check

---

[182]   A/HRC/19/60, paras. 20–73.

facilitated by frank intergroup communication and open public discourse. Without an encouraging communicative atmosphere in society, there is always the danger that negative anecdotal evidence associated with unfamiliar religious communities, minorities or dissenting individuals will remain exclusively within closed circles, including Internet chat rooms, while never being exposed to any open communication and public critical discussions. Rumours and gossip which remain unchecked by any counter-evidence and counterarguments can easily escalate into fully fledged conspiracy theories against unwelcome religious competitors or other religious groups. This increases the likelihood of religious hatred becoming an influential factor in social and political life. Moreover, when attempting to curb public criticism of their own political performance, authoritarian Governments may easily succumb to the temptation to blame existing problems and obvious political failures on religious or belief minorities, thus further contributing to an atmosphere of paranoia and scapegoating.

(c) Narrow identity politics

27. Governments may also instrumentalize religion as a means of shaping and reinforcing narrow concepts of national identity, tapping into feelings of religious belonging for the purposes of strengthening political loyalty. No religion or belief is per se immune from being utilized in such a way. Moreover, such instrumentalization of religion can occur in many different political or constitutional settings. Not only in countries that profess an official State religion but also in many formally secular States, religion has been harnessed to promote national unity and societal homogeneity through the invocation of one predominant cultural and/or religious legacy to which all citizens are supposed to relate in a positive manner. However, utilizing religion for the purposes of fostering national identity politics harbours serious risks of increased discrimination against members of religious minorities, as well as hostility towards those perceived as not belonging to the mainstream national-religious identity. Besides being viewed as religiously different, members of minorities, or individuals with dissenting religious views, may thus additionally be suspected of undermining national unity and endangering the future development of the nation. This can increase the likelihood of manifestations of collective religious hatred occurring in which national and religious hatred blend into one another. Typical target groups are members of immigrant religious communities or new religious movements who are often stigmatized as not fitting into the prevailing reli-

gious and national makeup of the country or even characterized as potential traitors. But members of long-standing religious minorities in a
country, many of which simultaneously constitute ethnic minorities, can
similarly be subject to stigmatization and accused of threatening national
unity.

3.   *Counter tendencies from within religions and beliefs: religious and
     belief communities as positive factors of societal resilience*

28.   The three above-mentioned aggravating political factors — endemic
corruption, an authoritarian atmosphere and the harnessing of religion
for narrow identity politics — serve as salient examples. While not constituting an exhaustive list of negative factors, they can mutually reinforce
one another, thus possibly further speeding up the vicious cycle of mistrust, narrow-mindedness, hysteria, scapegoating and rumours that
arouse contempt against certain religious or belief groups.

29.   However, the Special Rapporteur would like to reiterate that this vicious circle does not have the status of a natural law. It should never be
treated as something that is unavoidable. Although he experiences many
negative examples of religious hatred in his daily work, the Special Rapporteur also regularly meets with people from different religious or belief-related backgrounds — religious leaders as well as ordinary community members — who successfully and actively work to overcome these
destructive tendencies. Indeed, many people understand their religion or
belief as a source of broad-mindedness rather than narrow-mindedness,
and of open-heartedness and compassion rather than fear and contempt.
The Special Rapporteur has witnessed numerous positive examples, such
as during his country visit to Sierra Leone in July 2013, where he was impressed by how amicably religious communities — Muslims, Christians
and others — work together and cooperate on a daily basis in rebuilding
the country after a recent history of civil war. This is possible since religious community leaders had successfully managed to keep religion out
of the dynamics of fragmentation and escalation of violence (see
A/HRC/25/58/Add.1). Likewise, during his country visit to Jordan in September 2013, the Special Rapporteur witnessed much good will and
commitment to preserve the positive climate of interreligious harmony
within an increasingly difficult regional environment (see A/HRC/25/
58/Add.2).

30.   In general, the Special Rapporteur has the impression that the potential of religious or belief communities to become positive factors of

societal resilience against manifestations of collective hatred still requires further exploration in order to be fully understood. He thinks this is a fascinating area for research, practical experimentation and exchange of experiences.

C. Building trust on the basis of freedom of religion or belief

1. Respecting everyone's right to freedom of religion or belief

31. If it is true that collective hatred typically originates from combined sentiments of unreasonable fear and contempt, then it follows that policies of countering hatred must invest in trust-building based on universal respect for human dignity. Building trust with the purpose of overcoming unreasonable fears requires well-functioning public institutions, as well as activities that encourage and facilitate communication. Both levels are intertwined: whereas public institutions necessarily presuppose a certain level of public communication, the prospects of meaningful and sustained communication generally increase with an infrastructure of institutions that provide a public sphere to which everyone can have equal access.

32. In policies specifically addressing religious hatred and its root causes, freedom of religion or belief has a pivotal function. Like other human rights, freedom of religion or belief is a part of the development of an infrastructure of public institutions at national, regional and international levels, including courts, ombudsman institutions, national human rights institutions and international monitoring bodies. At the same time, freedom of religion or belief has far-reaching implications for communication — which, incidentally, also accounts for its close interrelatedness with freedom of expression. Finally, freedom of religion or belief institutionalizes due respect for all human beings as potential holders of profound, identity-shaping convictions and conviction-based practices.

33. Respect is a key term for the understanding of human rights in general and in particular for freedom of religion or belief. In the human rights framework, respect always relates to human beings, as evidenced in the opening sentence of the preamble of the Universal Declaration of Human Rights, which proclaims the "recognition of the inherent dignity and of the equal and inalienable rights of all members of the human family". In the face of widespread misunderstandings, it cannot be emphasized enough that freedom of religion or belief does not provide respect

to religions as such; instead it empowers human beings in the broad field of religion and belief. The idea of protecting the honour of religions themselves would clearly be at variance with the human rights approach (see A/68/290).

34. For many people around the world, religious convictions, spiritual values, a sense of sacredness, community-related ceremonies and other religious norms and practices constitute an essential part of their daily lives and may be the backbone of their individual and communitarian identities. Working on behalf of freedom of religion or belief requires an appreciation of the deep emotional attachment and loyalty that many believers feel to their religion or belief. However, to take religions and beliefs seriously in all their dimensions also implies taking pluralism seriously, including sometimes irreconcilable differences in world views and practices. What is sacred for one community may remain opaque to another community, and the values that one group holds in high esteem may appear incomprehensible to some others. This is one of the reasons why respect in the framework of human rights cannot immediately be accorded to the particular contents of religions or beliefs — that is, religious truth claims, norms, practices or identities — but only to human beings as those who hold, cherish, develop and try to live up to such convictions and norms.

35. Moreover, as the Human Rights Committee has pointed out in its general comment No. 22 (1993), freedom of religion or belief applies to a broad variety of convictions and conviction-based practices, beyond any predefined lists of "classical" religions. In the words of the Committee: "Article 18 protects theistic, non-theistic and atheistic beliefs, as well as the right not to profess any religion or belief. The terms belief and religion are to be broadly construed. Article 18 is not limited in its application to traditional religions or to religions and beliefs with institutional characteristics or practices analogous to those of traditional religions."[183]

2. Trust-building through public institutions

36. Sustainable trust within a society presupposes an infrastructure of public institutions operating in the interest of all. In connection with other human rights, freedom of religion or belief is important for the progressive development of society and requires the development of public institutions at international, regional and national levels. These institutional implications of the right to freedom of religion or belief con-

---

[183] General comment No. 22, para. 2.

stitute an important aspect of its comprehensive trust-building function in society.

37. Under international law, States serve as the formal guarantors of human rights, including freedom of religion or belief. In order to operate as trustworthy guarantors of freedom of religion or belief for everyone, States should provide an open, inclusive framework in which religious or belief pluralism can unfold freely and without discrimination. This requires overcoming any exclusivist settings. Above all, what must be overcome is an understanding in which the State identifies itself with one particular religion or belief at the expense of an equal and non-discriminatory treatment of followers of other persuasions. Such exclusivist settings do not only occur in States which have formally embraced an official religion or a State religion. Even in many supposedly religiously neutral or secular States, Governments may be tempted to invoke one particular religion as the basis of its political legitimacy or with the purpose of mobilizing followers by tapping into emotions of religious loyalty. Ample experience demonstrates that the use of religion in the context of national identity politics always harbours increased risks of discrimination against minorities, in particular against members of immigrant religious communities or new religious movements, who often are stigmatized as allegedly endangering national cohesion. As elaborated above, this can become the breeding ground for manifestations of collective religious hatred stoked by State agencies, non-State actors or a combination of both.

38. International human rights law does not prescribe one particular model of how the relationship between State and religion should be organized, and State religions or official religions are not per se prohibited under international human rights law. However, as the Human Rights Committee has pointed out, States should ensure that having an official religion — or making reference in constitutional or legal provisions to the historical role of a particular religion — does not lead to a de jure or de facto discrimination against members of other religions and beliefs. In its general comment No. 22, the Committee insisted that "the fact that a religion is recognized as a State religion or that it is established as official or traditional or that its followers comprise the majority of the population, shall not result in any impairment of the enjoyment of any of the rights under the Covenant, including articles 18 and 27, nor in any discrimination against adherents of other religions or non-believers."[184]

---

[184] Ibid., para. 9.

39. Notwithstanding, it seems difficult, if not impossible, to conceive of an application of the concept of an official "State religion" that in practice does not have adverse effects on religious minorities, thus discriminating against their members.[185]

40. An open constitutional framework that allows free manifestations of existing or emerging religious pluralism on the basis of equal respect for all is a sine qua non of any policy directed towards eliminating collective religious hatred by building trust through public institutions. This in turn requires a disentangling of any exclusivist relations between the State and particular religions or beliefs. Of course, this does not mean that all States will end up having the same structure of relations with religious communities. Moreover, the process of disentanglement may take time, and there remains space for experimentation and institutional diversity in this field, including in response to different historical legacies. In practice, however, States will hardly be able to function as trustworthy guarantors of freedom of religion or belief for everyone as long as exclusivist settings remain unchallenged.

3. Trust-building through communication

41. The communicative aspects of trust-building are no less important than the institutional aspects. In the context of religious diversity, communication activities should cover at least three different dimensions: (a) intergroup communication; (b) outreach activities of the State towards religious communities; and (c) creation of an atmosphere in which public debates on religious issues can flourish. Freedom of religion or belief has to play a role across all these dimensions.

(a) Intergroup communication

42. Regular communication across religious boundaries is the most important precondition for fostering understanding and preventing or overcoming mistrust between religious or belief groups (which is one of the root causes of collective religious hatred). When conducted on an equal footing and in a sustained manner, that is, in ways that go beyond mere superficial brief encounters, interreligious communication can help replace stereotypes and prejudices by real experiences. Even though these experiences may not always be positive, they can nonetheless chal-

---

[185] See the 2012 report of the Special Rapporteur on freedom of religion or belief (A/HRC/19/60), para. 66, and his 2012 interim report (A/67/303), para. 47.

lenge stereotypical us-versus-them demarcations which are unlikely to ever do justice to the complex realities of human beings.

43. The Special Rapporteur would like to emphasize in this context that, in his view, the potential of interreligious communication to lead to policies that contribute to the elimination of religious hatred still needs to be fully explored. He has often observed an attitude of merely lukewarm support for systematic activities in this field. Whereas hardly anyone would express a straightforward opposition to interreligious communication, its political significance typically remains underestimated.

44. However, the Special Rapporteur has had the opportunity to directly experience the beneficial impact of a highly developed culture of inter- and intrareligious communication, for instance during his country visit to Sierra Leone, where the Interreligious Council has become a key factor in a reunited country that until a decade ago had been torn by civil war (see A/HRC/25/58/Add.1). Likewise, during his visit to Jordan he met with many people from the Government, religious communities and civil society organizations whose commitment in this field helps to keep society together in an increasingly volatile region (see A/HRC/25/58/Add.2). In addition, there seems to be an improved climate of interreligious communication and cooperation in Cyprus, which the Special Rapporteur witnessed during the ground-breaking interreligious round tables held in Nicosia in September 2013.[186]

45. Under freedom of religion or belief, States have an obligation to promote interreligious communication and take active measures in this area. One should not underestimate the possible symbolic impact of interreligious communication being publicly acknowledged and promoted by State representatives. Governments can support interreligious dialogue in a number of ways, for example by providing financial support for existing projects or for the creation of new forums. In addition, Governments have the possibility to directly invite religious or belief groups

---

[186] On 22 October 2013 the Special Rapporteur hailed a key breakthrough in interfaith communication reached by a cross section of religious leaders in Cyprus. The agreement allowed Muslim and Greek Orthodox religious leaders to cross the Green Line dividing the island. The Special Rapporteur praised the religious leaders, and encouraged them to create an inclusive institutional framework to promote ongoing communication, such as an interreligious council for peace in Cyprus. The breakthrough became possible after the first interreligious round table held in Cyprus on 12 September 2013, organized by the Office of the Religious Track of the Cyprus Peace Process, under the auspices of the Embassy of Sweden, and in cooperation with OHCHR.

to meetings. The "neutral" space provided by State institutions can help facilitate dialogue even between groups which, perhaps due to a history of conflicts or other negative factors, would not be likely to meet on their own initiative. For example, when visiting the Republic of Moldova (in 2011), the Special Rapporteur attended a meeting of representatives of different religious leaders convened by the Ministry of Justice. It was evident from the uneasy atmosphere between participants of different communities that a culture of interreligious communication still needs to be further developed in that country and that this is unlikely to happen, unless the State undertakes more proactive initiatives in this field (see A/HRC/19/60/Add.2).

46. As pointed out in the Special Rapporteur's thematic report on the role of the State in this area (A/66/156, paras. 21–69), State activities should cover both formal and informal interreligious communication, that is, dialogue projects undertaken explicitly under the auspices of religious differences as well as forms of communication in which people meet without necessarily displaying their respective religious identities. State commitment in the field of interreligious communication should always take into account the existing and emerging diversity, including intrareligious differences, while also ensuring the substantive participation of women (who continue to be largely discriminated against in many dialogue projects). Moreover, school education also deserves special attention in this context, since the school is arguably the most influential institution in which interreligious communication (both formal and informal) can be experienced on a daily basis, during the formative years of young people and with the prospects of promoting sustained open-mindedness within the younger generation.[187] Fair information and real experiences with religious or belief pluralism, as part of normal public and private life, are among the most important preconditions for developing societal resilience against manifestations of collective religious hatred.

(b) Early warning and outreach by the State towards religious communities

47. While interreligious communication can build trust between communities, outreach activities by the State should also aim to establish trustful relations between representatives of the State administration

---

[187] See A/HRC/16/53, paras. 20–62. See also the Toledo Guiding Principles on Teaching about Religions and Beliefs in Public Schools.

and representatives or members of various religious communities. Communication channels should be a two-way process. On the one hand, it is important for Government agencies to be able to reach out to communities, in particular during crisis situations when public manifestations of collective hatred increase the risks of escalation into intergroup or other forms of violence. On the other hand, it is equally important for religious communities to have easy access to persons acting as focal points within the administration so they can alert them to emerging hostilities before a crisis situation fully unfolds its destructive dynamics.

48. During the first conference held in the context of the Istanbul Process for Combating Intolerance and Discrimination Based on Religion or Belief in December 2011 in Washington D.C.,[188] the Special Rapporteur had the chance to witness how civil servants operating as focal points within the administration worked together with members of various religious communities. They simulated a fictitious crisis situation in order to demonstrate how to communicate quickly and efficiently and how to decide on practical measures if the need were to arise. The Special Rapporteur was impressed by the degree of professionalism with which participants interacted. Obviously, they had known one another for quite some time and had established trustful working relations. For outreach activities to be successful it seems imperative that communication channels do not only exist in theory; they must also be regularly used in practice. During an informal visit to Sweden, the Special Rapporteur heard some positive examples of how Government agencies and municipalities maintain regular contact with faith-based communities in Sweden on issues relating to crisis preparedness and security, and of how they cooperate together to help forge greater societal trust and prevent incidents of religious violence.[189]

---

[188] Linked to Human Rights Council resolution 16/18 on combating intolerance, negative stereotyping and stigmatization of, and discrimination, incitement to violence and violence against, persons based on religion or belief, agreed by consensus, the Istanbul Process started a number of activities to explore appropriate policies and measures in this area.

[189] Sweden has created a national-level advisory group for faith communities, where the Swedish Civil Contingencies Agency and the Swedish Commission for Government Support to Faith Communities are responsible for maintaining contacts with faith communities in Sweden on crisis-related issues. This advisory group meets several times per year, and it played a key role in facilitating inter-religious dialogue following the attacks on immigrants in Malmo in 2010. At the local level, crisis preparedness is organized by the Swedish municipalities, which are responsible for building networks involving governmental agencies, busi-

49. Manifestations of collective hatred do not usually occur without prior warning signals, and they are quite often even publicly announced by those orchestrating them. However, even if all the early warning signs are visible, this does not often lead to appropriate early action, perhaps due to a lack of experience or to a lack of imagination about how to react appropriately and in due time. In order to close the gap between early warning and early action, regular outreach meetings are recommended between focal points in the administration and influential members of religious communities. Such meetings can include practical exercises, similar to the manoeuvres conducted by fire brigades or other crisis response agencies. It is important for States to be proactively prepared for crises resulting from manifestations of collective hatred and to keep the necessary communication channels open by using them on a regular basis. Practical training manoeuvres could be conducted at national and municipal levels, and it might also be useful to exchange both negative and positive experiences in this area within appropriate United Nations forums such as the Alliance of Civilizations.

50. Early warning signs identified by the different human rights mechanisms need to reach the political and conflict-prevention bodies of the United Nations. Effective channels of communication are needed between different parts of the United Nations system to enable decision makers to take appropriate and timely action. In this context, the Special Rapporteur commends a recent document on preventing atrocity crimes, prepared by the Office on Genocide Prevention and the Responsibility to Protect, in particular its paragraphs on the need to prepare contingency plans.[190]

(c) Atmosphere in which public debates on religious issues can flourish

51. As outlined earlier, an authoritarian climate that discourages people from publicly expressing their various concerns tends to increase the likelihood of manifestations of religious hatred occurring in a country. Where a culture of free public discourse does not exist, negative rumours are likely to remain within closed circles and to avoid sufficient exposure

---

ness, volunteer and community organizations and religious communities, to ensure functioning cooperation between all relevant parties whenever a crisis occurs.

[190] See Office on Genocide Prevention and the Responsibility to Protect, "Preventing incitement: policy options for action", presented in a side event at the sixth session of the Forum on Minority Issues, on 27 November 2013.

to critical public scrutiny. Even worse, those who have lived for a long time in a repressive climate may develop a distorted "mentality of suspicion", where they assume hidden agendas. As a consequence, the dichotomy between thinking and speaking, which people may have experienced in their own personal behaviour, is often also ascribed to other individuals or groups. Likewise, the dichotomy between private narratives and public propositions may become the interpretative background for any public statements made by individuals, groups or organizations, resulting in a society that is marked by general mistrust and suspicion. As a result, trustful communication may become increasingly difficult and may yield more and more to mere tactical rhetorical manoeuvres. In extreme cases this may culminate in a total breakdown of any meaningful intergroup communication, a collapse of the culture of public discourse and in unchecked prejudices and misconceptions.

52. The most promising antidote to a society beleaguered by a combination of paranoia and contempt is a well-developed culture of public discourse in which people feel encouraged to exercise their freedom of expression. Such a culture should also allow for the expression of any concerns, worries, anxieties and less pleasant experiences in the area of religious pluralism. Living together in a pluralistic society can certainly be enriching, but it is not always easy and at times can even become quite challenging. When people feel they have the freedom to publicly express any frustrations and irritations that may arise from their adverse experiences, instead of merely telling negative stories in private circles, there remains a good chance that counter-evidence and the promulgation of alternative narratives may help restore realistic proportion and perspective. This may prevent negative experiences from hardening into fixed prejudices. A culture of public discourse should thus enable people to conduct controversial discussions in the area of religious diversity, which naturally must also accommodate criticism of certain religions or even of religion in general.

53. Attempts to replace negative stereotypes about other religious communities or minorities by superficially imposing positive language and discouraging the articulation of adverse experiences are only likely to raise suspicion in the long run. A more promising strategy aims at overcoming misperceptions by facilitating the articulation of real experiences in the interaction of human beings, both as individuals and as communities. After all, sustainable trust can develop only on the basis of realism and by taking seriously the experiences that people have. Inter alia, such a realist strategy presupposes the availability of differentiated

information by nuanced research and reporting, including on religious community issues. Investigative journalism, which is often wrongly suspected of undermining social peace, can serve as a necessary ingredient of trust-building policies, since it may help to promote a climate of experience-based common sense in public life. Moreover, it is imperative that members of minorities, including religious or belief minorities, have access to fair opportunities to articulate their own experiences, interests and perspectives in the public domain through the existence of community media, as well as through effective participation in media that caters for more mainstream audiences (including new digital and online media).

D. Responding to advocacy of national, racial or religious hatred that constitutes incitement to discrimination, hostility or violence

1.   The genesis of the Rabat Plan of Action

54.   Sentiments expressing hatred can escalate into real acts of discrimination, hostility or violence. This often happens as a result of deliberate incitement to such acts. The question of how States and other stakeholders should prevent, or react to, incidents motivated by hatred has attracted the increased attention of the international community. It seems obvious that States have to tackle this problem by developing effective preventive and coping strategies. In extreme situations this may also include restrictive measures, such as prohibiting certain speech acts. However, when resorting to prohibitions and other restrictive measures, States should always make sure that this does not have a chilling effect on people's willingness to communicate freely and frankly, including on controversial religious issues. Any limitations to freedom of expression or other human rights deemed necessary in this respect must comply with all the criteria laid down in respective international human rights standards.

55.   In order to find appropriate solutions, OHCHR conducted a series of regional expert workshops, with broad participation of representatives from Governments, civil society, academia, United Nations treaty bodies and special procedures.[191] A wrap-up expert workshop was convened in

---

[191]   The expert workshops took place in Vienna, Nairobi, Bangkok and Santiago in 2011. Participants included representatives from Governments, representatives from intergovernmental organizations, civil society organizations (in particular the organization Article 19: Global Campaign for Free Expression), academics of

Rabat in October 2012 and led to the elaboration of the Rabat Plan of Action on the prohibition of advocacy of national, racial or religious hatred that constitutes incitement to discrimination, hostility or violence.[192] OHCHR launched the Rabat Plan of Action publicly in Geneva in February 2013.

56.   The title of the Rabat Plan of Action includes a quote from article 20 of the International Covenant on Civil and Political Rights, which in its second paragraph provides: "Any advocacy of national, racial or religious hatred that constitutes incitement to discrimination, hostility or violence shall be prohibited by law." It cannot be emphasized enough that this provision does not demand a prohibition of sharp or even hostile speech in general; instead it concentrates on such forms of hatred advocacy that constitute "incitement" to real acts of discrimination, hostility or violence. One of the main purposes of the Rabat Plan of Action is to raise awareness and understanding of article 20, paragraph 2, of the Covenant, while interpreting it consistently in conjunction with other human rights, in particular article 18 (freedom of religion or belief) and article 19 (freedom of expression) of the Covenant.[193]

57.   The Rabat Plan of Action acknowledges that "there has been a number of incidents in recent years, in different parts of the world, which have brought renewed attention to the issue of incitement to hatred."[194] As one of the reasons for this renewed attention, the text of the plan cites the challenge "to contain the negative effects of a manipulation of race, ethnic origin and religion and to guard against the adverse use of con-

---

different disciplines, experts working within OHCHR, members of the Human Rights Committee and the Committee on the Elimination of Racial Discrimination, and the Special Rapporteur on the promotion and protection of the right to freedom of opinion and expression, the Special Rapporteur on contemporary forms of racism, racial discrimination, xenophobia and related intolerance and the Special Rapporteur on freedom of religion or belief. All written contributions and meeting reports are available online from www.ohchr.org/EN/Issues/Free domOpinion/Articles19-20/Pages/ExpertsPapers.aspx.

[192]   See A/HRC/22/17/Add.4, annex, appendix.

[193]   In this context, the Rabat Plan of Action, inter alia, refers to Human Rights Council resolution 16/18. The Plan of Action furthermore draws on the Human Rights Committee's general comment No. 34 (2011) on the freedoms of opinion and expression. Both documents have also dealt with article 20, paragraph 2, of the International Covenant on Civil and Political Rights, which constitutes the main reference norm within the Rabat Plan of Action, as already indicated in its title.

[194]   A/HRC/22/17/Add.4, annex, appendix, para. 7.

cepts of national unity or national identity, which are often instrumentalized for, inter alia, political and electoral purposes."[195]

2. The interdependence between freedom of religion or belief and freedom of expression

58. The Rabat Plan of Action places great emphasis on the need to uphold a climate of free communication and public discourse based on freedom of expression, freedom of religion or belief and various other freedoms. It establishes a high threshold for imposing limitations on freedom of expression, for identifying incitement to hatred and for the application of article 20 of the International Covenant on Civil and Political Rights. It furthermore underlines that "freedom of expression is essential to creating an environment in which constructive discussion about religious matters could be held."[196] The Rabat Plan of Action explicitly endorses what the Human Rights Committee has clarified in its general comment No. 34, namely that prohibitions enacted under article 20, paragraph 2, of the International Covenant on Civil and Political Rights must comply with the strict requirements of article 19, paragraph 3, as well as such articles as 2, 5, 17, 18 and 26 of the Covenant.[197] Accordingly, the guarantees of freedom of expression as enshrined in article 19 of the Covenant can never be circumvented by invoking article 20. Prohibitions must be precisely defined and must be enacted without any discriminatory intention or effect. In addition, the Rabat Plan of Action presents a six-part test for assessing whether concrete acts of speech that are aggressive or antagonistic to certain religious or ethnic groups actually amount to "incitement to discrimination, hostility or violence" and are serious enough to warrant prohibitive measures.[198] The six test questions concern: (a) the social and political context; (b) the speaker, for example his or her status and influence; (c) the intent of a speech act, as opposed to mere negligence; (d) its content or form, for example style or degree of provocation; (e) the extent of the speech, for example its public nature

---

[195] Ibid., para. 9.

[196] Ibid., para. 10.

[197] General comment No. 34, para. 48, which is also quoted in the Rabat Plan of Action, para. 17.

[198] This test was proposed to the OHCHR expert workshops by the non-governmental organization Article 19: Global Campaign for Free Expression and later adopted into the Rabat Plan of Action.

and the size of its audience; and (f) the likelihood and imminence of actually causing harm.[199]

59.   In its assessment of existing legislation and jurisprudence on this issue, the Rabat Plan of Action observes a broad variety of statutes and case law, often enacted on an ad hoc basis and lacking in consistency. This can lead to arbitrary reactions and also to overreactions, with chilling effects on freedom of expression or on free manifestations of religious or belief convictions, in particular as regards religious minorities or people with dissenting views. In this context, the Rabat Plan of Action provides: "At the national level, blasphemy laws are counter-productive, since they may result in de facto censure of all inter-religious or belief and intra-religious or belief dialogue, debate and criticism, most of which could be constructive, healthy and needed. In addition, many blasphemy laws afford different levels of protection to different religions and have often proved to be applied in a discriminatory manner."[200] The Rabat Plan of Action therefore recommends that "States that have blasphemy laws should repeal them, as such laws have a stifling impact on the enjoyment of freedom of religion or belief, and healthy dialogue and debate about religion."[201] The Special Rapporteur would like to confirm that, according to his experiences, blasphemy laws typically have intimidating effects on members of religious minorities as well as on critics or dissenters.

60.   The Rabat Plan of Action certainly contributes to an understanding of article 20, paragraph 2, of the International Covenant on Civil and Political Rights, in full appreciation of the significance of freedom of expression and other freedoms. This implies that restrictive legal measures can play a necessary, but only limited, role in preventing or reacting to incidents of incitement. As a consequence, States and other stakeholders should develop more holistic policies that include non-restrictive and non-prohibitive activities: "To tackle the root causes of intolerance, a much broader set of policy measures is necessary, for example in the areas of intercultural dialogue — reciprocal knowledge and interaction —, education on pluralism and diversity, and policies empowering minorities and indigenous people to exercise their right to freedom of expression."[202]

---

[199]   For more details, see the Rabat Plan of Action (A/HRC/22/17/Add.4, annex, appendix), para. 29.

[200]   Ibid., para. 19.

[201]   Ibid., para. 25.

[202]   Ibid., para. 37.

61. Indeed, one of the most remarkable messages contained in the Rabat Plan of Action is that what we require above all in order to prevent and respond to incidents of incitement to hatred are policies which promote a creative and productive use of freedom of expression. For instance, in order to challenge advocates of religious hatred in their claims to speak in the name of "the silent majority", it is important that the majority does not remain silent. Civil society activities which visibly and audibly reject advocacy of religious hatred that constitutes incitement to discrimination, hostility or violence can have very practical effects in discouraging such advocacy, while at the same time showing solidarity and support for their targets. In any such activities, the gender dimension warrants special attention, as women frequently suffer from complex and intersectional stigmatization which renders them particularly vulnerable to hate propaganda and concomitant manifestations of contempt.

62. The Rabat Plan of Action specifically calls upon political and religious leaders to speak out firmly and promptly against intolerance, discriminatory stereotyping and instances of hate speech.[203] They should also refrain from using messages of intolerance or expressions which may incite to religious violence and lead to manifestations of collective religious hatred. Religious leaders can play a critical role in societies at risk of large-scale violence, by spreading positive messages of acceptance, reconciliation, peace and respect for diversity.[204]

63. Other measures recommended in the Rabat Plan of Action include voluntary ethical guidelines for media reporting and self-regulatory supervision, support for community media, facilitation of a non-discriminatory participation of religious minorities within mainstream media and encouragement of interreligious and intrareligious dialogue initiatives, public awareness-raising campaigns and educational efforts in schools. It is worth noting that actors in the area of new information technologies can also play an important role through the promotion of religious tolerance in the digital space. Artists, journalists, lawyers and human rights defenders can help to make a difference as well, especially when their statements and actions transcend religious boundaries and denounce religious intolerance.[205]

---

[203] Ibid., para. 36.
[204] Report of the Special Rapporteur on freedom of religion or belief (A/HRC/13/40), para. 60.
[205] Ibid., para. 62.

64. The Special Rapporteur would like to conclude by reiterating that freedom of religion or belief and freedom of expression, as enshrined respectively in articles 18 and 19, respectively, of both the Universal Declaration of Human Rights and the International Covenant on Civil and Political Rights, are "neighbouring rights" in a literal as well as metaphorical sense.[206] They are interdependent and mutually reinforcing and can serve as complementary safeguards of communicative freedom. This positive interrelation between freedom of religion or belief and freedom of expression should guide policies designed to combat negative stereotypes, prejudice and other narrow-minded attitudes, which can best be tackled in an environment that enables more meaningful intergroup communication, communicative outreach activities and public discussion of any controversies.

IV. Conclusions and recommendations

65. Manifestations of collective religious hatred, albeit sometimes leading to a seemingly unstoppable destructive dynamic, are not natural phenomena; they are caused by human action and/or omission. States and other stakeholders therefore have a shared responsibility to combat collective religious hatred, which presupposes an understanding of its root causes and of any aggravating political circumstances.

66. Sentiments of collective religious hatred are often caused by a combination of fear and contempt, which can trigger a vicious circle of mistrust, narrow-mindedness, collective hysteria, contempt-filled rumours and fear of imaginary conspiracies. Aggravating political factors that further increase the likelihood of manifestations of collective religious hatred include: (a) endemic corruption, which typically undermines reasonable trust in public institutions, thus creating inward-looking mentalities and possibly breeding collective narrow-mindedness; (b) an authoritarian political atmosphere that stifles free and frank public debate, creates a "mentality of suspicion" and undermines trust between individuals and groups; and (c) the harnessing of religion for the purpos-

---

[206] Articles 18 and 19 of the Universal Declaration of Human Rights and articles 18 and 19 of the International Covenant on Civil and Political Rights fit into a pattern also widely found elsewhere, including in the European Convention for the Protection of Human Rights and Fundamental Freedoms (arts. 9 and 10), the American Convention on Human Rights (arts. 12 and 13), the African Charter of Human and Peoples' Rights (arts. 8 and 9), and the Charter of Fundamental Rights of the European Union (arts. 10 and 11), as well as in numerous national constitutions.

es of national identity politics, which typically leads to the political marginalization of religious minorities whose members may become easy scapegoats or subjects of prejudice and misperception.

67. Policies intended to counter manifestations of religious hatred must invest in trust-building based on universal respect. By ensuring respect for all human beings as holders of profound, identity-shaping convictions, freedom of religion or belief plays a pivotal role in such anti-hatred policies, both in the area of trust-building through public institutions as well as in the area of trust-building through communication.

68. Trust-building through public institutions presupposes that the State operates as a trustworthy guarantor of freedom of religion or belief for everyone. Dissolving any exclusivist arrangements in the State's relation to religions or beliefs and overcoming all forms of instrumentalization of religion for the purposes of national identity politics serves as a precondition for providing an open, inclusive framework in which religious or belief-related pluralism can unfold freely and without discrimination.

69. Trust-building through communication implies at least three dimensions: (a) intergroup communication with the aim of replacing stereotypical perceptions and ascriptions by real experience and regular encounters with human beings belonging to different religious or belief communities; (b) outreach activities by the State towards religious communities with the purpose of establishing trustful relations and communication channels that can be used in crisis situations as part of contingency planning; and (c) the development of a public culture of open discourse in which rumours, stereotypes and misperceptions can be exposed to the test of public criticism. In all these dimensions States must take an active role in promoting respect for everyone's freedom of thought, conscience, religion or belief.

70. Against this background, the Special Rapporteur would like to formulate the following recommendations:

   a) States and other stakeholders should base their policies of prevention, or response to, manifestations of collective religious hatred firmly on respect for freedom of thought, conscience, religion or belief — a human right which requires a broad understanding and an inclusive implementation, in conjunction with other human rights, in particular that of freedom of expression;

b) States should develop an open constitutional and infrastructural framework to facilitate free and non-discriminatory manifestations of the existing and emerging diversity of religion and belief in the society;

c) States should actively foster the inclusion and integration of religious and other minorities as part of their responsibility to combat religious intolerance and tackle advocacy and manifestations of collective religious hatred;

d) States should implement the Rabat Plan of Action on the prohibition of advocacy of national, racial or religious hatred that constitutes incitement to discrimination, hostility or violence. When developing strategies concerning the implementation of this plan of action, they should invite relevant stakeholders to participate, including religious communities, national human rights institutions, civil society organizations, media representatives and professionals working in education, with the purpose of joining forces and establishing an effective division of labour;

e) Policies of preventing, or reacting to, incidents of incitement to acts of discrimination, hostility or violence, should include a broad range of measures. Restrictive measures, if deemed necessary, should be the last resort and must comply with all the criteria set out in the respective international human rights standards, including in articles 18, 19 and 20 of the International Covenant on Civil and Political Rights. States should repeal blasphemy laws, which typically have a stifling effect on open dialogue and public discourse, often particularly affecting persons belonging to religious minorities;

f) Political and religious leaders, as well as civil society organizations, should actively support and encourage an atmosphere of religious tolerance and help to build societal resilience against manifestations of religious hatred. As stressed in the Rabat Plan of Action, they should refrain from using messages of intolerance or expressions which may incite to religious violence and manifestations of collective religious hatred. They also have a crucial role to play in speaking out firmly and promptly against intolerance, discriminatory stereotyping and instances of hate speech;

g) States and other stakeholders should facilitate a culture of frank public discourse in which people can express their concerns, worries, anxieties and less pleasant experiences in the area of religious or belief pluralism. Encouraging people to express their fears and negative experiences in public, instead of confining them to private circles, opens up opportunities for counter-evidence and alternative narratives that can put things into realistic proportion and perspective. This may help to prevent adverse experiences from hardening into fixed prejudices;

h) States and other stakeholders should encourage inter- and intrareligious communication and take practical initiatives to engage all relevant stakeholders, in full recognition of the existing and emerging pluralism in society. This should also include intergenerational pluralism. A main purpose of inter- and intrareligious communicative efforts should be to replace negative stereotypes and preconceptions with real encounters between real human beings, both as individuals and within their communities. Women (often heavily underrepresented) must always have a substantive share in such initiatives, which should be promoted at the local, national and international levels;

i) States should create accessible focal points within the administration in charge of developing relationships of trust with representatives of different religious or belief communities. Regular meetings — at the municipal, national and regional levels — can help to keep the communication channels open. Such meetings may include practical "manoeuvres" in which fictitious crisis situations are played out to test and develop de-escalation strategies. This may help close the gap between early warning and early action;

j) International forums, such as the United Nations Alliance of Civilizations, as well as existing United Nations mechanisms for the protection and promotion of human rights, should be used to exchange positive experiences of human rights-based de-escalation strategies aimed at preventing, or coping with, manifestations of collective religious hatred and at combating advocacy of religious hatred that constitutes incitement to discrimination, hostility or violence;

k) Public and private media should be encouraged to help over-come religious or belief-related stereotypes by replacing these with more accurate and nuanced information. By promoting more balanced representations, professional journalism, including investigative journalism, can contribute to a public atmosphere of common sense, realism and experience, serving as an antidote to conspiracy theories, misperceptions and public hysteria. As new social media and the Internet have become major tools for fostering advocacy of religious hatred and incitement to discrimination, hostility or violence in many countries, specific efforts should be directed towards understanding and addressing this phenomenon appropriately;

l) The media is encouraged to develop voluntary guidelines for reporting on religious issues, in particular as regards situations of (alleged or factual) religious conflicts. Self-regulatory supervision mechanisms, such as regular peer review, can help to implement such guidelines in ways that fully respect the human right to freedom of expression;

m) Those responsible in public and private media should ensure a fair participation of religious or belief minorities within the media, so that their voices can be heard and become a part of the public discourse. The Camden Principles on Freedom of Expression and Equality can provide guidance in this regard;

n) School education should include fair information on religious and belief-related issues as part of the mandatory curriculum. Such information should take seriously the self-understandings of the respective religious communities, including internal pluralism, thus overcoming mere external descriptions, which often remain stereotypical. School education can also facilitate daily encounters between students of different religious or belief persuasions, thus helping them to experience diversity as something quite natural and serving to inhibit the formation of emotions of disgust towards groups of fellow citizens. Education can also encourage students to better imagine the experience and self-perception of others, especially those from diverse religious, ethnic and cultural contexts;

o) National human rights institutions are encouraged to use the Rabat Plan of Action as a reference document when planning

their activities towards overcoming the root causes of collective religious hatred;

p) The implementation of the Rabat Plan of Action and of Human
Rights Council resolution 16/18 at the national level should also be systematically scrutinized in the context of the universal
periodic review of each State.

8. Chapter: August 2014

I. Introduction

1.   The mandate of the Special Rapporteur on freedom of religion or belief was created by the Commission on Human Rights by its resolution 1986/20 and renewed by the Human Rights Council in its resolution 6/37. At the fourteenth session of the Council, Heiner Bielefeldt was appointed as mandate holder and assumed his function on 1 August 2010. The Council, in its resolution 22/20, renewed the mandate for a further period of three years.

2.   The General Assembly, in its resolution 68/170, strongly condemned all forms of intolerance and of discrimination based on religion or belief, as well as violations of freedom of thought, conscience and religion or belief, and requested the Special Rapporteur to submit an interim report to the Assembly at its sixty-ninth session.

3.   In section II of the present report, the Special Rapporteur provides an overview of his activities since the submission of his previous report to the General Assembly (A/68/290). In section III, he focuses on tackling religious intolerance and discrimination in the workplace. Section IV provides his conclusions and recommendations to various actors in this regard.

II. Activities of the Special Rapporteur

4.   The Special Rapporteur conducted various activities between 1 August 2013 and 31 July 2014 pursuant to Human Rights Council resolutions 6/37, 14/11 and 22/20.

A. Country visits

5.   The Special Rapporteur undertook three official country visits: to Jordan, from 2 to 10 September 2013;[207] Kazakhstan, from 25 March to 5 April 2014; and Viet Nam, from 21 to 31 July 2014.[208] He expresses his appreciation to all his interlocutors and officials for the cooperation they

---

[207]   The report of the visit to Jordan was presented to the Human Rights Council at its 25th session, in March 2014 (A/HRC/25/58/Add.2).

[208]   The reports of the visits to Kazakhstan and Viet Nam will be presented to the Human Rights Council at its 28th session, in March 2015.

extended to him during the visits. Additional official country visits are currently being scheduled. Updated information about the Special Rapporteur's visits and related requests is available on the website of the Office of the United Nations High Commissioner for Human Rights (OHCHR).[209]

B. Communications

6.   The Special Rapporteur deals with individual cases or issues of concern brought to his attention. He sends allegation letters and urgent appeals to States, seeking clarification on credible allegations of incidents and governmental action possibly incompatible with the provisions of the Declaration on the Elimination of All Forms of Intolerance and of Discrimination Based on Religion or Belief (General Assembly resolution 36/55).

7.   The Special Rapporteur regularly receives complaints about human rights violations committed against individuals and groups from various religious or belief backgrounds, which he takes up with the concerned States, as appropriate. Since the creation of the mandate, the Special Rapporteurs have sent more than 1,350 allegation letters and urgent appeals to a total of 130 States. The communications sent between 1 March 2013 and 28 February 2014 and the replies received from Governments before 30 April 2014 are included in the latest communications reports (A/HRC/24/21, A/HRC/25/74 and A/HRC/26/21).

C. Presentations and consultations

8.   On 27 and 28 August 2013, the Special Rapporteur conducted a number of seminars organized by State institutions and civil society organizations in Helsinki.

9.   On 12 September 2013, the Special Rapporteur conducted a follow-up visit to Cyprus, where he participated in the first interreligious round table, organized by the Office of the Religious Track of the Cyprus Peace Process, under the auspices of the Embassy of Sweden, in cooperation with OHCHR.

10.   Between 30 September and 2 October 2013, the Special Rapporteur attended the International Conference on Dialogue among Cultures and Religions, which was organized in Rabat by the International Organiza-

---

[209]   See www.ohchr.org/EN/HRBodies/SP/Pages/CountryandothervisitsSP.aspx.

tion of la Francophonie and the Islamic Educational, Scientific and Cultural Organization, under the patronage of the King of Morocco.

11. On 18 October 2013, the Special Rapporteur participated in an international conference on religion and politics on the theme "Blasphemy as political game", organized by the Graduate Institute of International and Development Studies, in Geneva.

12. Between 27 and 31 October 2013, the Special Rapporteur presented his interim report to the General Assembly (A/68/290) at its sixty-eighth session, with a focus on the intersection of freedom of religion or belief and the equality of men and women. In this context, he also participated in a number of side events on different themes.

13. On 14 and 15 November 2013, the Special Rapporteur visited Stockholm and attended a seminar on the topic "Freedom of religion or belief and equality between men and women — what could the EU and its Member States do", organized by the Ministry for Foreign Affairs of Sweden. He used this opportunity to also participate in a number of other events.

14. On 27 November 2013, the Special Rapporteur attended the sixth session of the Forum on Minority Issues, held in Geneva. The session focused on guaranteeing the rights of religious minorities.

15. Between 17 and 19 January 2014, the Special Rapporteur participated in a conference on freedom of religion or belief, organized by the International Religious Liberty Association, in Madrid.

16. On 12 February 2014, the Special Rapporteur participated in a conference on the theme "The state of freedom of religion or belief in the world", organized in Brussels at the European Parliament, following the presentation of the first annual report produced by the European Parliament Working Group on Freedom of Religion or Belief.

17. Between 17 and 27 February 2014, the Special Rapporteur conducted an unofficial visit to India, where he participated in a number of civil society meetings and seminars and gave public lectures.

18. Between 10 and 14 March 2014, the Special Rapporteur presented his reports to the Human Rights Council at its twenty-fifth session (A/HRC/25/58, Add.1 and Add.2) and participated in a number of side events.

19. On 8 May 2014, the Special Rapporteur attended a meeting of the Organization for Security and Cooperation in Europe Human Dimension

Committee in Vienna and gave a presentation on freedom of religion or belief as part of a human rights-based peace agenda.

20.   Between 15 and 18 May, the Special Rapporteur conducted a visit to the Republic of Moldova to follow up on his recommendations of his report on his official visit in 2011. He also participated in a round table with religious communities and civil society organizations in the Republic of Moldova and conducted a field visit to the Transnistrian region.

21.   On 19 and 20 June 2014, the Special Rapporteur attended a conference on freedom of religion or belief organized by a consortium of universities in Rome.

22.   The Special Rapporteur additionally held many meetings with government representatives, religious or belief communities, civil society organizations and academic experts working in the area of freedom of religion or belief. He produced comments on draft legislation affecting freedom of religion or belief, delivered video messages, released media reports and gave numerous interviews to international media.

III. Tackling religious intolerance and discrimination in the workplace

A. Introduction

23.   The management of religious or belief diversity in the workplace constitutes a major challenge for today's employment policy. An increasingly diverse and mobile global workforce, expanded manufacturing demands and new production schedules can lead to conflicts between professional and religious identities and duties. Given the salience of the topic and the increasing importance of religious or belief identity among certain groups, the Special Rapporteur has decided to dedicate the present report to exploring how the right to freedom of thought, conscience, religion or belief can be appropriately implemented in the workplace and what measures States, employers and other stakeholders should take to overcome intolerance and discrimination based on religion or belief in this context.

24.   The issue affects employer responsibilities for policies and practices affecting the right to freedom of religion or belief in the workplace, the rights of employees (including job applicants) and the rights of customers or service users. The report covers employment both in public insti-

tutions and the private sector, but does not address the autonomy of religious or religion-inspired institutions.

25. The report addresses both direct and indirect forms of religion or belief-related intolerance and discrimination in the workplace, examining existing gaps, efforts and approaches, highlighting ongoing challenges and promoting policy options to better protect religious manifestations in the workplace. It also assesses the role of reasonable accommodation, both as a legal strategy and as a tool for managing religion or belief-related diversity in the workplace.

1. Work as a fundamental part of human life

26. For most employees the workplace has a significance that goes far beyond its economic function. Besides providing an income, the workplace constitutes an important part of an employee's everyday life, with high relevance for individual self-esteem, self-image, social connections and inclusion into community and society at large. The workplace is furthermore a place in which many people manifest their religious convictions — or wish to do so. For example, some employees wear religious garments and perform their prayers at work. Members of religious minorities may also ask for the possibility to abide by religiously prescribed dietary rules or holidays. And occasionally employees refuse to perform certain work-related activities which run contrary to their deeply held conscientious convictions.

27. While in many cases religious manifestation at the workplace does not cause any problems or is appreciated as a positive expression of diversity, there can also be instances of resistance, confrontation and intolerance. Reluctant public and private employers typically invoke issues of corporate identity, "neutrality", contract-based stipulations, customer-orientation, health and safety and the rights of other staff members in order to prevent or restrict the open display of religious identities at work. In other situations, only the followers of mainstream religions or beliefs are granted an opportunity to manifest their convictions openly at the workplace, while individuals belonging to minority communities, sceptics, atheists or dissenters are forced to conceal their positions in order to avoid harassment by colleagues, customers or employers. Additional problems can occur when members of religious or belief minorities request seemingly "special treatment", such as exceptions from general rules, or when individuals object to performing certain work-related ac-

tivities which would go against their convictions.[210] Conflicts over such issues may result in employee dismissals or in other forms of sanctions and litigation.[211] At times, such conflicts can escalate into highly emotional debates within, and even beyond, the workplace, risking stoking resentment against religious or belief minorities.

2.   An underexplored issue

28. Given the enormous significance of the workplace as a place in which many people spend the majority of their daily lives, the issue of religious intolerance and discrimination in the workplace has been touched upon in the Special Rapporteur's mandate practice.[212] However, it certainly merits further systematic exploration. The sources of intolerance and discrimination can be manifold: existing prejudices against religious or belief minorities may poison the atmosphere among employees; customers may refuse to deal with employees of a religious orientation different from their own; public and private employers may pursue restrictive policies with the intention of preventing hypothetical conflicts (often far-fetched) between followers of different religions or beliefs; or some members of minorities may feel obliged to abide by religious prescriptions that cannot easily be accommodated. In addition, requirements of corporate identity often unduly limit the space for the manifestations of religious conviction and labour laws may have discriminatory side-effects, or even discriminatory intentions, against religious minorities or dissenters. Such problems can occur in public institutions, as well as in the private sector. Moreover, women may suffer from multiple and/or intersectional forms of discrimination or related abuses in the

---

[210]   For instance, doctors and nurses may refuse on conscientious grounds to be involved with abortions; individuals working in the food or catering industry refuse to touch alcohol, pork or other food.

[211]   See, for example, European Court of Human Rights in *Eweida and Others v. United Kingdom* (applications Nos. 48420/10, 59842/10, 51671/10 and 36516/10), judgement of 15 January 2013.

[212]   See, for example, the thematic report (A/HRC/10/8, paras. 41-43). In terms of country visits, the report on the United States of America referred to domestic legislation and jurisprudence on religious practice at the workplace (E/CN.4/1999/58/Add.1, para. 72). The report on the country visit to France noted that some women had been dismissed from their employment or had difficulties in finding employment because they wore the headscarf (E/CN.4/2006/5/Add. 4, para. 67). The report on the country visit to India identified problems faced by Muslims regarding the issuance of passports and security clearances for employment purposes (A/HRC/10/8/Add.3, para. 20).

workplace, often originating from both their sex and their religious or belief background. Thus, the issue has an obvious gender dimension (see also A/68/290, paras. 17-74).

29. Given the complexity of the issue, the Special Rapporteur has decided to narrow his focus to two accounts: First, the report approaches the theme from the angle of employees, not (or rather only incidentally) from the perspective of employers. Nevertheless, it should at least be noted that both employees and employers, qua human beings, are entitled to freedom of religion or belief. While this human right also has a collective or corporate dimension, a full analysis of this question would lead to discussion of the issue of the autonomy of religious institutions in their employment policies, which would go far beyond the confines of the present report.[213] Secondly, the focus will be on existing employment relations, rather than on the question of non-discriminatory access to employment. These two issues are strongly interrelated as there is a natural connection between the accommodation of religious diversity within existing employment and a non-discriminatory accessibility of employment. In some countries, people belonging to certain religious or belief minorities are formally barred from accessing public employment and parts of the private sector. The issue of non-discriminatory access to employment has been taken up by the International Labour Organization (ILO) Committee of Experts on the Application of Conventions and Recommendations, in particular with regard to ILO Convention No. 111 concerning Discrimination in Respect of Employment and Occupation, adopted in 1958. The Special Rapporteur would like to take this opportunity to commend the monitoring work performed by the ILO Committee of Experts on the basis of Convention No. 111, which covers discrimination in employment on different grounds, including religion or belief. ILO also conducts a regular dialogue with religious traditions on the decent work agenda and has produced a handbook outlining some convergences.[214]

3.   Terminology

30. The Special Rapporteur would like to reiterate, at the outset, that the terms "religion" and "belief", as they are used in the present report, must

---

[213] Religious institutions are sometimes subject to an exemption or exception, which allows them to require that employees are of a particular religious belief.

[214] ILO, *Convergences: Decent Work and Social Justice in Religious Traditions — a handbook* (Geneva, 2012).

be broadly understood, in keeping with the interpretation in the Human Rights Committee's general comment No. 22. As the Committee has pointed out, "[a]rticle 18 protects theistic, non-theistic and atheistic beliefs, as well as the right not to profess any religion or belief."[215] The general comment further clarifies that "[a]rticle 18 is not limited in its application to traditional religions or to religions and beliefs with institutional characteristics or practices analogous to those of traditional religions."[216] The Special Rapporteur fully subscribes to this interpretation. He is furthermore guided by a broad understanding of discrimination which includes direct and indirect discrimination. While direct discrimination openly targets certain individuals, or groups, with the intention or effect of denying their claims to full equality, indirect discrimination usually starts with prima facie "neutral" general rules, policies or practices, which — although on the surface appearing to apply to everyone equally — nonetheless have a discriminatory impact on certain individuals or groups. Based on the assumption that indirect discrimination is usually more difficult to detect and combat than direct discrimination, the present report will accord specific attention to this problem as it relates to freedom of religion or belief in the workplace.

B. Freedom of religion or belief in the workplace

1.   Applicability of freedom of religion or belief in the workplace

31. When discussing issues of religious intolerance and discrimination in the workplace, the Special Rapporteur often encounters two general misunderstandings. The first misunderstanding relates to the scope of freedom of religion or belief. It is sometimes assumed that religion should be a "private" affair which chiefly concerns the family and religious worship in a narrow sense, but has little to do with people's professional life. However, for many believers their religious conviction pervades all dimensions of human life: family relations, school education, etiquette, the general societal culture of communication, social and economic affairs, public and political life, and so on, and thus the workplace. Article 18 of the International Covenant on Civil and Political Rights supports such a comprehensive understanding. It covers everyone's freedom "either individually or in community with others and in public or private, to manifest his religion or belief in worship, observance, practice and teaching".

---

[215] Human Rights Committee, general comment No. 22 (A/48/40, vol. I, annex VI), para. 2.
[216] Ibid.

Whereas the terms "teaching" and "worship" relate to specific religious spaces and institutions, the terms "observance" and "practice" do not display any spatial or institutional specificities and must be broadly applied. The text also clearly states that the right to manifest one's religion or belief spans both private and public aspects of human life. In addition, the Declaration on the Elimination of All Forms of Intolerance and of Discrimination Based on Religion or Belief, 1981 (General Assembly resolution 36/55) clarifies, in article 4, paragraph 1, that the responsibility of States to combat religious discrimination covers "all fields of civil, economic, political, social and cultural life". Thus, there can be no reasonable doubt that the right to freedom of thought, conscience, religion or belief also applies in the workplace.

32. The second general misunderstanding is more difficult to refute. It rests on the assumption that by voluntarily signing a labour contract, employees largely waive their freedom of religion or belief, which they, supposedly, can fully retrieve by abandoning their employment and taking an alternative job that accommodates their religious needs and convictions. In other words, the voluntary nature of an employment relationship is used as an argument to deny any interference with the right of freedom of religion or belief and refute the possibility that serious issues of religious freedom at the workplace can emerge as long as the complainant could take steps to avoid the limitation, such as finding another job. Although in practice this may hold true in some cases, the overall reasoning remains highly problematic on a number of accounts. It is true that there is an option for the employer to define certain work-related obligations which may actually limit an employee's freedom to manifest her/his religion or belief. The scope of such limitations, inter alia, depends on the (public, private, religious, secular, etc.) characteristics of the employing institution, as well as on the particular purpose of the employment. However, limitations of the right to manifest one's religion or belief, if defined in a labour contract, must always be specific, compatible with the nature of the task to be accomplished and proportionate to a legitimate purpose. They can never amount to a simple waiver of the employee's freedom of religion or belief, which after all, enjoys the elevated status of an "inalienable" human right. Moreover, one should take into consideration that some employees may, in reality, have little option to find alternative employment. Pointing to the "voluntary" nature of an employment contract and the hypothetical option of leaving the existing contract can thus be unrealistic, depending on the specific situation. Instead, the factual availability, or non-availability, of alterna-

tive employment can be an important empirical factor in assessing the proportionality of specific contract-based limitations on freedom of religion or belief.

2.   Criteria for limitations imposed on freedom of religion or belief

33. Imposing limitations on the exercise of any right to freedom is always sensitive. On the one hand, it is a truism that neither the freedom of an individual, nor that of a group, can be completely unlimited, since making use of one's own freedom might negatively affect the rights of other people or important public interests. On the other hand, the general need for some limitations can easily become a pretext for imposing arbitrary, discriminatory or overly broad restrictions. Countless examples demonstrate that this also happens in the area of freedom of religion or belief. The question of where to draw limits and how to prevent the abuse of limitation clauses therefore requires caution and diligence. Article 18 of the International Covenant on Civil and Political Rights outlines some indispensable criteria in this regard, and the Human Rights Committee has dedicated several paragraphs of its general comment no. 22 in order to further clarify this issue.

34. According to the Committee, for limitations to be legitimate, they must satisfy a number of conditions. Moreover, one should bear in mind that the internal dimension of freedom of thought, conscience, religion or belief (traditionally termed *forum internum*) benefits from an unconditional protection,[217] according to article 18, paragraph 2, of the Covenant, which states that "[n]o one shall be subject to coercion which would impair his freedom to have or to adopt a religion or belief of his choice". The Committee stresses that policies or practices, such as "those restricting access to education, medical care, employment or the rights guaranteed by article 25 and other provisions of the Covenant, are similarly inconsistent with article 18(2)."[218]

35. With regard to manifestations in the *forum externum*, limitations are only permissible if they meet all the criteria set out in article 18, paragraph 3, of the Covenant. Accordingly, any limitations must be legally prescribed and must be "needed" to pursue a legitimate aim — the protection of "public safety, order, health, or morals or the fundamental rights and freedoms of others". In addition, such restrictions must remain within the realm of proportionality, which, inter alia, means that

---

[217]   Ibid., para. 3.
[218]   Ibid., para. 5.

they must always be limited to the minimum degree of interference that is necessary to pursue a legitimate purpose. These criteria are prescribed with a view to safeguarding the essence of freedom of religion or belief, even in situations of conflict with the rights or freedoms of others or with important public interests.

36. The onus of proof therefore falls on those who argue in favour of the limitations, not on those who defend the full exercise of a right to freedom. Confirming this critical function, the Human Rights Committee insists "that paragraph 3 of article 18 is to be strictly interpreted: restrictions are not allowed on grounds not specified there [...]. Limitations may be applied only for those purposes for which they were prescribed and must be directly related and proportionate to the specific need on which they are predicated. Restrictions may not be imposed for discriminatory purposes or applied in a discriminatory manner".[219]

3. Limitations on religious manifestations through employment contracts?

37. By signing a labour contract or a similar employment agreement, employees usually accept certain work-related obligations. In some cases such contract-based obligations can implicitly or explicitly limit the right to manifest one's religion or belief in the workplace. Assuming that labour contracts have a basis in public labour law, one might argue that limitations of freedom of religion originating from contract-based obligations may, in many cases, satisfy the requirement of a legal basis, as prescribed by article 18, paragraph 3, of the Covenant. However, even then, it remains to be seen whether such limitations serve a legitimate purpose and whether they are applied in a proportionate manner. Each specific situation and each individual case deserves a careful empirical and normative assessment.

38. Workplace-related considerations that conflict with an individual's right to freedom of religion or belief, and which arguably fall within the list of legitimate purposes according to the understanding in article 18, paragraph 3, of the Covenant, inter alia, depend on the raison d'être of the employing institution and on the specific purpose and nature of the employment. For instance, the purpose of employment in the public service may differ significantly from employment within a private company, and such differences could possibly become an argument for imposing different rules of conduct in respective public or private employment

---

[219] Ibid., para. 8.

contracts. However, any stipulations negatively affecting freedom of religion or belief must be precisely and narrowly defined. Limitations must always clearly relate to one of the legitimate purposes enumerated in article 18, paragraph 3, of the Covenant; they must furthermore be necessary to pursue the stated purpose; and they must be enacted without any discriminatory intention or effect.

39. In this context, the Special Rapporteur would like to again acknowledge the work carried out by the ILO Committee of Experts on the Application of Conventions and Recommendations, which engages in a process of ongoing dialogue with Governments on the application of ratified conventions, helping to identify information gaps and suggesting measures and mechanisms for improved implementation. In its Observations and Direct Requests, ILO can also take into account information from other United Nations supervisory bodies, forums and agencies. When monitoring ILO Convention No. 111, the Committee of Experts has always insisted on a narrow understanding of article 1, paragraph 2, which states: "Any distinction, exclusion or preference in respect to a particular job based on the inherent requirements thereof shall not be deemed to be discrimination." According to the Committee of Experts, "the concept of inherent requirements must be interpreted restrictively so as to avoid undue limitations of the protection that the Convention is intended to provide".[220]

40. The Special Rapporteur has gained the impression that restrictions imposed on religious manifestations at the workplace frequently fail to satisfy the criteria set out in relevant international human rights instruments. This critical assessment covers both public employers and the private sector. Limitations are often overly broad; it remains unclear which precise purpose they are supposed to serve and whether the purpose is important enough to justify infringements on an employee's right to freedom of religion or belief. The requirement always to minimize interferences to what is clearly "necessary" in order to achieve a legitimate purpose, as implied in the proportionality test, is frequently ignored. Moreover, restrictions are sometimes applied in a discriminatory manner. Indeed, many employers appear to lack awareness that they may incur serious human rights problems as a result of restricting manifesta-

---

[220] See, for example, the Committee's observation concerning Australia (adopted in 2013), which refers to the International Labour Conference General Survey on fundamental Conventions on the fundamental Conventions concerning rights at work in light of the ILO Declaration on Social Justice for a Fair Globalization, 2008 (ILC.101/III/1B), para. 827.

tions of freedom of religion or belief by their staff. Under international human rights law, States — in cooperation with other stakeholders — have a joint responsibility to rectify this state of affairs.

41. It should be noted in this context that religious institutions constitute a special category, as their raison d'être is, from the outset, a religious one. Freedom of religion or belief also includes the right to establish a religious infrastructure which is needed to organize and maintain important aspects of religious community life. For religious minorities this can even become a matter of their long-term survival.[221] The autonomy of religious institutions thus undoubtedly falls within the remit of freedom of religion or belief. It includes the possibility for religious employers to impose religious rules of conduct on the workplace, depending on the specific purpose of employment. This can lead to conflicts with the freedom of religion or belief of employees, for instance if they wish to manifest a religious conviction that differs from the corporate (i.e., religious) identity of the institution. Although religious institutions must be accorded a broader margin of discretion when imposing religious norms of behaviour at the workplace, much depends on the details of each specific case.[222]

C. Tackling direct and indirect forms of religious discrimination

I. Combating open intolerance and direct discrimination

42. Acts of intolerance and discrimination in the workplace can occur in open or more concealed forms, as well as in direct or indirect forms. For example, members of religious minorities may suffer unconcealed harassment from colleagues, customers or employers when manifesting their religion or belief — or when wishing to do so. Such harassment typically includes tasteless jokes, verbal abuse and other expressions of disrespect, often disproportionately affecting women from religious minorities. Converts are another particularly vulnerable group frequently suffering extreme forms of workplace harassment. Existing prejudices against certain religious or belief communities are sometimes used as a

---

[221] See the Special Rapporteur's thematic reports, A/HRC/22/51, paras. 14-89, and A/68/290, para. 57.

[222] See, for example, European Court of Human Rights, *Schüth v. Germany* (application No. 1620/03), judgement of 23 September 2010; and *Obst v. Germany* (application No. 425/03), judgement of 23 September 2010.

pretext to prevent members of those groups from communicating with customers, or else to generally prevent their "visibility" at work. Moreover, the Special Rapporteur has heard about incidents of pressure exercised by colleagues or employers on members of religious minorities to remove their religious garments, to consume religiously prohibited food, or to eat during religious fasting periods. Some private and public employers openly request their employees to distance themselves from certain religions or beliefs; at times they may even insist on the violation of religious rules, for instance dietary restrictions, as a test of loyalty. Failure to comply with such requirements can result in a reduction of salaries, refusal of promotion, loss of pension claims, dismissal or other sanctions. Some companies or public institutions may furthermore create a climate of vigilantism and intimidation by encouraging employees and customers to report unwanted religious activities performed by their staff.[223]

43.   Under freedom of religion or belief, States have the responsibility to do the utmost to prevent such abuses and tackle their root causes. Obviously, they have a special obligation concerning employment in State institutions, since the treatment of employees in State institutions can set an example for the society at large. If public employers unduly hinder the manifestation of religious diversity at work or openly discriminate against religious or belief minorities within their staff, this will likely have negative spillover effects on private employers who may feel encouraged to impose similar restrictions on their own staff. By contrast, policies that create an atmosphere of religious tolerance for employees working in public institutions can also serve as positive models for private sector employers.

44.   Besides this special responsibility concerning the employment policies of State institutions, States are obliged to create effective anti-discrimination laws for the society at large, including the private sector. Such laws must also cover discrimination on the grounds of religion or belief. The Declaration on the Elimination of All Forms of Intolerance and of Discrimination Based on Religion or Belief sends a strong message by proclaiming, in article 3, that "discrimination between human beings on the grounds of religion or belief constitutes an affront to human dignity

---

[223]   As mentioned previously, such a restrictive climate naturally has a negative impact also on the non-discriminatory accessibility of work, which itself constitutes a core aspect of the right to work. A full analysis of this issue would go beyond the confines of the present report. See also general comment No. 20 of the Committee on Economic, Social and Cultural Rights (E/C.12/GC/20), para. 22.

and a disavowal of the principles of the Charter of the United Nations". State responsibility to overcome religious discrimination in this area includes the regulation of employment in public institutions and the private sector through non-discrimination stipulations in general labour laws and other measures. Finally, the State is responsible for tackling the root causes of religious intolerance and related abuses, for instance, by providing anti-bias education in schools or by taking steps to counter negative stereotypes presented in the media.[224]

45. While States have undertaken formal obligations under international human rights law, non-State actors also have a responsibility to combat intolerance and discrimination in the workplace. This particularly concerns employers, trade unions and consumer organizations. They should all use their specific potential to contribute to a climate of open-mindedness and an appreciation of diversity in the workplace as part of normal life.

2.   Tackling concealed and indirect forms of intolerance or discrimination

46. Apart from straightforward expressions of religious intolerance and direct discrimination against religious minorities, intolerance and discrimination can also occur in more concealed or indirect forms which are not always easy to detect. They often remain hidden by seemingly "neutral" rules which, although on the surface applying to everyone equally, can have disproportionately negative effects on some people. For instance, the management of holidays at the workplace typically reflects the dominant religious and cultural tradition in a country. Whereas adherents of majority religions usually do not encounter great problems when trying to combine their work-related obligations with the celebration of their religious holidays, the situation of religious or belief minorities may be much more complicated. Additional problems may arise for people who feel a religious obligation not to work on specific days during the week. For instance, some Jews or Seventh-Day-Adventists have lost their jobs as a result of their refusal to work on Saturdays, and the same has happened to both Muslims and Christians who objected to working on Fridays or Sundays, respectively. Another example of possible indirect discrimination concerns dress code regulations which, in the name of

---

[224] See the Rabat Plan of Action on the prohibition of national, racial or religious hatred that constitutes incitement to discrimination, hostility or violence (A/HRC/22/17/Add.4), appendix.

"corporate identity" or for other reasons, prohibit employees from wearing religious garments. While on the surface such regulations may appear to affect all staff members equally, in practice they can impose disproportionate burdens on members of religious or belief minorities who may be confronted with the dilemma of either living in accordance with their convictions or risking dismissal or other sanctions.

47.   Indirect discrimination at the workplace can occur both in public institutions and in the private sector. When establishing rules or practices with indirectly discriminatory implications, public or private employers in some cases are cognizant of what they do and use such mechanisms on purpose. However, it seems plausible to assume that in many cases they are not fully aware of the possibly discriminatory effects that prima facie neutral rules can have on the situation of religious or belief minorities within their staff.

48.   Apart from difficulties in detecting indirect discrimination or other concealed forms of religious intolerance, finding an appropriate response is usually more complicated than in cases of straightforward intolerance and direct discrimination. Obviously, it requires a culture of open and trustful communication between employers, managers and staff, always including religious or belief minorities, who should feel encouraged to voice their specific concerns and needs. In some situations, indirect discrimination can only be rectified by modifying general rules or by accommodating specific "exceptions" for certain individuals. Many employers are reluctant to embark on such a course out of a fear that this could open the floodgates to all sorts of presumably "unreasonable" demands. Some employers may also fear that by accommodating specific needs of religious minorities, they could in the end undermine important policy considerations, such as corporate identity, neutrality, customer-friendliness and the rights of other employees. Demands to accommodate specific needs of religious or belief minorities seem to have triggered resistance in the wider society, because they are sometimes misperceived as "privileging" minorities at the expense of the principle of equality. For this reason, even people generally sympathetic with broader human rights and non-discrimination agendas may react in a somewhat ambivalent manner towards proposals of special accommodation for religious or belief minorities in the workplace. In order to counter such fears, those proposing specific measures of accommodation usually make clear that these measures should remain within a "reasonable" framework. This leads to the issue of "reasonable accommodation".

D. The role of reasonable accommodation

1. The meaning of reasonable accommodation

49. "Reasonable accommodation" has become a recognized term in the international human rights debate, and its relevance in a comprehensive non-discrimination strategy has been formally enshrined in the Convention on the Rights of Persons with Disabilities, 2006 (General Assembly resolution 61/106).[225] Article 2 of the Convention defines: "Reasonable accommodation means necessary and appropriate modification and adjustments not imposing a disproportionate or undue burden, where needed in a particular case, to ensure to persons with disabilities the enjoyment and exercise on an equal basis with others of all human rights and fundamental freedoms". Article 5, paragraph 3, of the Convention stipulates an obligation for State parties in this field: "In order to promote equality and eliminate discrimination, States Parties shall take all appropriate steps to ensure that reasonable accommodation is provided." It should be noted that article 5 of the Convention generally deals with equality and non-discrimination and that reasonable accommodation thus plays a systematic role in this specific context. In its concluding observations on reports of States parties, the Committee on the Rights of Persons with Disabilities has clarified that it treats failure to ensure reasonable accommodation as a violation of the principles of equality and non-discrimination.[226]

50. The Convention on the Rights of Persons with Disabilities reflects some of the most recent thinking in this area, including insights from international debates on measures needed to effectively combat discrimi-

---

[225] The term "reasonable accommodation" has been used by the Committee on Economic, Social and Cultural Rights in its general comment No. 5 (E/1995/22, annex IV, para. 15). See also the Committee's general comment No. 20 (E/C.12/GC/20, para. 28).

[226] See the references to "reasonable accommodation" in the Committee's concluding observations CRPD/C/TUN/CO/1, paras. 12-13; CRPD/C/ESP/CO/1, paras. 19-20, 40 and 43-44; CRPD/C/PER/CO/1, paras. 6-7; CRPD/C/ARG/CO/1, paras. 11-12; CRPD/C/CHN/CO/1 and Corr.1, paras. 11-12 and 74; CRPD/C/HUN/CO/1, paras. 15, 16, 27, 34, 39 and 41-43; CRPD/C/PRY/CO/1, paras. 13-14, 32, 44 and 65; CRPD/C/AZE/CO/1, paras. 13, 41 and 43; CRPD/C/CRI/CO/1, paras. 11-12, 28 and 55-56; CRPD/C/SWE/CO/1, paras. 9-10, 21, 23 and 26; CRPD/C/SLV/CO/1, paras. 13-14, 28-32, 49-50 and 55; CRPD/C/AUS/CO/1, paras. 45-46. See also the Committee's views on the cases of H.M. v. Sweden (CRPD/C/7/D/3/2011); Nyusti and Takács v. Hungary (CRPD/C/9/D/1/2010); Bujdosó et al. v. Hungary (CRPD/C/10/D/4/2011); and X. v. Argentina (CRPD/C/11/D/8/2012).

nation, in particular indirect forms of discrimination. It seems fair to infer that what the Convention specifically stipulates as regards reasonable accommodation on behalf of persons with disabilities might also apply to persons suffering discrimination on other grounds, including religion or belief.

2.   Reasonable accommodation in the workplace

51. Measures of reasonable accommodation in the workplace in order to ensure everyone's freedom of religion or belief on the basis of equality and
non-discrimination are not a mere utopian dream. Fortunately, we have a number of impressive success stories in this field which may help to inspire positive action and dispel unjustified fears.

52. In many institutions, a more or less appropriate infrastructure already exists or is in the process of development. Accommodating religious or belief-related diversity in the workplace has become a standard practice in many public institutions and private companies. One example is respect for specific dietary needs originating from religious prescripts or other conscience-based reasons. Workplace canteens frequently provide halal or kosher food and offer vegetarian meals, and in many cases this is appreciated even by employees who have not requested such options for religious reasons. Public and private employers have successfully negotiated pragmatic ways of accommodating diverse religious holidays, for instance, by permitting employees to use parts of their annual vacation for this purpose. Trade unions and staff representatives often participate in such negotiations. There are also examples of employees performing their prayer rituals in the workplace without any negative implications on professional operations. Moreover, the wearing of religious garments is considered part of normal life in many public institutions or private companies and is largely respected by colleagues and customers. In short: provided there is goodwill on all sides, practical solutions can be found in most cases. So before dealing with remaining challenges and objections, it may be useful to find encouragement from the broad spectrum of success stories in this area.

3.   Resistance towards reasonable accommodation

53. Despite many positive experiences, measures of reasonable accommodation continue to meet with scepticism or resistance. Sceptics and opponents seem to be driven by different fears. For instance, they may fear that such measures would privilege minorities at the expense of

equality among colleagues, could undermine the "neutrality" of certain institutions, open the floodgates to all sorts of special demands, dilute corporate identity, poison the workplace atmosphere and lead to high economic costs and managerial complications. Within the confines of the present report, the Special Rapporteur can only sketch out brief responses to such typical objections.

(a) Privileging minorities?

54. Against a widespread misunderstanding, the purpose of reasonable accommodation is not to "privilege" members of religious minorities at the expense of the principle of equality. In fact, the opposite is true. What reasonable accommodation encourages is the implementation of substantive equality. One should first note that within the framework of human rights, equality must not be mistaken for "sameness" or "uniformity". Based on recognition of the inherent dignity and of the equal and inalienable rights of all members of the human family,[227] human rights empower all human beings — on the basis of equal respect and equal concern — to pursue their personal life plans, to enjoy respect for their unique and irreplaceable biographies, to freely express their diverse political opinions and to live in accordance with their diverse faith-related convictions and practices etc. In the context of human rights, equality always means a diversity-friendly "complex equality". Implementing equality in this sense will bring to bear the existing and emerging diversity among human beings in all sectors of society. This, inter alia, requires the elimination of discrimination, including indirect discrimination — and therein lies the precise purpose of reasonable accommodation. In short, instead of diluting the principle of equality, reasonable accommodation contributes to a more complex — and thus more appropriate — conceptualization of substantive equality, based on equal respect and concern for all human beings with their diverse biographies, convictions, identities and needs. It does not privilege certain groups of people but finally contributes to a more diverse society to the benefit of all.

(b) Endangering neutrality?

55. Some employers pursue a policy of "neutrality" vis-à-vis their customers in order to demonstrate that they cater to all parts of the society without distinguishing between adherents of different creeds. Such a pol-

---

[227] See the first sentence of the preamble to the Universal Declaration of Human Rights.

icy of neutrality may be of particular importance for the public service or other State institutions — for example, the police or the judiciary — which are supposed to operate in the service of everyone without prejudice to different religious backgrounds. When discussing the issue of neutrality the different functions which State institutions carry out certainly must be taken into consideration. At any case, on closer analysis, it becomes obvious that in the context of freedom of religion or belief the term neutrality can have very different meanings. It can sometimes be a proxy for a policy of non-commitment towards, and non-recognition of religious or belief diversity and can even lead to rather restrictive measures in this area. Unfortunately, there are examples of unreasonably restrictive readings of neutrality within both public institutions and the private sector. By contrast, neutrality can also represent a policy of fair inclusion of people of diverse religious or belief orientation — both within an organization's staff and vis-à-vis its customers. In this positive understanding, the principle of neutrality serves as an antidote to all sorts of biases, exclusions, negative stereotypes and discrimination. It provides an open and inclusive framework for the free and non-discriminatory unfolding of religious and belief diversity among staff and when dealing with the outside-society. This latter is an understanding of neutrality to which the Special Rapporteur fully subscribes. From such a perspective, reasonable accommodation, far from endangering the neutrality of the workplace, can actually become a positive factor of "neutrality", appropriately understood.

(c)   Opening the floodgates to trivial demands?

56. Employer reluctance towards reasonable accommodation may reflect fears that such a policy could invite all sorts of trivial demands from staff. Indeed, it is important to ensure that reasonable accommodation does not fall prey to trivial interests. The underlying idea is not simply to accommodate all kinds of personal tastes or preferences, but rather to help avoid situations in which an employee would otherwise be faced with discriminatory treatment and a serious, existential dilemma. The preamble to the Declaration on the Elimination of All Forms of Intolerance and of Discrimination Based on Religion or Belief recalls that "religion or belief, for anyone who professes either, is one of the fundamental elements of his conception of life". Those claiming some accommodation in order to fully exercise their freedom of religion or belief can therefore be expected to present the argument that without such appropriate measures they would suffer an existential conflict, that is, a dilemma of a

serious nature. Certainly in some cases it may be difficult to distinguish a serious religious or belief-related demand from more trivial interests. When confronted with such questions, public or private employers may therefore need professional advice, based on a clear understanding of freedom of religion or belief and its broad application. The availability of appropriate professional support is of strategic significance for the practical implementation of reasonable accommodation in this area.

(d) Diluting corporate identity?

57. Public institutions and private companies can have a legitimate interest to be publicly recognizable in their dealings with customers and other people. Experiences from both public institutions and private companies demonstrate that the interest in maintaining corporate identity is, in most cases, easily reconcilable with accommodating religious diversity. Rather than leading to all-or-nothing-dilemmas, reasonable accommodation usually just requires a degree of flexibility from both employers and employees, as well as tolerance from third parties and the society at large.[228] It should be reiterated that religious institutions may require a different assessment in this regard, since their corporate identity is religiously defined from the outset.

(e) Risk of conflicts in the workplace?

58. Measures of reasonable accommodation in the workplace are not always popular among staff and can lead to tensions, sometimes based on (mis)perceptions that members of minorities receive a "privileged" treatment. As briefly mentioned previously, this is a misunderstanding, because reasonable accommodation presupposes a more demanding concept of complex equality. However, instead of dispelling such misunderstandings among their staff, some employers resort to policies of "abstract conflict prevention" by refusing to even consider measures of reasonable accommodation in the first place. Such restrictive policies of-

---

[228] See also the Human Rights Committee's decision on admissibility in the case of *Riley et al. v. Canada* (CCPR/C/74/D/1048/2002, para. 4.2: "The Committee has noted the authors' claims that they are victims of violations of articles 3, 9, paragraph 1, 18, 23, paragraphs 3 and 4, 26, and 2, paragraph 1, because Khalsa Sikh officers of the RCMP [Royal Canadian Mounted Police] are authorised to wear religious symbols as part of their RCMP uniform. [...] The Committee is of the view that the authors have failed to show how the enjoyment of their rights under the Covenant has been affected by allowing Khalsa Sikh officers to wear religious symbols.").

ten lack any realistic risk-analysis. The mere possibility — perhaps even a far-fetched one — that such conflicts could hypothetically emerge, is taken as a pretext to reject any accommodation of diversity in the workplace. However, the resulting restrictive policies may amount to undue limitations of the freedom to manifest one's religion or belief. As elaborated previously, the imposition of limitations always requires precise empirical and normative arguments, in compliance with article 18, paragraph 3, of the International Covenant on Civil and Political Rights, as well as all other relevant international human rights norms.

(f)   Undue economic and managerial burdens?

59. Perhaps the most widespread objection to measures of accommodation concerns anxieties of possibly far-reaching economic or managerial consequences. However, already the definition of reasonable accommodation in the Convention on the Rights of Persons with Disabilities makes it clear that measures of accommodation should not amount to a "disproportionate or undue burden" for the respective institution. Depending on the specific context, this provision can serve as an argument for rejecting too far-reaching requests for accommodation, if they are likely to cause disproportionate economic or other costs. However, such rejection should always be concrete and confined to specific cases. A broadly applied "preventative" strategy which, with regard to merely hypothetical costs and complications, would deny any discussion of accommodation in the first place would be illegitimate. Moreover, experience shows that in many cases measures of accommodation are nearly or totally cost-free.[229] Rejecting accommodation would thus be "unreasonable" even in a narrow economic understanding of reasonableness. In the long run, measures of accommodation can even have positive economic effects by enhancing the reputation of an institution or company, by reinforcing a sense of loyalty and identification within the staff and by facilitating a creative atmosphere in which diversity is appreciated as a positive asset.

4.   *Reasonable accommodation as a legal requirement*

60. For all the significance and potential that reasonable accommodation holds to combat discrimination, legislators and courts have by and large been reluctant to apply the principle as a legal entitlement. The

---

[229]   See Marie-Claire Foblets and Katayoun Alidadi, eds., "Summary report on the RELIGARE Project: Religious Diversity and Secular Models in Europe — Innovative Approaches to Law and Policy", (summer 2013), p. 13. Available from www.religareproject.eu/system/files/RELIGARE%20Summary%20Report_0.pdf.

Special Rapporteur hopes that the Convention on the Rights of Persons with Disabilities may serve as a general door opener in this regard, including beyond the specific area of disability.

61. Those opposed to a legal approach on this issue argue that turning reasonable accommodation into a legally enforceable right could negatively backfire and reduce the readiness of public or private employers to experiment with creative measures. Instead of treating accommodation as a legal entitlement, they prefer pragmatic policies of encouraging employers to use reasonable accommodation as a managerial tool outside the realm of law. However, the flipside of this non-legal approach is that employees would remain unilaterally dependent on the willingness of employers to accommodate their specific religious or belief-related needs at the workplace. They would not have any legal recourse against employers who, from the outset, reject any form of accommodation, even if the religious concerns at stake are high and the economic or managerial costs of the accommodating measures are merely minor.

62. The Special Rapporteur advocates for combining the advantages of a legal approach to reasonable accommodation with those of a more pragmatic managerial approach. In the spirit of article 5 of the Convention on the Rights of Persons with Disabilities, as quoted in paragraph 49 above, the provision of reasonable accommodation should be understood as part of the legal responsibility of States, including as regards the guarantee of freedom of religion or belief. This also follows from article 4, paragraph 1, of the Declaration on the Elimination of All Forms of Intolerance and of Discrimination Based on Religion or Belief, which proclaims: "All States shall take effective measures to prevent and eliminate discrimination on the grounds of religion or belief in the recognition, exercise and enjoyment of human rights and fundamental freedoms in all fields of civil, economic, political, social and cultural life". Denying a person accommodation in situations where such measures would not amount to a disproportionate or undue burden could accordingly qualify as discrimination, depending on the circumstances of the particular case. Moreover, individuals should have the option of resorting to legal remedies in order to challenge any denial of accommodating measures that could be reasonably enacted. The serious implications of indirect discrimination on the full enjoyment of freedom of religion or belief for all certainly call for a legal course, without which reasonable accommodation would remain a mere act of mercy.

63. At the same time, public and private employers, as well as other stakeholders, should be encouraged to further explore and expand the

scope of reasonable accommodation beyond what is currently legally enforceable. Public and private employers, trade unions, representatives of staff and others should exchange positive experiences, discuss typical obstacles and set up contextualized pragmatic benchmarks. States should support such experiments by providing advice and establishing good practice examples in their own employment policies.

5.   The role of training and advisory services

64. Policies of reasonable accommodation can lead to complicated questions, problems and, at times, impasses. For instance, it may not always be easy to distinguish between serious demands put forward in the name of a person's religious identity and mere trivial interests or unsubstantiated claims.[230] Drawing a line requires sensitivity for people's identity-shaping convictions and practices as well as a solid understanding of the precise normative implications of freedom of religion or belief and its universal and inclusive application. Problems can also occur if parts of the management or staff are still unconvinced that reasonable accommodation of religious diversity is a meaningful purpose. Calculation of costs or possible side-effects is another complicated matter that requires experience and professional knowledge.

65. The availability of appropriate training and advice is therefore of strategic importance for a successful handling of reasonable accommodation. Given the overall responsibility of States for combating all forms of intolerance and discrimination based on religion or belief, States should establish an appropriate infrastructure of training and advisory services based on human rights. National human rights institutions seem ideally placed to play a key role in this area. Many national human rights institutions have already developed programmes of human rights-based diversity training which, inter alia, cater to public and private employers. Training programmes should also include sensitivity training for multiple and intersectional discrimination, for example, problems that women from religious minorities encounter in the intersection of gender-related and religious discrimination in the workplace.

66. Notwithstanding the formal responsibility of States under international human rights law, other stakeholders — such as employers and their umbrella organizations, trade unions, religious communities, civil

---

[230] See A/HRC/13/40/Add.2, para. 16, referring to the European Court of Human Rights, *Kosteski v. the former Yugoslav Republic of Macedonia* (application No. 55170/00), judgement of 13 April 2006.

society organizations, etc. — should each use their specific potential to contribute to combating religious intolerance and discrimination at the workplace. For example, they can offer their expertise to help in designing appropriate policies of reasonable accommodation and to dispel typical misperceptions, or they can facilitate an exchange of relevant experiences in this area.

IV. Conclusions and recommendations

67. Given the enormous significance of the workplace, in which many people spend a large share of their daily lives, the issue of religious discrimination in the area of employment so far has received comparatively little systematic attention. However, there can be no doubt that the freedom to manifest one's religion or belief without discrimination also applies in the workplace.

68. Although labour contracts can stipulate specific work-related obligations which, under certain conditions, may limit some manifestations of an employee's religion or belief, they can never amount to a general waiver of this human right in the workplace. Moreover, any limitations of the right to manifest one's religion or belief in the workplace, if deemed necessary, must always be specific and narrowly defined; they must furthermore be clearly needed to pursue a legitimate purpose, as well as proportionate to the said purpose. While these requirements apply broadly to both public and private employment, one should bear in mind that religious institutions constitute a special case. As their raison d'être and corporate identity are religiously defined, employment policies of religious institutions may fall within the scope of freedom of religion or belief, which also includes a corporate dimension.

69. Under freedom of religion or belief, States have a formal responsibility to prevent and eliminate all forms of intolerance and discrimination based on religion or belief, including in the workplace. Their responsibility goes far beyond ensuring non-discrimination in employment within State institutions; they must also combat discrimination within the larger society, including as regards employment in the private sector. Other stakeholders — companies, trade unions, religious communities, civil society organizations — are also encouraged to use their potential to contribute to a climate of tolerance and to an appreciation of the diversity of religion or belief in the workplace.

70. Combating discrimination requires a comprehensive approach of tackling both direct and indirect forms of discrimination based on reli-

gion or belief. Whereas direct discrimination can typically be identified on the surface, indirect discrimination often remains hidden under "neutral" rules which, on the surface, affect all staff members equally. It may be useful to mandate specific monitoring bodies with the task of gathering relevant data in order to detect indirect discrimination. Moreover, eliminating indirect discrimination may require measures of "reasonable accommodation". At the level of specific institutions, a culture of trustful and respectful communication is needed in order to identify the specific needs of persons belonging to religious or belief minorities.

71. The enshrinement of the principle of reasonable accommodation in the Convention on the Rights of Persons with Disabilities should serve as an entry point for discussing the role of similar measures in other areas of combating discrimination, including on the grounds of religion or belief. Policies of eliminating discrimination cannot be fully effective unless they also contemplate measures of reasonable accommodation.

72. Against a widespread misunderstanding, the purpose of reasonable accommodation is not to "privilege" religious or belief-related minorities, at the expense of the principle of equality. One should bear in mind that in the context of human rights, equality must always be conceived of as a diversity-friendly equality, which is the opposite of "sameness" or uniformity. From the perspective of a diversity-friendly, complex and substantive equality, measures of reasonable accommodation should be appreciated as instruments of translating the principle of equality into different social contexts. In order to find appropriate practical solutions in this area, public and private employers require training and advice which should be provided by the State.

73. Against this background, the Special Rapporteur formulates the following recommendations.

A. Recommendations addressed to State institutions

74. States should establish effective anti-discrimination legislation which, inter alia, covers employment in public and private institutions. Such legislation must include the prohibition of discrimination on the basis of religion or belief. Issues of multiple and intersectional discrimination — for instance, on combined grounds of gender and religion or belief — require specific attention.

75. In order to ensure an effective implementation of anti-discrimination legislation, appropriate monitoring mechanisms should be put in place. National human rights institutions, operating in line with

the Paris Principles, may be particularly well-suited to take an active role in this endeavour. They should also help to identify indirect discrimination (or other forms of concealed discrimination) based on religion or belief at the workplace, including by gathering relevant disaggregated data.

76. States should set positive examples of respect for religious diversity in their own employment policies within State institutions. Good practice in this area should serve as a model to be followed in the private sector and in other societal areas.

77. States should provide diversity training and advisory services for public and private employers concerning religious tolerance and non-discrimination in the workplace. This should include advice as regards policies of reasonable accommodation of religious and belief diversity in the workplace.

78. Policymakers, legislators and judges should treat claims of reasonable accommodation as an important part of combating indirect discrimination based on religion or belief.

B. Recommendations addressed to public and private employers

79. Public and private employers should generally understand religious tolerance and diversity as a positive asset and as an integral and important part of their corporate identity. Diversity should, inter alia, combine consideration of gender issues with tolerance and respect for religious diversity.

80. Employers should foster an atmosphere of trustful and respectful communication, which allows employees, including members of religious or belief minorities, to express their problems and discuss their needs openly, as a preliminary to detecting concealed forms of intolerance and instances or patterns of indirect discrimination.

81. Employers are encouraged to develop policies of reasonable accommodation of religious or belief diversity at the workplace in order to prevent or rectify situations of indirect discrimination and to promote diversity and inclusion.

82. Experiences with policies of reasonable accommodation can be shared among peers and with other stakeholders in order to establish and encourage good practice.

C. Recommendations addressed to other stakeholders

83. Trade unions are encouraged to incorporate programmes to combat workplace-related intolerance and discrimination based on religion or belief as part of broader policies.

84. Religious communities are encouraged to pay more attention to issues of intolerance and discrimination at the workplace and offer their expertise to negotiate practical solutions.

85. Civil society organizations working on human rights and anti-discrimination agendas are encouraged to monitor workplace-related forms of discrimination based on religion or belief.

86. National human rights institutions should develop training programmes and an advisory function in this field, which they can offer to public and private employers, both on their own initiative and on demand. This should also include advice on human rights-based policies of reasonable accommodation.

87. Close cooperation between ILO and OHCHR in relation to human rights treaties is an important strategy to ensure consistency and coherence within the United Nations system as regards human rights at work.

9. Chapter: December 2014

I. Introduction

1. The mandate of the Special Rapporteur on freedom of religion or belief was created by the Commission on Human Rights pursuant to its resolution 1986/20 and renewed by the Human Rights Council in its resolutions 6/37, 14/1 and 22/20.[231]

2. In its resolution 25/12, the Human Rights Council condemned "all forms of violence, intolerance and discrimination based on or in the name of religion or belief, and violations of the freedom of thought, conscience, religion or belief, as well as any advocacy of religious hatred that constitutes incitement to discrimination, hostility or violence, whether it involves the use of print, audiovisual or electronic media or any other means". Against that background, the present report, in its section II, focuses on preventing violence committed in the name of religion and, in its section III, includes specific recommendations addressed to all relevant stakeholders.

II. Preventing violence committed in the name of religion

A. A complex phenomenon

3. Violence committed "in the name of religion", that is, on the basis of or arrogated to religious tenets of the perpetrator,[232] is a complex phenomenon in different parts of the world. The brutality displayed in manifestations of such violence often renders observers speechless. While in some countries violence in the name of religion remains a local or regional phenomenon, acts of terrorism carried out intentionally to send global messages have been increasingly prominent in recent years. In that context, prima facie "archaic" acts of cruelty seem to be cynically "staged" in order to cater to modern media voyeurism, which adds yet another dimension of humiliation to the suffering of victims and their families.

---

[231] For an overview of the activities of the Special Rapporteur between 1 August 2013 and 31 July 2014, see A/69/261, paras. 4–22.

[232] By contrast, violence "on the grounds of religion or belief" is based on the religious affiliation of the victim (see A/HRC/13/40, para. 33).

4.   Violence in the name of religion can be in the form of targeted attacks on individuals or communities, communal violence, suicide attacks, terrorism, State repression, discriminative policies or legislation and other types of violent behaviour. It can also be embedded and perpetuated in the status quo in various forms of structural violence justified in the name of religion. Perpetrators comprise different types of non-State actors, but also State agencies or — quite often — a combination of both. In some countries, armed groups invoke religion to justify atrocities such as targeted mass killings, extrajudicial and summary executions, enforced disappearances, torture, sexual violence, indiscriminate attacks against civilians, mass expulsions, enslavement or systematic destruction of certain communities. In other countries, vigilante groups harass religious minorities by vandalizing cemeteries and places of worship, grabbing lands or properties and threatening their security.

5.   The main problem in a number of countries stems from the State's failure in combating terrorism or violence of non-State actors, while certain State agencies in other countries support such violence directly or indirectly, for example, by promoting hatred against religious minorities or by turning a blind eye to violence, hence indulging a culture of impunity. Human rights violations can even originate directly from the State apparatus itself, for example, when a Government resorts to violent repression in order to "defend" a State religion or existing religious hegemonies against perceived threats by religious competitors or internal dissidents. The State's involvement with violence in the name of religion thus shows a broad variety of patterns, ranging from lack of capacity to indirect or direct forms of complicity or deliberate policies of religious discrimination, sometimes even culminating in formal endorsement or systematic orchestration of such violence by the State.

6.   Violence in the name of religion disproportionately targets religious dissidents, members of religious minorities or converts.[233] People suspected of undermining national cohesion are also frequent targets of intolerant violence. Attacks will also likely increase where there is a recognized "official" or State religion or when a religion is used as a medium to define national identity. Moreover, vigilante groups, sometimes with the support of law enforcement agencies, attack people, in particular women, whose ways of life are deemed "immoral" from the standpoint of certain narrowly defined religious codes of conduct.

---

[233]   See A/67/303, para. 15.

7.   However, violence in the name of religion also affects followers of the very same religion, possibly also from a majority religion, in whose name such acts are perpetrated. Voices of moderation or critics who actively oppose the abuse of their religion for the justification of violence bear an increased risk of being accused of "betrayal" or "blasphemy" and having retaliatory penalties inflicted upon themselves.

8.   The relevance of the issue with respect to freedom of religion or belief is obvious since violence in the name of religion is a source of many of the most extreme violations of this human right, usually in conjunction with other human rights violations as well. Freedom of religion or belief, due to its nature as a human right, protects human beings rather than religions. The starting point for any assessment of religious or belief pluralism must therefore be the self-understandings of human beings in this area, which may be quite diverse.

9.   Victims of violence come from all religious or belief backgrounds. They comprise adherents to large "traditional" communities and followers of small or new religious movements, which are often stigmatized as "sects". Furthermore, atheists and agnostics suffer in many countries from a climate of intimidation, repression or violence. Another frequently neglected group of people are the adherents to different indigenous beliefs, who are also targets of violence carried out by State agencies and/or non-State actors.

10.   Countless examples demonstrate that violence in the name of religion usually displays a pronounced gender dimension.[234] Many women and girls are victims of "honour" killings, acid attacks, amputations or floggings, sometimes pursuant to penal codes that are based on religious laws. Women and girls also disproportionately suffer from sexual violence, such as rape, abduction, sexual enslavement, female genital mutilation, forced marriage, often in conjunction with forced conversion, or other cruelties.

11.   Furthermore, homophobic and transphobic violence against lesbian, gay, bisexual and transgender (LGBT) persons may also be perpetrated in the name of religion. Those perceived as LGBT may be targets of orga-

---

[234] See, for example, www.ohchr.org/EN/NewsEvents/Pages/DisplayNews.aspx? NewsID=10522&LangID=E, www.ohchr.org/EN/NewsEvents/Pages/DisplayNews. aspx?NewsID=14125&LangID=E, www.ohchr.org/EN/NewsEvents/Pages/Display News.aspx?NewsID=14618&LangID=E, www.ohchr.org/EN/NewsEvents/Pages/ DisplayNews.aspx?NewsID=14936&LangID=E and www.ohchr.org/EN/News Events/Pages/DisplayNews.aspx?NewsID=15094&LangID=E.

nized abuse, including by religious extremists.[235] Violence against LGBT persons includes brutal gang rapes, so-called "curative" rapes and family violence owing to their sexual orientation and gender identity.[236] There is a strong connection between discrimination in law and practice, and incitement to violence in the name of religion and violence itself. Violence against women and against LGBT persons is often justified and given legitimacy by discriminatory laws based on religious laws or supported by religious authorities, such as laws criminalizing adultery, homosexuality or cross-dressing. The Human Rights Committee has noted with concern hate speech and manifestations of intolerance and prejudice by religious leaders against individuals on the basis of their sexual orientation, in a broader context of acts of violence, including killings of LGBT persons.[237] There have also been reports of direct violence exercised by religious authorities against LGBT persons, although many of them are religiously interested in practising.

B. Overcoming simplistic interpretations

1. *Inadequacy of isolating "religion" as a factor in conflict descriptions*

12. The experience that religion is invoked in civil wars, communal violence, terrorist acts or other violent conflicts causes some observers to use the label "religion" broadly and loosely when analysing those phenomena. Multidimensional violent conflicts are often described along religious lines. Although such descriptions may capture some relevant elements of the phenomena, they fail to understand the complexity of the issues. Headlines such as "religious violence", "religious civil war" or "sectarian conflicts" tend to obfuscate the significance of non-religious factors, in particular political factors, for an adequate understanding of the core problems.

13. Non-religious factors that deserve to be taken seriously may include intricate historic legacies of a country, a climate of political authoritarianism, military interventions, extreme poverty, social, cultural, economic and political discrimination, exclusion and marginalization, inequalities, caste hierarchies, ethnic fragmentation, rapid demographic changes, patriarchal values and a "macho" culture, migration processes, a widen-

---

[235] See A/HRC/19/41, para. 21.
[236] See A/HRC/14/22/Add.2, paras. 38 and 89.
[237] See CCPR/C/RUS/CO/6, para. 27.

ing gulf between urban and rural areas, the breakdown of meaningful public discourse, lack of intergroup communication, endemic corruption and political cronyism, widespread disenchantment with politics, general loss of trust in weak or inexistent public institutions, and a culture of impunity and denial for past serious violations of international human rights and humanitarian law. Any specific incident of violence in the name of religion warrants a careful, contextualized analysis of all relevant factors, including the broader political environment. It will thereby become clear that religion is almost never an isolated root cause of violent conflicts or attacks.

14. An isolated focus on religion in descriptions of violence, conflicts and civil wars often creates the risk of nourishing fatalistic attitudes. The impression that seemingly "perpetual" religious or denominational differences lie at the root of respective problems can exacerbate feelings of helplessness and lead to inaction. However, if it is wrongly assumed that certain violent conflicts have their decisive root causes in religious strife that allegedly started centuries or even millennia ago, this will likely distract attention from the responsibilities that Governments, community leaders, media representatives, civil society organizations and international agencies have today.

15. Moreover, it is important to avoid "essentialist" views that falsely ascribe violence to the essence of certain religions or to religion in general. The formulation "violence in the name of religion" in the present report is deliberately chosen to emphasize the fact that the perpetrators of violent crimes are always human beings, not religions as such. It is human beings — individuals, groups, community leaders, State representatives, non-State actors and others — who invoke religion or specific religious tenets for the purposes of legitimizing, stoking, spreading or escalating violence. In other words, the relationship between religion and violence can never be an immediate one; it always presupposes human agency, that is, individuals or groups who actively bring about that connection — or who challenge that connection.

2. Inadequacy of the instrumentalization thesis

16. Whereas an isolated focus on religion ignores the relevance of political and other non-religious factors, the "instrumentalization thesis", by contrast, from the outset denies that religious motives can play a genuine role in incidents of violence. Instead, it is assumed that perpetrators of such violence merely "instrumentalize" religion for political, economic or other mundane purposes. The term "instrumentalization" conveys the

impression that religious persuasions themselves have little, if anything, to do with the acts of violence perpetrated in their name.

17. However, downplaying the significance of religious motives, fears and obsessions in this context would be factually wrong and conceptually inappropriate in many cases. It would furthermore mean that religious communities and their leaderships are from the outset excluded from taking any genuine responsibility for violence in the name of religion and, by implication, cannot contribute meaningfully towards tackling the problem.

18. It remains true that acts of violence cannot be attributed to religions per se or to any particular religion, as these acts are always carried out by human beings pursuing certain aims in particular social, economic, political and historical contexts. Yet it is equally true that human agency comprises a broad range of motives, including religious ones. While in some cases violent attacks may be orchestrated by Machiavellian strategists who whip up religious sentiments, there are obviously religious fanatics who seem to believe that, by torturing or killing fellow human beings, they actually perform a service to God. Moreover, it is a disturbing reality that religious fanatics may find some admirers and supporters within their broader communities who mistakenly resort to violence as a manifestation of strong religious commitment. Religious communities and their leaders, including theologians of various denominations, have a responsibility to tackle this problem on the basis of a clear analysis of its various root causes, including narrow-minded and polarizing interpretations of religious messages.

3.   A broad range of factors and actors

19. The two above-mentioned simplistic interpretations often appear in discussions about violence in the name of religion. What both interpretations have in common is that, albeit in different ways, they ignore relevant factors and actors. The isolated focus on religion neglects the significance of human agency in general, political and other non-religious factors in particular, thus possibly leading to fatalism in the face of seemingly perpetual sectarian strife. By contrast, the instrumentalization thesis trivializes the role that religious motives may play in committing and supporting acts of violence, leading to inadequate responses from religious communities and their leaders.

20. The Special Rapporteur is convinced that policies aimed at overcoming violence in the name of religion must be based on a comprehensive

understanding of all underlying factors and responsible actors. This is the sine qua non for mobilizing all relevant stakeholders to do their utmost to eliminate such violence.

C. Root causes, factors and political circumstances

21. Violence committed in the name of religion is a complex reality. Given the word limits of the present report, the Special Rapporteur will restrict himself to a few non-exhaustive typological observations.[238]

I. Narrow-minded interpretations of religions

22. For many people, religion is a very emotional issue, deeply connected to feelings of identity, devotion and group attachment. Religious convictions can drive people to push their boundaries and perform acts of solidarity, compassion and charity. However, this enormous potential can also turn into a destructive force, feeding collective polarization, narrow-mindedness and violent fanaticism.

23. Religious fanaticism is a danger that exists in different religions and beliefs. Attempts to derive a propensity for violence directly from specific theological features of particular religions are highly problematic. Not only do they fail to do justice to the wide range of violent manifestations connected to most different religions and beliefs, including secular worldviews; they also neglect the decisive factor of human agency as pointed out before.

24. Although most religions claim a transcendent — and in this sense "trans-human" — origin, religious sources and normative codes of conduct always accommodate different readings that are actively undertaken by human beings. Thus, human agency is inevitably involved in interpreting religious traditions, dogmas, laws or identities. Open-minded interpretations that encourage tolerance, empathy and solidarity across boundaries may exist alongside narrow-minded interpretations of the same religion, which lead to polarized worldviews and a militant rejection of people holding other persuasions. Whatever the ultimate origins of a religious belief are thought to be, human beings bear in any case responsibility for the practical consequences that they draw from the interpretation of their faith. This particularly applies to religious teachers, preachers and community leaders, whose influence should always be connected with an enhanced sense of responsibility.

---

[238] See also A/HRC/25/58, paras. 16-70.

25. Whenever violence is justified by the invocation of religion or arrogated to religious tenets, the specific interpretations, for example, religious ideas, concepts, images or anxieties, should be taken seriously. Although they should not be seen in isolation from broader political and other factors, it would be too easy simply to dismiss polarizing religious interpretations as mere excuses for acts of aggression. At the same time, the pitfalls of essentialism can be avoided by bearing in mind that it is always human beings, in their various roles and positions, who remain the responsible agents for any justifications and commission of violence.

2.   Loss of trust in public institutions

26. The seeds of religious fanaticism fortunately do not always find fertile ground. Whereas in many societies those promoting religious narrow-mindedness, violence or even terrorism do not succeed in mobilizing many followers, in other countries their opportunities may be higher. There are societies in which the voices of fanaticism resonate strongly and in some countries they have even managed to infiltrate important parts of the State apparatus or to lead the Government.

27. One main factor, which typically makes larger groups of people receptive to messages of religious extremism, is a general loss of trust in public institutions. What often starts with endemic corruption and political cronyism may end up in a total disenchantment with State politics by large parts of the population. However, if people have lost any trust in the fair functioning of public institutions, they will try to manage their lives by resorting to their own support networks. Frequently, such networks are defined along ethnic or religious lines.

28. When overarching public institutions lose their credibility, groupings defined by ethnic and/or religious loyalties at the same time gain more importance. Such fragmentation processes typically produce inward-looking mentalities, collective anxieties and attitudes of general suspicion against everything happening outside of the boundaries of one's own group. Where the willingness to trust people is gradually shrinking to an internal circle, collective narrow-mindedness will be a likely consequence. In this situation, polarizing apocalyptic religious messages may become "attractive" since they actually seem to match the mind-set of people who feel that they live under siege in a hostile and dangerous political environment. Everyday anxieties and militant religious messages may thus blend into each other.

29.   In such a precarious constellation, a sudden crisis such as an incident or even mere rumours can easily ignite mass-scale violence, including atrocious acts of barbarism justified in the name of religion. Owing to the lack of trustworthy overarching public institutions, political hysteria may set in and further poison the relationship between competing communities. The end result of this vicious cycle can be a climate of political paranoia in which militarized groups fight each other by using all available means, including religious condemnation and demonization. Militarized group identities defined along religious lines and dichotomized religious worldviews can thus reinforce each other.

30.   The absence of trustworthy public institutions often goes together with a decline of public communication. If negative rumours remain unchecked by any counter-evidence that could be presented and discussed in public discourses, they may harden into fully-fledged conspiracy projections. In such situations, apocalyptic images and violent messages, which can be found within different religious traditions, may provide interpretative patterns for assessing contemporary anxieties, thereby becoming an additional factor of violent escalation.

3.   Policies of exclusion

31.   While many of the most extreme acts of violence in the name of religion currently occur in the context of failing or failed States, State agencies can also be directly involved in violent sectarian polarization. This is often the case where the State understands itself as the guardian of one particular religion. If this is compounded with an "official" or State religion, the negative impact on people belonging to religious minorities tends to be even worse. Whereas the followers of the protected religion(s) usually receive a privileged treatment, adherents to other religions or beliefs may suffer serious discrimination, such as underrepresentation in public employment, exclusion from higher education or even deprivation of citizenship. The experience of systematic exclusion almost inevitably leads to divisiveness within the society.

32.   Policies of exclusion in the field of religion exist under different auspices. On the one hand, there are a number of Governments that base their legitimacy on their role as guardians of certain religious truth claims. Those people who do not adhere to the protected religion or those who follow interpretations deemed "deviant" may be publicly attacked as "infidels", "apostates" or "heretics"; some State may even exercise pressure in order to forcibly convert them to the official religion of the country.

33. On the other hand, there is an even broader group of States, including formally secular States, which promote a particular religious heritage as an inherent part of their national identity, without resorting to specific truth claims. Such national heritage can either consist of one religion, which has largely shaped the national history, or comprise a number of different religions or beliefs, which are officially recognized as constituting the "traditional religious mosaic" of the nation. In fact, the fault lines resulting from harnessing religion for the promotion of national identity often run between "traditional" and "non-traditional" religions, including religions or beliefs of immigrants. Individuals or groups perceived as not fitting into the traditional self-understanding of the nation may be suspected of undermining national cohesion or even acting as fifth columns in the interest of "foreign powers" or "foreign donors".

34. Policies of exclusion are often manifested in hostile public statements made by populist politicians, usually in conjunction with incitement to religious hatred in the media. Sometimes, even very small minorities are demonized as allegedly posing a dangerous threat to the long-term survival of the nation, or they are accused of being involved in clandestine conspiracies. The Special Rapporteur has often noted a pronounced gender dimension in hate speech, for example, the stoked fear of far-reaching demographic changes allegedly in a strategic attempt of minorities to get the upper hand in the long run, and as a result of a hyperbolic sexual drive ascribed to members of religious minorities, who thereby are depicted as "primitive". LGBT people have also been falsely portrayed in religious discourse as "threatening" the survival of a nation or being part of a "conspiracy" to control population growth.

35. Policies of exclusion may also manifest themselves in formal acts of administration or legislation. For instance, unwelcome religious minorities may confront insuperable obstacles when trying to obtain a legal personality status without which they cannot develop an infrastructure needed for running their community affairs in a sustainable manner. Sometimes the very existence of such communities in a country is deemed "illegal". As a result, people belonging to such discriminated minorities typically suffer systematic harassment and intimidation. A factor that further increases the likelihood of harassment is anti-blasphemy laws or anti-proselytism laws, which may threaten criminal punishments for vaguely circumscribed "offences". Countless examples demonstrate that such laws disproportionately affect minorities. Meanwhile, they may encourage self-appointed vigilante groups to commit acts of violent ag-

gression, frequently with direct or indirect support by law enforcement agencies.

4.   Impunity, trivialization and the culture of silence

36.   A major problem underneath violence in the name of religion is a culture of impunity that exists in quite a number of countries. Often, victims and their families report that the authorities do not provide efficient protection, that police reach the scene of violence late or become bystanders watching the places of worship being torched or people attacked by an aggressive mob. It is not always clear whether impunity results from a lack of capacity or even reflects a certain degree of complicity by parts of the State apparatus.

37.   An additional factor that further aggravates the situation is the tendency of certain Governments to ignore or downplay the systemic root causes of violence in the name of religion. When addressing the issue, they may trivialize it as "sporadic incidents" allegedly caused by a few irresponsible individuals, without acknowledging the broader structural or political dimension of the issue. Official statistics displaying the frequency and patterns of violence, including disaggregated data on the underlying motives, often do not exist.

38.   In a climate of fear and intimidation in some countries — either caused by aggressive non-State actors or by repressive Governments — the population may largely refrain from even talking about violence committed in the name of religion. This constitutes yet another layer of the problem. The growing culture of silence, often exacerbated by restrictive laws, prevents responsible stakeholders from tackling the problem publicly and strategically. Overcoming the culture of silence is a major precondition for holding Governments accountable for relevant political actions and omissions, including situations of impunity.

D.   The human rights framework

39.   The scourge of violence in the name of religion calls for concerted action of States, religious and belief communities, interreligious initiatives, civil society and the media to contain and eventually overcome this phenomenon. Human rights provide the normative framework in which any policies tackling the problem and its root causes must be developed. Their potential in this regard is manifold:

   a)   Human rights represent a broad moral consensus endorsed by the international community and are binding under international law, thus combining moral persuasiveness with legal force;

b) Human rights are connected with the establishment of infrastructure-relevant institutions at the global, regional, national and subnational levels. This complex infrastructure facilitates strategic cooperation between different stakeholders in the implementation and monitoring of human rights;

c) The infrastructure of human rights institutions and mechanisms at different levels — from global to local — can furthermore help to build or restore trust among people, particularly in situations in which public institutions in a society have largely ceased to function adequately;

d) Although human rights as legal norms do not themselves constitute an overarching belief-system, the underlying principles — such as the respect for human dignity, the equality of all human beings and the aspiration to universal justice — have substantive overlaps with many religious, culture and philosophical traditions. Human rights may therefore provide incentives for strengthening the awareness of the charitable messages contained in different religions or beliefs in order to build resilience against messages of hatred and violence;

e) Freedom of religion or belief, in conjunction with other human rights, provides the normative basis for the coexistence and cooperation of people belonging to most different religions or beliefs and obliges the State to provide an inclusive framework. Furthermore, freedom of religion or belief assures that different communities and subcommunities will receive protection.

40. This non-exhaustive list shows the potential of human rights to bring together various stakeholders who, in concerted actions, should do their utmost to combat violence in the name of religion. Below, the Special Rapporteur discusses specific roles of some relevant stakeholders in this area.

E. Obligations and responsibilities under international law

I. Overarching obligations of the State

41. The State is not just another stakeholder alongside various other actors and institutions. As the formal guarantor of human rights under international law, the State has an overarching obligation that can be di-

vided conceptually into three levels, that is, the obligations to respect, to protect and to promote human rights.

(a) Obligations to respect

42. For the context of the present discussion, the obligations to respect chiefly require that the State abandon all sorts of — formal or informal — policies of exclusion by which persons belonging to certain groups suffer discrimination.[239] This has manifold consequences. In particular, Government representatives must clearly refrain from any statements that may be perceived as condoning or even encouraging acts of violence that target religious dissenters, religious minorities or other groups of people. Legislation that renders the existence of certain religious communities as such "illegal" in the country or prevents them from developing a sustainable infrastructure is incompatible with the universal right to freedom of religion or belief and should be revoked. Such legislation furthermore fuels resentments and may encourage acts of intimidation, including by law enforcement agencies. Moreover, the State should repeal anti-blasphemy laws, anti-conversion laws and criminal laws that discriminate against certain people according to their religious affiliations or beliefs or criminalize their "dissident" practices. Apart from further increasing the vulnerability of marginalized groups or individuals, these laws may give a pretext to vigilante groups and other perpetrators of hatred for intimidating people and committing acts of violence. Textbooks used for school education should not contain stereotypes and prejudices that may stoke hostile sentiments against the followers of certain religions or beliefs and groups that suffer systematic discrimination, including women and LGBT persons.

43. In order to operate as a credible guarantor of freedom of religion or belief for everyone, the State should not identify itself exclusively with one particular religion or belief (or one particular type of religions) at the expense of equal treatment of the followers of other faiths.[240] As ample experience demonstrates, the use of religion in the context of national identity politics always harbours aggravated risks of discrimination against minorities, for instance, against members of immigrant religious communities or new religious movements, thus creating divisiveness within the society. Any exclusivist settings should therefore be critically addressed and finally replaced by an inclusive institutional framework in

---

[239] See Human Rights Committee general comment no. 22, CCPR/C/21/Rev.1/Add.4, paras. 9 and 10.

[240] See A/HRC/19/60, paras. 65 and 66.

which religious diversity can unfold without discrimination and without fear.

(b) Obligations to protect

44. Violations of human rights do not only originate from the State; they are quite often carried out by non-State actors. Nonetheless, the State bears a responsibility for such acts inasmuch as they may reflect inadequate human rights protection.

45. A first step towards providing protection against violence in the name of religion is a quick and unequivocal condemnation of any such acts, whenever they occur, by high representatives of the State. State representatives should indeed take the lead in rejecting violence, expressing sympathy for victims and providing public support for targeted individuals or groups. Violent attacks targeting members of groups that face systematic discrimination in the name of religion should be understood as attacks on the entire society. Public messages to that effect, however, can only be credible if they openly address the root causes, including systemic political conditions, which may become enabling factors of violence. Unfortunately, some Governments display a tendency to resort to policies of trivializing violence by ascribing the incidents to just a few irresponsible individuals without acknowledging the broader political dimensions of the issue. Overcoming such trivialization is the sine qua non for designing effective preventative and coping strategies.

46. A major issue in the context of protection against violence in the name of religion is the fight against impunity, wherever it exists. Those who commit, or are complicit in, acts of violence must always be brought to justice. This requires training for law enforcement agencies and the establishment of an efficient and independent judiciary. Moreover, anti-discrimination legislation plays an indispensable role in protecting the equality of all in their enjoyment of human rights, across religious or denominational divides, thus preventing or overcoming divisiveness within society.

47. While the States' obligation to protect human rights requires them to take effective measures to combat terrorism, the Special Rapporteur would like to reiterate that States must ensure that any measure taken to combat terrorism fully complies with their obligations under international law, particularly human rights, refugee and humanitarian law. In this context, the targeting of specific groups, including members of par-

ticular religious communities through so-called religious profiling, is of concern.[241]

(c) Obligations to promote

48. Beyond respecting and protecting human rights, States should also take a broad range of positive measures aimed at facilitating their effective implementation. This includes providing an appropriate framework in which other stakeholders, including religious communities, interreligious initiatives, civil society organizations, human rights defenders and media professionals, can unfold their specific potential.

49. Moreover, the State itself should use all available means — including formal and informal education and community outreach — in order to promote a culture of respect, non-discrimination and appreciation of diversity within society. In close consultation with all relevant stakeholders, the State should develop national action plans against violence in the name of religion. A useful document in this context is the Rabat Plan of Action on the prohibition of advocacy of national, racial or religious hatred that constitutes incitement to discrimination, hostility or violence.[242] The Rabat Plan of Action, elaborated with broad participation by experts, Member States and civil society organizations under the auspices of the Office of the United Nations High Commissioner for Human Rights, can provide guidance on how to build resilience in society against incitement to religious hatred and concomitant acts of violence. Building resilience requires a broad range of activities, including educational efforts, early warning capacities and policies on crisis preparedness, by establishing channels of communication that enable relevant actors to respond strategically and swiftly.

50. National human rights institutions are particularly suited for the promotion of human rights. Some of them have an explicit mandate for also promoting intergroup relationships. The Special Rapporteur would like to encourage them, including their International Coordinating Committee, to take an active ownership of the Rabat Plan of Action and develop strategies to eliminate the root causes of violence in the name of religion.

51. Furthermore, States should safeguard the memory of all population groups, and of religious communities in particular, including by develop-

---

[241] See A/HRC/4/21, paras. 40–42.
[242] See A/HRC/22/17/Add.4, annex.

ing and protecting national archives, memorial museums and monuments.

2. Responsibility to protect populations from genocide, war crimes, ethnic cleansing and crimes against humanity

52. At the 2005 World Summit, Heads of State and Government committed to the responsibility to protect their populations from genocide, war crimes, ethnic cleansing and crimes against humanity.[243] This entails the responsibility of States to protect their own populations from atrocity crimes; the responsibility to help other States do so through the provision of international assistance; and the responsibility to take collective action when a State manifestly fails to protect its population. In particular, the word "populations" refers to all people living within a State's territory, whether citizens or not, and including religious groups. The principle builds on existing obligations under international law and embodies a political determination to prevent and respond to atrocity crimes, but does not itself have an independent legal character.

53. In his 2009 report on implementing the responsibility to protect (A/63/677), the Secretary-General established a framework for implementing the responsibility to protect principle on the basis of three equal, mutually reinforcing and non-sequential pillars. The first pillar encompasses the responsibility of each individual State to protect its populations from genocide, war crimes, ethnic cleansing and crimes against humanity. The second pillar focuses on the provision of international assistance on the basis of paragraphs 138 and 139 of the 2005 World Summit Outcome, which asserts that the international community should, as appropriate, encourage and help States to exercise this responsibility, and that the international community should also support the United Nations in establishing an early warning capability and assist those which are under stress before crises and conflicts break out. The third pillar outlines options for taking collective action, in a timely and decisive manner and in accordance with the Charter of the United Nations, should peaceful means be inadequate and where national authorities are manifestly failing to protect their populations.[244]

---

[243] See General Assembly resolution 60/1, paras. 138 and 139.
[244] See also www.un.org/en/preventgenocide/adviser/responsibility.shtml; and A/69/266, paras. 78-85.

3.   Obligations of non-State armed groups

(a)   International human rights law

54. While international human rights law traditionally focused only on the obligations of States,[245] an evolving approach recognizes the importance and impact of certain non-State actors, arguing that some human rights obligations also apply to them, including non-State armed groups with (or arguably even without) effective control over a territory. In that regard, the Committee on the Elimination of Discrimination against Women stressed in its general recommendation No. 30 (2013) on women in conflict prevention, conflict and post-conflict situations, that "under certain circumstances, in particular where an armed group with an identifiable political structure exercises significant control over territory and population, non-State actors are obliged to respect international human rights".[246]

55. Special procedures and commissions of Inquiry have also addressed human rights violations committed in the name of religion by armed groups with effective control over territory.[247] "Effective control" means that the non-State armed group has consolidated its control and authority over a territory to such an extent that it can exclude the State from governing the territory on a more than temporary basis.[248] Furthermore, armed groups without effective control over territory have been held to have committed human rights violations.[249] In May 2014, a report by the United Nations Mission in the Republic of South Sudan[250] stressed that the most basic human rights obligations, in particular those emanating from peremptory international law (jus cogens), bind both the State and armed opposition groups in times of peace and during armed conflict.

---

[245] See CCPR/C/21/Rev.1/Add.13, para. 8.

[246] See CEDAW/C/GC/30, para. 16.

[247] See, for example, A/56/253, paras. 27 and 30, concerning the Taliban; A/HRC/2/7, para. 19, concerning Hezbollah; A/HRC/18/48, para. 31, concerning Al-Shabaab; and www.ohchr.org/Documents/HRBodies/HRCouncil/CoISyria/HRC_CRP_ISIS_14Nov2014.pdf, concerning Islamic State in Iraq and the Levant.

[248] See article 42 of the Regulations respecting the Laws and Customs of War on Land; CCPR/C/21/Rev.1/Add.13, para. 10; and CAT/C/GC/2, para. 16.

[249] See www2.ohchr.org/SPdocs/Countries/LRAReport_December2009_E.pdf and www2.ohchr.org/SPdocs/Countries/LRAReport_SudanDecember2009.doc, concerning the Lord's Resistance Army.

[250] See www.unmiss.unmissions.org/Portals/unmiss/Human%20Rights%20Reports/UNMISS%20Conflict%20in%20South%20Sudan%20-%20A%20Human%20Rights%20Report.pdf.

(b) International humanitarian law

56. In the event that a non-State armed group is party to an armed conflict, international humanitarian law can also be invoked. Article 3 common to the four Geneva Conventions of 1949 defines certain minimum guarantees that all parties involved in a non-international armed conflict should observe, including to treat in all circumstances persons who take no active part in the hostilities humanely, without any adverse distinction founded on religion or faith. Furthermore, a number of norms contained in the Geneva Conventions of 1949 and the Additional Protocols I and II of 1977 have reached the status of customary international law and, as such, are binding on all parties to the armed conflict.[251]

57. Most notably, international humanitarian law requires that both the State and non-State armed groups take all measures to minimize the impact of violence on civilians, respect the principles of distinction and proportionality when carrying out military operations and ensure the safety and protection of civilians by enabling them to leave areas affected by violence in safety and dignity as well as to access basic humanitarian assistance at all times.[252]

(c) International criminal law

58. Certain conduct of members of non-State armed groups may also trigger individual responsibility under international criminal law. The Rome Statute of the International Criminal Court provides definitions of "genocide" in article 6, of "crimes against humanity" in article 7 and of "war crimes" in article 8. These provisions also include several references to the terms "religious" or "religion", for example, in article 6 ("acts committed with intent to destroy, in whole or in part, a [...] religious group, as such"), article 7, paragraph 1 (h), ("persecution against any identifiable group or collectivity on [...] religious [...] grounds") as well as article 8, paragraphs 2 (b)(ix) and (e)(iv), ("[i]ntentionally directing attacks against buildings dedicated to religion, [...] provided they are not military objectives").

---

[251] See Jean-Marie Henckaerts and Louise Doswald-Beck, *Customary International Humanitarian Law, Volume I: Rules*, International Committee of the Red Cross (Cambridge: Cambridge University Press, 2005), with rules 3, 27, 30, 38, 40, 88, 104 and 127 specifically referring to "religious" issues.

[252] See www.ohchr.org/EN/NewsEvents/Pages/DisplayNews.aspx?NewsID=14884&LangID=E.

59. Individual criminal responsibility is essential to ensuring accountability for gross or serious violations of international human rights and humanitarian law. However, according to article 25, paragraph 3 (f), of the Rome Statute, "a person who abandons the effort to commit the crime or otherwise prevents the completion of the crime shall not be liable for punishment under this Statute for the attempt to commit that crime if that person completely and voluntarily gave up the criminal purpose". Hence, this provision in combination with the threat of possible international prosecution may hopefully influence individual members of non-State armed groups to abandon their efforts to commit international crimes.

F.   Roles of other stakeholders

1.   Religious communities and their leaderships

60. Perpetrators of violence typically represent comparatively small segments of the various religious communities to which they belong, while the large majority of believers are usually appalled to see violence perpetrated in the name of their religion. It is all the more important for the majorities and their leaders, who do not endorse the violence, to speak out against it. In some countries, religious communities organize broad demonstrations and use all available media to publicly condemn religious justifications of violent atrocities. However, there are also situations in which the silence of the majority and their leaders is quite "deafening", thus factually leaving the public stage to small aggressive groups.[253] Speaking out in these situations often requires courage, determination and the ability to seize opportunities to intervene at the right moment when violence arises and can still be contained and curbed.

61. Overcoming a culture of silence, wherever it exists, in the face of violent attacks is of paramount importance. Often, perpetrators of violence pretend to act on behalf of a "silent majority". Religious fanatics furthermore like to portray themselves as "heroes" and a religious avant-garde that ultimately promotes the interests of their community. As long as the majorities and broader communities remain largely silent, extremists can easily play this game. They may feel that they have carte blanche to perform acts of violence and to sell these atrocities as manifestations of religious devotion.

---

[253] See, for example, A/HRC/19/60/Add.2, para. 65 (Republic of Moldova).

62. Overcoming the culture of silence is not an easy task and, depending on the specific situation, such attempts can be quite risky. One problem is that extremist religious groups typically receive or seek to use broad media coverage, whereas voices of peace and reconciliation often remain at the margins of public attention. Although this can be a highly frustrating experience, it should never serve as an excuse for remaining silent. The cynical belief that bad news makes for good sales must not prevent other members of religious communities from bringing forward their views actively. Moreover, in a climate of intimidation, many believers, for fear of reprisals, may refrain from speaking out publicly. In such situations, fellow believers living in safer political environments should lend their voices and clearly condemn violence committed in the name of their religion.

63. The Special Rapporteur has seen impressive anti-violence statements issued by representatives of religious communities, that is, statements which are clear, theologically profound and passionate.[254] However, he has also come across public rejections of violence which remain disappointingly abstract, because they are based on the problematic assumption that violence results from a mere "instrumentalization" of religion and, accordingly, has little, if anything, to do with religious motives. Yet, such rejections based on a trivialization of religious motives will themselves remain trivial. As discussed earlier, the instrumentalization thesis one-sidedly attributes the problem to external, non-religious factors while too quickly discarding the potential relevance also of religious obsessions and theological views.

64. Religious communities and especially their representatives and intellectual leaders should not succumb to the temptation to reduce the issue of violence in the name of religion to mere "misunderstandings" and external abuses. This would amount to an irresponsible trivialization of the problem. Instead, when dealing with the issue of such violence, theologians and religious leaders should actually expose themselves to the disturbing fact that perpetrators of violence — or at least some of them — may be convinced to perform an act of service to God when killing fellow humans. Taking seriously these ideas, however bizarre and distorted they may seem, is the precondition for giving sufficiently profound responses. Only by confronting the perverse "attractiveness" of violent religious extremism for some people, including people living in

---

[254] See, for example, A/HRC/25/58/Add.1, para. 35 (Sierra Leone) and A/HRC/25/58/Add.2, para. 16 (Jordan).

precarious and volatile political circumstances, will it be possible to tackle the various root causes of violence, including polarizing religious interpretations and incitement to religious hatred.

65. Beyond a clear condemnation of violence committed in the name of religion, communities and their leaders should positively promote empathy, tolerance and an appreciation of diversity. They should challenge the religious extremists' authenticity claims by exposing the ignorance of their views of the charitable core messages contained in religious traditions. Religious communities and scholars may also play an important role in rehabilitation and reintegration programs for violent extremist offenders and foreign fighters who returned to their country of origin, also with a view to neutralize possible future radicalization efforts.[255]

2.   Interreligious initiatives

66. The potential of interreligious communication for overcoming violence in the name of religion is enormous.[256] Many examples demonstrate that violence frequently occurs in the absence of any trustful communication across religious or denominational boundaries, and the related vacuum of ideological power. The reasons for the lack or decline of intergroup communication can be manifold, ranging from broader processes of societal fragmentation and policies of exclusion to the demonization of others in polarizing religious interpretations. Whatever the reasons in a particular situation may be, initiatives aimed at improving the relationship between different religious communities can substantially contribute to preventing violent escalation. In-depth research into a number of cases of communal violence has led to the conclusion that acts of violence could be contained to a certain degree in localities where communities had developed a sustainable culture of cross-boundary communication. Apart from its preventative potential, intergroup communication therefore also helps to alleviate situations in which mass-scale violence actually occurs.

67. For interreligious communication to be productive, partners should meet on an equal footing and there should always be room for a meaningful exchange beyond mere ritualistic encounters. A broad representa-

---

[255]   See, for example, www.thegctf.org/documents/10162/38330/Rome+Memorandum-English. and www.thegctf.org/documents/10162/140201/14Sept19_The+Hague-Marrakech+FTF+Memorandum.pdf.

[256]   See A/HRC/22/51/Add.1, para. 90 (Cyprus), A/HRC/25/58, para. 44 and A/66/156, paras. 21-69.

tion, including gender balance and participation of different generations, can ensure that larger populations can take active ownership of such initiatives, thus enhancing their sustainability. There is much space for improvements in this regard, since women, including feminist theologians, are typically very underrepresented in interreligious dialogue initiatives. Their voices are sadly absent in many projects. The roles of women human rights defenders should also be promoted as they can contribute to a less patriarchal interpretation of religions that disproportionately affect the rights of women, girls and LGBT persons.

68. Projects that involve interreligious cooperation can have far-reaching impacts. One very positive recent development is the enhanced interreligious cooperation in providing aid for refugees and internally displaced persons.[257] Apart from supporting people who are living under dire conditions, such cooperation also sends a much-needed message of hope to these communities and to the international community, and constitutes good practices that may inspire others.

69. Some initiatives have led to the formal establishment of interreligious councils in which people of different religious and denominational backgrounds meet regularly. This can be useful to ensure a sustainable cooperation and keep the forces of violent extremism at bay. At the same time, there are also many illustrations of informal grass-root initiatives with the purpose of cherishing trustful relations. Quite surprisingly, everyday communication across religious divides may even exist at the local level in countries that are torn by religious extremism and violent conflicts. Figuratively speaking, even in a desert of violent political paranoia, people communicating across boundaries can uphold certain oases of common sense that certainly deserve to be acknowledged, strengthened and supported politically.

70. Interreligious communication and intergroup cooperation have a key function in all agendas to overcome violence in the name of religion. Although people who meet regularly across boundaries will not necessarily agree on all issues, they will realize that followers of other religions and denominations are not "aliens" with totally different mentalities or feelings. This is an important experience and a precondition for overcoming hostile stereotypes. Discovering common concerns, worries and

---

[257] For example, cooperation between the organizations Lutheran World Federation and Islamic Relief Worldwide; see www.lutheranworld.org/news/lwf-and-islamic-relief-sign-memorandum-understanding.

interests may also be the first step for developing joint action plans for tackling the root causes of violence more strategically.

3. Civil society

71. Civil society organizations differ from religious communities in that they predominantly locate themselves in the "civil" sphere. What brings people together in civil society organizations is not, or not primarily, a common religious belief or practice, but rather joint commitments to address issues of common concerns, including human rights. This does not preclude the possibility that quite a number of civil society organizations at the same time understand themselves as being faith-based.

72. The expertise gained by civil society organizations is indispensable for assessing the human rights situation, including freedom of religion or belief. For victims of human rights violations and people living under conditions of constant intimidation, it is reassuring to know that civil society organizations monitor their situations and alert relevant authorities and the public when necessary. They provide information, advice, guidance, assistance and sometimes protection, including by following up on individual cases. The findings of civil society organizations can also assume an early warning function, notably in volatile situations.

73. Moreover, in the face of violent aggression, civil society plays a major role in overcoming a culture of silence wherever this exists. It is important for individuals and groups targeted by incitement to religious hatred and violent attacks to experience solidarity support and that others speak out on their behalf. Overcoming silence is likewise needed to challenge the claims of perpetrators of hatred to act in the name of a "silent majority". Speaking out against such violence, and the broader political or religious dimensions involved with these problems, can be dangerous. Therefore, local civil society organizations may need international networks to defend them in situations where they are threatened.[258]

74. Different faith-based and secular civil society organizations work together and have created common platforms. Beyond the pragmatic advantages of joining forces, such cooperation also demonstrates that a commitment to human rights can create and strengthen solidarity across all religious, cultural and philosophical divides. This is an important message in itself. The Special Rapporteur has come across impressive exam-

---

[258] See www.ohchr.org/EN/issues/SRHRDefenders/.

ples in this regard, for example, initiatives taken by Christian civil society organizations in support of atheists or Buddhists under threat and public statements made by Bahá'í representatives against the persecution of Shia Muslims. Such acts of solidarity have a highly symbolic value.

4.   Contributions by the media

75.   While the media, including the Internet, are frequently used to stoke intergroup hostilities by spreading false, biased or partisan information and hateful messages that incite violence, they can also be harnessed to foster cross-boundary communication and promote policies of tolerance, reconciliation and cooperation. In short, the media are a part of the problem, but they must certainly be part of the solution.

76.   Hostile media campaigns can have disastrous effects on people's mindset and in the long run can undermine people's common sense, creating a climate of confusion and collective hysteria. The most important antidote to hostile media campaigns targeting religious minorities or other groups is the diligent research of facts.

77.   Fact-finding may also include a public analysis of collective historical traumas. Meaningful communication across boundaries requires the possibility that people can agree — or at least partially agree — on important facts concerning intricate historic legacies. It is no coincidence that reconciliation commissions usually also have the aspiration of "truth" in their titles (typically being called "truth and reconciliation commissions"), because only on the basis of agreeing on at least some elementary historic facts can communities tackle traumatic historic legacies that otherwise would have the potential of tearing societies apart. The "ghosts of the past" can only be put to rest by public debates based on a careful research of facts. Here again, public discourse facilitated by a rich landscape of independent and critical media has an important function.

78.   The media play an indispensable role in bringing about a culture of public discourse. Where such a culture remains underdeveloped or even non-existent, prejudiced messages against groups that face systematic discrimination usually find fertile ground, because hostile rumours remain unchecked by factual evidence, and fearful narratives can hardly be exposed to public scrutiny or counter-narratives. Positively speaking, a developed culture of open and frank public communication across boundaries is a prerequisite necessary for preventing resentments from escalating to fully-fledged conspiracy projections.

79. The media are moreover needed for overcoming the culture of silence, wherever it exists, in the face of violence in the name of religion. In conjunction with civil society organizations, representatives of the media should openly address incidents of violence, their root causes and political circumstances. Since a culture of impunity and a culture of silence often go hand in hand, putting an end to such silence may also be a first step towards tackling the problem of impunity. Journalists and other media workers who operate in dangerous environments require networks to defend them against violent threats.

80. Moreover, impressive media projects bear witness to the enormous positive potential of the media in facilitating cross-boundary understandings. This may also include the production of fiction aimed at overcoming societal divides. Particularly after experiences of traumatic collective violence, positive media initiatives can help restore the faculty of empathy by making people aware that the members of other religions or beliefs, far from being "aliens", in fact have quite similar fears, hopes and feelings. Generally, the potential impact of media work across religious or other divides can hardly be overemphasized.

81. Freedom of religion or belief cannot flourish without freedom of expression, and the human rights enshrined in close neighbourhood in articles 18 and 19 of the Universal Declaration of Human Rights and the International Covenant on Civil and Political Rights mutually reinforce each other. Like most other human rights, freedom of expression is not without possible limits, and there can be situations in which the State has to impose restrictions, for instance, in order to protect targeted minorities against advocacy of religious hatred that constitutes incitement to discrimination, hostility or violence. However, bearing in mind the high value of free communication and the indispensable functions of the media to facilitate public discussions, any limitations imposed on freedom of expression must be enacted with a high degree of empirical and normative diligence. Limitations must meet all the criteria enshrined in article 19, paragraph 3, of the International Covenant, which are further spelled out by the Human Right Committee in its general comment no. 34.[259] Moreover, the Rabat Plan of Action also sets a high threshold for any re-

---

[259] See CCPR/C/GC/34, paras. 21-52; see also principles 11 and 12 of the Camden Principles on Freedom of Expression and Equality, available from www.article19. org/data/files/pdfs/standards/the-camden-principles-on-freedom-of-expression-and-equality.pdf.

strictions on freedom of expression, including for the application of article 20, paragraph 2, of the International Covenant.[260]

82. Indeed, the best antidote to hate speech is "more speech", in the sense of nuanced and precise media reporting, self-regulating bodies and a fair representation of religious and other minorities within the media, careful fact-finding in order to dispel myths and check negative gossiping, public statements by civil society organizations, sustainable interreligious communication and clear anti-violence messages sent by religious communities, as elaborated above.

III. Conclusions and recommendations

83. Violence in the name of religion does not "erupt" in analogy to natural catastrophes and it should not be misconstrued as the inevitable result of sectarian hostilities that supposedly originated centuries or millennia ago, thus seemingly lying outside of the scope of the responsibility that different actors have today. It is important to overcome fatalistic attitudes that often stem from simplistic descriptions of the phenomena. Rather than being rooted in seemingly "perpetual" religious antagonisms, violence in the name of religion is typically caused by contemporary factors and actors, including political circumstances, which provide the fertile ground for the seeds of hatred.

84. While it would be wrong to focus on religion in isolation when analysing the problem, it would be equally simplistic to reduce religious motives to mere "excuses" for violent crimes perpetrated in their name. What is needed is a holistic understanding of the various factors involved in violence committed in the name of religion. Typical factors are the lack of trust in the rule of law and fair functioning of public institutions; narrow-minded and polarizing interpretations of religious traditions that may bring about societal fragmentation processes with far-reaching negative repercussions on social relations; and policies of deliberate exclusion, often in conjunction with narrowly defined national identity politics and other factors; denial and impunity for serious violations of international human rights and humanitarian law.

85. Only a full account of the various root causes of the problems can build an awareness of the joint responsibility, which a broad range of actors have in fighting violence committed in the name of religion. Against

---

[260] See A/HRC/22/17/Add.4, appendix, para. 29.

this background, the Special Rapporteur formulates the recommendations below addressed to the various stakeholders.

A. Recommendations to all relevant stakeholders

86. Government representatives, religious communities, civil society organizations, the media and other relevant stakeholders should reject and speak out promptly, clearly and loudly against any acts of violence committed in the name of religion as well as related incitement to violence and discrimination in law and practice, thus overcoming the culture of silence that exists in some countries. They should act swiftly and in concert to deter and stop such violence.

87. Public condemnations against violence committed in the name of religion should be made on the basis of an adequately complex analysis of the problem, including its underlying systemic root causes.

88. The different stakeholders should jointly contribute to the containment and eventual elimination of violence committed in the name of religion by making creative use of their space and specific potential. They should also cooperate in neutralizing any possible radicalization efforts that target foreign fighters who returned to their country of origin.

B. Recommendations to different State institutions

89. States have the responsibility to protect its populations, whether nationals or not, from genocide, war crimes, ethnic cleansing and crimes against humanity, and from their incitement.

90. States have the obligation to act swiftly to stop acts of violence committed in the name of religion, against individuals, groups and places of worship. Overcoming a culture of impunity, wherever it exists, must be a priority. Those who commit or are complicit in acts of violence must be brought to justice.

91. States should safeguard the memory of all population groups, and of religious communities in particular, including by developing and protecting national archives, memorial museums and monuments.

92. States must respect freedom of religion or belief and all other human rights when undertaking actions to contain and combat against violence in the name of religion.

93. Legislation that renders the existence of certain religious communities "illegal" in the country should be revoked.

94. States should repeal anti-blasphemy laws, anti-conversion laws and any other discriminatory criminal law provisions, including those based on religious laws.

95. States should provide disaggregated data on acts of violence committed in its jurisdiction, including on possible religious motivations.

96. In order to operate as a credible guarantor of freedom of religion or belief for everyone, the State should not identify itself exclusively with one particular religion or belief at the expense of equal treatment of the followers of other faiths. Any exclusivist settings should be replaced by an inclusive institutional framework in which religious diversity can unfold without discrimination and without fear.

97. Anti-discrimination legislation should protect the equality of all in their enjoyment of human rights, across religious or denominational divides, thus preventing or overcoming divisiveness within society. States should in particular take steps to assure that the rights of all will be protected so that all can feel safe in their religions or beliefs.

98. In close consultation with all relevant stakeholders, States should develop national action plans on how to prevent violence committed in the name of religion, but also other forms of religious persecution carried out by State agencies or non-State actors.

99. Textbooks used for school education should not contain negative stereotypes and prejudices, which may stoke discrimination or hostile sentiments against any groups, including the followers of certain religions or beliefs.

100. States should use all available means, including education and community outreach, in order to promote a culture of respect, non-discrimination and appreciation of diversity within the larger society.

101. National human rights institutions are encouraged to take an active ownership of the Rabat Plan of Action on the prohibition of advocacy of national, racial or religious hatred that constitutes incitement to discrimination, hostility or violence, for the development of strategies towards eliminating the root causes of violence committed in the name of religion.

102. States should refrain from stoking violent religious extremism in other countries.

C. Recommendations to religious communities

103. When religious communities and their leaders address any violence committed in the name of their religion, they should take seriously the relevance, inter alia, of religious motives often stemming from narrow-minded, polarizing and patriarchal interpretations of religious traditions.

104. In situations in which speaking out against violence may be dangerous, fellow believers living in safer political environments should lend their voices and clearly condemn violence committed in the name of their religion.

105. Religious communities and their leaders should promote empathy, respect, non-discrimination and an appreciation of diversity. They should challenge the authenticity claims of religious extremists by exposing their views as being ignorant of the charitable core messages contained in religious traditions. Additionally, they should share with others their beliefs in the importance of respecting the rights of others, thereby contributing to a sense that the rights of all will be respected.

106. Religious communities should feel encouraged to start initiatives of interreligious communication and cooperation, including the establishment of interreligious councils. A broad representation, including gender balance and participation of different generations, can ensure that larger populations can take active ownership of such initiatives.

D. Recommendations to civil society organizations

107. Civil society organizations should continue to collect information about the situation of human rights and support people living under conditions of intimidation by following up on their cases.

108. The findings of civil society organizations should be more systematically used in their early warning function, notably in volatile situations.

109. Civil society should continue to play a role in overcoming a culture of silence in the face of violence committed in the name of religion, thereby sending a signal of solidarity to targeted individuals and groups.

110. Faith-based and secular civil society organizations should work together, including by creating common platforms, thereby demonstrating that a commitment to human rights can create solidarity across all religious, cultural and philosophical divides.

111. Human rights defenders operating in dangerous situations deserve particular attention and support by networks designed to defend the defenders.

E.   Recommendations to the media

112. In close collaboration with civil society organizations, representatives of the media should defend their independence, professionalism and integrity and address incidents of violence, their various root causes and the political circumstances in which they take place.

113. The media should help to bring about a culture of public discourse that is a prerequisite to checking hostile rumours and fearful narratives, which should be exposed to public scrutiny or counter-narratives in order to prevent them from escalating to fully-fledged conspiracy projections.

114. Careful fact-finding is the most important antidote to negative media campaigns that target religious minorities or other groups. Such fact-finding may also include a public analysis of collective historical traumas.

115. The media can help restore the faculty of empathy by making people aware that the members of groups facing systematic discrimination, far from being "aliens", have quite similar fears, hopes and feelings.

F.   Recommendations to the international community

116. The international community is reminded of its duty to assist and build the capacity of States in fulfilling their commitments to the responsibility to protect their populations from genocide, war crimes, ethnic cleansing and crimes against humanity, as concluded in the 2005 World Summit.

117. Human rights mechanisms, including the special procedures, treaty bodies and universal periodic review, are encouraged to address the issue of violence in the name of religion and State involvement in such violence.

118. The international community should hold States and non-State armed groups to account and make them aware of their existing obligations under international law, including human rights, humanitarian, criminal and refugee law.

10. Chapter: August 2015

I. Introduction

1.   The Commission on Human Rights created the mandate of the Special Rapporteur on freedom of religion or belief in resolution 1986/20. In 2007 and 2010 the Human Rights Council renewed the mandate in resolutions 6/37 and 14/11 and in 2013 the Council extended the mandate for a further period of three years in resolution 22/20.

2.   The General Assembly, in its resolution 69/175, recognized with concern the situation of persons in vulnerable situations, including children, as regards their ability to freely exercise their right to freedom of religion or belief. It also referred to the need to address urgently situations of violence and discrimination that affect many individuals, particularly women and children, on the basis or in the name of religion or belief, or in accordance with cultural and traditional practices.

3.   In section II of the present report, the Special Rapporteur provides an overview of his activities since the submission of his previous report to the General Assembly (A/69/261). In section III, he focuses on the rights of the child and his or her parents in the area of freedom of religion or belief. In section IV he sets out his thematic conclusions and recommendations.

II. Activities of the Special Rapporteur

4.   The Special Rapporteur conducted various activities between 1 August 2014 and 31 July 2015, pursuant to Human Rights Council resolutions 6/37, 14/11 and 22/20.

5.   He presented his annual reports to the sixty-ninth session of the General Assembly in October 2014 and to the twenty-eighth session of the Human Rights Council in March 2015, where he also participated in side events and held bilateral meetings.

6.   He undertook a country visit to Lebanon from 23 March to 2 April 2015 and will present his report on the mission to the thirty-first session of the Human Rights Council.

7.   The Special Rapporteur sent communications to Governments through urgent appeals, allegation letters and other letters. The latest communications   reports   (A/HRC/27/72,   A/HRC/28/85   and

A/HRC/29/50) include all communications sent between 1 March 2014 and 28 February 2015 and the replies received from Governments before 30 April 2015. He also made public statements and gave various interviews.

8.   In November 2014, the Special Rapporteur participated in a meeting of the International Panel of Parliamentarians for Freedom of Religion or Belief, held in Oslo, where parliamentarians from 17 countries signed the Charter for Freedom of Religion or Belief.[261]

9.   On 4 December 2014, the Special Rapporteur met again with Cypriot religious leaders at the second interreligious round table convened by the Office of the Religious Track of the Cyprus Peace Process under the auspices of the Embassy of Sweden, in cooperation with the Office of the United Nations High Commissioner for Human Rights (OHCHR).

10.   During the reporting period, the Special Rapporteur gave numerous lectures and took part in many panel discussions. On 8 January 2015, he delivered a speech on national identity and freedom of religion or belief in Athens and on 15 and 16 January, he spoke on various non-discrimination dimensions of freedom of religion or belief in Luxembourg. From 9 to 11 February 2015, he took part in a conference at Wilton Park on the theme of "Developing a multilateral approach to freedom of religion or belief". On 14 March 2015, he attended the twelfth national peace symposium hosted by the Ahmadiyya Muslim community in London. On 8 June 2015, he delivered a speech in Strasbourg, at a high-level seminar of the Council of Europe on the theme of "Building inclusive societies together". He also took part in in a panel on the theme of "Dialogue on freedom of religion and gender-related rights" in Geneva on 18 June 2015, at which he stressed the importance of integrating a gender perspective into programmes designed to protect and promote freedom of religion or belief.

11.   In addition, the Special Rapporteur took part in the fifth conference within the Istanbul Process on the theme of "From resolution to realization — how to promote effective implementation of Human Rights Council resolution 16/18", organized by the Organization of Islamic Cooperation on 3 and 4 June 2015 in Jeddah, Saudi Arabia.

---

[261] Available from ippforb.com/charter-for-freedom-of-religion-or-belief/.

III. The rights of the child and his or her parents in the area of freedom of religion or belief

12.   Violations of freedom of religion or belief often affect the rights of children and their parents. An extreme example is the abduction of children, typically girls, from religious minorities in order to convert them forcibly to another religion, frequently in combination with a forced early marriage. In some countries such crimes occur in a climate of impunity. While it massively violates a number of the rights of the affected child, including freedom of religion or belief, freedom from discrimination on the basis of sex or gender, the right to physical and psychological integrity and the right of the child to be cared for by his or her own parents, it simultaneously violates the rights of the parents, including the right to ensure a religious and moral education of the child in conformity with their own convictions.

13.   Sometimes, violations are also directly committed by State agencies. For instance, in some countries, converts away from mainstream religions risk losing the right to have custody of their children. Depending on the specificities of the case, that may amount to a simultaneous violation of parental rights and the rights of the children. Another field requiring attention in that regard is education in school. Pressure exercised on children in schools, for instance with the purpose of alienating them from their religion or beliefs, may again simultaneously violate the rights of the child and the rights of his or her parents. In many such cases, the rights of persons belonging to religious minorities may additionally be at stake.

14.   While in many situations of violations the rights of the child and the rights of his or her parents may be affected in conjunction, it is not always the case. Every individual child is a rights holder in his or her own capacity, not just through membership in a family or community. Moreover, the interests of parents and children are not necessarily identical, including in the area of freedom of religion or belief. There can be situations in which the rights of the child must be safeguarded also against his or her parents. One example is the infliction of harmful practices, such as female genital mutilation or child marriage, sometimes carried out in the name of culture, tradition or religion. When designing policies against harmful practices, States should bear in mind that such practices are usually contested between and within religious communities. Awareness of such internal diversity is important, to avoid stigmatizing overgeneral-

izations and muster support from within religious communities when combating harmful practices.

A. Legal framework

15. When exploring the complex relationship between the rights of children and their parents in the area of freedom of religion or belief, all relevant international human rights instruments must be taken into account, including the Universal Declaration of Human Rights, the International Covenant on Civil and Political Rights, the Declaration on the Elimination of All Forms of Intolerance and of Discrimination based on Religion or Belief, as adopted in General Assembly resolution 36/55 (the 1981 Declaration), and the Convention on the Rights of the Child. The following observations start with an interpretation of the most recent comprehensive convention in this regard, the Convention on the Rights of the Child, which in its article 14 enshrines the right of the child to freedom of thought, conscience and religion, while also addressing the rights and duties of parents or legal guardians to provide direction to the child in the exercise of his or her freedom of religion or belief, in a manner consistent with the evolving capacities of the child.

I.   The child as rights holder

16. The Convention on the Rights of the Child highlights the status of the child as a rights holder in the framework of human rights. That is not entirely new. The Universal Declaration of Human Rights recognized "the inherent dignity and ... the equal and inalienable rights of all members of the human family", thus using a formulation that at least implicitly includes children. However, the Convention on the Rights of the Child renders that status explicit and draws out practical consequences with regard to the particular needs, interests, vulnerabilities and capabilities of the child. That is all the more important in view of attitudes, customs, norms and practices that are unfortunately still widespread, whereby children are treated as if they were the property of their parents, families or communities, without having rights in their own capacity.

17. The Convention on the Rights of the Child enshrines a broad range of human rights to which every child is entitled. Article 14 must be interpreted in the broader context of corroborating the status of the child as a rights holder. Its first paragraph states that: "States parties shall respect the right of the child to freedom of thought, conscience and religion."

18.   Freedom of religion or belief has a wide scope of application. In its general comment No. 22 (1993) on freedom of thought conscience or religion, the Human Rights Committee stated that article 18 of the International Covenant on Civil and Political Rights "protects theistic, non-theistic and atheistic beliefs, as well as the right not to profess any religion or belief. The terms 'belief' and 'religion' are to be broadly construed". That inclusive understanding of article 18 of the Covenant must also guide interpretation of article 14 of the Convention on the Rights of the Child. Accordingly, the status of the child as a rights holder in the area of freedom of religion or belief deserves respect across the whole range of diverse faith orientations. It furthermore covers followers of traditional religions or beliefs, as well as of newly established religious movements.

19.   The Convention on the Rights of the Child also includes a provision on behalf of children who belong to ethnic, religious or linguistic minorities. The wording of article 30 of the Convention resembles article 27 of the International Covenant on Civil and Political Rights, with the remarkable exception that the Convention includes "persons of indigenous origin". With regard to a child from a religious minority or of indigenous origin, article 30 of the Convention on the Rights of the Child confirms the child's right to "profess and practise his or her religion" and to do so "in community with other members of his or her group". While the community dimension is clearly acknowledged, the immediate rights holder remains the individual child who belongs to a religious minority or indigenous community.

2.   The role of parents

20.   While recognizing the status of the child as a rights holder, the Convention on the Rights of the Child also reflects the awareness that the child needs a supportive environment to realize his or her rights. That supportive environment is usually provided by the family. According to the preamble of the Convention, the child "should grow up in a family environment", since the family provides "the natural environment for the growth and well-being of all its members and particularly children".

21.   From that insight into the significance of the family, the Convention derives a number of rights, which protect the relationship between children and their parents or legal guardians. Article 7, paragraph 1, emphasizes that the child shall have "the right to know and be cared for by his or her parents". Article 9, paragraph 1, obliges States to "ensure that a child shall not be separated from his or her parents against their will",

except in clearly defined exceptional situations, which furthermore must be carefully assessed under principles of due process and connected to effective remedies. Even in such exceptional situations, States "shall respect the right of the child who is separated from one or both parents to maintain personal relations", unless this would clearly go contrary to the child's best interests. Article 18, paragraph 1, furthermore provides that "States parties shall use their best efforts to ensure recognition of the principle that both parents have common responsibility for the upbringing and development of the child. Parents or, as the case may be, legal guardians, have the primary responsibility for the upbringing and development of the child. The best interests of the child will be their basic concern." While that is formulated from the perspective of the child, it necessarily also corroborates the specific rights and duties of parents.

22. Given the child's dependency on an enabling family environment, albeit with recognition of the variety of family forms, parents have the primary responsibility for supporting the child in the exercise of his or her human rights. According to article 5 of the Convention on the Rights of the Child, they should provide "appropriate guidance and direction" to the child in that regard. That specific responsibility entrusted to the parents also constitutes a parental right that the State must respect and protect. Article 14, paragraph 2, of the Convention further specifies that general understanding by enshrining due respect for the rights and duties of the parents "to provide direction to the child in the exercise of his or her right" to freedom of religion or belief.

3.   Due respect for the "evolving capacities of the child"

23. The status of each individual child as a rights holder and his or her reliance on support usually provided by the family must be seen in conjunction. On the one hand, the rights of the child can never flourish without an enabling environment. On the other hand, the need of the child for an enabling environment must not lead to the wrong conclusion that parents or other family members can simply override, ignore or marginalize the rights of the child. The status of the child as rights holder must always be respected and should, inter alia, be reflected in the manner in which parents provide guidance and direction to the child. The decisive term employed in the Convention on the Rights of the Child is "the evolving capacities of the child".[262]

---

[262]   See also United Nations Children's Fund, "The evolving capacities of the child" (2005). Available from www.unicef-irc.org/publications/384.

24. Article 5 of the Convention, which is central for the understanding of the entire Convention, defines the complex and dynamic relationship between the rights of the child and parental rights and duties as follows: "States parties shall respect the responsibilities, rights and duties of parents or, where applicable, the members of the extended family or community as provided for by local custom, legal guardians or other persons legally responsible for the child, to provide, in a manner consistent with the evolving capacities of the child, appropriate direction and guidance in the exercise by the child of the rights recognized in the present Convention."

25. Adequate consideration of "the evolving capacities of the child" presupposes that the child, once capable of forming personal views, can express such views freely, with a chance of being heard and taken seriously. Article 12, paragraph 1, of the Convention confirms that right, while furthermore requiring that the views of the child be "given due weight in accordance with the age and maturity of the child". Thus, the child should in the course of time assume a more and more active position in the exercise of his or her rights.

26. Article 14 of the Convention reflects and further specifies the general understanding of the dynamic interrelatedness of the rights of the child and his or her parents. While paragraph 1 confirms the status of the child as a rights holder as regards freedom of thought, conscience and religion, paragraph 2 demands respect for "the rights and duties of the parents and, when applicable, legal guardians, to provide direction to the child in the exercise of his or her right in a manner consistent with the evolving capacities of the child". That wording bears a striking resemblance to article 5 of the Convention. In fact, article 14, paragraph 2, is the only provision in the Convention that reiterates the importance of the evolving capacities of the child. It means that the child should always be respected, including within the family, as having the gradually evolving capacities of forming his or her own thoughts, ideas and religious or belief-related convictions and taking his or her own decisions in that area. In article 14, paragraph 3, the limitation clause already contained in article 18, paragraph 3, of the International Covenant on Civil and Political Rights is reiterated.

B. The interrelatedness of the rights of the child to freedom of religion or belief and parental rights

27. The relationship between the rights of the child and parental rights in the area of freedom of religion or belief has given rise to controversies. On the one hand, fears have been expressed that the status of the child as a rights holder might undermine parental rights, thus opening the floodgates for far-reaching interference by State agencies in the religious socialization of children. On the other hand, there exist views that parents should be obliged to provide a religiously "neutral" upbringing of their children. With the following clarifications, the Special Rapporteur would like to contribute to a holistic understanding of the rights of the child and parental rights in their normative interrelatedness, without ignoring possible conflicts.

I.   No legitimate pretext for eroding parental rights

28. Some critics of article 14 of the Convention on the Rights of the Child have voiced concerns that the explicit recognition of the child's freedom of religion or belief in the Convention might lead to an erosion of parental rights and undermine the specific responsibility that parents have in the religious socialization of their children. That has been among the reasons for some States entering reservations or explanatory declarations concerning article 14 when ratifying or acceding to the Convention. The Special Rapporteur is convinced that such anxieties cannot be sustained on the basis of an appropriate reading of the Convention, seen in conjunction with other relevant international standards.

29. Fears that some State agencies could be tempted to use the child's right to freedom of religion or belief as a pretext for undue interference are generally understandable. As a matter of fact, in some countries, far-reaching State interventions into families in the spheres of religious initiation, socialization and education of children actually do occur — at times also by invoking an alleged interest of the child. Such problematic State interventions disproportionately affect families belonging to religious minorities, new religious movements or small communities often stigmatized as "sects". Depending on the country, families not professing any religion may also be under increased threat of undue State interference. In extreme cases, children have been taken away from their families, for instance under the pretext of saving them from ill-defined "superstitious" religions — a pretext often invoked against indigenous families in the past.

30. Converts constitute another particularly vulnerable group. In particular, in States that privilege a certain religion as the official or State religion, parents converting away from that hegemonic religion run the risk of being alienated or even separated from their children. Possibly starting with adverse comments by teachers in kindergartens and schools, such alienation can climax in a formal loss of custody rights, for instance when a divorce takes place. Official documents issued for children do not always reflect the new religious orientation of parents after conversion, thus leading to different religions being ascribed to the parents and the children, often against the explicit will of both.

31. Thus, there can be no doubt that the erosion of parental rights by undue State interference is a serious problem and a source of grave violations of freedom of religion or belief. That problem requires systematic attention. It is furthermore true that some States may use the rhetoric of superficial child rights in an attempt to "justify" such interference. However, based on an appropriate understanding of the Convention on the Rights of the Child, the fear that article 14 of the Convention could legitimize the erosion of parental rights seems unsubstantiated. Instead of being part of the problem, the Convention can and should be part of the solution. In conjunction with other human rights instruments, article 14 can help to tackle the problem of abusive State interventions. Rather than eroding parental rights in the sphere of freedom of religion or belief, article 14 corroborates, and at the same time further qualifies, those rights by acknowledging their significance from the specific perspective of the rights of the child. Moreover, the Convention gives the child, his or her parents and other family members a strong position in pursuing their human rights-based interests. When it comes to families belonging to religious minorities, article 30 of the Convention can be used in combination with article 14 in order to strengthen further the claims of persons belonging to minorities against unjustified interventions.

32. Earlier provisions of freedom of religion or belief remain fully valid. That includes article 18, paragraph 4, of the International Covenant on Civil and Political Rights which provides that the States parties "undertake to have respect for the liberty of parents and, when applicable, legal guardians to ensure the religious and moral education of their children in conformity with their own convictions."[263] Whereas the International

---

[263] See also similar wording in article 13, para. 3, of the International Covenant on Economic, Social and Cultural Rights and article 12, para. 4, of the International Convention on the Protection of the Rights of All Migrant Workers and Members of Their Families.

Covenant on Civil and Political Rights focuses on the rights of parents, the Convention on the Rights of the Child combines parental rights and the rights of the child to freedom of religion or belief.[264] That reflects an increased awareness, manifested in the Convention, of the status of the child as a rights holder.

33. While article 18, paragraph 4, of the Covenant should be interpreted in the light of the Convention, with its explicit focus on the interrelatedness of parental and child rights, article 14, paragraph 2, of the Convention should, vice versa, be seen in continuity with article 18, paragraph 4, of the Covenant, which remains fully valid. Indeed, the liberty of parents or legal guardians to ensure the religious and moral education of their children in conformity with their own convictions continues to constitute a human-rights based claim which is far from redundant, since the parental right to provide "direction" to the child in his or her exercise of freedom of religion or belief includes the religious socialization of the child, albeit neither in an unchangeable way nor in a manner inconsistent with the evolving capacities of the child.

34. In practice, the right of the child to freedom of religion or belief and parental rights to provide direction to the child in that regard should be seen as largely, although not always, consonant. The Convention on the Rights of the Child operates on the assumption that parents serve as the natural custodians of the best interests of the child, as enshrined in article 3, paragraphs 1 and 2, and that the child has a natural interest in living in a family together with his or her parents. That does not preclude conflicts of interests, in particular when the child grows up and tries to become more independent. Moreover, situations may emerge in which the best interests of the child may actually require State interventions to protect him or her, for example against neglect, domestic violence or harmful practices. Intervening measures must always be carried out with empirical and normative diligence and furthermore they are connected to substantive and procedural safeguards.[265]

2.   No obligation to provide a religiously "neutral" upbringing

35. Other critics have questioned the provisions of the Convention on the Rights of the Child from the opposite angle by contending that it al-

---

[264] See also article 5, para. 2, of the 1981 Declaration, which more narrowly focuses on access to education in matters of religion or belief. In that context, the Declaration refers to parental rights and the best interests of the child.

[265] For details see below, section III.D.

legedly gives too much weight to parental rights, in particular in the context of freedom of religion or belief. In order for the child to fully retain the right to free choice in questions of religion or belief, it has been argued that parents should not be allowed to determine the child's religious identity by initiating the child into any particular religion. The idea seems to be that the child should rather grow up in a more or less religiously "neutral" environment, in order to preserve all options of his or her future self-determination. Sometimes such demands are presented in the name of the child's "right to an open future".[266]

36. Freedom of religion or belief indeed facilitates an open development by guaranteeing everyone's freedom to "change" one's religion or belief[267] and to "have or to adopt a religion or belief of his choice".[268] In the course of their personal development, individuals, including children, can modify, change or even abandon their religion or belief. However, that does not presuppose a right of the child to grow up in a religiously "neutral" family environment, let alone a right possibly enforced by the State against parents. The principle of "neutrality" can meaningfully be invoked only against States in order to remind them of their obligation to exercise fairness, impartiality and inclusivity and in this specific sense "neutrality", when dealing with diversity of religion or belief. By contrast, parents cannot be obliged by the State to remain religiously "neutral" when raising their children.

37. Some parents may take a deliberate decision not to socialize their children in a religious manner. Of course, such a decision must be respected as falling within their parental rights, however, that cannot serve as the general model to be promoted, let alone enforced, by the State. Attempts made by the State to enforce a religiously "neutral" upbringing of children within their families would amount to a far-reaching violation of parental rights to freedom of religion or belief, as enshrined, inter alia, in article 14, paragraph 2, of the Convention on the Rights of the Child.

38. For many believers, religion represents an all-encompassing reality which permeates all spheres of life. Religious rituals and ceremonies may

---

[266] In that regard, reference is often made to an emblematic article by Joel Feinberg, "The child's right to an open future" in *Whose Child? Children's Rights, Parental Authority, and State Power*, William Aiken and Hugh LaFollette, eds. (Totowa, New Jersey, Rowman and Littlefield, 1980).

[267] Article 18 of the Universal Declaration of Human Rights explicitly refers to "freedom to change his religion or belief".

[268] See article 18, paras. 1 and 2, of the International Covenant on Civil and Political Rights.

thus be involved when parents welcome newborn children as members of the family and the larger community, when they familiarize children with their religious lifeworld, or when they teach them the basic rules of interaction, ethical principles and how to perform prayers and religious ceremonies. Freedom of religion or belief protects such religious socialization processes broadly, as part of the right to manifest one's religion or belief "in worship, observance, practice and teaching".[269] Here again, article 14 of the Convention on the Rights of the Child must be seen in continuity with other provisions of freedom of religion or belief, as enshrined in article 18 of the Universal Declaration of Human Rights, article 18 of the International Covenant on Civil and Political Rights and other international instruments.

C. Dimensions of practical application

39. The requirement to respect the "evolving capacities of the child", as laid down in article 5 of the Convention on the Rights of the Child, is reiterated only in article 14, paragraph 2, of the Convention, which accounts for the significance accorded by the Convention to upholding that principle in the context of freedom of religion or belief. Respect for the evolving capacities of the child is critical, since it reflects the due recognition of the child as a rights holder also within the family context.

1.   Religious socialization

40. In the early years, a child's survival, socialization, development and general well-being totally depend on regular support which is usually provided by his or her parents. Accordingly, the "direction" given by parents in the exercise of the child's rights, in accordance with article 5 of the Convention on the Rights of the Child, is particularly far-reaching when concerning infants or young children. That also applies to freedom of religion or belief. Under articles 5 and 14, paragraph 2, of the Convention, States are obliged, first of all, to "respect" those parental rights and duties.

41. Welcoming the newborn child into the family and the larger community frequently involves religious initiation rites. As part of religious socialization processes, such initiation rites, provided they take place with the free consent of the parents, fall within the right to manifest one's religion or belief, as protected under article 18 of the International Covenant on Civil and Political Rights and similar provisions. Limitations,

---

[269]   See article 18, para. 1, of the International Covenant on Civil and Political Rights.

if deemed necessary, for instance to prevent harmful practices, must meet all the criteria listed in article 18, paragraph 3, of the Covenant and reiterated in article 14, paragraph 3, of the Convention.

42. Whereas protection against harmful practices can become an argument for prohibiting or limiting the application of certain initiation rites, depending on the specific circumstances of the case, the child's freedom from religion, or an alleged right of the child to remain uninfluenced by religious initiation, cannot be invoked as arguments for limiting such religious ceremonies undertaken with the free consent of the parents of a child who has not yet reached religious maturity. Moreover, as pointed out earlier, being initiated into a particular religious community does not waive the right of the child to change his or her religion when adopting a different conviction in the course of his or her later development, as protected in article 14, paragraph 1, of the Convention on the Rights of the Child.

2. Religious instruction within the family

43. The small child typically receives his or her first religious instructions within the family and/or the local religious community. Parents engaged in religious instruction thereby exercise their parental rights, while at the same time directing the child in the exercise of his or her own right to freedom of religion or belief. With the tacit or express consent of the parents, the religious community can also take an active role in familiarizing the child with religious or belief matters. States are obliged to respect and protect such activities, including by facilitating the development of the appropriate infrastructure needed for religious communities, especially minority communities, to be able to pass on the tenets of their faith to the next generation.

44. In its assessment of country situations, the Committee on the Rights of the Child repeatedly expressed concerns that State-imposed restrictions on religious instruction might seriously infringe the freedom of children, in particular children belonging to religious minorities, to study and practise their religion (see, for example, CRC/C/CHN/CO/3-4, para. 41, and CRC/C/KWT/CO/2, paras. 37 and 38). The Special Rapporteur and his predecessors also addressed this problem in various country visits (see, for example, A/HRC/10/8/Add.4, para. 46 and A/HRC/28/66/Add.1, para. 63).

45. Religious instruction should be given in a manner consistent with the evolving capacities of the child. Young children may need appropri-

ate child-centred forms of teaching, including through dialogue and example.[270] The more children mature, the more should they be able to take an active part in such instructions and their own positions, questions and concerns should be heard and taken seriously, in accordance with article 12, paragraph 1, and article 14, paragraph 1, of the Convention on the Rights of the Child. An older child should thus also be respected in his or her refusal to receive religious instruction.

3. Participation in religious community life

46. The child has the right to participate widely in religious community practices, including by attending religious services, performing common prayers and ceremonies and celebrating religious holidays. While for younger children that generally presupposes the tacit or express consent of parents or guardians, more mature children deserve respect for their own decisions in that regard, including the decision not to participate if they so wish. When assessing country situations, both the Committee on the Rights of the Child and the Special Rapporteur have expressed concerns about tight restrictions as they exist in some countries. Such restrictions may largely prevent minors from having access to religious community practices, in violation of their freedom of religion or belief (see, for example, CRC/C/UZB/CO/3-4, para. 32, A/HRC/10/8/Add.4, paras. 45 and 46, and A/HRC/28/66/Add.1, para. 64).

4. Religious education in schools

47. Article 28 of the Convention on the Rights of the Child recognizes the child's right to education, as also enshrined in other human rights instruments, including article 13 of the International Covenant on Economic, Social and Cultural Rights. That, inter alia, requires that States "make primary education compulsory and available free to all" (article 28, para. 1 (a), of the Convention). The usual place for the implementation of that right is the school, which thus plays a major role in the life of children (for more detail, see A/HRC/16/53, paras. 20-62). However, apart from realizing the child's right to education, the school is also a place in which the child is exposed to authority — not only the authority of teachers, but possibly also that of the State on whose behalf teachers act. The child may also feel exposed to peer pressure. That calls for a sensitive human rights-based approach when organizing school life and it requires

---

[270] See Committee on the Rights of the Child, general comment No. 7 (2006) on implementing child rights in early childhood.

that the particular vulnerabilities of children belonging to various minorities are always taken into account.

48. When religious ceremonies, such as public prayers, are performed in school, specific safeguards are needed to ensure that no child is forced to participate against his or her will, or the will of his or her parents. The same principle applies to religious instruction in schools, namely religious education given on the tenets of a particular religion or belief. Such instruction must not be a mandatory requirement and it should always be connected with the option of receiving a low-threshold exemption (see, for example, CCPR/C/82/D/1155/2003). Requests for an exemption must not lead to any punitive consequences and must not influence the assessment of the general performance of students in school. In practice, however, those requirements are often ignored, thus leading to situations in which children are exposed to involuntary religious instruction or even indoctrination. The Committee on the Rights of the Child has even referred to cases of forced conversion taking place in schools (see CRC/C/MMR/CO/3-4, para. 45) and the Special Rapporteur has heard complaints, inter alia, about confessions held by priests during regular school hours (see, for example, A/HRC/22/51/Add.1, para. 63).

49. "Religious instruction" given in school differs conceptually from "information about religions and beliefs". While religious instruction aims to familiarize students with a particular faith, information about religions and beliefs serves the purpose of broadening children's knowledge and understanding of the diversity of faith systems and practices. Unlike religious instruction, which should never be given against the will of the child or his or her parents, information about religions and beliefs can become part of the mandatory curriculum, provided it is taught in a spirit of fairness and neutrality. In that context, the Special Rapporteur would like to recommend the Toledo Guiding Principles on Teaching about Religions and Beliefs in Public Schools as a useful instrument for assessing and improving the quality of such teaching.

50. Parents also have the right to have their children educated in private denominational schools which conform to such educational standards as may be laid down or approved by the State.

5. Voluntary display of religious symbols in schools

51. A much-disputed question concerns the voluntary display of religious symbols by students in public schools, such as headscarves, turbans, kippas or crosses. Following religious dress codes or displaying reli-

gious symbols generally belongs to everyone's freedom to manifest their religion or belief. Although that freedom is not beyond possible limitations, such limitations can only be justified if they satisfy all the criteria laid down in article 18, paragraph 3, of the International Covenant on Civil and Political Rights and reiterated in article 14, paragraph 3, of the Convention on the Rights of the Child.[271]

52. Accordingly, limitations must have a legal basis; they must pursue one of the listed legitimate purposes (public safety, order, health or morals, or the fundamental rights and freedoms of others) and they must be proportionate to such a purpose. Under the principle of proportionality, States have always to look for the least intrusive measure available. Restrictions, for instance, if deemed necessary to protect students from being pressured by peers or their general school environment into wearing religious symbols, should be based on a precise empirical and normative analysis of the situation at issue. General or far-reaching prohibitions of the voluntary wearing of headscarves or other religious symbols by students in schools should remain a last resort. After one of her country visits, the Special Rapporteur's predecessor expressed her concerns that restrictive measures imposed on students would convey "a demoralizing message to religious minorities" (E/CN.4/2006/5/Add.4, para. 98).

53. By generally accommodating the voluntary display of multiple religious symbols by students, the school can become a place in which children experience religious diversity on a daily basis and in a relaxed manner, as part of normal societal life. That may be conducive to fulfilling the purposes of education as listed in article 29, paragraph 1 (d), of the Convention on the Rights of the Child, including the "preparation of the child for responsible life in a free society, in the spirit of understanding, peace, tolerance, equality of sexes and friendship among all peoples, ethnic, national and religious groups and persons of indigenous origin".

6. Respecting the evolving capacities of the maturing child

54. Respect for the evolving capacities of the child is to be ensured in all relevant spheres of life, such as family life, participation in the religious community, school education, the voluntary wearing of religious symbols and other areas. Hence, it is a principle running through all the above-mentioned spheres of application of freedom of religion or belief. For instance, children who have developed their own self-understanding on

---

[271] The following remarks relate only to the display of religious symbols by students, not by teachers.

issues of religion or belief should not receive religious instruction against their will, in or outside school education. Children should have broad access to information concerning religious or philosophical beliefs, also beyond their family's faith. From a certain age or maturity, children deserve respect when taking their own decisions, whether positive or negative, concerning participation in acts of worship, ceremonies or other religious community activities. Depending on his or her evolving capacities, a child may also be able to exercise his or her right to have or adopt a religion or belief of his or her own choice.

55. Some States have defined fixed age thresholds for the child's exercise of certain elements of freedom of religion or belief, for example concerning opting out of religious instruction or converting to another faith with or without the agreement of the parents. However, given the dynamic nature of the child's "evolving capacities", it is preferable to avoid fixed definitions and instead take decisions on a case-by-case basis, with respect to each individual child's personal situation and maturity. In its general comment No. 12 (2009) on the right of the child to be heard, the Committee on the Rights of the Child also opted for a flexible approach: "The more the child himself or herself knows, has experienced and understands, the more the parent, legal guardian or other persons legally responsible for the child have to transform direction and guidance into reminders and advice and later to an exchange on an equal footing. This transformation will not take place at a fixed point in a child's development, but will steadily increase as the child is encouraged to contribute his or her views."

7.   Non-discrimination on the basis of religion or belief

56. Under article 2, paragraph 1, of the Convention on the Rights of the Child, States shall respect and ensure the rights laid down in the Convention to every child without discrimination, including on the ground of his or her religion or the religion of his or her parent(s) or legal guardian(s). Article 2, paragraph 2, furthermore obliges States to take all appropriate measures in order to provide effective protection of the child against discrimination. Those provisions apply to all spheres of society, such as family laws, public and private schools, institutions of higher education, vocational training, accessibility of employment and health-care institutions. Unfortunately, systematic violations of the principle of non-discrimination persist, often with far-reaching negative implications in particular for the rights of children belonging to religious minorities (see, for example, CRC/C/CHN/CO/3-4, para. 25).

57. Besides direct, open and straightforward forms of discrimination, there are also concealed forms of discrimination, such as structural or indirect discrimination. In order to detect and combat such forms of discrimination, disaggregated statistical data may be needed. The State should develop comprehensive anti-discrimination legislation and policies, with a view to safeguarding the right of the child to be free from any kind of discrimination, including on the basis of religion or belief. Civil society organizations and national human rights institutions operating in line with the Principles relating to the Status of National Institutions (Paris Principles) should play an active role in the design and implementation of anti-discrimination policies.

D. Conflicts

1. The need for diligence when dealing with conflicting human rights concerns

58. The Convention on the Rights of the Child combines the recognition of the child as a genuine rights holder with respect for the rights and duties of parents or legal guardians in directing the child in the exercise of his or her human rights. However, situations can occur in which State interventions in the sphere of parental rights are necessary, for instance to protect the child from neglect, domestic violence or harmful practices. According to article 19, paragraph 1, of the Convention, "States parties shall take all appropriate legislative, administrative, social and educational measures to protect the child from all forms of physical or mental violence, injury or abuse, neglect or negligent treatment, maltreatment or exploitation, including sexual abuse, while in the care of parent(s), legal guardian(s) or any other person who has the care of the child." In the context of the right to health, article 24, paragraph 3, of the Convention obliges States to "take all effective and appropriate measures with a view to abolishing traditional practices prejudicial to the health of children".

59. Moreover, the right to education has the component of compulsory primary education, which by implication can also be enforced against the will of the parents or guardians (article 28, paragraph 1 (a), of the Convention). With regard to adolescents, the Committee on the Rights of the Child emphasizes that States parties should provide them "with access to sexual and reproductive information, including on family planning and contraception, the dangers of early pregnancy, the prevention of HIV/AIDS and the prevention and treatment of sexually transmitted dis-

eases (STDs)."[272] In that context the Committee insists that adolescents should "have access to appropriate information, regardless of ... whether their parents or guardians consent."[12]

60. State interventions should always be carried out with the purpose of supporting families in fulfilling their task of providing a suitable environment for the flourishing of the rights of the child, to the maximum degree possible. It is in that spirit that article 19, paragraph 2, of the Convention on the Rights of the Child, calls, inter alia, for "the establishment of social programmes to provide necessary support for the child and for those who have the care of the child". Separating a child from his or her parents against their will in order to protect the best interests of the child must remain the ultimate resort. As the Committee on the Rights of the Child has pointed out in its general comment No. 14 (2013) on the right of the child to have his or her best interests taken as a primary consideration: "Given the gravity of the impact on the child of separation from his or her parents, such separation should only occur as a last resort measure, as when the child is in danger of experiencing imminent harm or when otherwise necessary; separation should not take place if less intrusive measures could protect the child." Under article 9, paragraph 1, of the Convention, "competent authorities subject to judicial review" have to "determine, in accordance with applicable law and procedures, that such separation is necessary for the best interests of the child". Even in such a situation, the child should be able to "maintain personal relations and direct contact with both parents on a regular basis, except if it is contrary to the child's best interests" (article 9, paragraph 3).

61. The Special Rapporteur sees a need to stress that this understanding must also guide the handling of cases involving religious minorities. Unfortunately, that is not always the case. When dealing with religious minorities, small communities or new movements, often branded as "sects", some State agencies seem to operate on the assumption that, in case of doubt, children should be separated from their parents. Lack of diligence and respect, possibly based on prejudice, is thus a source of major human rights concerns, also from the perspective of the Convention on the Rights of the Child.

62. In some situations, State interventions may actually prove necessary to safeguard the best interests of the child, for instance if the child's rights to life, health or education are imperilled. However, any such situ-

---

[272] General comment no. 4 (2003) on adolescent health and development in the context of the Convention on the Rights of the Child.

ation warrants a careful empirical and normative assessment. Empirical diligence is needed, inter alia, to avoid stereotypical ascriptions, possibly based on rumours, overgeneralizations or merely abstract, possibly far-fetched fears. Members of small religious communities or new religious movements often run an increased risk of having their rights infringed. In extreme cases, parents have lost their custody rights without any serious empirical investigation having taken place and without being granted effective legal remedies. Besides empirical negligence, there is also the danger of normative negligence if due weight is not given to all the human rights concerns at stake and the criteria set out for limitations are ignored. For instance, cases of religious conversion of one parent have led to him or her being deprived of custody rights, often against the explicit will of the parents and the child, and sometimes as a consequence of a forced divorce being required by the State in the wake of one parent's conversion.

2.   Ensuring non-discriminatory family laws and settlement of family-related conflicts

63. According to article 7, paragraph 1, of the Convention on the Rights of the Child, the child has the right to be cared for by his or her parents. That must also guide the handling of family crises, such as a divorce. In such situations, the best interests of the child must be a primary consideration (article 3); the child, once able to express his or her views, must have a chance to be heard in judicial or other official hearings (article 12, paragraph 2); and if separation from a parent proves necessary, the child is generally entitled to maintain personal relations with both parents (article 9, paragraph 3).

64. In cases in which the two parents follow different religions or beliefs, such a difference cannot in itself serve as an argument for treating parents differently, for instance in decisions on custody rights in divorce settlements. Discrimination against parents on the grounds of their religion or belief may simultaneously amount to a serious violation of the rights of the child in their care. That also applies to members of religious minorities, new religious movements, atheists, agnostics or converts.

65. In quite a number of countries, that issue is a source of major human rights concern, since family laws reflect traditional religious or ideological hegemonies, thus leading to systematic discrimination based on religion or belief, often in conjunction with gender-based discrimination (see A/HRC/25/58/Add.2, paras. 28-37). In some legal systems people from

certain religious or belief backgrounds are even prevented from entering a legally recognized marriage, which may result in children being treated as "illegal". Family law reforms with the purpose of eliminating such discrimination based on religion or belief must be a priority. Judges dealing with family laws should receive training based on all relevant human rights instruments.

66.   When a child is given into foster care, adoption or *kafalah* (an institution of Islamic law), the child's freedom of religion or belief must always be respected. According to article 20, paragraph 3, of the Convention on the Rights of the Child, in such situations "due regard shall be paid to the desirability of continuity in the child's upbringing and to the child's ethnic, religious, cultural and linguistic background".

3.   Combating harmful practices

67.   A much-discussed issue concerns harmful practices, which are sometimes invoked in the name of cultural or religious traditions. Many of those practices particularly affect girls. In 2014, the Committee on the Elimination of Discrimination against Women and the Committee on the Rights of the Child addressed the problem in a joint general recommendation/general comment. The two Committees listed "female genital mutilation, child and/or forced marriage, polygamy, crimes committed in the name of so-called honour and dowry-related violence" among "the most prevalent and well documented" harmful practices "grounded in discrimination based on sex, gender, age and other grounds".[273] A more comprehensive list also includes neglect of girls, extreme dietary restrictions, virginity testing, binding, scarring, branding/tribal marks, corporal punishment, stoning, violent initiation rites, widowhood practices, witchcraft, infanticide, incest, breast ironing or pressure to be fashionably thin.

68.   The Special Rapporteur fully subscribes to the recommendation formulated by the two Committees that "the obligation to protect requires States parties to establish legal structures to ensure that harmful practices are promptly, impartially and independently investigated, that there is effective law enforcement and that effective remedies are provided to those who have been harmed by such practices".[13] He shares the observation "that prevention can be best achieved through a human

---

[273]   Joint general recommendation/general comment No. 31 (2014) of the Committee on the Elimination of Discrimination against Women and No. 18 of the Committee on the Rights of the Child on harmful practices.

rights-based approach to changing social and cultural norms, empowering women and girls, building the capacity of all relevant professionals who are in regular contact with victims, potential victims and perpetrators of harmful practices at all levels, and raising awareness of the causes and consequences of harmful practices, including through dialogue with relevant stakeholders".[13]

69. Whether harmful practices, or some of them, are based on religious grounds usually remains contested between and within various religious communities. It is important to be aware of such inter- and intrareligious diversity and contestation, when designing appropriate counter-strategies, in order to avoid false generalizations and mobilize support from religious communities, or parts of communities, in the fight against harmful practices. Community leaders have a particular responsibility to clarify that harmful practices, wherever they exist, must be abandoned. In that context, the Special Rapporteur's predecessor publicly welcomed statements clarifying religious views on female genital mutilation and the recommendations of the international conference of scholars concerning a ban on abuse of the female body, held at Al-Azhar University, Cairo, in 2006 (see A/HRC/4/21, para. 38, footnote).

70. Moreover, whatever their reasons may be, harmful practices can never be justified as legitimate manifestations of freedom of religion or belief. Being part of the broader human rights framework, freedom of religion or belief can never become a pretext for legitimizing cruel practices and violations of human rights. If necessary, the limitation clauses, as laid down in article 18, paragraph 3, of the International Covenant on Civil and Political Rights and article 14, paragraph 3, of the Convention on the Rights of the Child, must be applied. As already emphasized, they must always be applied with empirical and normative diligence and those affected by limitations must have access to effective legal remedies when claiming that their human rights have been violated.

4.   Controversies around male circumcision

71. A question which has caused some controversy is how to assess the ritual circumcision of male infants, which is widely practised in some religions. For many believers, it counts as a core element of their religious identities and as an integral part of religious initiation processes. At the same time, it obviously has irreversible physical consequences. Male circumcision has been particularly contested when carried out by untrained personnel in unhygienic settings and without adequate pain relief, which increases the risk of serious medical complications and may even have

fatal consequences, including death. The Committee on the Rights of the Child has therefore recommended taking effective measures, including training for practitioners and awareness-raising, to ensure the health of boys and protect against unsafe medical conditions during the practice of male circumcision (CRC/C/15/Add.122, para. 33).

72. The issue has also been discussed within those religious communities in which ritual male circumcision is widely practised and seen as an essential element of their identity. Although some reformers have proposed postponing the practice to an age at which the child concerned can take his own decisions, the vast majority of parents continue to understand and practise circumcision as an indispensable element of religious initiation rituals performed on their children.

73. While some national legislators have specified certain conditions for the practice of circumcision, in the spirit of the recommendation of the Committee on the Rights of the Child, no State has outlawed the practice as such, which would be a far-reaching intervention into parental rights. The Special Rapporteur would argue that, if performed by trained practitioners, in sanitary conditions and with the clearly expressed consent of parents or guardians, male circumcision of children who have not yet reached religious maturity should generally be respected as falling within the freedom to manifest one's religion or belief, which includes the ritual initiation of children into religious life. At the same time, he would like to encourage further discussion, including within practising religious communities, about how to improve the conditions of male circumcision in order to avoid the risks of physical and psychological damage.

IV. Conclusions and recommendations

74. The Special Rapporteur calls upon States to pay more attention to violations of the rights of the child and his or her parents in the area of freedom of religion or belief. That may particularly concern persons belonging to minorities, converts, dissidents, critics, atheists or agnostics, members of non-recognized groups and others.

75. Due respect for the rights of the child and his or her parents in the area of freedom of religion or belief has been corroborated in article 14 of the Convention on the Rights of the Child. While article 14, paragraph 1, enshrines the fundamental status of the child as a rights holder in the area of freedom of religion or belief, article 14, paragraph 2, provides that parents or legal guardians have the rights and duties to direct the child in the exercise of his or her freedom of religion or belief. Such direction

should be given in a manner consistent with "the evolving capacities of the child", in order to facilitate a more and more active role of the child in exercising his or her freedom of religion or belief, thus paying respect to the child as a rights holder from early on. Article 14 of the Convention should be interpreted in line with all other relevant international standards on freedom of religion or belief, including article 18 of the Universal Declaration of Human Rights, article 18 of the International Covenant on Civil and Political Rights and the Declaration on the Elimination of All Forms of Intolerance and of Discrimination Based on Religion or Belief.

76. The rights of children and parental rights in the area of freedom of religion or belief, although in practice not always consonant, should generally be interpreted as being positively interrelated. They cover various spheres of life, from the child's religious initiation into the family and his or her participation in religious community life to religious instruction given in the context of school education. While State interventions may sometimes be necessary, for instance to protect the child from neglect, domestic violence or harmful practices, unjustified State interference with parental rights in the area of freedom of religion or belief will in many cases simultaneously amount to violations of the rights of the child.

77. Harmful practices, such as female genital mutilation or child marriage, can never be "justified" by the invocation of freedom of religion or belief and States are obliged to take all appropriate measures to eliminate such practices. When tackling the root causes of harmful practices, including certain cultural and religious traditions, States should avoid stereotypical overgeneralizations, always bearing in mind the broad range of inter- and intrareligious pluralism.

78. When ritual male circumcision of a child is performed, appropriate sanitary conditions and professional performance should be ensured.

79. Against the background of the observations above, the Special Rapporteur formulates the following recommendations:

   a) In line with the Convention on the Rights of the Child and other relevant international human rights standards, States and other stakeholders, including religious communities and families, should recognize the status of the child as a rights holder;

   b) States should withdraw reservations concerning article 14 of the Convention on the Rights of the Child. When implementing the Convention, they should understand article 14 as an integral part of it, which stands in continuity with freedom of religion or belief, as enshrined in other international instruments, including article 18 of the Universal Declaration of Human Rights, article 18 of the International Covenant on Civil and Political Rights and the Declaration on the Elimination of All Forms of Intolerance and of Discrimination Based on Religion or Belief;

c) Article 14 of the Convention on the Rights of the Child should be broadly interpreted as covering theistic, non-theistic and atheistic beliefs, including the right not to profess any religion or belief;

d) States should respect, protect and promote parental rights and the rights of the child as, in general, positively interrelated rights, including in the area of freedom of religion or belief. Respect for the "evolving capacities of the child" should be understood as an integral part thereof. States should avoid fixed age limits when identifying religious maturity in order to do justice to the personal religious maturation of each individual child;

e) As part of the positive interrelatedness of parental rights and the right of the child to freedom of religion or belief, States should generally respect religious initiation rites, in which the small child is introduced into the family and community, if initiated by parents and/or carried out with their consent;

f) State interventions into parental rights in the area of freedom of religion or belief, for example if deemed necessary to prevent harmful practices and to safeguard the best interests of the child, must always be enacted with empirical and normative diligence, always bearing in mind the prescribed criteria for limitations;

g) States should repeal unduly restrictive regulations, wherever they exist, in order to facilitate the participation or non-participation of children in religious community life, in accordance with their wishes or the wishes of the parents, depending on the maturity of the child;

h) When providing religious instruction in public schools, States should ensure low-threshold options for the child and his or her parents to get exemptions, with the purpose of preventing children from being exposed to religious instruction against their own will or that of their parents;

i) When providing information about religions and beliefs as part of the regular school curriculum and with a view to broadening the child's knowledge, States should ensure that such information is of high quality, which should always be based on solid research and should furthermore do justice to the self-understanding of the followers of different religious communities, always taking into account internal diversity. The Toledo Guiding Principles on Teaching about Religions and Beliefs in Public Schools can serve as a useful tool to ensure quality management in that area;

j) Religious instruction and/or information about religions, as given in schools or other educational settings, should always respect the evolving capacities of the child who, in the course of his or her maturation, should be able to assume a more active role in the exercise of his or her freedom of religion or belief;

k) States should reform unduly restrictive dress code regulations for students in schools in order to facilitate a school life in which students can experience free and voluntary manifestations of religious or belief-related diversity, as a normal aspect of living together in a modern society;

l) States should reform family laws which discriminate against parents or legal guardians belonging to religious minorities, or against parents who are converts, atheist or agnostics, with a view to upholding the best interests of the child and fully guaranteeing the right of the child to freedom of religion or belief without discrimination. Such reforms may also prove necessary in the interests of equality between men and women;

m) States should reform administrative practices which may lead to different religions being ascribed to converts and their children against their will. Such practices, apart from violating the freedom of religion or belief of parents who have converted, will in many cases also violate the rights of the child;

n) States should provide appropriate training for judges or other officials involved in the settlement of family conflicts, such as divorces, in order to ensure that the religious orientation of parents or legal guardians, including religious conversion, does not lead to discriminatory treatment;

o) States should provide effective anti-discrimination legislation and policies, to eliminate all forms of discrimination based on the religion or belief of the child and his or her parents or legal guardians. Special attention should be given to aggravated, multiple or intersectional discrimination, for instance discrimination based on religion or belief in combination with ethnicity, age and gender;

p) States should collect disaggregated statistical data, which may help in detecting concealed forms of discrimination based on the religion or belief of a child, or his or her parents;

q) States should take all appropriate measures to eliminate harmful practices. When tackling the issue of harmful practices, including practices allegedly based on certain cultural or religious traditions, States should avoid stereotypical overgeneralizations and should bear in mind the inter- and intrareligious diversity which usually exists with regard to such practices;

r) Religious communities should discuss the issue of how to better ensure respect for the freedom of religion or belief of children within their teaching and community practices, bearing in mind the status of the child as a rights holder and the need to respect the evolving capacities of each child;

s) Religious community leaders should support the elimination of harmful practices inflicted on children, including by publicly challenging problematic religious justifications for such practices whenever they occur.

11. Chapter: December 2015

I. Introduction

1. The present report is submitted by the Special Rapporteur on freedom of religion or belief, Heiner Bielefeldt, pursuant to Human Rights Council resolution 22/20.

2. An overview of the activities of the Special Rapporteur between 1 August 2014 and 31 July 2015 is provided in his interim report (see A/70/286, paras 4-11). The Special Rapporteur also undertook a country visit to Bangladesh from 31 August to 9 September 2015 and presented his annual report, which included a thematic focus on the rights of the child and his or her parents to freedom of religion or belief, to the General Assembly at its seventieth session in October 2015.

3. The Special Rapporteur participated in the regional Conference on Freedom of Religion or Belief in South-East Asia, held in Bangkok on 30 September and 1 October 2015, at which multi-stakeholders participants from member States of the Association of Southeast Asian Nations (ASEAN) made a commitment to defend and promote freedom of religion or belief for all persons.[274] He also hosted a regional conference on the theme Broadening cross-boundary communications, in Nicosia on 7 and 8 October 2015, at which religious leaders, lawmakers and human rights defenders from the broader Middle East and North Africa region discussed ways to strengthen and promote cooperation in cross- boundary communications in order to prevent religious violence.

4. The present report focuses on the relationship between the right to freedom of thought, conscience, religion or belief[275] and the right to freedom of opinion and expression. After some systematic observations on the structural similarities between these two rights, the Special Rapporteur explores the interplay of the two rights in the implementation of Human Rights Council resolution 16/18 on combating intolerance, negative stereotyping, stigmatization of, and discrimination, incitement to violence and violence against, persons based on religion or belief, bearing in mind, also, important insights formulated in the Rabat Plan of Ac-

---

[274] See www.icj.org/faith-based-and-other-groups-commit-to-strengthen-freedom-of-religion-or-belief- in-southeast-asia/.

[275] Hereafter referred to as "freedom of religion or belief".

tion.[276] He critically addresses the restrictive measures, including criminal laws, which adversely affect the two rights and provides practical conclusions and makes recommendations to different stakeholders.

II. Two closely interrelated rights: freedom of religion or belief and freedom of opinion and expression

5.   In political discussions, legal debates and journalistic interviews, the Special Rapporteur regularly faces questions concerning the relationship between freedom of religion or belief and freedom of opinion and expression. Often, such questions reveal a sceptical attitude. The assumption seems to be that these two rights do not easily fit together. For instance, when people wonder how it might be possible to reconcile freedom of religion or belief and freedom of expression, such wording displays a perception that the two rights stand in essential opposition to each other. The underlying idea may be that, whereas freedom of expression facilitates frank and open discussions, including satirical provocation and caricatures that may be offensive to some, freedom of religion or belief, by contrast, would more likely be invoked against excessive provocation relating to religious issues. In short, while freedom of expression seems to signal a "green light" to all sorts of provocation, freedom of religion or belief appears to function more like a "stop sign" to provocation – or such is the perception.

6.   In 2006, the previous Special Rapporteur, in a joint report, stressed that "freedom of religion primarily confers a right to act in accordance with one's religion but does not bestow a right for believers to have their religion itself protected from all adverse comment".[277] This is an important clarification. Freedom of religion or belief is a right to "freedom", a quality which accounts for its close relationship to other rights to freedom, including freedom of opinion and expression. Moreover, among the various facets covered by freedom of religion or belief, the rights to free personal orientation and free communicative interaction with others constitute indispensable core aspects, which point to the positive interrelatedness with freedom of opinion and expression. To a large extent, both

---

[276]   The Rabat Plan of Action on the prohibition of advocacy of national, racial or religious hatred that constitutes incitement to discrimination, hostility or violence was adopted in Rabat on 5 October 2012 (see A/HRC/22/17/Add.4, appendix).

[277]   See A/HRC/2/3, para. 37.

rights move in the same direction — although each has specific features. Articles 18 and 19 of the International Covenant on Civil and Political Rights display far-reaching analogies in their legal formulations.

7.   Both articles have in common the unconditional protection of the *forum internum* – a person's inner realm of thinking and believing, and the criteria for drawing limitations with regard to their external manifestations, that is, the *forum externum*, are very similar. Hence there are good reasons to conclude that the rights to freedom of religion or belief and to freedom of expression do not stand in opposition to each other, but are actually quite close in spirit and formulation. Yet, this positive interrelatedness does not preclude concrete conflicts, as controversial issues may at times emerge at the intersection of both rights.

8.   The positive interrelatedness between freedom of religion or belief and freedom of expression is not only a theoretical postulate. More importantly, the two rights mutually reinforce each other in practice. This insight should also guide the implementation of Human Rights Council resolution 16/18 on combating intolerance, negative stereotyping, stigmatization of, and discrimination, incitement to violence and violence against, persons based on religion or belief, which addresses both rights explicitly.

9.   With regard to freedom of religion or belief, States should create favourable conditions for everyone to be able to enjoy this right without fear and without discrimination. This requires, inter alia, taking measures to eliminate all forms of intolerance, stigmatization and negative stereotyping of persons based on their religion or belief, as well as adopting effective policies to prevent acts of violence or incitement thereto, as requested in resolution 16/18. Although this may at times require restricting freedom of expression, in accordance with the criteria established for imposing restrictions in articles 19 (3) and 20 (2) of the Covenant, the right to freedom of expression, above all, provides positive preconditions for combating intolerance by facilitating the creation of communicative counter-strategies in the broadest sense, such as public condemnation of incitement to hatred and public demonstrations in support of targeted individuals or groups.

10. The interrelatedness of freedom of religion or belief and freedom of expression was also explored in some detail in the Rabat Plan of Action, which contains the results of a series of regional workshops organized by the Office of the United Nations High Commissioner for Human Rights (OHCHR) in 2011 and 2012, with the broad participation of international

experts, civil society organizations, government representatives, as well as international and regional organizations.

11. The present report is intended to contribute to the ongoing discussion on resolution 16/18, which takes place within, inter alia, the Istanbul Process for Combating Intolerance, Discrimination and Incitement to Hatred and/or Violence on the Basis of Religion or Belief,[278] with the purpose of collecting ideas for the effective implementation of the resolution. The Istanbul Process itself should also consistently draw on the Rabat Plan of Action, which in turn refers to resolution 16/18 as "a promising platform for effective, integrated and inclusive action by the international community".[279]

A. Structural similarities

1. Human beings as rights holders

12. As their titles indicate, the right to freedom of religion or belief and the right to freedom of opinion and expression are both rights to freedom, a quality that they also have in common with the right to freedom of peaceful assembly and association. All these rights play an indispensable role in shaping free and democratic societies, in which the diversity of, inter alia, thoughts, ideas, opinions, interests, convictions, conscientious positions, religions and beliefs can be manifested and defended freely, including by getting together with others and by establishing adequate institutions and infrastructures with that purpose.

13. Rights holders are human beings, who may exercise these freedoms as individuals and in community with others. While this may sound like a truism in the context of human rights in general, the right to freedom of religion or belief has sometimes been misperceived as protecting religions or belief systems in themselves. This misperception is the source of much confusion, as it obfuscates the nature of freedom of religion or belief as an empowering right. Ignoring that may lead to the wrong assumption of an antagonism between freedom of religion or belief and freedom of expression. Thus, it may warrant highlighting that freedom of religion or belief protects believers rather than religions or beliefs.

---

[278] The Istanbul Process is a series of intergovernmental meetings launched in 2011 with the aim of supporting the implementation of Human Rights Council resolution 16/18.

[279] A/HRC/22/17/Add.4, appendix, para. 41.

14. Against a possible misperception, it should be noted that the focus on human beings as rights holders does not imply a particular "anthropocentric" world view. Instead, this focus follows from the diversity of existing world views. More precisely, it means taking religious and philosophical pluralism seriously, including irreconcilable differences in beliefs and practices. For instance, while some religions are based on scriptures transmitted through prophets, other religions do not have the notions of prophecy, scriptural revelation or even God. What is sacred for one community may remain rather opaque to another community. It is not least for this reason that legal recognition in the framework of human rights cannot immediately be accorded to the particular contents of religions or beliefs — such as their truth claims, scriptures or practices —, but only to human beings as the responsible agents who hold, cherish, develop and try to live in accordance with their convictions. Only by focusing on human beings as rights holders can freedom of religion or belief do justice to the broad variety of religious and non-religious convictions, identities and practices, without singling out one specific religion or belief (or one type of religion) for privileged treatment.

15. Likewise, freedom of opinion and expression also focuses on human beings, who have the right to develop, hold and change opinions and ideas on different themes; seek, receive and impart information and ideas of all kinds; and express their views freely in communicative interaction with others through any media which they see fit for those purposes. Here again, legal protection is not directly accorded to certain opinions, ideas or expressions as such, which may be very diverse and frequently irreconcilable. Instead, the focus lies on the freedom that individuals and groups of individuals have to hold and exchange opinions and ideas.

16. It should be furthermore emphasized that the two rights under discussion here are rights of "everyone" and thus held by all human beings who should be able to exercise them free from fear and free from discrimination. Freedom of religion or belief and freedom of expression are not only rights to freedom, but also epitomize the principle of equality which underpins the human-rights approach as a whole — in "recognition of the inherent dignity and of the equal and inalienable rights of all members of the human family" as stressed in the first sentence of the preamble of the Universal Declaration of Human Rights

2. Unconditional respect for the forum internum

17. Articles 18 and 19 of the Covenant show strikingly similar legal formulations, the most salient common feature being the conceptual dis-

tinction drawn in both articles between the *forum internum* and the *forum externum*. This conceptual distinction appears nowhere else in the text of the Covenant. While the wordings used to define the specific protection of the *forum internum* within article 18 and article 19 are slightly different, the basic content is identical. In both articles the protection accorded to the inner dimension of a person's thoughts, opinions or convictions (religious or otherwise) is strictly unconditional.

18. Article 18 (2) of the Covenant demands that "no one shall be subject to coercion which would impair his freedom to have or to adopt a religion or belief of his choice". Similarly, article 19 (1) of the Covenant provides for the "right to hold opinions without interference". The Human Rights Committee has clarified that the non-coercion and non- inference provisions both have the status of unconditional normative requirements. In paragraph 3 of its general comment No. 22 (1993) on the right to freedom of thought, conscience and religion, the Committee points out that article 18 does not permit any limitations whatsoever on the freedom of thought and conscience or the freedom to have or adopt a religion or belief of one's choice, and that those freedoms are protected unconditionally. In paragraph 9 of its general comment No. 34 (2011) on freedoms of opinion and expression, the Committee likewise states that article 19 (1) is a right to which the Covenant permits no exception or restriction. Such unconditional guarantees are rare in international human rights law.

19. A main function of both articles is to protect every individual's inner faculty of forming, holding or changing, inter alia, opinions, ideas, conscientious positions, religious and non-religious convictions against coercion and interference. Exposure to coercion in this inner nucleus, for example, by being forced to conceal one's true position or conviction or to feign a belief that is not authentic, can mean betraying oneself. If this happens repeatedly or over a long period, it can undermine the preconditions for developing a stable sense of self-respect. That experience warrants an interpretation of articles 18 (2) and 19 (1) of the Covenant in close analogy to the unconditional prohibition of slavery[280] and the equally unconditional prohibition of torture.[281] While legal restrictions against external manifestations originating from a person's conviction (i.e., the *forum externum*) may be justifiable in certain situations (provided those restrictions fulfil strict criteria), coercive means can never be legitimate-

---

[280]   See article 8 (1) of the Covenant.
[281]   See article 7 of the Covenant.

ly employed to manipulate a person's inner conviction (i.e., the *forum internum*) itself.

20. The wording of article 18 of the Covenant differs from that of article 19 in that it explicitly enshrines everyone's freedom "to have or to adopt a religion or belief of his choice", thus using an equivalent of the right to "change", as contained in article 18 of the Universal Declaration of Human Rights. This additional clarification is necessary since religions and beliefs can shape an individual's personal identity and create a deep sense of attachment and group loyalty based on shared world views, symbols, ethical norms and practices. The preamble of the 1981 Declaration on the Elimination of All Forms of Intolerance and of Discrimination Based on Religion or Belief states that "religion or belief, for anyone who professes either, is one of the fundamental elements of his conception of life". What goes without saying with regard to more general opinions and ideas, namely that they can legitimately change over time, needs explicit confirmation when it comes to religions and beliefs specifically, which may profoundly shape the identity of the person, often in conjunction with truth claims and deep-seated expectations of loyalty.[282]

3.   Forum externum *dimensions*

21. Both articles 18 and 19 of the Covenant also require broad application with regard to the *forum externum*. According to article 18 (1) of the Covenant, the external dimensions of freedom of religion or belief include everyone's freedom "either individually or in community with others, and in public or private to manifest his religion or belief in worship, observance, practice and teaching". Manifestation of one's religion or belief covers a broad range of activities: for instance, bearing witness to one's faith in private and in public, educating the younger generation, celebrating religious holidays, fasting, performing prayers alone or in community with others or establishing community infrastructures. Article 19 of the Covenant, in turn, deals with "information and ideas of all kind"; it is applicable "regardless of frontiers"; and it includes the use of any media. According to the last criterion, a person can seek, receive and transmit information or ideas "orally, in writing or in print, in the form of art, or through any other media of his choice". Religious or belief-related convictions undoubtedly fall within the broad category of "information and ideas of all kind", thus directly benefit from the broad conceptualization of freedom of expression set out in article 19 of the

---

[282] See A/66/156.

Covenant. Just as both rights show large overlaps within the *forum internum*, they also broadly overlap in the *forum externum*.

22.   *Forum internum* and *forum externum* should be generally seen as a continuum. Their conceptual distinction should not be misperceived as a clear-cut separation of different spheres of life. Just as freedom in the *forum internum* would be inconceivable without a person's free interaction with his or her social world, freedom within the *forum externum* presupposes respect for the faculty of every individual to come up with new thoughts and ideas and to develop personal convictions, including dissident and provocative positions. While providing unconditional protection to the inner nucleus of each individual against coercion and interference, the legally enhanced status of the *forum internum* at the same time improves the prospects of free communication and manifestation within the *forum externum*. In other words, it strengthens freedom of religion or belief and freedom of opinion and expression in all their dimensions, both internal and external.

23.   Another common feature of the rights to freedom of religion or belief and to freedom of opinion and expression is that they guarantee open communication, thus contributing to the flourishing of communities and a culture of free public discourse. At the same time, the two rights each have their specific applications concerning the *forum externum*. External "manifestations" of religion or belief, while in many cases also amounting to "expressions" in the understanding of article 19 of the Covenant, often reflect an existential desire to actually live in accordance with one's religious or other conviction, for instance by observing certain dress codes or dietary restrictions, thus exceeding mere communicative "expressions". One example illustrating the difference is conscientious objection to military service, which falls within the subcategories of "observance" or "practice" listed in article 18. Conscientious objectors would most likely not be satisfied with having the mere option to publicly "express" their opposition to the use of military force. What counts for many of them is the possibility to actually shape their lives in accordance with their conscience-based moral and/or religious position. Generally speaking, while freedom of religion or belief has a strong communicative component, which it shares with freedom of opinion and expression, the protected dimensions of religious manifestations — worship, observance, practice and teaching — cannot be summed up under the heading of communicative freedom only because they also include other aspects of leading one's life in conformity with one's religion or belief.

24. The importance of living in accordance with one's religion or belief naturally includes family life. In article 18 (4) of the Covenant, States parties "undertake to have respect for the liberty of parents, and when applicable, legal guardians to ensure the religious and moral education of their children in conformity with their own convictions". There is no parallel provision in article 19, however, that should not lead to the wrong conclusions. Of course, the freedom "to impart information and ideas of all kinds", as guaranteed in article 19 (2) of the Covenant, also applies to free communication within the family, particularly between parents and children. Nonetheless, the specific significance which religious or belief-related convictions have for the self-understanding of individuals and communities necessitates an explicit recognition of religious and moral socialization processes within the family. Freedom to "manifest" one's religion or belief thus includes the various practical dimensions of organizing one's entire private and public life, individually and together with others, in conformity with one's identity-shaping religious or belief-related convictions.

4.   Criteria for limitations

25. Although the *forum externum* of freedom of religion or belief and freedom expression is not protected unconditionally in articles 18 and 19 of the Covenant, its legal protection remains strong. Limitations or restrictions cannot be legitimate unless they satisfy all the criteria set out in article 18 (3) or article 19 (3), respectively. Notwithstanding differences in concrete formulations, the tests required in both articles contain similar elements. Firstly, limitations or restrictions must be "prescribed by law" or "provided by law". The requirement of a clearly formulated legal basis should prevent Governments from intervening in an arbitrary and unpredictable manner. Moreover, limitations or restrictions must serve a legitimate purpose from an exhaustive list of possible purposes. In the case of article 18 (3), this list comprises "public safety, order, health, or morals or the fundamental rights and freedoms of others". Article 19 (3) enumerates "respect of the rights and reputations of others", as well as "protection of national security or of public order (ordre public), or of public health or morals". Finally, both articles require that limitations or restrictions be strictly "necessary" to pursue one of the said purposes. In other words, proposed limitations cannot be legitimate if the respective purpose could also be served by a less far-reaching intervention.

26. The Human Rights Committee emphasizes the need for limitation clauses to be applied in a strict manner to ensure that the substance of the respective provisions is preserved also in situations of a real or alleged collision with other rights or important public interests. In its general comment No. 22, the Committee insists that "limitations may be applied only for those purposes for which they were prescribed and must be directly related and proportionate to the specific need on which they are predicated. Restrictions may not be imposed for discriminatory purposes or applied in a discriminatory manner" (para. 8). In its general comment No. 34, the Committee is even more specific in defining the criteria for legitimate restrictions to freedom of expression. With regard to the required legal basis, the Committee states that a law "must be formulated with sufficient precision to enable an individual to regulate his or her conduct accordingly and it must be made accessible to the public" (para. 25).

27. With regard to the necessity clause, the Human Rights Committee stresses in general comment No. 34 that, before resorting to restrictions, States "must demonstrate in specific and individualized fashion the precise nature of the threat, and the necessity and proportionality of the specific action taken, in particular by establishing a direct and immediate connection between the expression and the threat" (para. 35).

28. Concerning the concept of morals as one of the grounds for limitation, the Human Rights Committee calls for a cautious approach. In its general comment No. 22, it notes that "the concept of morals derives from many social, philosophical and religious traditions; consequently, limitations on the freedom to manifest a religion or belief for the purpose of protecting morals must be based on principles not deriving exclusively from a single tradition" (para. 8). In reiterating this clarification in its general comment No. 34, it adds that "any such limitations must be understood in the light of universality of human rights and the principle of non-discrimination" (para. 32). This is in line with the Siracusa Principles on the Limitation and Derogation Provisions in the International Covenant on Civil and Political Rights, which require States to demonstrate that a limitation on grounds of public morals is essential to the maintenance of respect for the fundamental values of the community, "since public morality varies over time and from one culture to another".[283]

29. Unfortunately, limitation criteria are often loosely invoked by Governments, for example by simply citing the truism that "no freedom can

---

[283] See E/CN.4/1985/4, annex, para. 27.

be absolute" in order to "justify" far-reaching restrictions disregarding the criteria on the matter set out in articles 18 and 19 of the Covenant or specified in general comments and the Siracusa Principles. Against this background, the clarifications made by the Human Rights Committee are all the more important. It may be useful in this context to reiterate that human rights have the elevated status of "inalienable rights" since they originate from the due respect for each and every human being's inherent dignity. Limitation clauses have an indispensable practical function in upholding this status of "inalienable rights", including in complicated situations, in which public order interests may enter the picture. These clauses must therefore be applied strictly and with the utmost degree of empirical and normative diligence.

B. Need for communicative freedom in implementing Human Rights Council resolution 16/18

1. Reaffirmed significance of freedom of religion or belief and freedom of expression

30. As mentioned earlier, the close interrelatedness of freedom of religion or belief and freedom of opinion and expression is not confined to mere parallelisms in normative formulations within the Covenant; the interrelatedness is also a practical one, as the two rights mutually reinforce each other in facilitating free and democratic societies. This insight should guide the implementation of Human Rights Council resolution 16/18. Many observers have appreciated resolution 16/18 as a landmark document upon which to base the ongoing efforts to eliminate the various root causes of religious intolerance and of related problems.

31. In the preamble of resolution 16/18, the Human Rights Council underlines the significance of freedom of religion or belief and freedom of opinion and expression. It reaffirms "that the International Covenant on Civil and Political Rights provides, inter alia, that everyone shall have the right to freedom of thought, conscience and religion or belief, which shall include freedom to have or to adopt a religion or belief of his choice, and freedom, either individually or in community with others and in public or private, to manifest his religion or belief in worship, observance, practice and teaching". It also reaffirms "the positive role that the exercise of the right to freedom of opinion and expression and the full respect for the freedom to seek, receive and impart information can play in strengthening democracy and combating religious intolerance".

32. The explicit reference to the rights to freedom of religion or belief and to freedom of opinion and expression is no coincidence, as the Council, in resolution 16/18, attaches great importance to communicative interaction, which has a key function in building trust between different religious or belief communities as well as in society at large. This includes a broad range of measures in the areas of education, awareness-building, outreach strategy, interreligious communication and public discourse. In that context, the Council specifically recognizes "that the open public debate of ideas, as well as interfaith and intercultural dialogue, at the local, national and international levels can be among the best protection against religious intolerance" (para. 4).

33. At the same time, the Council also calls for a clear rejection of certain speech acts and condemns "any advocacy of religious hatred that constitutes incitement to discrimination, hostility or violence, whether it involves the use of print, audio-visual or electronic media or any other means" (para. 3). Furthermore, it calls for "measures to criminalize incitement to imminent violence based on religion or belief" (para. 5 (f)). Other measures recommended in resolution 16/18 include putting an end to the practice of religious profiling, which inevitably leads to stigmatization and providing effective protection for places of worship and religious sites, including in conflict situations.

2.   Facilitating free and voluntary communication

34. From the combined perspectives of the two rights at issue, individuals are entitled to all aspects of communicative interaction. For instance, they have the right to seek, receive and impart information, express opinions and ideas, voice personal and/or political concerns, share their religious or philosophical convictions with others, try to persuade others or let themselves be persuaded, bear witness to their belief in private or publicly, engage in communication across State boundaries etc. For these and other acts to be manifestations of freedom, however, individuals also need to have the right not to participate in certain communicative acts, if they so wish. They are generally free to withdraw from unwanted communicative actions, remain disinterested in certain information, keep their political opinions or religious convictions for themselves, decline invitations to interreligious ceremonies or refrain from participating in public demonstrations.

35. Rights to freedom typically have their "positive" and "negative"[284] sides: they entitle individuals to perform certain acts or not to do so. Both aspects are equally important. Indeed, for communicative acts to merit their qualification as "free and voluntary", individuals should generally be respected in their freedom to decide for themselves whether, when and how to communicate, seek or impart information or speak out on certain issues. The right to withdraw or to remain reserved is the indispensable flipside of the right to engage in all aspects of free communication. This also applies to persons who belong to a group, such as members of religious or belief minorities.

36. In that context, it may be useful to recall that freedom of religion or belief includes the right not to have one's religious or belief orientation involuntarily exposed, for instance in passports, identification or other official documents. Likewise, freedom of opinion and expression entitles individuals to protection of their political or other opinions against unwanted exposure.[285] Such protection functions as a practical safeguard against discrimination, while at the same time contributing to overcome "religious profiling" and its stigmatizing effects, as required by Human Rights Council resolution 16/18. Policies of using communicative interaction with a view to combating intolerance, stereotyping, stigmatization, discrimination and incitement against individuals based on their religion or belief should therefore always accommodate the interest in non-exposure, which some individuals or groups of individuals may have.

37. To facilitate communication while at the same time accommodating the possible interest in non-exposure presupposes a broad variety of different communicative formats. For instance, while some communicative settings may operate on the express understanding that participants represent different faith communities, there should also be formats which allow people to communicate about religious intolerance and related problems without "outing" themselves in their personal religious or belief orientation. The different formats should mutually complement each other, thus facilitating a culture of open and frank communication with broad voluntary participation.

---

[284] The adjective "negative" does not carry a pejorative meaning in this context.
[285] The Special Rapporteur on freedom of expression highlighted that unwanted exposure may serve as a deterrent to expression, thereby undermining the right and the ability to express opinions or beliefs (see A/HRC/29/32).

3.   Relevant types of communicative action (examples)

38. As the word limit of the present report does not allow a detailed analysis of the multiple forms of communicative action needed to combat intolerance, stereotyping, stigmatization, discrimination, violence and incitement thereto, the Special Rapporteur would like to make a few non-exhaustive typological observations.

Interreligious communication

39. Human Rights Council resolution 16/18 repeatedly underlines the role of interfaith and intercultural dialogue for combating intolerance based on religion or belief. Such dialogue can assume different forms, which all have specific advantages and limitations. While some interreligious projects chiefly fulfil symbolic functions, others may serve practical purposes, including interreligious charity work. Whereas in some projects the main intention may be for persons belonging to different groups to regularly encounter each other face to face, other projects may aim at the systematic clarification of thematic issues of common concern. While some activities are carried out explicitly under the auspices of religious and denominational differences, other types of communication cut across the entire spectrum of religious diversity without highlighting or even mentioning the participants' religious backgrounds.

40. In his country visits, the Special Rapporteur observed different formats of interreligious dialogue and the variety of purposes pursued thereby. For instance, during his visit to Lebanon, he participated in a big interreligious ceremony, in which representatives of different Christian and Muslim communities symbolically reassured each other of their mutual appreciation. Not only were there religious dignitaries, but also ordinary community members, including young people, who expressed their rejection of violence committed in the name of religion, in a theatrical performance. One should not underestimate the impact that such ceremonies — in particular when conducted on a regular basis and with broad participation — can have on the climate of interreligious conviviality in a country. In Lebanon and in Jordan, the Special Rapporteur visited private schools run by various religious communities, which accommodate refugee children across all denominational boundaries at their own expense. Those admirable examples of practical interreligious cooperation send much-needed rays of hope in a region currently torn by violent conflicts with obvious sectarian components.

41. In Sierra Leone, the Special Rapporteur was highly impressed by the constructive role that the Interreligious Council plays in rebuilding the nation after the traumatic civil war. He also learned that the tangible atmosphere of interreligious "open-heartedness" in Sierra Leone was not least facilitated by public and private schools, in which students from different religious backgrounds — Sunnis, Shias, Ahmadis, Catholics, Anglicans, Methodists, Baptists among others — meet on a daily basis and learn together, thus building trust from early on. In Kazakhstan, the Government organizes regular interreligious meetings, with the purpose of strengthening the forces of religious moderation. While at the regional level, such meetings are open to broad public participation, the big ceremonial conferences held every second year in the capital mainly bring together world and traditional religious leaders.

42. During a follow-up visit to the Republic of Moldova, the Special Rapporteur witnessed clear signs of improvement in the interaction of religious communities. In Cyprus, the enhanced interreligious communication between Christian and Muslim leaders has led to recent breakthroughs, including the re-opening of churches and mosques that had been inaccessible for decades owing to the protracted conflict on the island. Religious leaders have initiated emergency measures and cleaned up each other's places of worship, thus creating an atmosphere of goodwill and trust. Some interreligious encounters in Cyprus have been open to participation beyond the traditional religious communities, including Evangelicals, Baha'is, Buddhists and others, thus building awareness on the further emergence of religious pluralism.

43. Those and numerous other examples testify to the peacebuilding potential of interreligious communication, which often remains politically underrated. The Special Rapporteur appreciates the diversity of formats in which interreligious dialogue projects can take place and the various specific goals that they may pursue. It is certainly useful to allow for broad ownership in order to solidify regular communication beyond the narrow circles of "dialogue experts". Women often remain underrepresented in many of those projects and that situation should change. Internal diversity of positions and assessments is important and may help eliminate stereotypical perceptions of religious communities as monolithic blocks.

44. When convening or facilitating interreligious encounters, government agencies should ensure that their communicative outreach is inclusive, by also involving members of small communities, representatives of

new religious movements or non-believers.[286] Besides "formal" interreligious dialogue projects, in which people explicitly meet as representatives of their respective religious communities, "informal" communication should also be encouraged, as it allows the active participation of persons who are less used to expressing themselves under the auspices of religious diversity or might prefer not to "come out" with their personal religious or non-religious orientations. Here again, the diversity of formats of interreligious communication can play a productive role and should systematically be taken into account.

A culture of public discourse

45. Intolerance, stereotyping, stigmatization, discrimination and incitement against persons based on their religion or belief do not only affect members of religious communities, but also have an impact on society as a whole. Communicative counter- strategies cannot therefore be limited to various formats of interreligious dialogue. What is also needed is the development of frank public discourse, facilitated by free and independent broadcast, print and online media, a broad range of civil society organizations and other stakeholders. The best antidote to intolerant propaganda is a culture of critical public discourse with broad participation. Governments have the responsibility to create a safe and enabling environment in law and practice for media practitioners and civil society activists, based on respect for everyone's freedom of expression and all other human rights.

46. For instance, when it comes to combating negative stereotyping, the counter-strategy cannot consist in "image campaigns" aimed at replacing negative pictures by positive pictures. In the long run, such image campaigns will merely reinforce suspicion in sceptical parts of society. Instead, what is needed is overcoming the root causes of stereotyping in general, including through nuanced debates and reporting. The purpose should be to solidify or restore experience-based common sense in society at large, including concerning issues of religious diversity.

47. Coexistence among people of different religious orientations is not always easy and can produce tensions, which should be articulated publicly. When sharing experiences — including negative experiences — in public debates, such experiences and concomitant feelings at least can be

---

[286] Of course, there may be reasons to reserve certain "bilateral" or other meetings to participants from specific communities only. What counts is that the general communicative policy is inclusive (see A/66/156).

exposed to public counter-narratives, which may help to prevent them from hardening into fixed prejudices and negative stereotypes. By contrast, lack of public debate typically provides fertile ground for spreading spiteful rumours against certain communities and their members. When told merely in hermetic circles or closed chatrooms and remaining unchecked by any counter-narratives or counter-evidence, negative rumours may easily lead to collective prejudices. They can even escalate into paranoid conspiracy projections and concomitant incitement to violence.[287]

48. An important purpose of public debates is overcoming all forms of essentialism in the area of religion and belief. Essentialism basically denies or marginalizes internal diversity, thus assuming that the followers of a certain religion all think and behave alike. This typically results in a de-individualization of the individual or a de-personalization of the person, who seems to disappear behind an ascribed homogeneous collective mentality. It is all the more important to recapture the truth that religions and beliefs, as lived social phenomena, always consist of human beings with most different biographies, characters, inclinations, interests, positions and assessments. Beside face-to-face communication, public discussions play a crucial role in this endeavour and should be based on respect for freedom of expression. A fair representation of members of different religious communities in the media, including in particular minorities, is an indispensable part of such a strategy.

49. In this context, the Special Rapporteur would like to recommend the Camden Principles on Freedom of Expression and Equality.[288] The Camden Principles advocate making use of freedom of expression, including media freedom, to promote equality and non-discrimination in society. According to principle 6, "all mass media should, as a moral and social responsibility, take steps to: ensure that their workforces are diverse and representative of society as a whole; address as far as possible issues of common concern to all groups in society; seek a multiplicity of sources and voices within different communities, rather than representing communities as a monolithic blocs; adhere to high standards of information provision that meet recognized professional and ethical standards". Principle 5.3, for its part, proposes a public policy framework that, inter alia,

---

[287] See A/HRC/25/58.
[288] See Article 19, Global Campaign for Free Expression, "The Camden Principles on Freedom of Expression and Equality" (April 2009), available at www.article19.org/data/files/pdfs/standards/the-camden-principles-on-freedom-of-expression-and-equality.pdf.

ensures "that disadvantaged and excluded groups have equitable access to media resources, including training opportunities". Obviously, the insistence placed by the Camden Principles on ensuring pluralistic representation within the media, as part of their moral and social responsibility, includes religious and belief-related pluralism.

Public condemnations of incitement to acts of religious hatred

50.   An inclusive culture of public discourse presupposes public rejection of speech-acts or other symbolic acts by which certain individuals or groups are de facto ex-communicated from any meaningful communication. Examples include extreme forms of essentialism, which effectively de-individualize certain individuals, or the equation of human beings with animals, which even aim at excommunicating them from the human family in general. Quite often, such rhetorical excommunication of human beings paves the way to real acts of hatred, such as discrimination, hostility or violence.

51.   Incitement to acts of hatred can never be condoned and requires quick and clear communicative interventions.[289] While a broad range of different stakeholders — civil society organizations, the media, religious communities and others — should participate in communicative counter-activities, the public condemnation of incitement also falls within the responsibility of the Government. Lack of government commitment in this regard or delayed and lukewarm reactions can easily be perceived as tacit complicity by government agencies with acts of incitement, or even as encouragement to commit violent crimes. By contrast, when the Government publicly sends quick and clear messages that any attacks against certain individual or groups will be perceived as attacks on society as a whole, this may function as a deterrent to potential perpetrators.

52.   It is well known that entrepreneurs of hatred like to stage themselves as the political avant-garde, typically pretending to act in the name of a "silent majority". As long as the majority of people within a society actually remain silent, this cynical game can continue unabated. It is all the more important that public rejections of violence and incitement to violence find a broad echo in society and that many people actively join in such rejections. The Special Rapporteur was repeatedly impressed to see public demonstrations in which numerous people — ordinary citizens, representatives of civil society organizations, religious leaders and others — took the streets to visibly express their abhorrence

---

[289]   See A/HRC/28/66.

of any advocacy of hatred in the name of religion(s). Such activities can have an enormous impact on the climate in a society by sending a clear message to potential perpetrators, while at the same time mobilizing broad support for targeted minorities.

53. In cases where violent acts have actually occurred, credible public expressions of solidarity for the targeted groups are crucial alongside other measures. Members of targeted groups should be able to experience sympathy and feel that they are not alone in their mourning. Whereas lack of public solidarity may make members of minority groups feel helpless and encourage the radical forces within them to resort to violence in response to attacks, the experience of practical sympathy can help restore trust in society among members of the targeted minority after violence has been perpetrated. Acts of solidarity should include participation in funerals and visits to bereaved families. Again, government representatives have a particular responsibility to be visibly and credibly present in such critical situations.

4.   Restrictive measures connected to high thresholds

54. As previously stated, the rights to freedom of religion or belief and to freedom of expression are not beyond limitations in the *forum externum*. However, bearing in mind the special rank of these "inalienable" rights as well as their practical significance for creating a culture of trustful communication and public discourse, limitations should always be drawn with caution and must be fully in line with international human rights standards. Among the criteria required for restrictions to be justifiable, these measures must actually prove "necessary" for achieving one of the enumerated legitimate aims. The principle of necessity implies that certain restrictive measures cannot be legitimate if less far-reaching interventions could accomplish the same results.

55. Unfortunately, realities in many countries differ from those standards. The Special Rapporteur was repeatedly surprised that some Governments all too quickly resort to restrictive measures in their fight against religious intolerance, often without even trying to explore the potential of communicative counter-strategies. Rather than using communicative counter-strategies and forming broad alliances with different societal stakeholders in creating a culture of open-mindedness against religious intolerance, some Governments seem to see their leadership role chiefly as passing and enforcing criminal legislation. However, this means turning the sequence of measures upside down. From the perspective of freedom of religion or belief, seen in conjunction with freedom of

expression, the primacy of non-restrictive policies should always be upheld. Moreover, restrictive measures if deemed necessary must meet all the criteria laid down in articles 18 (3) and 19 (3) of the Covenant, as developed above.

56. Another important norm, which has recently attracted more attention, is article 20 (2) of the Covenant, which states that "any advocacy of national, racial or religious hatred that constitutes incitement to discrimination, hostility or violence shall be prohibited by law". The title and the text of Council resolution 16/18 reflect the renewed awareness of this norm. In its general comment No. 34, the Human Rights Committee emphasizes that prohibitions enacted in the name of article 20 (2) must comply "with the strict requirements of article 19, paragraph 3, as well as such articles as 2, 5, 17, 18 and 26" (para. 48). This means that, besides preserving all the guarantees enshrined in article 19 (3) of the Covenant, which can never be circumvented by invoking article 20 (2), prohibitions must be precisely defined and must be enacted without any discriminatory intention or effect.

57. Article 20 (2) of the Covenant is also reflected in the title of the Rabat Plan of Action on the prohibition of advocacy of national, racial or religious hatred that constitutes incitement to discrimination, hostility or violence. In appreciation of the special rank of the right to freedom of expression, the Rabat Plan of Action clarifies that "article 20 of the Covenant requires a high threshold because, as a matter of fundamental principle, limitation of speech must remain an exception".[290] In order to further spell out the required threshold, the Rabat Plan of Action proposes a six-element test which should support the judiciary in assessing whether concrete acts of hate speech actually amount to "incitement to discrimination, hostility or violence" and are serious enough to be considered as criminal offences. The six elements are: the social and political context; the speaker (e.g. his or her status and influence); the intent of a speech act (as opposed to mere negligence); its content or form (e.g. style, degree of provocation); the extent of the speech act (e.g. its public nature and the size of its audience); and the likelihood and imminence of actually causing harm.[291]

58. The Rabat Plan of Action thus strictly upholds the criteria laid down in article 20 (2) of the Covenant. It calls upon States to bring their relevant legislation fully in line with articles 18, 19 and 20 of the Covenant

---

[290] See A/HRC/22/17/Add.4, appendix, para. 18.
[291] Ibid., para. 29.

when taking action against incitement. As the flipside of this approach, the Rabat Plan of Action reaffirms the role that non-restrictive measures of counter-incitement should play, thus corroborating the legitimacy of limitations as measures of last resort only. In this context, the Rabat Plan of Action explicitly underlines the close interrelatedness of freedom of religion or belief and freedom of expression in any attempt to combat incitement to acts of hatred:

> It is often purported that freedom of expression and freedom of religion or belief are in a tense relationship or even contradictory. In reality, they are mutually dependent and reinforcing. The freedom to exercise or not exercise one's religion or belief cannot exist if the freedom of expression is not respected, as free public discourse depends on respect for the diversity of convictions which people may have. Likewise, freedom of expression is essential to creating an environment in which constructive discussion about religious matters could be held.[292]

C. Problematic restrictions

I.   Blasphemy laws

59. In its general comment No. 34, the Human Rights Committee stresses that "prohibitions of displays of lack of respect for a religion or other belief system, including blasphemy laws, are incompatible with the Covenant, except in the specific circumstances envisaged in article 20, paragraph 2, of the Covenant" (para. 48). To exemplify this clarification, the Committee underlines that prohibitions cannot be permitted in order "to prevent or punish criticism of religious leaders or commentary on religious doctrines and tenets of faith". The Rabat Plan of Actions likewise criticizes blasphemy laws and finds it counterproductive at the national level as they may result in de facto censure of all interreligious and intrareligious dialogue, debate and criticism, most of which could be constructive, healthy and needed.[293]

60. As stated earlier, rights holders in the framework of human rights can only be human beings, as individuals and in community with others. This logic fully applies also to the right to freedom of religion or belief. While human beings — and indeed all of them — should receive recognition and legal protection in their freedom to believe and practise in the ways they see appropriate, blasphemy laws typically single out certain

---

[292] Ibid., para. 10.
[293] Ibid., para. 19.

religions for special protection, thus not only encroaching on freedom of expression but also on freedom of religion or belief, in particular of members of religious minorities, converts, critics, atheists, agnostics, internal dissidents and others. Abundant experience in a number of countries demonstrates that blasphemy laws do not contribute to a climate of religious openness, tolerance, non-discrimination and respect. To the contrary, they often fuel stereotyping, stigmatization, discrimination and incitement to violence. As noted in the Rabat Plan of Action, "many blasphemy laws afford different levels of protection to different religions and have often proved to be applied in a discriminatory manner. There are numerous examples of persecution of religious minorities or dissenters, but also of atheists and non-theists, as a result of legislation on what constitutes religious offences or overzealous application of laws containing neutral language" (para. 19). Based on that assessment, it recommends that "States that have blasphemy laws should repeal them, as such laws have a stifling impact on the enjoyment of freedom of religion or belief, and healthy dialogue and debate about religion" (para. 25). Moreover, blasphemy provisions may encourage non-State actors to threaten and commit acts of violence against people expressing critical views.

61. Obviously, satirical comments on religious issues or depictions of religious figures may sometimes offend the feelings of believers. Those who feel offended are free to voice their anger publicly and call for a change in attitudes. This can also become an issue for interreligious communication and public debates. Subjective feelings of offensiveness, however, should never guide legislative action, court decisions or other State activities. The threshold for imposing legal restrictions on freedom of expression must remain very high, in compliance with the criteria provided in international human rights law. At the same time, there is still space for other. non-restrictive, activities. For instance, the media may establish voluntary mechanisms of religious sensitization. In general, sensitivity concerning the religious sentiments of different religious and belief communities should become an important feature of a culture of communication, especially in multi-religious societies. However, the employment of criminal sanctions against expressions which do not advocate for violence or discrimination but which are deemed "blasphemous" cannot play a productive role in such endeavours, and such criminal sanctions, wherever they exist, are incompatible with the provisions of freedom of religion or belief and freedom of expression.

2. Unclear anti-hatred laws

62. While legal sanctions must not be employed to protect the religions or belief- systems per se against adverse comments, such sanctions may be necessary to protect human beings against incitement to acts of hatred, as reaffirmed in Human Rights Council resolution 16/18 and the Rabat Plan of Action. Indeed, article 20 (2) of the Covenant explicitly calls upon States to prohibit any advocacy of religious hatred that constitutes incitement to discrimination, hostility or violence, which implies, inter alia, adopting adequate legislation.

63. However, State practices in this regard vastly differ and often reveal a lack of consistency. Sometimes failure to act on "real" incitement cases, on the one hand, and overzealous reactions to innocuous cases, on the other, exist simultaneously, thus creating a climate of impunity for some and a climate of intimidation for others. The Rabat Plan of Action notes:

> It is of concern that perpetrators of incidents, which indeed reach the threshold of article 20 of the International Covenant on Civil and Political Rights, are not prosecuted and punished. At the same time members of minorities are de facto persecuted, with a chilling effect on others, through the abuse of vague domestic legislation, jurisprudence and policies (para. 11).

In practice, this often leads to the non-prosecution of perpetrators belonging to the State religion and to the persecution of members of religious minorities under the guise of anti- incitement laws.

64. Domestic laws which prohibit incitement to hatred are often vaguely defined, thus failing to meet the requirements contained in articles 18 (3), 19 (3) and 20 (2) of the Covenant and further specified in general comments No. 22 and No. 34. Of the Human Rights Committee. Sometimes incitement to discrimination, hostility or violence is amalgamated with broad legislative provisions against creating "discord" in society, undermining the unity of the State, or endangering interreligious "harmony". Such broad concepts typically remain undefined, opening the way to arbitrary application of such laws, often to the disadvantage of those who would actually need protection from incitement to acts of hatred, including members of religious minorities, dissenters, critics, converts, atheists and others. In fact, they may even suffer additional intimidation owing to unclear legislation and its inconsistent, arbitrary application. Indeed, the Special Rapporteur has had to deal with a number of cases, including by means of allegation letters to Governments, in which individuals have been imprisoned under the pretext of vaguely de-

fined anti-hatred laws for simply expressing religious criticism, internally dissenting views or creating their own reform branches of religious communities.[294]

65. Overcoming impunity is the main responsibility of Governments when combating incitement to imminent violence. In order to fulfil the envisaged goal, however, anti- incitement laws must be clearly defined and meet all the criteria set out in articles 18 (3), 19 (3) and 20 (2) of the Covenant and all other relevant provisions of international human rights law.

3.   Criminalizing ill-defined superiority claims

66. Anti-hatred laws sometimes combine criminalization of incitement with prohibiting the spread of superiority claims based on "race", ethnicity, religion or belief. This is yet another source of legal insecurity. The Special Rapporteur therefore attaches great importance to drawing a clear conceptual distinction between claims of superiority of certain religions or beliefs, on the one hand, and superiority claims based on "race" or ethnicity, on the other.

67. Surely, there are many overlaps at the phenomenological level. For instance, a common religion or belief may become one of the elements shaping the identity of an ethnic group. In spite of possible phenomenological overlaps, however, religion preserves a specific anthropological and epistemological status. Unlike various ethnic or "racial" group characteristics, religion typically includes ideas — for example, ideas of a metaphysical and/or a normative nature — which may invite personal reflection and meditation, exchange with others, public discourses, critical comments, academic research, missionary attempts and other forms of communicative positioning. That likewise applies to non- religious belief-systems too, including atheism or agnosticism. The possibility of becoming an object of communication — affirmative or critical — constitutes an indispensable part of freedom of religion or belief. It is even one of the defining characteristics of this human right, which again accounts for its closeness to freedom of expression.

68. According to article 4 (a) of the International Convention on the Elimination of All Forms of Racial Discrimination, States parties "shall de-

---

[294] See, under expert papers, the joint submissions by Special Rapporteurs to the four 2011 Expert workshops on the prohibition of incitement to national, racial or religious hatred. Available from www.ohchr.org/EN/Issues/FreedomOpinion/Articles19-20/Pages/ExpertsPapers.aspx.

clare as an offence punishable by law all dissemination of ideas based on racial superiority". Whereas article 20 (2) of the International Covenant on Civil and Political Rights calls for prohibiting incitement to acts of discrimination, hostility of violence, article 4 (a) of the International Convention on the Elimination of All Forms of Racial Discrimination requires criminalizing the dissemination of certain such ideas. It is important to adhere to a narrow interpretation of this provision, including a narrow definition of the nature of those ideas, i.e. their characterization on the basis of "racial superiority". Reading into the required prohibition of "ideas based on racial superiority" an implicit prohibition also of ideas based on "religious" superiority would lead to problematic results. Punishing such ideas would amount to nothing less than the end of any free communication concerning religious and belief-related issues. It would de- legitimize theological analysis, academic studies of religion, missionary and da'wah activities as well as other kinds of communication in this field and thus erode basic guarantees of freedom of religion or belief in conjunction with freedom of expression. States should therefore repeal any laws which impose criminal sanctions against claims of religious or belief-related superiority. Moreover, article 4 (a) of the International Convention on the Elimination of All Forms of Racial Discrimination should be consistently interpreted with due regard to the right to freedom of expression, as protected under article 5 of the International Convention on the Elimination of All Forms of Racial Discrimination, article 19 of the International Covenant on Civil and Political Rights and other relevant provisions of international human rights law.

III. Conclusions and recommendations

A. Conclusions

69. The human rights to freedom of religion or belief and to freedom of opinion and expression, as enshrined in articles 18 and 19 of the International Covenant on Civil and Political Rights and other international human rights instruments, are closely interrelated in law and in practice.

70. The widespread perception that these two rights are in opposition to each other is usually based on the misunderstanding that freedom of religion or belief protects religions or belief systems per se. However, like freedom of expression, freedom of religion or belief is a right to freedom and the right holders are human beings. It facilitates the flourishing of free and democratic societies in conjunction with other rights to freedom.

71. Both rights share similar features of unconditional protection of the forum internum, i.e. the person's internal dimension of religious or belief-related conviction or thinking that does not allow for any limitations or restrictions on any grounds whatsoever. External manifestations of freedom of religion or belief and freedom of expression do not enjoy unconditional protection, but the thresholds of limitations are high. Limitations can only be justifiable when the criteria set out in articles 18 (3) and 19 (3) of the Covenant, respectively, are met.

72. In spite of these similarities, freedom of religion or belief and freedom of expression each have their specific features. Freedom of religion or belief protects a broad range of "manifestations" in worship, observance, practice and teaching, many of which may go beyond the "expression" of one's belief. What is specific to freedom of religion or belief, above all, is the recognition of the practical implications that a religion or belief may have on the way its followers shape their lives as individuals and in community with others.

73. The close interrelatedness of freedom of religion or belief and freedom of opinion and expression facilitates manifold practical synergies. Any attempt to combat intolerance, stereotyping, stigmatization, discrimination and incitement to violence based on religion or belief should therefore make use of both rights in conjunction. It is no coincidence that the Human Rights Council, in the preamble of resolution 16/18, mentions these two rights as the main references on which to base the measures to be taken against religious intolerance and concomitant problems.

74. Synergies between freedom of religion or belief and freedom of expression come to the fore in different formats of interreligious communication, in a culture of frank public discourse and in policies for Government and other actors to speak out quickly, clearly and publicly against incitement to acts of hatred. The Rabat Plan of Action is a helpful tool in interpreting and implementing article 20 (2) of the Covenant, which prohibits any advocacy of national, racial or religious hatred that constitutes incitement to discrimination, hostility or violence.

B. Recommendations

75. Against the background of these observations, the Special Rapporteur would like to make the recommendations set out below.

1. Recommendations mainly addressed to States

76. Legislators, judges and policymakers should implement laws and policies based on the understanding that the rights to freedom of religion or belief and to freedom of opinion and expression are complementary.

77. States should always respect and uphold the unconditional protection status of the forum internum dimensions of freedom of religion or belief and freedom of opinion. They should provide space for different dissenting religious or political views, refrain from any coercion or interference and provide protection against coercion exercised by third parties.

78. States must abide by the criteria enshrined in articles 18 (3), 19 (3) and 20 (2) of the International Covenant on Civil and Political Rights before imposing restrictions that they deem necessary on certain external manifestations of religion or belief or expressions.

79. States should not require anyone to register or reveal their religious affiliation in official documents, such as passports or identity cards.

80. States, in collaboration with relevant stakeholders, should develop comprehensive policies to combat intolerance, negative stereotyping and stigmatization of, and discrimination, incitement to violence and violence against persons based on religion or belief further to Human Rights Council resolution 16/18. Such policies should reflect the primacy of non-restrictive communicative interventions wherever and whenever possible.

81. States should proactively share their experiences and best practices when implementing Council resolution 16/18 and the Rabat Plan of Action, for example within the Istanbul Process.

82. States are responsible for creating the public space that facilitates intergroup communication, frank and open discourse, free and independent media and civil society activities.

83. State representatives should always speak out quickly, clearly and publicly against any advocacy of religious hatred that constitutes incitement to discrimination, hostility or violence.

84. In line with Human Rights Committee general comment No. 34 and the Rabat Plan of Action, States that still have blasphemy laws should repeal them, as such laws may fuel intolerance, stigmatization, discrimination and incitement to violence and discourage intergroup communication.

85. States should prevent or overcome a climate of impunity, in which intolerant groups may feel encouraged to commit acts of discrimination, hostility or violence against persons based on their religion or belief.

86. Legislation aimed at prohibiting incitement to acts of hatred needs to be precisely defined, in line with the criteria set out in articles 18 (3), 19 (3) and 20 (2) of the International Covenant on Civil and Political Rights and further developed in Human Rights Committee general comment No. 34 and the Rabat Plan of Action. Such legislation should not contain provisions aimed at sanctioning those claiming superiority of certain religions or beliefs.

2. Recommendations addressed to different stakeholders

87. Interreligious communication should accommodate the diversity of interreligious and intrareligious positions as different formats of "formal" or "informal" communication may complement each other in this regard. Broad engagement with people from different age, gender, ethnic and indigenous groups will enhance the dialogues and overcoming the underrepresentation of women must be a priority.

88. All relevant stakeholders should cooperate in developing a culture of public discourse in accordance with the Camden Principles on Freedom of Expression and Equality by addressing and discussing problems openly, hence exposing negative experiences of interreligious coexistence to counter-evidence and counter-narratives. This can help prevent the spread of rumours and their escalation to fully fledged conspiracy projections.

89. Civil society organizations are encouraged to show public solidarity with targeted individuals or communities, including by mobilizing public demonstrations against entrepreneurs of hatred.

90. National human rights institutions are encouraged to use the Rabat Plan of Action when designing national policies of combating incitement to acts of hatred.

3. Recommendations addressed to the international community

91. The international community should continue to cooperate within the Istanbul Process which aims at the systematic implementation of Human Rights Council resolution 16/18. The Rabat Plan of Action should serve as an interpretative tool in this regard. National human rights institutions and civil society organizations should participate in exchanges on how to implement resolution 16/18 and the Rabat Plan of Action.

92. Commitment of States towards Human Rights Council resolution 16/18 should become a systematic element of the interactive dialogues within the universal periodic review. The international community should continue to monitor the situations of prisoners of conscience and advocate for their release.

12. Chapter: August 2016

I. Introduction

1.   The Special Rapporteur on freedom of religion or belief, Heiner Bielefeldt, was first appointed by the Human Rights Council on 18 June 2010
(see Council resolution 14/11) for a three-year term starting on 1 August
2010. In 2013, his mandate was renewed for another three-year term by
the Council in its resolution 22/20, ending on 31 July 2016. However, on 1
July 2016, the President of the Human Rights Council announced that in
order to avoid a protection gap, Mr. Bielefeldt would retain his functions
as Special Rapporteur on freedom of religion or belief until the entry into
office of his successor, Ahmed Shaheed, who at that time was the Special
Rapporteur on the situation of human rights in the Islamic Republic of
Iran.

2.   In section II of the present report, the Special Rapporteur provides
an overview of his activities since the submission of his previous report
to the General Assembly (A/70/286). In section III, he focuses on the
broad range of violations of freedom of religion or belief and their manifold root causes, as well as additional variables, including from a gender
perspective. In section IV, he sets out his thematic conclusions.

II. Activities of the Special Rapporteur

3.   The Special Rapporteur conducted various activities between 1 August 2015 and 31 July 2016, pursuant to Human Rights Council resolutions
6/37, 14/11, 22/20 and 31/16.

4.   An overview of the activities of the Special Rapporteur between 1
August and 30 November 2015 is included in his latest report to the Human Rights Council (see A/HRC/31/18, paras. 2 and 3). In February 2016,
the Special Rapporteur contributed to the discussion at a conference on
the theme "Combating religious intolerance: how to make the best use of
the existing framework", which took stock of the implementation of Human Rights Council resolution 16/18.

5.   The Special Rapporteur presented his annual report (A/HRC/31/18)
to the thirty-first session of the Human Rights Council, in March 2016,
where he also participated in side events and held bilateral meetings.
Subsequently, he undertook a country visit to Denmark from 13 to 22
March 2016. The next mandate holder will present the report on the mis-

sion to the thirty-fourth session of the Human Rights Council, in March 2017.

6.   The Special Rapporteur sent communications to Governments through urgent appeals, allegation letters and other letters. The latest communications reports (A/HRC/30/27, A/HRC/31/79 and A/HRC/32/53) include all communications sent between 1 March 2015 and 29 February 2016 and the replies received from Governments before 30 April 2016. He also made public statements and gave various interviews.

7.   From 8 to 10 June 2016, the Special Rapporteur, in collaboration with the non-governmental organization Muslims for Progressive Values, hosted the first conference on freedom of religion or belief and sexuality in Geneva, attended by the United Nations Deputy High Commissioner for Human Rights, who moderated the public conversation with civil society. The conference explored in depth the relationship between the various human rights issues involved in the area of sexuality and freedom of religion or belief, both at the normative level and at the level of personal experience. Religious leaders and representatives, lesbian, gay, bisexual, transgender and intersex activists, academics, legal experts and diplomats at the conference discussed openly how to overcome the misperception of an abstract normative dichotomy and identify possible synergies between commitment on behalf of freedom of religion or belief and rights for lesbian, gay, bisexual, transgender and intersex persons.

8.   On 13 and 14 June 2016, the Special Rapporteur delivered a presentation at a high-level seminar on the protection and promotion of human rights in culturally diverse societies, held in Strasbourg, France, by the Council of Europe. On 29 and 30 June, he attended the launch of the annual report on the state of freedom of religion or belief in the world issued by the European Parliament Intergroup on Freedom of Religion or Belief and Religious Tolerance. On 19 July, he addressed the Human Dimension Committee of the Organization for Security and Cooperation in Europe in Vienna and gave a presentation on the theme "The interrelatedness of democracy and human rights: freedom of religion or belief as a test case for Europe".

III. The broad range of violations of freedom of religion or belief, their root causes and variables

9.   After six years of sending individual communications, conducting country visits and drafting thematic reports, the Special Rapporteur does not think it would be possible to provide a "global map" of existing viola-

tions of freedom of religion or belief. The forms, motives and root causes of violations differ widely and cannot be captured adequately by "cartographic" projects, some of which try to depict degrees of violations in analogy to the height of mountains or the depth of the ocean. The main purpose of the present report is to sensitize readers to the complexity of human rights violations in the area of freedom of religion or belief. While some types of violations attract wide public attention, including within the international community, others are hardly known, even among human rights experts.

10. Sensitization to the complexity of human rights violations in the area of freedom of religion or belief first requires clarification of the normative scope and contours of this human right as it has been enshrined in article 18 of the Universal Declaration of Human Rights, article 18 of the International Covenant on Civil and Political Rights and other international human rights instruments. The scope of the right to freedom of religion or belief is often underestimated, with negative implications for its conceptualization and implementation. For instance, some Governments narrowly focus on individualistic and private dimensions of freedom of religion or belief while paying inadequate attention to community-related, institutional and infrastructural aspects of religious life. By contrast, other Governments place all the emphasis on recognizing collective religious identities, thus missing the crucial element of personal freedom even though it figures in the title of freedom of religion or belief. Yet other Governments privilege one particular religion or belief — or one particular type of religion — by promoting it as part of the national heritage, thereby ignoring the principles of equality and non-discrimination that are spelled out in some detail in the Declaration on the Elimination of All Forms of Intolerance and Discrimination Based on Religion or Belief of 1981 (the 1981 Declaration). Moreover, in situations in which abuses are mainly committed by non-State actors, Governments still bear a responsibility for not being willing — or not being fully able — to provide effective protection for individuals and groups whose rights are being violated.

A. The normative scope of freedom of thought, conscience, religion or belief

1. Inclusive conceptualization as a consequence of universalism

11. Freedom of religion or belief does not — and indeed cannot — protect religions or belief systems themselves, that is, their various truth

claims, teachings, rituals or practices. Instead, it empowers human beings — as individuals, as well as in community with others — who profess religions or beliefs and may wish to shape their lives in conformity with their own convictions. The reason for this focus on "believers rather than beliefs" (as it has been summed up succinctly) is not that human rights reflect a certain "anthropocentric world view", as some observers have wrongly inferred. Instead, a main reason is that religions and beliefs are very different, often even irreconcilably so, in their messages and normative requirements. Religions and beliefs reflect an abundance of diverse teachings, doctrines, ideas of salvation, norms of conduct, liturgies, holidays, fasting periods, dietary customs, dress codes and other practices. Moreover, interpretations of what matters religiously may differ widely, not only between but also within religious communities. Hence, the only common denominator identifiable within such vast diversity seems to be the human being, who is the one professing and practising his or her religion or belief, as an individual and/or in community with others. Accordingly, human rights can only do justice to the existing and emerging diversity by empowering human beings, who indeed are the right-holders of freedom of religion or belief. This consistent focus on human beings as right-holders is also fully in line with the human rights-based approach in general.

12. Human rights are universal rights in the sense of being intimately linked to the humanness of the human being and hence of all human beings equally. In the first sentence of article 1 of the Universal Declaration of Human Rights, it is stated that: "All human beings are born free and equal in dignity and rights". Because of its nature as a universal human right, to which all human beings are entitled, freedom of religion or belief must be interpreted broadly. It cannot be confined to particular lists of religious or belief-related "options" predefined by States, within which people are supposed to remain. Instead, the starting point must be the self-definition of all human beings in the vast area of religions and beliefs, which includes identity-shaping existential convictions as well as various practices connected to such convictions. In paragraph 2 of its general comment No. 22 (1993) on the right to freedom of thought, conscience and religion, the Human Rights Committee corroborated such an open, inclusive understanding by clarifying that article 18 of the International Covenant on Civil and Political Rights protects theistic, non-theistic and atheistic beliefs, as well as the right not to profess any religion or belief, and that the terms "belief" and "religion" are to be broadly construed. The Human Rights Committee also stressed that article 18 is

not limited in its application to traditional religions or to religions and beliefs with institutional characteristics or practices analogous to those of traditional religions. One should add that freedom of religion or belief also covers the rights of members of large and small communities, minorities and minorities within minorities, traditionalists and liberals, converts and reconverts, dissenters and other critical voices and, last but not least, women, who sadly still occupy marginalized positions within many religious traditions.

13. Widely-used abbreviations such as "religious freedom" or "religious liberty" do not fully capture the scope of the human right at issue. Even the term "freedom of religion or belief", which for ease of reference has generally been employed by the Special Rapporteur and his predecessors, remains a shorthand formulation. Hence, it may be useful from time to time to recall the full title of the right, which is "freedom of thought, conscience, religion or belief". Legislation and jurisdiction in many States do not adequately reflect the full scope of this human right by often restricting its application to predefined types of religions while excluding non-traditional beliefs and practices. Limiting the enjoyment of freedom of religion or belief to members of "recognized" religions is also in violation of the spirit and letter of universal human rights.

2. The primacy of freedom and scope of permissible limitations

14. Freedom of religion or belief is a multifaceted right. It empowers human beings in the entire sphere of religious and non-religious convictions, conscience- based positions and religious practices, which may be exercised by individuals alone and/or in community with others. This includes, inter alia, the free development of religious or belief-related identities, bearing witness to one's existential conviction by freely communicating with fellow believers or other persons, the autonomous organization of religious community life, the intergenerational transmission of religions or beliefs, various infrastructural aspects, such as the running of schools or charitable organizations, and other aspects. Moreover, just as individuals are free to remain within their religious tradition, they are also free to reconsider their faith, express personal doubts and adopt a new religion or belief.

15. It is in this spirit of freedom that the right to freedom of religion or belief covers all aspects of religious and belief-related life: not only the "believing", but also the "belonging" and the "behaving", that is, individual and community practices connected with convictions and traditions. Manifestations can take place in private, as well as in public. While indi-

viduals have the right to publicly manifest their religious or belief orientation alone or together with others, they also have the right to keep their convictions to themselves. Moreover, no one can be genuinely free to do something unless he or she is also free not to do it, and vice versa. That is why freedom of religion or belief also covers the freedom not to profess a religion or belief, not to attend acts of worship and not to participate in community life.

16. The Special Rapporteur has often heard statements by government representatives that freedom of religion or belief, like any other right, "cannot be absolute" and sometimes must be limited in its application. This is a truism and indeed a dangerous one, since the general invocation of limitations can easily become a pretext for imposing far-reaching or arbitrary restrictions. Many Governments actually refer to broad and unspecified "security", "order" or "morality" interests in order to curb religious criticism, discriminate against minorities, tighten control over independent religious community life or otherwise restrict freedom of religion or belief, often in excessive ways.

17. The Special Rapporteur therefore would like to reiterate that the relationship between a human right to freedom and its limitations must remain a relationship between rule and exception. No one has to justify the exercise of his or her freedom of religion or belief, which, qua its nature as a universal human right, must be respected as inherent in all human beings. The burden of justification rather falls on those who deem limitations necessary. For limitations to be justifiable, they must meet all of the criteria set out in article 18 (3) of the International Covenant on Civil and Political Rights and other relevant norms of international human rights law. Accordingly, limitations must be prescribed by law and they must be necessary to pursue a legitimate aim: the protection of "public safety, order, health, or morals or the fundamental rights and freedoms of others". In addition, restrictions on manifestations of religion or belief (in the *forum externum*) must remain within the realm of proportionality, which means, inter alia, that they must be the least restrictive among all the adequate measures that could be applied. The internal dimension of freedom of thought, conscience, religion or belief (*forum internum*) even enjoys unconditional protection pursuant to article 18 (2) of the International Covenant on Civil and Political Rights, in which it is stated that: "No one shall be subject to coercion which would impair his freedom to have or to adopt a religion or belief of his choice".

18. Respect for freedom of religion or belief — or lack of such respect — typically manifests itself in the ways in which Governments deal with

grounds for limitations. Unfortunately, the Special Rapporteur has frequently noticed loose and overly broad invocations of grounds for limitations, which often seem to be undertaken without due empirical and normative diligence. He would like to reiterate paragraph 8 of general comment No. 22, in which the Human Rights Committee insists "that paragraph 3 of article 18 is to be strictly interpreted: restrictions are not allowed on grounds not specified there ... Limitations may be applied only for those purposes for which they were prescribed and must be directly related and proportionate to the specific need on which they are predicated. Restrictions may not be imposed for discriminatory purposes or applied in a discriminatory manner".

3.   Equality and non-discrimination

19. Freedom of religion or belief does not only prohibit undue encroachments on the freedom of a person or a group of persons; it also prohibits discrimination — that is, the denial of equality — on the basis of religion or belief. For example, in article 2 of the Universal Declaration of Human Rights it is asserted that: "Everyone is entitled to all the rights and freedoms set forth in this Declaration, without distinction of any kind, such as race, colour, sex, language, religion, political or other opinion, national or social origin, property, birth or other status". Article 2 (1) of the International Covenant on Civil and Political Rights extends the same guarantee of non-discrimination to all individuals within the territory of a State party and to those subject to its jurisdiction.[295] Furthermore, it is confirmed in article 2 (1) of the 1981 Declaration that "no one shall be subject to discrimination by any State, institution, group of persons or person on the grounds of religion or belief", thus the component of "belief" is also included. A strong message is sent in article 3 of the 1981 Declaration, in which it is stated that: "Discrimination between human beings on the grounds of religion or belief constitutes an affront to human dignity and a disavowal of the principles of the Charter of the United Nations".

20. The international discussion on discrimination has made enormous strides in recent decades. Apart from the ongoing need to tackle direct and open manifestations of discrimination, there is greater sensitivity to

---

[295] See Human Rights Committee, general comment No. 31 (2004), para. 10, and Heiner Bielefeldt, Nazila Ghanea and Michael Wiener, Freedom of Religion or Belief: An International Law Commentary (Oxford, Oxford University Press, 2016), pp. 573 -574.

concealed forms of discrimination, for example, prima facie "neutral" rules prescribing certain dress codes in public institutions. Although they usually do not openly target a specific community, such rules can amount to discrimination against persons belonging to a religious minority if those persons (often women) feel obliged by their religion to wear specific religious garments. Similar problems may occur with regard to dietary rules, fasting, public holidays, labour regulations, public health norms and other issues. Overcoming the various forms of discrimination in the field of religion or belief, including indirect and structural discrimination, is a complex task that requires moving beyond mere formal equality towards substantive equality, including by adopting measures of reasonable accommodation (see A/69/261, paras. 49-66).

4. State obligations

21. States' obligations towards the implementation of human rights standards can be divided into obligations to respect, to protect and to fulfil. First of all, States have to respect human rights, including freedom of religion or belief. This presupposes a clear understanding that human beings — as individuals and/or in community with others — do not need any permission by the State to be allowed to have, adopt, profess and practise their religion or belief in private or in public. Like other human rights, freedom of religion or belief follows from the due respect for human dignity, which inheres in all human beings equally and thus commands an unconditional respect, prior to, and ultimately independent of, any acts of legislative or administrative approval.

22. The State should, furthermore, protect freedom of religion or belief against abuses by third parties, for instance, against threats stemming from authoritarian milieux, religious vigilante groups or even terrorist groups. Depending on the precise nature of the problem, this requires different initiatives, such as legislative support for religious minorities against discrimination in the workplace, measures to protect people from forced conversion and policies of combating religious vigilantism or terrorism.

23. Lastly, States should provide appropriate infrastructure that allows all persons living under their jurisdiction to actually make full use of their human rights. This aspect of their responsibility has been termed the obligation to fulfil. It includes the availability of suitable remedies, in particular, an independent and efficient judiciary. States should also facilitate the acquisition by religious communities of a collective legal standing, which they may need to undertake important community func-

tions, such as employing professional staff, purchasing real estate to build places of worship or establishing charitable organizations or institutions of religious learning. The obligation to fulfil also covers a broad range of promotional activities, such as education about religious and belief diversity as part of the school curriculum, and the building of societal resilience against religious intolerance.

B.   Root causes and motives

24.   It is often assumed that violations of freedom of religion or belief mainly originate from religious intolerance, that is, an attitude of narrow-mindedness that does not accommodate any interreligious or intrareligious diversity. While intolerant interpretations of religions or beliefs are in fact one of the most important root causes of numerous violations in this area, one should not ignore the relevance of various societal and political factors, such as interference by control-obsessed authoritarian Governments, the utilization of religions for defining a homogeneous understanding of national identity, loss of trust in public institutions and concomitant processes of societal fragmentation, the prevalence of a "macho culture", economic and social disparities, widening power gaps between different groups within a society and other variables. Again, the observations set out below remain non-exhaustive.

1.   Intolerant interpretations of religions or beliefs

25.   It cannot be emphasized enough that religious intolerance does not directly originate from religions themselves, but always presupposes the intervention of human beings. The basic insight that there can be no understanding of a text without human interpretation also applies to the sources (written or oral) of various religious or belief-related traditions. Although there may be differences between inclinations towards open-mindedness and tolerance in various traditions, there is scope for interpretation in all of them. Thus, human beings themselves are ultimately responsible for open-minded or narrow-minded interpretations, which actually exist side by side in virtually all religious and philosophical traditions. While some believers may demonize anyone professing a slightly different view, other believers of the same faith group may appreciate broad interreligious and intrareligious diversity as a stimulant necessary for profound theological or philosophical reflection and a precondition for productive exchanges. Some may dream of a religiously homogenous society as their ultimate political aspiration, whereas others would fear such homogeneity to be the end of any authentic belief.

26. Awareness of the relevance of human intervention, including human interpretation of religious sources, may help to overcome widespread "fatalistic" misperceptions. While in one country the followers of various religions or denominations have coexisted amicably since time immemorial and may even intermarry with the full approval of their respective communities, the relationship between the same communities in a neighbouring country may seem hopelessly complicated. Moreover, situations can change over time, be it for the better or the worse. There is a broad variety of amicable or hateful interactions and productive or tense relationships in different countries, which bears witness to the impact that human beings — individuals, communities and societies — actually have in shaping interreligious coexistence positively, including by developing open-minded interpretations of religious doctrines and of religious norms of conduct (see A/HRC/25/58/Add.1). Awareness of that possible impact is the precondition for overcoming fatalistic misunderstandings, which, at the end of the day, would discourage any commitment in this field.

27. In a number of countries, however, intolerant interpretations of a religion are actively supported and encouraged by the Government. As a consequence, Governments may fail to adequately protect religious minorities from hate crimes by intolerant groups and may even arrogate to themselves the authority to act as guardians of the purity of religious doctrines against so-called "unbelievers", "heretics" and people demonstrating religiously "deviant" behaviour. The general experience has been that, apart from violating, if not totally denying, the universal right to freedom of religion or belief, such "theocratic" regimes, wherever they exist, typically stifle any serious intellectual debate on religious issues and thus often create a climate of bigotry and hypocrisy. Hence, it is no coincidence that the opposition against theocratic regimes always includes critical believers of the very same religion that the Government pretends to protect, since they may feel that such governmental "guardianship" merely leads to superficial conformism, which actually undermines any persuasiveness and attractiveness of their religion.

2. Utilizing religion for demarking national identity

28. Apart from Governments that pretend to protect particular religious truth claims, many Governments promote certain religions in order to define and demark their national or cultural identity. The use of religion in rhetoric on national identity occurs more frequently than governmental aspirations to protect the "purity" of specific truth claims. The sin-

gling out of certain religions or beliefs for special protection as part of a national heritage sometimes leads to their formal entrenchment in the Constitution or in other legal statutes. Privileged religions also exist under the auspices of "secular" States. In spite of their claim to be religiously neutral, quite a number of formally secular States nonetheless demarcate their national identity by drawing sharp distinctions between "national" religions worthy of support and "foreign" religions deemed dangerous or destructive to national cohesion.

29. A country's officially or factually protected national heritage can cover more than one religion. Besides the traditionally hegemonic national religion, it may also include certain traditional minorities, which are viewed as constituting parts of the country's "traditional mosaic" (see A/HRC/22/51/Add.1). In such a constellation, the dividing line between accepted and non-accepted communities may chiefly run between traditional and non-traditional religions. While those minorities who have traditionally resided in the country are more or less appreciated, people belonging to so-called "non-traditional" minorities, by contrast, may face suspicion and hostility.

30. In a number of countries, small and non-traditional minorities, often branded as "sects", carry the stigma of operating as "fifth columns" in the interest of "foreign powers" or "foreign donors", thus allegedly eroding the country's national cohesion. Public media campaigns and hostile stereotypes, which at times are even promoted within the official school curriculum, may encourage nationalist groups to commit acts of violence against members of such minorities, not infrequently even with the tacit approval, if not the direct participation, of parts of the State apparatus.

3. Exercising excessive political control

31. Yet other Governments commit violations of freedom of religion or belief for utterly mundane purposes, for example, in the interest of exercising political control over society as a whole. In this context, the "war on terrorism" has proven a convenient pretext for a number of Governments when wishing to impose far- reaching control measures that encroach on freedom of religion or belief and other human rights.

32. It seems fair to say that the more authoritarian a Government is, the more excessive its control obsessions usually are. In particular, one-party systems typically conjure an allegedly seamlessly harmonious relationship between the political party and the people as a whole. Questioning that harmony is taboo, since it might ultimately lead to challenging the

party monopoly itself, an outcome that authoritarian Governments try to avoid by placing any communication under strict surveillance.

33. Freedom of religion or belief rightly has been termed a "gateway" to other freedoms, including freedom of expression and freedom of peaceful assembly and association. There can be no free religious community life without respect for those other freedoms, which are closely intertwined with the right to freedom of religion or belief itself. This is exactly what worries authoritarian Governments and often causes them to curb freedom of religion or belief. While mostly not caring much about issues of religious orthodoxy versus heterodoxy, the main interest of many authoritarian Governments is to prevent religious communities from running their own affairs independently for fear that this might in the long run erode the control of the State over society. Control obsessions may go so far as to even place the appointment of religious leaders or the "reincarnation" of certain religious dignitaries under tight administrative control.

34. When visiting authoritarian countries, observers are sometimes deceived by the display of religious pluralism and diversity of beliefs, which on the surface may actually exist. However, the decisive test question for many authoritarian regimes is not whether there is more than one recognized religion or whether religious minorities exist alongside the majoritarian religion or ideology. Instead, relevant test questions are whether religious communities can run their own affairs outside of tightly monitored official channels, whether community members can meet spontaneously and in self-chosen religious centres, whether religious leaders can deliver sermons or address the community without previously being submitted to censorship, whether parents are free to pass on their religious faith and rituals to the younger generation in ways they see fit, and whether the right to conscientious objection to military service is respected.

35. In a number of countries governed by authoritarian regimes, the dividing line between what is permissible and what is prohibited does not run between "orthodox" and "heterodox", "traditional" and "non-traditional" or "national" and "foreign" religions. Rather, it runs between those communities cooperating with State agencies by remaining within predefined and closely monitored channels, on the one hand, and those wishing to keep their community life free from excessive Government control and infiltration, on the other (see A/HRC/28/66/Add.2). Government interference may even sow seeds of mistrust between and within communities and poison the relationship between followers of "loyal"

communities and "independent" religious groups, thus creating a climate of suspicion, in a vicious cycle that gives law enforcement agencies an additional pretext for applying far-reaching control measures.

4. Failing and failed States

36. Massive violations of freedom of religion or belief are currently taking place, in particular, in countries characterized by systemic political mismanagement, such as endemic corruption, cronyism and ethnocentrism. The resulting disenchantment with public institutions in large parts of the population may set in motion a vicious cycle of escalating societal fragmentation, in the course of which government institutions, including the judiciary, may increasingly lose their authority, a process that can ultimately result in a failed State.

37. When public institutions fall apart, societal groups typically fill the vacuum, including mafia organizations, self-appointed vigilante groups and even terrorist organizations, some of which commit violence in the name of religion (see A/HRC/28/66). In such situations, religious or confessional identity — often in combination with ethnic identity — may become a factor in defining militarized groupings. Frequently, people cannot avoid being ascribed to one of the religious groups in confrontation, even if they would wish to keep out of such dangerous dynamics.

38. In a climate of general mistrust caused by the absence of trustworthy public institutions, militant interpretations of religious messages find fertile ground. The failures of public institutions, which in extreme situations may even cease to exist, thus typically breed narrow-minded attitudes, with possible spillover effects on predominant interpretations of religions, which therefore may become more and more militant. This pattern illustrates once more that intolerant interpretations do not directly originate from certain religions in themselves, but usually result from a broad set of political, social, economic and historical root causes and factors, al l of which need to be analysed.

5. Social power imbalances and other variables

39. When undertaking country visits, the Special Rapporteur has become aware that land-grabbing may be an important factor accounting for violations of freedom of religion or belief in some regions. Indigenous peoples are particularly vulnerable in this regard. They often cannot present ownership titles (in the modern understanding) to land that they may have used and cultivated since time immemorial. This has led to bit-

ter and often violent disputes. Freedom of religion or belief issues enter the picture, for example, if land disputes affect the real estate on which religious institutions, such as churches, temples, mosques, pagodas or graveyards, have been erected. In addition, some indigenous peoples may entertain an understanding of "holy sites" that goes beyond any spatially demarcated areas and may include broader parts of the physical environment (see A/HRC/31/18/Add.2).

40.   Land-grabbing is merely one example illustrating the relevance of economic and social variables that need to be taken into account for an appropriate understanding of violations of freedom of religion or belief and their root causes. In that context, one also should always pay attention to power imbalances, which typically render parts of the population vulnerable to pressure, exploitation and discrimination. Moreover, gender is a crucial factor that must never be neglected in any analysis of violations of freedom of religion or belief. The generally subordinated role of women in many societies is often also reflected in obstacles to their full enjoyment of freedom of religion or belief. In a few countries, questions of religious minority status are deeply interwoven with the caste society, which creates situations of increased vulnerability, including for converts from lower-caste backgrounds (see A/HRC/10/8/Add.3).

41.   Quite a number of societies still grapple with complicated historical legacies, such as the consequences of colonial rule or dictatorship. Colonizing powers, as well as home-grown dictators, have frequently applied the "divide and rule" principle by pitting certain groups against one another. Again, this may have far- reaching repercussions on relationships among religious communities and the general atmosphere in a country. Incitement to hatred may revive old stereotypes against certain religious minorities by adding aggressive conspiracy theories, some of which portray small or even tiny groups as allegedly posing a danger to morals, societal cohesion, the economy or development.

C. Patterns of State-induced violations

42.   Many violations of freedom of religion or belief directly originate from State agents and may include killings, enforced and involuntary disappearances, large - scale arbitrary detention and other atrocities targeting religious minorities or dissidents. State agencies have also been involved in the destruction of places of worship or the vandalization of graveyards. Within the constraints of the present report, it is impossible to describe all such incidents. Instead, the non-exhaustive typology set

out below is aimed at identifying widespread general patterns of systematic violations committed by State agencies.

1.   Criminal law sanctions

43.   The most frequently discussed form of State-induced violations of freedom of religion or belief are criminal sanctions against dissidents, critics, converts, non-believers or persons belonging to religious minorities. A number of States still have anti-apostasy provisions in their criminal laws, or have newly introduced such laws. This is in obvious breach of the freedom of religion or belief, which unequivocally corroborates people's freedom to "change" their religion or belief (see article 18 of the Universal Declaration of Human Rights) or any person's freedom to "have or to adopt a religion or belief of his choice" (see article 18 of the International Covenant on Civil and Political Rights). The prohibition of coercive interference in the inner realm of a person's conviction even enjoys the status of an absolute norm, comparable to the equally absolute prohibitions of torture and slavery (see A/67/303).

44.   While the number of States that formally prohibit apostasy through criminal sanctions is limited, the picture changes once anti-proselytism laws or other laws that ban missionary activities are included. Unlike prohibitions of apostasy, which currently seem to exist only in certain Muslim-majority countries, anti-proselytism laws have been enacted under the auspices of different religions, such as Buddhism, Christianity, Hinduism and Islam. The effects of these laws can come c lose to those of apostasy prohibitions. While directly targeting persons who "induce" others to change their religion or belief, these laws — often intentionally — also cast a shadow on the converts themselves by portraying the act of conversion as a result of mere external manipulation. Anti-apostasy and anti-proselytism laws also have in common a tendency to prohibit changes away from hegemonic religions, which typically receive privileged treatment. Double standards not only are a problem when applying the respective laws in practice; they frequently define the very essence of those laws.

45.   Still broader is the scope of anti-blasphemy laws. What constitutes an offence of "blasphemy" frequently remains merely vaguely circumscribed, thus giving Governments carte blanche to apply such laws in an arbitrary and discriminatory manner. Not only verbal or other statements, but also certain acts of conduct, such as eating in public during the fasting season, may be deemed as "blasphemous" in some countries. In countries that do not have anti-apostasy or anti-proselytism laws, the

criminalization of broad blasphemy offences can serve as a proxy that basically fulfils the same function. Numerous reports have given clear evidence that members of religious minorities typically suffer disproportionately from such laws, which also target converts, dissidents, nonbelievers, critics within the majority religion and individuals engaging in unwelcome missionary activities.

46.   While anti-apostasy, anti-proselytism and anti-blasphemy laws more or less openly carry "religion" in their titles, other criminal laws do not directly display an intention to curb religious dissidence or criticism and yet may have such consequences in practice, for example, overly broad anti-hatred laws (see A/HRC/13/40/Add.2, paras. 46-48). While article 20 (2) of the International Covenant on Civil and Political Rights obliges States to prohibit "advocacy of national, racial or religious hatred that constitutes incitement to discrimination, hostility or violence",[296] anti-hatred provisions often lump together a wide range of different "offences", thereby opening the floodgates for arbitrary applications. Penal law provisions sometimes even criminalize religious superiority claims, thus hypothetically threatening sanctions against all individuals or groups who publicly bear witness to their convictions. Countless examples have proven that such vague provisions are used mostly to intimidate unwelcome minorities, converts, atheists, agnostics or dissidents, including critics belonging to the country's majority religion. Further examples of prima facie "neutral" criminal law provisions are laws that, by criminalizing alleged acts of eroding national security, may threaten punishments against conscientious objectors to military service.

2.   *Bureaucratic harassment and burdensome administrative stipulations*

47.   Arguably the most widespread pattern of State-induced violations of freedom of religion or belief relates to harassment by an uncooperative bureaucracy that may treat people belonging to certain religious communities with contempt, hostility or suspicion. It is all the more important to draw public attention to this form of violation of religion or belief.

48.   When wishing to build places of worship or religious schools or to repair existing religious buildings, minority communities often have to

---

[296] For useful guidance in this regard, see the Rabat Plan of Action on the prohibition of advocacy of national, racial or religious hatred that constitutes incitement to discrimination, hostility or violence (A/HRC/22/17/Add.4, appendix).

apply for special permissions, which may take decades to obtain. If the believers start to build or repair places of worship before receiving official permission, they may encounter hefty sanctions or even be forced to tear down a newly erected building. The Special Rapporteur heard reports that it seemed easier for some communities to build a chicken farm and subsequently convert it into a place of worship than to apply to establish the place of worship.

49.   Some Governments request religious communities to register with the Administration before being allowed to exercise their group -related freedom of religion or belief. Registration status may be connected to a number of practical advantages, such as tax benefits or regular participation in municipal consultations. While registration thus can have beneficial effects for those communities wishing to obtain such a status, it is highly problematic if the Government renders registration compulsory by turning it into a sine qua non of any communitarian enjoyment of freedom of religion or belief (see A/HRC/28/66/Add.1). It cannot be reiterated enough that freedom of religion or belief, qua its nature as a universal human right, inheres in all human beings prior to any process of administrative approval. It thus must be possible for individuals and groups of individuals to also practise their religion or belief independently from any official status, if they prefer not to obtain any such status or if their application for registration has been unsuccessful. The situation can become even more complicated if Governments require the periodic renewal of registration, which thus may become a never-ending bureaucratic exercise for certain communities. The more detailed information the Administration demands in such procedures, the easier it will be to find "shortcomings" in the application that the Administration may use as a pretext to impose sanctions, thereby creating a climate of intimidation for any unwelcome religious activities.

50.   For many (not all) religious communities, it is important to obtain the appropriate legal personality status to exercise certain community functions, such as purchasing real estate, which they may need to establish a lasting religious infrastructure, employing teaching professionals or other staff and running their own schools or media or charitable organizations (see A/HRC/22/51). The denial of appropriate legal personality status or unreasonable stipulations connected with such a status may thus amount to a violation of freedom of religion or belief.

3.   Discriminatory structures in family laws

51. In many countries, family laws reflect traditional religious hegemonies. Before discussing the negative repercussions that this may have for freedom of religion or belief, the Special Rapporteur would like to clarify that religious family laws differ conceptually from religious family values, rites and customs. Law in the narrow sense of the word carries with it the element of enforcement by the State. State - enforced laws based on a particular religion or denomination can lead to problematic situations, for example, if an interreligious marriage cannot be contracted or if such a marriage breaks down and the spouse who had converted to the religion of her or his partner wishes to return to the religion he or she professed previously. Such a return is usually difficult in itself, and it can be made even more complicated by legal insecurity, which a change of religion may incur with regard to important issues, such as inheritance, maintenance or custody of children. Moreover, apart from causing concerns under freedom of religion or belief, denominational family laws frequently reflect and reinforce inequalities between men and women concerning marriage, child-rearing, custody, maintenance, inheritance and other areas of family life (see A/HRC/25/58/Add.2).

52. From the specific viewpoint of freedom of religion or belief, State-enforced denominational family laws give rise to a number of serious concerns. Even though the structure may be pluralistic to a certain degree, the system typically does not easily, if at all, accommodate certain constellations of interreligious partnerships. On the basis of the widespread assumption that children have to follow the religious orientation of the father, denominational family laws may allow some interreligious marriages, provided that the husband is of the predominant religion, while often ruling out any marriage between a woman from the traditionally hegemonic religion and a man professing another religion or belief. Thus, complicated cases of multiple and intersectional discriminations — in other words, in the intersection of religious minority status and gender — may arise (see A/HRC/31/18/Add.1). Moreover, converts, agnostics, atheists and others may face even greater difficulties to fit into the limited options provided by State-enforced religious family laws. Although reforms with the purpose of accommodating the existing and emerging pluralism in a non-discriminatory way should be a priority, many Governments seem to be reluctant to tackle these issues.

4. Violations in the context of school education

53. The school is an institution designed to fulfil human rights, in particular, the right to education, as enshrined in article 13 of the International Covenant on Economic, Social and Cultural Rights, article 28 of the Convention on the Rights of the Child and similar provisions. In order to ensure this right for every child, States have the obligation to render elementary school education mandatory. However, school is also an environment in which serious human rights problems may arise. In public schools, children regularly experience the authority of teachers, who, as public officials, may also represent the authority of the State. Furthermore, children may suffer peer pressure and bullying, a problem that disproportionately affects children from minorities.

54. Parents belonging to religious minorities, or parents who have converted away from the predominant religion, sometimes fear that school education may be utilized to alienate their children from them. The Special Rapporteur heard reports about the disrespectful treatment of children during religious fasting seasons, when children were exposed to expectations clearly articulated by their teachers that they should eat the food served in school, thereby breaking the fasting rules of their religion.

55. Whenever religious ceremonies, such as public prayers or acts of collective worship, are performed in school, and in particular during regular school hours, safeguards are needed to ensure that no child feels compelled to participate in such ceremonies against his or her free will or the will of his or her parents. The same caveat applies to religious instruction in schools (see A/HRC/16/53). In paragraph 6 of its general comment No. 22, the Human Rights Committee noted that public education that includes instruction in a particular religion or belief is inconsistent with article 18 (4) of the International Covenant on Civil and Political Rights unless provision is made for non-discriminatory exemptions or alternatives that would accommodate the wishes of parents and guardians. In practice, however, such provisions, if they exist at all, are often ignored, possibly as a result of ignorance or lack of systematic monitoring or even in a deliberate attempt to convert children belonging to religious minorities to the hegemonic religion of the country.

56. In view of the compulsory status of school education, attempts at converting children in the school context may amount to serious violations of the absolutely protected *forum internum* dimension of freedom of religion or belief. At the same time, such attempts may violate the rights of parents to ensure a religious and moral upbringing of their child —

who has not yet reached religious maturity — in conformity with their own convictions, as enshrined in article 18 (4) of the International Covenant on Civil and Political Rights and article 14 (2) of the Convention on the Rights of the Child (see A/70/286).

57. Whereas religious instruction — in the understanding of familiarizing students with their own or their parents' faith — requires safeguards to avoid any involuntary exposure of students to such teachings, general information about religions may well become part of the compulsory school curriculum, "if it is given in a neutral and objective way", as the Human Rights Committee cautions in paragraph 6 of its general comment No. 22. However, the objectivity of textbooks and other learning materials is often questionable, for example, when textbooks assume a peculiar warning tone towards "non-traditional" minorities or "sects", thus stigmatizing certain communities. Many textbooks used in school reflect existing religious hegemonies while totally ignoring the perspectives of minorities. For students and parents exposed to such stigmatization, possibly even on a daily basis, school education can be a traumatizing experience. Other school textbooks may favour a narrowly secularist world view by either completely excluding religious themes or by containing solely critical and negative comments on religion, which, together with corresponding teaching practice, may put religious students under pressure.

5.   State-induced discrimination and stigmatization

58. The patterns described above — restrictive criminal law provisions, harassment and intimidation by an unsympathetic bureaucracy, discriminatory structures in family laws and disrespectful treatment of children in schools — often overlap, thus creating a climate in which members of religious minorities, followers of non-traditional religious movements, individual dissidents, critics, converts, agnostics, atheists and others may suffer systematic discrimination, marginalization and exclusion. Hateful statements by government officials or media campaigns may further exacerbate their situation. However, members of the majority religion may also suffer from a climate in which religious and belief-related issues can scarcely be discussed in a relaxed and open manner.

59. As elaborated in section III.B above, the motives behind State-induced violations of freedom of religion or belief can be manifold, may differ from country to country and can also change in the course of a country's development. Any comprehensive analysis requires the consideration of all relevant factors, including economic and social factors, that

may lead to multiple and intersectional forms of discrimination, such as discrimination in the intersection of religious minority status, gender, caste, economic impoverishment and other factors.

D. Violations by non-State actors and societal restrictions

60. Many of the most brutal abuses of freedom of religion or belief are currently perpetrated by non-State actors, such as terrorist groups or militant vigilante groups. The fact that there is no general definition of non-State actors, nor a consensus on their human rights obligations (see A/HRC/28/66, paras. 54-59), renders any attempt at providing a typological overview rather complicated. While it ma y be that non-State actors are those carrying out acts of violence, States are sometimes directly or indirectly supporting these actors for the different motives explained above. The main purpose of the present section is to remind Governments of the responsibility that they bear also when combating violations of freedom of religion or belief committed by non-State actors.

1. Terrorism, extremism, vigilantism and social ostracism

61. Some terrorist groups that pretend to operate in the name of religion try to wipe out any traces of religious diversity, not only in the present and for the future, but even traces of the past (see A/56/253, paras. 25-30). Atrocities committed by such groups include mass killings, extremely cruel forms of execution, mutilations, forcible deportations, ethnic cleansing, blackmailing, confiscation of property, kidnapping of women and children and their sale into slavery, the destruction of religious buildings, some of which had been recognized internationally as historical monuments, and other acts of brutality.

62. The information presented in section III.B above on the complex root causes of violations of freedom of religion or belief likewise applies to the atrocities committed by terrorist groups. Lack of good governance — for example, the breakdown of trustworthy public institutions, endemic corruption and cronyism, the absence of any rule of law, far-reaching societal fragmentation and concomitant polarization, and widespread feelings of despair within the population — creates the fertile ground on which militant groupings can operate successfully. At the same time, one should not ignore the additional impact of intolerant and narrow-minded religious interpretations, which, through modern information and communications technologies, reach out to a global audience. Terrorist groups have also received ideological, logistical and financial support from a number of Governments, without which they would be less suc-

cessful. While stigmatizing members of religious minorities as "unbelievers" or "heretics", terrorist groups frequently also attack people of the same religion to which they themselves belong, thereby creating a climate of fear in which no one can enjoy their freedom of religion or belief.

63. In a number of countries, self-appointed militant vigilante groups patrol their neighbourhoods to ensure that everyone behaves in ways deemed religiously appropriate, including by threatening violence (see E/CN.4/2006/5/Add.3). Women and girls typically run an increased risk of being sanctioned, for instance, when failing to conform to certain imposed dress codes or other norms of behaviour. Even if not being mandated by the Government, militant vigilante groups nonetheless may receive direct or indirect support from certain government agencies, which systematically turn a blind eye to abuses committed by such groups.

64. Furthermore, grave abuses of freedom of religion or belief can occur within homogeneous societal milieux that do not accommodate any interreligious or intrareligious diversity. Individuals not fitting into traditional patterns of "acceptable" belief and conduct may incur a variety of sanctions, such as social ostracism, systematic mobbing or even physical violence. Women and girls or persons with different sexual orientations and gender identities bear an increased risk of abuses when wishing to free themselves from narrow understandings of what is deemed "appropriate conduct", often on the basis of excessively restrictive interpretations of religious norms. This is another area in which freedom of religion or belief frequently intersects with issues of gender-based violence or discrimination (see A/68/290). Apart from failing to provide appropriate legal and political protection, Governments may even support such repressive practices, for instance, through laws that treat violent crimes committed in the name of "honour" in a particularly lenient manner or by sending messages that blame the victim of an attack for having infringed moral norms in the first place.

65. Policies intended to prevent and counter violent extremism must be based on a clear understanding of the numerous root causes, which often mutually reinforce each other. As the United Nations Deputy High Commissioner for Human Rights, Kathryn Gilmore, pointed out at a panel discussion on the human rights dimensions of preventing and countering violent extremism, held in Geneva on 17 March 2016, "violent extremism is the child of many parents — discrimination or injustice — whether actual or perceived; political disenfranchisement; a sense among young people of powerlessness, or denial of identity; of hopelessness". When calling for positive action, the Deputy High Commissioner placed particu-

lar emphasis on the need to support human rights defenders and civil society, as well as "the immediate deterrence of reprisals against those who
speak out".

2.   Government responsibility

66.   When abuses are not perpetrated by State agencies, the Government
remains accountable for any violation of freedom of religion or belief occurring within its jurisdiction. This is even more obviously the case when
government agencies are directly or indirectly complicit in such violations, for example, by apparently condoning acts of violence or by creating an atmosphere of impunity that gives militant groups a free rein.
Public condemnations by government officials of abuses committed within society are sometimes absent or may sound merely lukewarm. Moreover, the Government may send ambiguous signals to law enforcement
agencies, which, accordingly, do not know whether they are actually expected to provide protection to individuals or groups who are looked
down upon by "mainstream" society (see A/HRC/31/18/Add.2).

67.   During some country visits, the Special Rapporteur repeatedly
sensed a lack of awareness that the right to freedom of religion or belief
requires protective and promotional government activities to ensure its
systematic implementation in all parts of society. For instance, discrimination on the grounds of religion or belief occurring in the labour market
or the housing market is sometimes still treated as a merely "private" issue that the Government allegedly could ignore. However, such lack of
commitment is at variance with the 1981 Declaration, in article 4 (1) of
which it is unambiguously clarified that: "All States shall take effective
measures to prevent and eliminate discrimination on the grounds of religion or belief in the recognition, exercise and enjoyment of human rights
and fundamental freedoms in all fields of civil, economic, political, social
and cultural life." This also covers acts of intolerance and discrimination
in the workplace, including in business sectors. Governments that lack an
efficient and comprehensive anti-discrimination policy thus fail to honour their human rights obligations.

E.   Responsibility of the international community

68.   One of the most significant progressive developments in international human rights politics is the increased awareness that violations of
human rights, including freedom of religion or belief, do not fall within
the "internal affairs" of States. Although Governments are still the main
duty bearers concerning the implementation of human rights within

their jurisdiction, their responsibility is not an exclusive one. By ratifying international treaties, Governments formally corroborate the understanding that respect for and protection and promotion of human rights is both a national duty and a matter of international concern. In addition, there is broad consensus that human rights also constitute an indispensable part of international customary law.

69. Besides States, the international community also comprises other actors, in particular, civil society organizations, without whose contributions international monitoring would not even be conceivable. Moreover, situations can arise in which the international community has to take direct action to stop massive violations of freedom of religion or belief and other human rights abuses, for instance, by ensuring that terrorist organizations operating in the name of religion do not receive financial, logistical or other support or by holding to account political leaders who have committed widespread and systematic human rights violations.

70. Throughout the past few years, the Special Rapporteur has sensed an increasing interest in issues concerning his mandate. At the same time, he feels that the broad range of violations of freedom of religion or belief fails to receive attention. For example, administrative harassment and unreasonable bureaucratic stipulations hardly ever make it into the headlines. The scarcity of empirical findings may follow from difficulties in research and reporting, but may also reflect a lack of awareness that certain issues have a human rights dimension in the first place. The latter problem may be the result of an inadequate understanding of the normative range and full scope of freedom of religion or belief, which is a broadly applicable right to freedom to which every human being is entitled.

71. One issue on which the international community has obviously failed concerns the rights of refugees and internally displaced persons. Violations of freedom of religion or belief are among the manifold reasons for people to leave their home and flee their country, in particular where violent conflict has assumed a religious or sectarian dimension. However, when applying for asylum because of violations of their freedom of religion or belief, refugees have sometimes experienced that their claims are not taken seriously. Some of them have been given bizarre recommendations, such as to avoid public exposure and to keep their faith to themselves. Converts may face suspicion of having fabricated their conversion for the strategic purpose of gaining refugee status. In addition, many violations of freedom of religion or belief are inextricably interwoven with other social or political variables, for example, excessive

control interests of authoritarian Governments. Given the complexity of such issues, some observers may dramatically underestimate the gravity of violations experienced by people on the basis of their religion or belief. This may have an impact on the treatment of refugees, whose experiences in this area fail to receive appropriate attention and recognition.

72. It is depressing to see that in the current refugee crisis, many States fail to honour the responsibility they have in accommodating refugees, including those who are fleeing massive violations of their freedom of religion or belief. Some Governments have opened their borders and demonstrated solidarity, often in conjunction with admirable commitment shown by civil society organizations and countless volunteers. By contrast, other States have been reluctant to even host a handful of refugees. Yet other Governments have indicated that they would be merely willing to accommodate refugees from religious backgrounds close to their own predominant religious traditions. However, this would amount to a (re)territorialization of religion and thus would clearly be at variance with the freedom of religion or belief, which protects human beings in their diverse convictions and practices instead of fostering religiously homogeneous territories. The Special Rapporteur can merely appeal to reluctant Governments to reconsider their position and honour their obligations under international law, including by respecting, protecting and fulfilling everyone's right to freedom of religion or belief.

IV. Conclusions

73. The full scope of freedom of thought, conscience, religion or belief is often underestimated, with the result being an inadequate awareness of the broad range of violations that take place in this area. Given its nature as a universal human right, freedom of religion or belief cannot be limited to any list of legitimate religious "options" predefined by Governments. Instead, it recognizes human beings broadly as subjects of profound identity-shaping convictions and conviction-based practices, thus always taking the self- definition of all human beings as the starting point. Freedom of religion or belief is a multifaceted right, covering individual, relational, institutional and infrastructural dimensions of freedom, that people should be able to exercise as individuals and/or in community with others, in private as well as in public. In keeping with the human rights-based approach in general, freedom of religion or belief furthermore requires non-discriminatory implementation, which implies positive efforts towards overcoming all forms of discrimination —

direct, indirect and structural discrimination, by both public and private actors — by taking appropriate measures.

74. For a comprehensive analysis of existing and emerging problems, all root causes, motives and factors underlying violations of freedom of religion or belief must be taken seriously. This includes intolerant and narrow-minded interpretations of religions — in other words, theological issues — as well as political, social and economic factors. While Governments that see themselves as guardians of certain religious truth claims impose restrictive measures against "unbelievers" and "heretics", other Governments utilize particular religions in order to demarcate their national identities, thus creating dividing lines between "national" and "foreign" religions or between "traditional" and "non-traditional" religions. Yet other Governments violate freedom of religion or belief by exercising excessive political control over religious community life in order to defend authoritarian political structures or party monopolies against possible challenges that may arise from people meeting freely and communicating outside of tightly monitored official channels. Moreover, loss of trust in public institutions may set in motion a process of increasing institutional fragmentation, thus possibly creating a political vacuum, which terrorist or vigilante organizations operating in the name of religion may try to fill.

75. Furthermore, societal power imbalances may lead to situations of increased vulnerability for certain individuals or communities, including persons from lower-caste backgrounds, individuals belonging to religious minority communities or indigenous peoples, whose freedom of religion or belief thus may be at stake, often in conjunction with violations of other human rights. Any analysis of the root causes underlying violations of freedom of religion or belief should also address gender issues. Countless women and girls suffer from human rights violations in the intersection of freedom of religion or belief and gender issues, for example in the context of State-enforced denominational family laws.

76. Violations of freedom of religion or belief can originate from States or non-State actors, or a combination of both. While some State-induced infringements, such as the criminalization of "apostasy", "proselytism" or "blasphemy", openly display the intention of controlling religion, other measures do not show any relationship to religion or belief on the surface and yet have a negative impact on freedom of religion or belief. Encroachments may also include bureaucratic stipulations that impose unreasonable burdens on certain religious communities, for instance by requesting them to undergo complicated administrative procedures in

order to be allowed to exercise any community-related aspects of freedom of religion or belief. State-enforced family laws may discriminate against persons on the basis of their religion or belief, thus effectively preventing certain individuals from changing their religion for fear that it could result in a loss of inheritance rights or the denial of custody of their own children. School education is another area warranting systematic monitoring, since it may expose children from religious minorities, for example, to a non-accommodating national curriculum, to the authority of teachers or to pressure exercised by fellow students.

77. Governments are also obliged to prevent abuses of freedom of religion or belief committed by non-State actors, including terrorist groups or vigilante groups, or originating from authoritarian societal milieux that do not accommodate any religious diversity. In quite a number of countries, a prevailing atmosphere of impunity encourages militant groups to continue to stigmatize, harass and intimidate minorities, dissidents, critics, converts or people — often women and girls or persons with different sexual orientations and gender identities — whose conduct is deemed "inappropriate" from a certain narrow-minded interpretation of religious norms. Such abuses can even assume degrees of physical violence, sometimes perpetrated with the silent complicity of law enforcement agencies or other parts of the State apparatus. Even Governments that are not complicit in such acts may lack the awareness that they bear the full responsibility for any violation of freedom of religion or belief if they fail to take appropriate measures to protect persons under their jurisdiction from abuses by non-State actors, whether they are armed groups, business corporations or individuals.

78. While States remain the main duty bearers for the implementation of human rights obligations within their jurisdiction, the international community, too, has to live up to its obligations. Apart from regularly monitoring the worldwide human rights situation within United Nations forums, which would be impossible without the contributions of civil society organizations, there are situations in which the international community has to take direct action, for example, to ensure that terrorist organizations operating in the name of religion do not receive financial or logistical support. Unfortunately, serious shortcomings have been seen recently in the provision of international protection for refugees and in the prevention of massive violations of freedom of religion or belief, in particular in situations of armed conflict. The international community should remind Governments of their international obligation to provide protection to refugees, regardless of their specific religion or belief. The

pretext that hosting certain refugees would erode the traditional religious make-up of a country amounts to a "territorialization" of religion or belief, which violates the spirit and the letter of the universal right to freedom of religion or belief.

www.ingramcontent.com/pod-product-compliance
Lightning Source LLC
Chambersburg PA
CBHW060138280326
41932CB00012B/1559